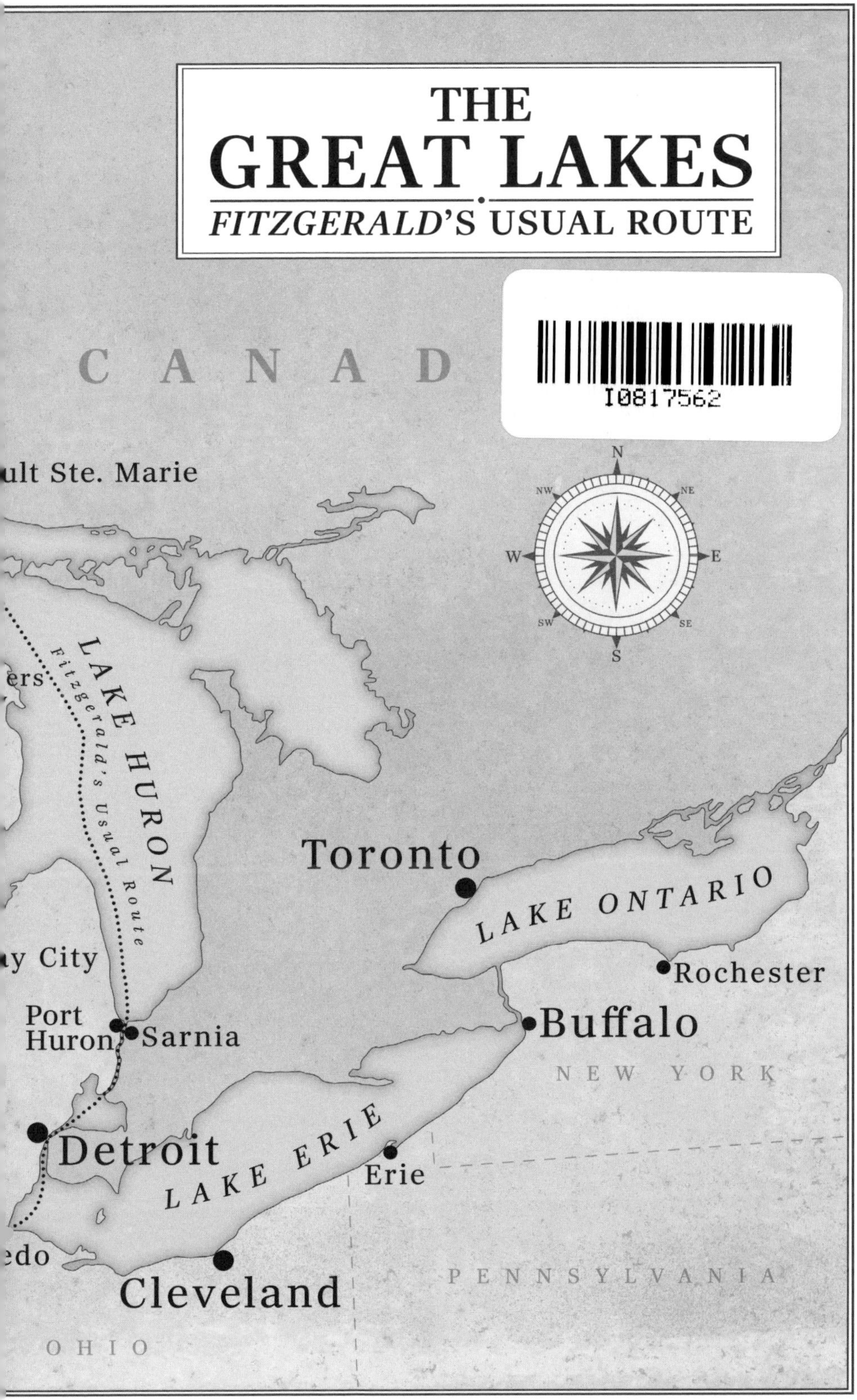

THE GREAT LAKES

FITZGERALD'S USUAL ROUTE

CANAD

N
NW
NE
W
E
SW
SE
S

ult Ste. Marie

ers

LAKE HURON

Fitzgerald's Usual Route

Toronto

LAKE ONTARIO

Rochester

y City

Port Huron

Sarnia

Buffalo

NEW YORK

Detroit

LAKE ERIE

Erie

edo

Cleveland

PENNSYLVANIA

OHIO

THE GALES OF NOVEMBER

ALSO BY JOHN U. BACON

The Greatest Comeback: How Team Canada Fought Back, Took the Summit Series, and Reinvented Hockey

Let Them Lead: Unexpected Lessons in Leadership from America's Worst High School Hockey Team

Overtime: Jim Harbaugh and the Michigan Wolverines at the Crossroads of College Football

The Best of Bacon: Select Cuts

The Great Halifax Explosion: A World War I Story of Treachery, Tragedy, and Extraordinary Heroism

Playing Hurt: My Journey from Despair to Hope (with John Saunders)

Endzone: The Rise, Fall, and Return of Michigan Football

Fourth and Long: The Fight for the Soul of College Football

Three and Out: Rich Rodriguez and the Michigan Wolverines in the Crucible of College Football

Bo's Lasting Lessons: The Legendary Coach Teaches the Timeless Fundamentals of Leadership

Cirque du Soleil, The Spark: Igniting the Creative Fire That Lives Within Us All

America's Corner Store: Walgreen's Prescription for Success

Blue Ice: The Story of Michigan Hockey

The *Edmund Fitzgerald* is baptized in the Detroit River on June 7, 1958. *MHSD*

THE GALES OF NOVEMBER

The Untold Story of the *Edmund Fitzgerald*

JOHN U. BACON

Liveright Publishing Corporation

A Division of W. W. Norton & Company
Independent Publishers Since 1923

Printed in the United States of America
First Edition

For information about permission to reproduce selections from this book, write to Permissions, Liveright Publishing Corporation, a division of W. W. Norton & Company, Inc., 500 Fifth Avenue, New York, NY 10110

For information about special discounts for bulk purchases, please contact W. W. Norton Special Sales at specialsales@wwnorton.com or 800-233-4830

Manufacturing by Lakeside Book Company
Book design by Lovedog Studio
Production manager: Julia Druskin

ISBN: 978-1-324-09464-7

Liveright Publishing Corporation
500 Fifth Avenue, New York, NY 10110
www.wwnorton.com

W. W. Norton & Company Ltd.
15 Carlisle Street, London W1D 3BS

Authorized EU representative: EAS, Mustamäe tee 50, 10621 Tallinn, Estonia
10 9

To the twenty-nine men on the
Edmund Fitzgerald, *and their families.*
This story is theirs, above all.

CONTENTS

Miles
0
25
50
75
100
0
50
100
150
Kilometers
LAKE SUPERIOR
Fitzgerald's Usual Route
Silver Bay
Duluth
Superior
Marquette
Whitefish Point
MICHIGAN
WISCONSIN
GRAND TRAVERSE BAY
Traverse City
Green Bay
LAKE MICHIGAN
Muskegon
Milwaukee
IOWA
U.S.
Chicago
Gary
ILLINOIS
INDIANA

THE GREAT LAKES

FITZGERALD'S USUAL ROUTE

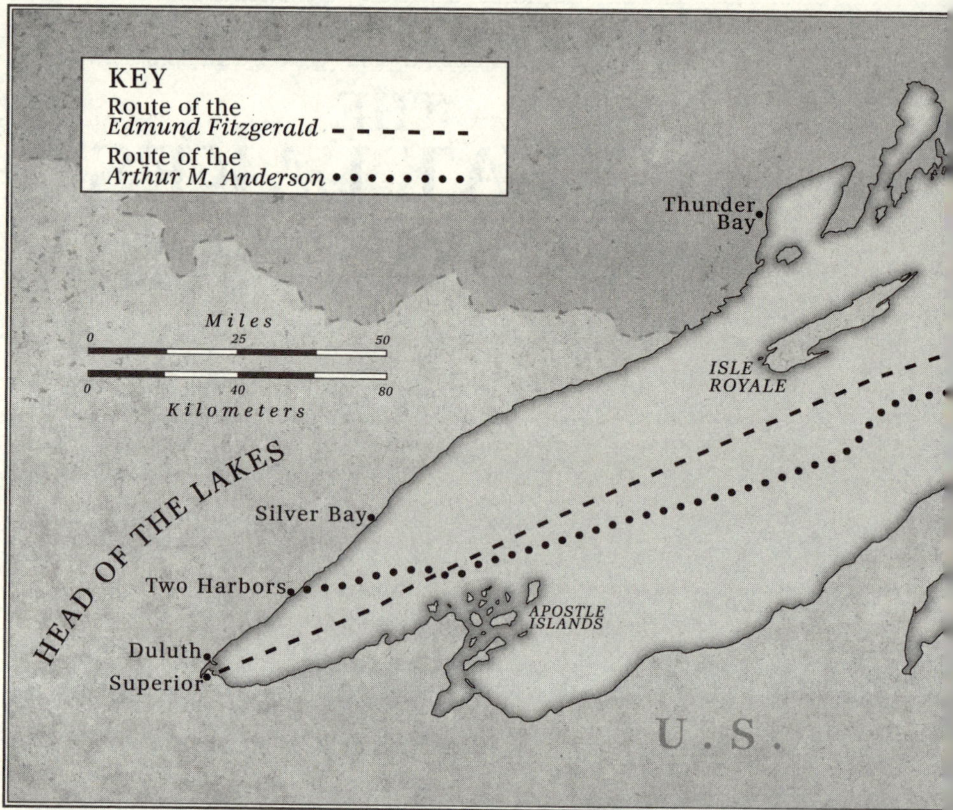

KEY
Route of the *Edmund Fitzgerald* - - - - - -
Route of the *Arthur M. Anderson* • • • • • • • •

Miles
0 25 50
0 40 80
Kilometers

Thunder Bay
ISLE ROYALE
HEAD OF THE LAKES
Silver Bay
Two Harbors
APOSTLE ISLANDS
Duluth
Superior
U.S.

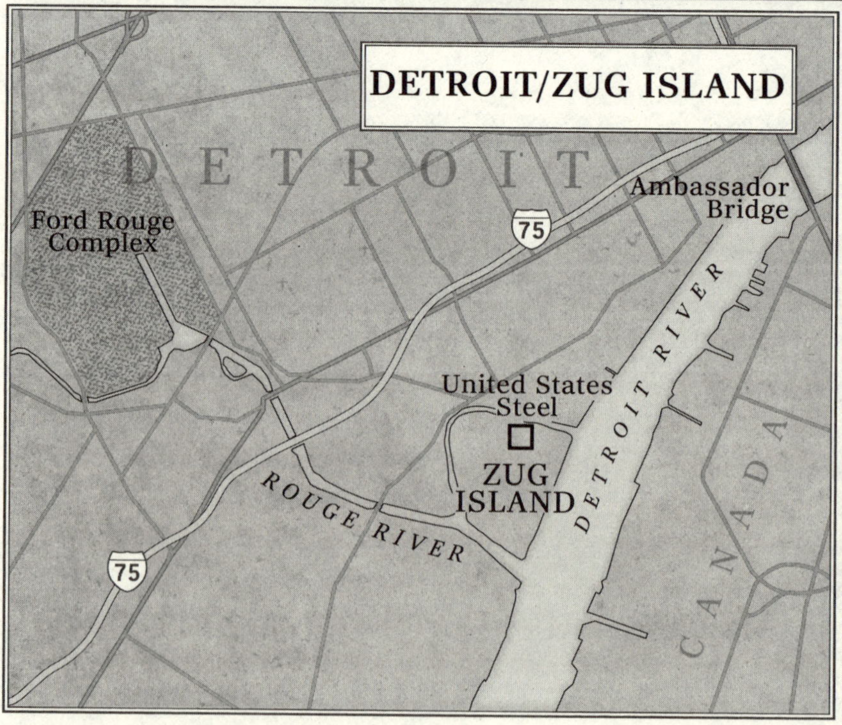

DETROIT/ZUG ISLAND

DETROIT
Ford Rouge Complex
75
Ambassador Bridge
DETROIT RIVER
United States Steel
ZUG ISLAND
ROUGE RIVER
75
CANADA

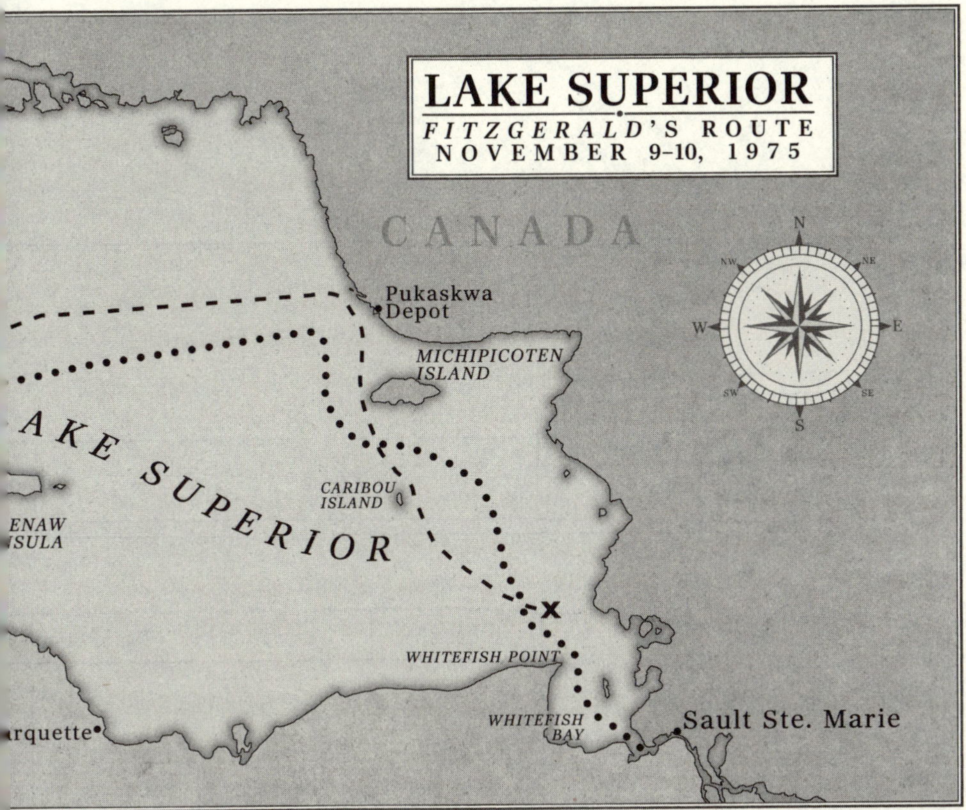

LAKE SUPERIOR

FITZGERALD'S ROUTE
NOVEMBER 9–10, 1975

CANADA
N
NE
E
SE
S
SW
W
NW
Pukaskwa
Depot
MICHIPICOTEN
ISLAND
AKE SUPERIOR
CARIBOU
ISLAND
ENAW
SULA
WHITEFISH POINT
WHITEFISH
BAY
Sault Ste. Marie
rquette

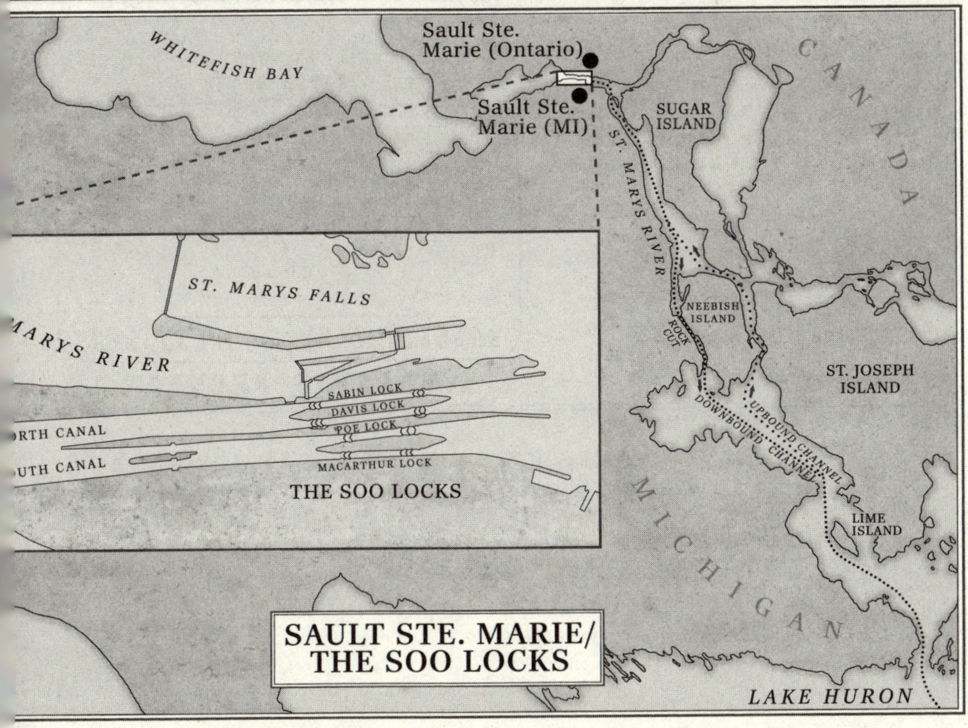

WHITEFISH BAY
Sault Ste.
Marie (Ontario)
Sault Ste.
Marie (MI)
SUGAR
ISLAND
CANADA
ST. MARYS RIVER
NEEBISH
ISLAND
ROCK
CUT
ST. JOSEPH
ISLAND
DOWNBOUND CHANNEL
UPBOUND CHANNEL
LIME
ISLAND
MICHIGAN
LAKE HURON

ST. MARYS FALLS
MARYS RIVER
SABIN LOCK
DAVIS LOCK
POE LOCK
MACARTHUR LOCK
ORTH CANAL
UTH CANAL
THE SOO LOCKS

SAULT STE. MARIE/
THE SOO LOCKS

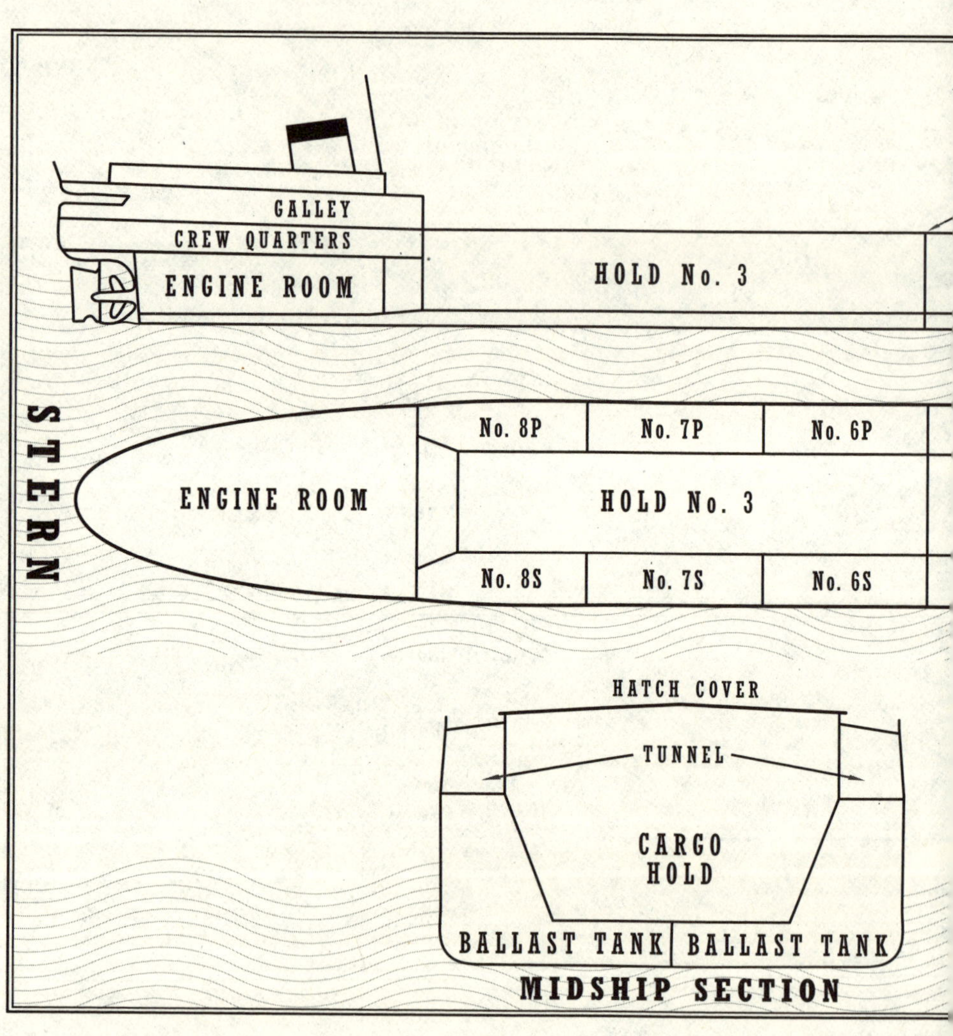
GALLEY
CREW QUARTERS
ENGINE ROOM
HOLD No. 3
STERN
No. 8P
No. 7P
No. 6P
ENGINE ROOM
HOLD No. 3
No. 8S
No. 7S
No. 6S
HATCH COVER
TUNNEL
CARGO HOLD
BALLAST TANK
BALLAST TANK
MIDSHIP SECTION

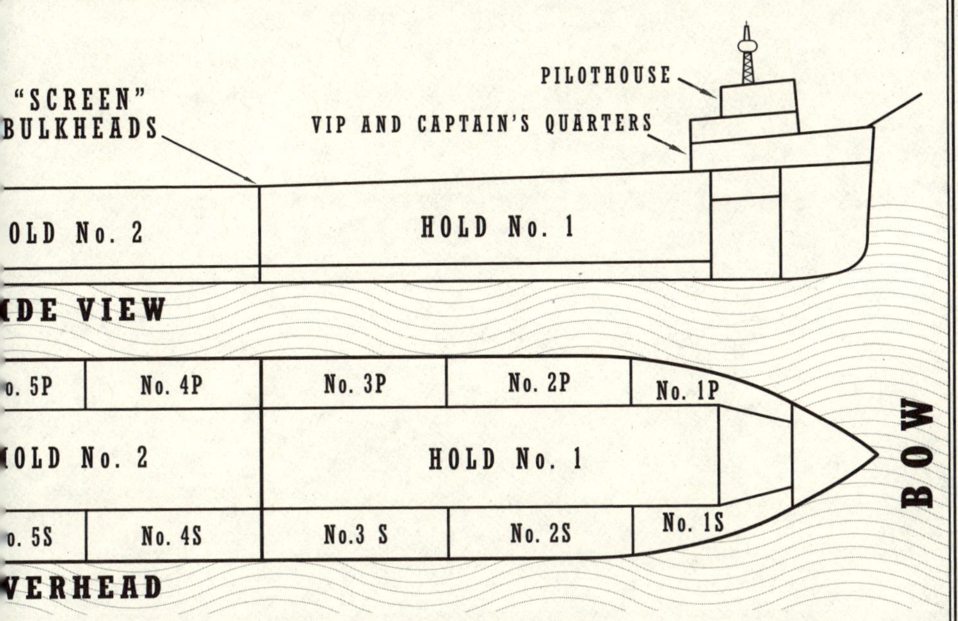

SS *EDMUND FITZGERALD*

Length overall	729 feet
Breadth	75 feet
Depth	39 feet

AUTHOR'S NOTE

Like a lot of Michiganders, I grew up fascinated by the Great Lakes in general, and the *Edmund Fitzgerald* in particular. Once you've caught the bug, it's hard to shake, as many can attest.

I first wrote a proposal two decades ago, but when I finally started this book in 2022, I soon learned that writing about the *Edmund Fitzgerald* presented several challenges I had not foreseen.

Wading through countless books, documentaries, and articles about the *Fitz* and conducting hundreds of interviews confirmed two things: there remains a great deal of interest in the subject, and there is little everyone agrees on beyond the fact that the *Edmund Fitzgerald* sank on November 10, 1975. In addition to the wide-ranging theories of how the *Fitzgerald* ultimately foundered, other factual questions regarding the intensity of the winds, the size of the waves, and the *Fitzgerald*'s exact position throughout its final two days, among other details, have generated an array of answers from authors, experts, investigators, and government officials—just one reason why the *Fitzgerald* remains covered in mystery. When faced with several possibilities regarding the data on a particular question, I did my best to make the most reasonable judgments, grounded in as many facts as possible. When answers are largely unknown, or the questions have produced deep, irreconcilable disagreements, I generally present the competing theories and let the reader decide.

I worked hard to produce the most accurate report possible on the *Edmund Fitzgerald*, bouncing many drafts off subject experts and eyewitnesses for fact-checking, but I make no claim to be a scientist or naval investigator. While this book should pass muster with those experts, many of whom have vetted it, it is intended for general readers.

To those ends, I have measured speed in miles per hour instead of knots (Great Lakes sailors and investigators often use both); used *ship* and *boat* almost interchangeably, as Great Lakes sailors do (but ocean sailors do not); and frequently used pounds instead of tons, because on the Great Lakes they use something called "long tons," which are actually 2,240 pounds each, not 2,000. As a nod to the sailors, I identify what we landlubbers call maps as "charts" throughout, except on the book's opening maps themselves, because those are not navigational charts. (The glossary provides more information.)

The term *engineer* here refers not to engineers who work on land, but to those who work below deck and in the stern of a Great Lakes freighter, and are responsible for keeping the ship's many mechanical systems running smoothly, especially the engine.

Also, I frequently refer to "crewmen" and the like, simply because the *Edmund Fitzgerald*'s twenty-nine crew members were all men, as were the crews of the other three hundred–plus ships on the Great Lakes fifty years ago. I'm pleased to report that on the two venerable ships I sailed on in 2024—the *Wilfred Sykes* and the *Arthur M. Anderson*, both of which were sailing alongside the *Edmund Fitzgerald* on November 10, 1975—skilled women could be found working everywhere from the galley to the engine room to the pilothouse, and both ships are now operated by racially and geographically diverse crews, none of which was true fifty years ago.

All quotes presented here are just that: quotes, taken verbatim directly from the source or as reported by the source, as a firsthand witness to a conversation. Where a conversation is paraphrased, it does not appear in quotes. No dialogue, or anything else, is fabricated.

I hope this subject captivates you as much as it has me.

—John U. Bacon
Ann Arbor, Michigan
May 2025

PROLOGUE

On Tuesday, July 4, 1995, a serene summer day, a boat named the *Northlander* eased across calm seas until she sat directly over her destination:

46 degrees, 59 minutes north latitude
85 degrees, 6 minutes west longitude

These coordinates mark the final resting place of the SS *Edmund Fitzgerald*, which lies in two big broken sections under 530 feet of Lake Superior's frigid water, just barely on the Canadian side of the invisible line that divides the world's largest freshwater lake.

Onboard were the Reverend Richard Ingalls Sr., the rector of Detroit's Mariners' Church, and the families of the *Edmund Fitzgerald*'s twenty-nine crewmen.

When the *Fitzgerald* foundered on November 10, 1975, the people who would gather aboard the *Northlander* twenty years later had not yet met each other. In 1975 they had little in common beyond losing a loved one on the *Fitzgerald*. But after two decades of working together to get various governments to declare the sunken ship a gravesite, they had developed a deep trust. United in their grief and their determination to shield the ship from the grifters seeking to profit from their loss, they had built a bond they dared not extend beyond their tight circle.

Who else could really understand how they felt?

Although she was the mother of Bruce Hudson, a twenty-year-old deckhand on the *Fitzgerald*, everyone in the *Fitzgerald* family knew Ruth Hudson as "Aunt Ruth," thanks to her frequent companion and devoted niece, Pam Wittig.

"Aunt Ruth was all of four foot nine," Wittig says. "But she told everyone she was five foot four—and they believed her! She stood like she was six feet tall, and she would kick your butt. She was a tough little woman with a big heart, and really put together. She was not well educated, but you'd never know it because she was so well-read."

Born Ruth Gladys Kincaid, the fourth of ten children, Aunt Ruth grew up during the Great Depression in Kincaid, West Virginia, a coal mining town named after her family. Her first serious beau, a young man named Alva Edison Hudson, who went by Edison, left her heartbroken when he married another girl. In May of 1943, just three weeks after his wedding and one month before Edison was scheduled to be deployed in Europe, he was electrocuted in an accident at the Mary Francis coal mine.

After his death Ruth grew close to Edison's brother Oddis Hudson, who was pressed into military service in Italy in 1945. They married in late 1946, and eventually settled in North Olmsted, Ohio, a Cleveland suburb, where they raised their only child, Bruce, born in 1953.

Oddis took a job at the General Motors plant in Youngstown, while Ruth worked at the Bonne Bell Cosmetics factory in Westlake. Ruth's sister Betty Woodman and her family—including her middle child, now Pam Woodman Wittig—lived just a few miles away.

"There weren't two days Aunt Ruth and I would go without seeing each other," Pam says. "We were so close, everyone thought she was my mom."

Although Bruce was eight years older than Pam, the two cousins were close. He liked to tease her, but he'd also play catch with her, and she liked the attention.

"Bruce was a good-looking guy, with the long hair and the lambchops and all," she says. "He was lean, but really muscular. Whenever my girlfriends heard he was back in town, all of a sudden there was a pack of girls over at our house, hoping to see him."

Bruce had two sides. He played trombone in the North Olmsted high school band, achieved the rank of Eagle Scout, and enrolled at the College of Wooster, a strong liberal arts school south of Cleveland, where he studied forestry. But he also had a girlfriend, a Kawasaki motorcycle, and a habit of hitchhiking home from college with Kelly, his German shepherd, against Ruth's express wishes.

"Oh, Bruce was a handful growing up," Pam says. "Aunt Ruth tried to keep him on a short leash."

It worked only so well. After one year at Wooster Bruce transferred to Ohio State University, then dropped out in 1974 to become a Great

Lakes deckhand, a position that required more energy than education. His family had produced plenty of miners, farmers, and factory workers, but no sailors. So his decision, seemingly made from thin air, took his parents by surprise.

Bruce never thought shipping would be his life's work, often telling his friends he planned to return to school and finish his degree. But by 1975 he had grown fond of life on the water, and signed on for another season—this time aboard the *Edmund Fitzgerald*. He liked the pay, the hard but honest work, and most of all, the crew.

Captain Ernest McSorley, sixty-three, took years to put together his ultimate crew, a half-dozen of whom planned to retire at the end of the season, including McSorley himself. A good-sized man at six feet or so, with a modest paunch, McSorley had a square jaw, a long, sharp nose that looked like it could have cracked open tin beer cans, and dark, searing eyes. He wore his short, neat, jet-black hair slicked back, in the style of the time, and when he was onboard he would not be seen out of uniform. He presented well in his white jacket, and in his more formal black uniform during VIP dinners at the captain's table, the very picture of maritime authority.

Widely considered the best captain on the Great Lakes, McSorley had a reputation for being firm but fair with his crew. He let the six youngsters on the ship, aged twenty to twenty-two, keep their hair long, provided it wasn't in danger of getting caught in the ship's machinery. Two other crewmen were in their thirties, and the rest of the twenty-nine-man crew were all forty and above, most of them World War II veterans. They liked to play cards, pull pranks, and perhaps surprisingly, help the young bucks, so long as the new guys got their work done—and they did.

Mark Thomas, a twenty-one-year-old from Richmond Heights, Ohio, another Cleveland suburb, became Bruce Hudson's closest friend onboard. The two bonded over long talks during the *Fitzgerald*'s four dozen round trips across the Great Lakes that season. They made increasingly detailed plans to take Hudson's burgundy 1974 Dodge Challenger on a cross-country road trip as soon as the shipping season ended. Hudson's eye-catching muscle car waited for them at the dock in Toledo, Ohio, where the *Fitzgerald* was scheduled to tie up for the year on November 12, 1975.

During the summer of 1975, however, Hudson injured his back and needed a couple months off to heal. While recuperating he resumed his relationship with Cindy Reynolds, a cute, vivacious blonde in Toledo. When Bruce returned to the *Fitzgerald* in September, he called Cindy from a pay phone and received a shock: She was pregnant. To Cindy's great relief, Bruce was not upset. He assured her they'd move in and raise the baby together, and she told him he should still go on his cross-country trip with Thomas.

But on November 10, 1975—a couple days before Hudson and Thomas planned to head west in Hudson's hotrod—a storm rushing up from the American southwest and an Arctic cold front that had cut across Canada collided over Lake Superior. The clash created 100-mph winds, blinding snow, and fifty-foot waves just outside the safety of Whitefish Bay. The Mighty *Fitz*, alone now, found itself at the worst possible place, at the worst possible time. The tempest would exploit the weak points that could sink the *Fitzgerald*'s first-rate captain and crew, while summoning the strengths that might save them.

I

THE RISKS

A Higher Degree of Danger

FEW AMERICANS UNDERSTAND JUST HOW GREAT THE Great Lakes really are.

Describing them is like trying to capture the magnitude of the Grand Canyon in words alone. It can't be done. You simply have to see them to believe them.

Unlike the Grand Canyon, the majesty of the Great Lakes isn't immediately apparent. The lakes don't open before you in a single, sweeping view. Their immensity fully unfolds only for those who navigate their waters. The rest of us are left with statistics, analogies, and comparisons to try to comprehend their enormity.

How big are they? In terms of volume, these five lakes—west to east, Lake Superior, Lake Michigan, Lake Huron, Lake Erie, and Lake Ontario (Great Lakes schoolchildren learn the acronym HOMES)—hold more than 80 percent of North America's freshwater, and more than *20 percent* of the world's. If you could empty the Great Lakes over North and South America, you would flood the land in a foot of standing water.

Another perspective: If you stand on any of the Great Lakes' shores and look across, at most points it's impossible to see the far shore. This has nothing to do with atmospheric visibility; they're simply so vast that the earth's curvature renders the port cities across the water invisible even on the clearest days. When you're sailing in the middle of Lake Superior, Lake Michigan, or Lake Huron, you cannot see *either* shore. You might as well be bobbing aimlessly in the middle of an ocean, lost as can be—which must be how many Great Lakes' victims felt before their boats disappeared.

When Alexis de Tocqueville, the Parisian aristocrat and polymath, traveled to the United States in the 1830s to write his famed treatise,

Democracy in America, he was most awestruck by the Great Lakes. "This lake without sails, this shore which does not yet show any trace of the passage of man, this eternal forest which borders it; all that, I assure you, is not grand in poetry only; it's the most extraordinary spectacle that I have seen in my life."

And de Tocqueville was describing Lake Erie, the smallest of the five.

Collectively, the five lakes cover a surface area equal to that of Vermont, New Hampshire, Massachusetts, Connecticut, Rhode Island, and Maine—the whole of New England—plus the state of New York. Lake Superior alone, the largest and deepest of the Great Lakes, spans 160 miles north to south, and 350 miles east to west, forming an area larger than all of Ireland. From outer space the Great Lakes are North America's most visible topographical feature.

Recognizing the importance of the Great Lakes, in 1969 the U.S. Congress created the nation's sixth maritime academy in Traverse City, Michigan, on Lake Michigan—the only maritime academy not on the Atlantic, Pacific, or Gulf coasts—so future captains and engineers could learn the mysteries of the lakes, and how to navigate them.

John Tanner, seventy-five, served as the superintendent of the Great Lakes Maritime Academy (GLMA) for fifteen years.

"The word 'lake' doesn't do them justice," he says. "People on the coasts don't get it. The Great Lakes don't behave like lakes. They function more like seas, big enough to develop waves, which grow as they cross the lakes."

THE GREAT LAKES can be more treacherous than the oceans.

One reason is the distinct structure and frequency of the Great Lakes' freshwater waves. In the oceans, salt weighs down the water, squashing the waves and spreading them out, so they typically form larger but smoother swells, similar to a roller coaster.

On the Great Lakes there's no salt to hold down the waves, so they rise more sharply and travel closer together, like jagged mountains of water coming at you in rapid succession. These waves don't roll; they peak, crest, then crash down on whatever is unlucky enough to lie below them.

"Go to Southern California," says Guy Meadows, a professor at Michigan Technological University and the founding director of MTU's Great Lakes Research Center (GLRC). "The mellow swells rolling by are generated by a storm hundreds or thousands of miles away. So by the time they get to the coast, they've been smoothed out and make beautiful surfing waves.

"The Great Lakes' waves are what we call 'locally generated seas.' They're not created by some storm thousands of miles away, but rather by the storm right here, right on top of us, right now.

"Boom. Just like being inside a hurricane."

That's another reason why Great Lakes waves are so steep and ragged and travel so fast. On the ocean the waves are usually about ten to sixteen seconds apart, so even a large container ship can fit between them. On Lake Superior the waves run four to eight seconds apart, which means that a seven-hundred-foot lake freighter can be riding atop two waves at once.

That problem produces more problems.

On the Great Lakes a ship that long can impale its bow in one wave, which can lift it up thirty feet or more, while the ship's stern can be simultaneously stuck in the wave coming right behind it, raising the ship's back end in the air another thirty feet. That leaves its midsection, which could be loaded with 58 million pounds of iron ore—the equivalent of 4,200 adult elephants—suspended between the two waves, with nothing supporting it. That creates a phenomenon naval architects call "sagging," in which the unsupported middle of the ship sags toward the water below it, exerting a tremendous strain on the hull.

After sagging between two waves, just seconds later the ship might face another threat: riding over the peak of a single colossal wave. This creates a condition known as "hogging," the opposite of sagging, where the vessel drapes over the wave's crest, with both the bow and stern drooping downward, again placing immense pressure on the center of the ship's hull.

A ship fighting through a serious storm can get caught in a harrowing cycle of hogging and sagging every few seconds. This weakens the ship's hull and increases the likelihood of a major structural failure, like bending a paper clip back and forth too many times before it finally snaps.

WHEN SAILORS REPORT waves on Lake Superior reaching twenty and even thirty feet, you have to wonder how they measured them, and how accurate any such assessment could be. Nobody in a ship being tossed every which way would bother pulling out a tape measure to plumb the depths of the latest wave. But experienced commercial sailors rarely exaggerate the height of the biggest waves. In fact, studies show recreational sailors in small boats tend to overestimate the waves, while professional sailors in freighters tend to *underestimate* them.

Michigan Tech's Guy Meadows has spent his professional life studying the Great Lakes. To determine wave heights, Michigan Tech's GLRC deploys six bright yellow buoys across Lake Superior. Each is about the size of a beanbag chair, and is equipped with $85,000-worth of sophisticated scientific instruments to collect data. The professors use that data to calculate something called "significant wave height," an average of the biggest third of all the waves that pass by, which is what naturally registers with us while watching them.

"Your brain automatically averages the biggest one-third of the waves it sees," Meadows says. "They're the waves that do the most significant damage."

Meadows's research shows that Lake Superior's biggest storms occur every thirty years or so, but even in milder storms the waves on the Great Lakes can be alarming. In a pretty unremarkable 2020 storm, for example, two of their buoys anchored off Lake Superior's southern shore, far from the path of Superior's biggest waves, measured waves reaching 28.5 feet, almost as high as a three-story building.

"Well," Meadows says, "that gets your attention."

There's more: Wind speed does not merely increase a wave's power proportionally, but *exponentially*. The math goes like this: Wave *periods* (the elapsed time between each wave crest, or the wave's speed) increase with wind speed directly, but wave *heights* increase as a function of wind speed *squared*. This means if wind speed doubles, wave height increases by a factor of four. Wave *power* equals wave speed times wave height *squared*, and will also increase by a factor of *four*.

Put it all together: When the winds increase from 20 mph to 40 mph, they produce waves that contain at least *sixteen times* more power.

A thirty-foot wave with a period of ten seconds will generate 3,700 pounds of pressure per square foot—more than enough to crush a four-inch-thick slab of concrete.

So when Great Lakes sailors watch the wind rise from 20 to 40 mph, they know everything they're fighting just multiplied. They're in for a hell of a trip, something to tell their grandkids about—if they're lucky. Fortunately for Great Lakes sailors, most don't see thirty-foot waves very often, and some have gone their entire careers without seeing even twenty-footers.

"I've seen fifteen- to twenty-footers, *once*," says retired Great Lakes sailor John Hayes. "That's enough. Trust me."

Weather on the Great Lakes ranks among the world's most erratic. You can be enjoying a peaceful morning fishing in calm, balmy weather, then find yourself hurrying to take shelter from a blizzard blowing in from Western Canada before lunch.

Storms can kick up just about any time on the Great Lakes, but they are at their meanest in November, when the wind is the strongest, the waves are the biggest, and both are often accompanied by sleet, snow, and hail.

"If you've never been on a laker, you can't know what it feels like to ride in rough weather," says Rick Barthuli, who served on the SS *Arthur M. Anderson*, which followed closely behind the *Fitzgerald* on November 10, 1975. "On the Great Lakes big ships like that don't ride like a boat, up and down the waves. They ride like a train. When you slam into a wave, your ship goes *boom-boom-boom!*—like all the train cars slamming together, one by one. And then it stretches back out, and you do it again—*boom-boom-boom!* Spend one night like that and you won't forget it."

When we rank our most essential needs, water ranks a close second to oxygen. It's so fun to play in and beautiful to watch that its dangers are easy to underestimate.

A cubic yard of water weighs 1,700 pounds, about the same as a large male polar bear. The face of a thirty-foot wave alone weighs almost 20,000 pounds, to say nothing of the force of weight coming right behind it.

"When that wave is moving at about thirty-six miles per hour," Meadows explains, "it's like getting hit by a fully loaded moving truck."

In a Great Lakes squall, those waves come over your ship every four to eight seconds. If you happen to be on the deck when one hits, you'll soon be off the deck. In such conditions a ship's equipment can become heavy and sluggish, including the steering; hands grow stiff with bone-deep cold; and the deck becomes slick, then icy, and finally impossible to pass, or even stand on. Once the ice settles on the upper lakes by January, most Great Lakes freighters—called "lakers," as opposed to "salties," their ocean-going counterparts—dock in the lower ports until the ice breaks up in March. But many ships making late-season runs have to smash through thick sheets of white, gray, or blue ice, with the latter containing the least amount of oxygen and is therefore the densest, and most feared. Repeatedly crashing into blue ice is loud, jarring, and nerve-rattling.

If a vessel gets wedged between two thick sheets of ice, it no longer matters how large the ship is or how skilled the captain and crew may be. Once the ice starts moving, humans and their machines no longer have any say in the matter, and the ice plates can push a freighter clear across a Great Lake, shove it ashore in rivers, or just saw the ship apart like a steak knife ripping through a flimsy aluminum can.

ICE SURROUNDING A ship can be perilous. So can ice *on* a ship.

With no salt in the water, the sea spray on the Great Lakes freezes more quickly than it does on the oceans, coating the surfaces of ships with layers of white ice in a flash. That usually includes the pilothouse windows, which can render the captain all but blind. Ships built after World War II were usually equipped with de-icers—heating wires installed around the windows—but those didn't always work, and even when they did, sometimes the heat caused the windows to shatter when the frigid wind and waves hit them.

The sheer weight of the ice creates another hazard. On a windy night, if the temperature is just a couple degrees below freezing, every wave that sprays the ship flash freezes on the cold steel deck. With waves coming every four to eight seconds, the ice builds up with horrifying efficiency. Full-size freighters have come out of fall storms carrying an extra four hundred tons of ice pushing down on the bow—if they came out at all. That's eight hundred thousand pounds, as heavy as a three-story brick house. The additional weight slows the ship down, thus giving subsequent waves even more time to form ice onboard, creating a vicious cycle.

Worse, the ice also causes the bow to dive lower and lower into each successive wave, which can sink a ship by itself. If the ice is not balanced evenly, and it rarely is, it can create a dangerous "list," a tilting of the ship to one side, which makes a ship harder to steer and more likely to capsize.

"Once you've seen the amount of ice that can form on a ship," former GLMA superintendent John Tanner says, "and how it can grow layer by layer, and so quickly, it's *alarming*. A foot of rock-hard ice, maybe two, covering everything? The image stays with you."

This is why, when Great Lakes sailor John Hayes was a boy, he knew he had to be quiet when the weather came on the TV or radio. His dad, a Great Lakes captain, "was *listening*. I didn't understand that until I got on a ship myself. The weather is *everything*. It's why some guys get home, and others don't. You learn pretty quick to pay attention."

For all these reasons, sailors who've spent years working on both the Atlantic Ocean and the Great Lakes will tell you the Great Lakes can present more perils.

"The ocean sailors just laughed at us," says Hayes, who served twenty-three years on the Great Lakes and twelve on the Atlantic. "But not for long. Once they saw the Great Lakes for themselves, they shut up pretty fast—and then they started looking for safe harbor. I'm telling you, it's not even close—and anyone who's sailed on both would tell you the same."

"When the salty captains first come on the Great Lakes they say, 'How hard can it be?'" Rick Barthuli grins, then turns serious. "How hard can it be? Ask thirty thousand men on the bottom of the Great Lakes. That's how hard. But once the ocean sailors actually sail on the Great Lakes, they stop asking that question."

Once an ocean freighter, or salty, leaves shore the captain has little to do but point his ship toward the next continent and ride for a week or so on autopilot until the crew sees land. The odds of the ship hitting anything along the way are virtually zero. When a salty approaches its destination the captain is rendered all but useless because the local harbor pilots and tugboats take over his ship to guide her in. The captain is obligated to stay on the bridge, but he could read a book or smoke a cigarette, and no one would notice or care.

No such luck for a Great Lakes captain, who spends about two-thirds of each trip in open waters, and the rest avoiding rocky shores, the edges of narrow canals and rivers, harrowing shoals (submerged ridges, sandbars, or other deceptively shallow plateaus), some of the world's biggest piers and bridges, plus hundreds of other ships racing for the same ports. Captains also have to contend with complex currents and recreational sailors, boaters, and fishermen buzzing around their ships like flies, a worrisome combination.

Further, when a captain on a laker nears port, his diciest duties have just begun. He has to make all the decisions himself, and quickly, until his ship is safely secured to the dock. For a captain, navigating a salty compared to a laker is the difference between cruising in the backseat on a cross-country road trip and surviving a demolition derby.

A Great Lakes shipping company won't let you near the pilothouse, for any position, without a pilotage license. Those are obtained by demonstrating local knowledge of all five Great Lakes, including the strength and direction of the currents around the bridges, locks, and harbors; how to approach the various piers at six dozen ports; and not least, where the shoals are, and how deep and wide they run, lest they end your trip prematurely.

"*And all of this has to be in your head*," Barthuli says. "You're coming into port in a storm, trying to get around another freighter—man, there's no time to check your damn notes. And you have to act on all this in the dark, in big waves, in horrible weather, in fog, in ice. You name it, the Great Lakes get it."

BETWEEN 1875 AND 1975 alone, the Great Lakes claimed at least six thousand ships—some estimates from respected researchers go as high as ten thousand or even twenty-five thousand sunken vessels—plus a minimum of thirty thousand sailors. Even the lowest estimate marks an average of one shipwreck per week, and nearly one casualty a day, every day, for a century.

Those freighters battled waves twenty feet or more, faced eighty-mile-per-hour winds, and crashed into lighthouses, ports, piers, bridges, shoals, jagged shores, and each other. They faced fires and explosions onboard, hundreds of tons of ice weighing their ships down, water flooding into their pilothouses and cargo holds, and fog, the one element that could make even the most seasoned mariner stop in his tracks, praying for luck.

And luck was the factor they trusted least.

The Storm of the Century, 1913

In early November 1913 a breath of wind blew some snowy powder over the flatlands of Canadian ranches and farms—such a common occurrence that the cowboys and farmers had no reason to remember it. A few days later, when they saw articles about a biblical storm over the Great Lakes, they probably had no idea that what they were reading about had begun in their backyards while they were milking cows and herding cattle.

Like a snowball gathering mass, the budding storm collected power as it rolled across the prairies on its way to a collision with a severe low-pressure system hovering over the Great Lakes. The storm ballooned, loading up with tons upon tons of water, and accelerated.

Adding to the threat was a dangerous dynamic all too familiar on the Great Lakes: The later winter shows up, the angrier it arrives.

The temperature of the Great Lakes always trails the temperature of the air. In spring that disparity generally keeps the lakes stable; the cooler water stays put. By August both air and water warm up, and even thin-blooded folks find all the Great Lakes swimmable except Superior, which never is. Then in September the air cools down, but the lakes, still trailing the air, stay warm a month or two longer. Because the water is now warmer than the air, it wants to rise, just as steam floats up from boiling water. On cool fall mornings you can watch the surface of these lakes evaporate into thin air.

When the gap between the water and air grows wider it creates waves, a phenomenon common to all the Great Lakes in November. For sailors, it's unpleasant but usually manageable.

Not this time.

HUMANS HAVE BEEN studying the weather as long as we've been walking the earth, but only recently have we applied science to the task. Thermometers, barometers, and other climate-measuring tools spread with the nation's westward pioneers, but without the means to communicate the information, those devices could help only those who possessed them.

Samuel Morse solved that problem in 1844, when he used his eponymous code to send the first telegraph message from the nation's capital to Baltimore's old Mt. Clare Depot forty-four miles away: "WHAT HATH GOD WROUGHT?"

The telegraph sparked an international communications revolution that would eventually include the telephone and the internet. Although the efficient transmission of accurate weather forecasts may seem an obvious application of this new technology, it took a shocking tragedy more than four decades after Morse's breakthrough to make it a reality. On May 31, 1889, an epic rainstorm broke an earthen dam in Johnstown, Pennsylvania, killing 2,208 people. The following year President Benjamin Harrison approved the creation of the United States Weather Bureau, forerunner to today's National Weather Service.

But there remained one last hurdle: People in harm's way had to listen, and take heed.

ON FRIDAY, NOVEMBER 7, 1913, just days after that first puff of wind stirred some light snow out West, the National Weather Bureau telegraphed storm warnings across its Great Lakes stations. Then they hoisted the only warning flag in their repertoire: a black square center surrounded by a red square, which signifies "hurricane," accompanied by a pennant indicating wind direction.

The warning was intended to instill enough fear to convince captains to remain in port. But with only one level of warning, the Weather Bureau's system went from zero to ten in an instant, with no detailed information about the storm's location or severity.

This made it easy for seasoned sailors to dismiss the Weather Bureau as crying wolf, and rely on their own decades of experience instead. After all, most of them had been sailing on these lakes long before President Harrison founded the National Weather Bureau. Their shipping companies weren't paying them to obey some bureaucrat hoisting a flag, but to deliver their goods. They had been trusting their eyes and instincts for years, and those had gotten them through every storm they'd faced so far.

What's more, the 1913 shipping season had been unusually pleasant and safe, straight into November. The Great Lakes had seen a handful of wrecks and fatalities that year, but far fewer than in any season the sailors could remember, and the fall had been glorious.

What the sailors considered welcome weather, however, should have been received as an omen.

Even if the sailors had taken the Weather Bureau at its word, it wouldn't have been enough to keep them safe. The Weather Bureau's forecast greatly underestimated the sheer violence barreling toward them, worse than anything the Weather Bureau's rudimentary instruments could measure, and well beyond the range its officials could comprehend, let alone communicate. No one working at the twenty-three-year-old Weather Bureau, nor any of the sailors they were trying to alert, had ever seen anything like it. Everyone, even the Weather Bureau officials, would be astonished by what happened next.

By the hundreds the captains, trusting their lifelong belief that they knew the Great Lakes and the weather better than anyone, didn't hesitate to cast off right on schedule. Their freighters, most now made of steel, were built to haul record quantities of grain, coal, limestone, raw iron ore, and cement—the building blocks for a productive society, including the building blocks themselves. They shipped these raw materials from the northern Great Lakes to the mills and factories in Milwaukee, Chicago, Gary, Detroit, Toledo, Cleveland, and Buffalo, where their cargo would be turned into bread, cereal, concrete, cars, and the skyscrapers sprouting in cities nationwide.

Going into or out of Lake Superior requires ships to travel through the Soo Locks in Sault Ste. Marie, Michigan. (Both the Michigan and Ontario towns on either side of the St. Marys River—which has no apostrophe, for some reason—are called Sault Ste. Marie; they're pronounced *Soo Saint Marie*, and referred to collectively as "the Soo.") A lock allows a ship to go from a higher body of water to a lower one, or vice versa, by bringing the ship into a huge holding tank, called a lock, then raising or lowering the water inside the lock until it's level with the body of water the ship wants to enter. Then the gates open easily, and the ship sails off.

Over the past two centuries the Americans have built a half dozen different locks on their side of the St Marys River, all parallel to each other, and each with its own name—the Poe Lock, the MacArthur Lock, and so on. But whatever locks were in use at a given time, all fall under the broader title "Soo Locks."

When the Army Corps of Engineers completed their first lock, the Poe, in 1896 for $4.7 million (about $154 million today), it ran one hundred feet wide, eight hundred feet long, and twenty-one feet deep, the world's largest lock by volume. When it opened the Poe could accommodate any ship on the Great Lakes and then some, but naval architects soon designed bigger vessels to take full advantage of the Poe's dimensions. They built the next generation of ships to be incredibly long and narrow, with flat bottoms and no external keels to speak of. The final products looked like supersized barges, with their decks dangerously low to the water when fully loaded, but they were perfectly formed to maximize cargo loads while just barely slipping through the Soo Locks and the shallow St. Marys River that feeds into them.

What these new ships were decidedly *not* designed to maximize was stability in heavy storms. Their long, thin dimensions made them vulnerable to cracking when sailing between or over the bigger waves, and their flat bottoms made them prone to roll between the waves from starboard to port and back, until they reached either safe harbor or the bottom of the lake. These new ships often took on too much water and sank, capsized after rolling too far, or just snapped in half in heavy seas. In an era that didn't offer much comfort or safety in any endeavor, anybody who worked on those boats wouldn't have expected either, but the Storm of the Century would test their limits.

Not long after the storm reached Duluth, Minnesota, at the western corner of Lake Superior, winds climbed as high as eighty miles per hour and waves up to thirty-five feet, conditions even the most seasoned sailors had never experienced before. The storm would rage without relent for four days, ravaging four of the five Great Lakes all the way to Cleveland on Lake Erie. Along the way the ships caught in the middle would display nearly every conceivable way they could founder, flip, crash, crack, or sink—while the sailors would demonstrate myriad ways a human can suffer and die on the Great Lakes.

THE LC *WALDO*, a freighter measuring 387 by 48 feet, loaded iron ore in Two Harbors, Minnesota, a port at the western end of Lake Superior, then pushed off two hours before the Weather Bureau issued its storm warning on Friday, November 7. Riding low with twenty-two men, two women, and a dog, the *Waldo* was headed for Cleveland, but didn't get too far past Michigan's Keweenaw Peninsula (pronounced *KEE-win-aw*), which juts out into Lake Superior, before disaster struck.

Around midnight the dreaded "Three Sisters," a trio of gigantic waves often seen during Lake Superior storms, obliterated the *Waldo*'s upper pilothouse. Captain John Duddleson resisted the waves' attempts to pull him into the surf while managing to break into the lower pilothouse. Equipped with only a lantern and a compass retrieved from a lifeboat, he steered his ship over the course of four hours to the far side of the Keweenaw Peninsula, the "lee" side, where it was sheltered from the wind.

Going full steam ahead to find safe harbor before the waves sent her under, the ship screeched to a sickening halt on a granite outcrop at the tip of the Keweenaw. The *Waldo*'s heavy load caused its two ends to sag over the rock, and its deck began to crack.

The crew members in the engine room at the stern of the ship decided they would be safer in the bow, not knowing the pilothouse had been destroyed four hours before. Just walking to the bow required them to scooch down the deck while clutching the cable railings to avoid getting blown off the ship by sixty-mile-per-hour winds or washed away by waves reaching twenty and thirty feet. The three-hundred-foot trip took them thirty minutes, and when they got there, they discovered the pilothouse was . . . just gone.

They soon found the rest of their party in the room below the pilothouse, a considerable improvement over the engine room they'd just abandoned, which would soon fill with water, break off from the rest of the hull, and drop into the lake. If they'd stayed in the stern, they would have gone down with it.

In the pilothouse they chopped up the wooden cabins for firewood, converted the ship's bathtub into a fireplace, and rigged tin buckets for makeshift chimneys. They took turns warming by the fire, with Captain Duddleson ordering those waiting their turn to exercise to stay warm.

With winds now reaching seventy miles per hour spraying tons of water onto the crippled ship every five seconds, encasing the vessel in layers of ice and threatening to entomb everyone inside, they knew they couldn't stay there much longer. But they couldn't leave, either, without being dashed to the rocks and pulled underwater.

When their fate seemed sealed salvation arrived on the horizon, where they saw the form of a passing ship, the *George Stephenson*. The *Waldo* survivors hurried to signal distress by hoisting the forty-eight-star U.S. flag upside down, which crew members on the *Stephenson* managed to identify through the blinding blizzard.

The *Stephenson*'s first mate lowered the ship's lifeboat and boarded it in the waves, but quickly realized the seas were too treacherous to approach the *Waldo*. Instead, the first mate rowed to shore, then hiked eight miles through the woods to the nearest town, Delaware, where he found a phone to make two calls: one to the Eagle Harbor lightkeeper, and another to the lifesaving station at Portage, near Houghton.

The crew at Eagle Harbor told him they couldn't take out their thirty-six-foot-long rescue boat because the engine wasn't working. So they launched their second craft, half as big, an open boat providing no protection from the elements, and set out to make the thirty-two-mile trip to the disabled ship. Watching the rescuers ready their tiny craft for the mission, one onlooker advised, “Boys, you better wire . . . to send another crew. You’ll never see that one again. That little boat will never survive in this storm.”

Eight miles out the boat and crew were already covered in ice and frozen to their seats, their lifejackets, and even their clothes. They wisely returned to their station, where their colleagues had to chip their bodies off the seats to free them. They soon got the engine on their bigger rescue boat working, then set out again.

The lifesaving crew in Portage also headed out to rescue the *Waldo*, but they had to travel the long way, east to the Keweenaw Bay then up the Keweenaw Peninsula to the tip—a total of eighty miles. They caught a big break when they were picked up by a tugboat called the *Charles Hebard*, which towed them the rest of the way through the storm to the *Waldo*. During the fourteen-hour trip the lifeboat became covered in ice and the bilge pumps froze, until the crew hammered the ice off the pumps to get them working again.

Back on the *Waldo* the twenty-four survivors and their dog had already lasted ninety-two hours, almost four full days, but they knew they couldn’t go much longer in these draining conditions without freezing, starving, or being interred in ice. They had no idea what had happened to the *Stephenson*’s first mate, who had rowed ashore and then disappeared. When hope had all but run out, they once again found deliverance on the water.

“We saw a grotesque ghostly shape top a wave,” one *Waldo* crew member said, “poise on its crest for a moment, then sink out of sight. As the . . . object again came into view, it was nearer and the mystery was explained, and with understanding the watchers felt warming blood leap into their chilled veins.”

It was the ship from Portage, being towed by the tugboat *Charles Hebard*, which was soon joined by the rescue craft from Eagle Harbor. Good news, to be sure, but their crews still needed to execute a nerve-racking rescue. The men on both lifeboats knew if they got too close to the granite outcrop the waves could smash their wooden vessels against the rock and reduce them to kindling in an instant. But what choice did they have?

The *Waldo* crew hacked their way out of their temporary ice tomb, then dropped a rope ladder. When the Portage lifeboat approached, the first escapee waited for a wave to lift the rescue boat as high as it would go, then scurried down the ladder to the boat before it dropped again. Success! They pulled off this trick ten times in a row, then the Eagle Harbor boat picked up the remaining twelve men and women, and the dog, too.

Incredibly, all were still in good enough shape to escape—barely. Taking in the pitiful sight of the survivors on their rescue boat, one of the rescuers recalled, "Some had towels wrapped around their heads. And some were wearing socks for mittens. The majority had neither. We put our mackinaws and caps on them until we could get them to the tug. The women cried for joy when we wrapped them in warm blankets and when we put them on the tug they offered up a prayer of thanksgiving and asked the blessing of heaven upon our captain and his crew."

Against considerable odds, everyone on the *Waldo* and both rescue teams made it back safely, with the Portage rescuers alone completing a 160-mile round trip in historically horrible conditions.

The U.S. Treasury department awarded both crews medals for their heroism. A year later a salvage crew finally pulled the *Waldo* off the rock, and remarkably, put it back into service, thus completing the *Waldo* rescuers' unalloyed triumph.

Their ringing success would be the exception, not the rule, during the first Storm of the Century.

The Bureau of Lost Souls

EARLY IN THE STORM, THE CAPTAIN AND CREW OF A barge called the *Plymouth* had been humbled enough to not tempt the tempest.

A tugboat pulled the *Plymouth* across Lake Michigan toward Wisconsin until the seas turned rough. Recognizing that she would be safer without the *Plymouth* behind her, the tugboat literally cut her loose in the storm, and sailed off. The *Plymouth*'s captain opted to anchor off St. Martin Island near Death's Door, a perilous passage to Green Bay where the waves squeeze through a small opening between two narrow peninsulas, which has the same effect as putting your thumb on the end of a garden hose, multiplying the water's force.

But on this day even playing it safe didn't guarantee safety. Although the sailors figured the waves crashing over the *Plymouth* probably couldn't sink her, they knew those same waves could easily sweep them off the wet and icy deck and into the frigid lake, where they would be paralyzed by the cold in mere minutes and then sink to the bottom.

One passenger, fifty-five-year-old Special Deputy Marshal Christopher Keenan, fearing the end was near, wrote a letter to his wife and four children, hoping they would somehow find his final words at their home in Ohio. He explained how the *Plymouth*'s tugboat had left her to fend for herself, and the storm had already claimed another victim. Keenan ended his letter with a heartbreaking farewell:

Goodbye dear ones, I might see you in Heaven. Pray for me.
P.S. I felt so bad I had another man write for me. Goodbye Forever.

He stuffed his message in a bottle, and tossed it into Lake Michigan.

With their options dwindling from bad to worse, in desperation Keenan and the others decided the only way they could withstand the crushing waves was to tie themselves to the *Plymouth*'s masts and rails, hoping to outlast the storm until they could free themselves and sail to safety.

Their plan worked—to a point. They tied themselves so tightly to the rigging that when the waves finally subsided forty hours later, most were still securely fastened to the ship. But when rescuers reached the barge, they were met with a macabre sight: The men, still tied to the ship's rigging and railings, had frozen to death, and were covered in ice.

Keenan's corpse had gotten free of the ship, and crossed Lake Michigan. It washed ashore a few days later near Manistee, Michigan, followed by his farewell letter in a bottle.

More haunting tales might have been told by the men aboard the *John A. McGean*, *Isaac M. Scott*, *Argus*, *Hydrus*, *Wexford*, and *Regina*. But there was no one to tell them, because all eight of those ships simply vanished, buried by the waves, broken by the rocks, and occasionally sent under after colliding with other ships. Their stories are lost, their victims forever sworn to silence.

They say history is written by the victors. On the Great Lakes, it's written by the survivors.

A DAY AFTER the storm had wrecked ships and lives across Lake Superior, Lake Michigan, and Lake Huron, it hit Lake Erie with a vengeance. Until then Cleveland—the headquarters of more shipping companies than any other Great Lakes city—had been spared the worst of it, so people there had a hard time believing the few stories that had trickled in. But it didn't take long for the storm to win Clevelanders' respect.

Snow drifts swept over street cars, locomotives, and even rooftops. Thick coats of rock-hard ice enveloped everything that wasn't moving and brought the bustling city to its knees. Inches of ice coated Cleveland's sturdy wooden telephone and electric poles, then record winds snapped them like toothpicks, bringing power lines and telephone wires crashing down all over town. Pitch-black nights returned to a city that hadn't seen darkness since the advent of gaslights decades before.

For days no one could enter or leave, as if Cleveland had been transformed overnight into a walled medieval city. Among those trapped were the famed English singer and comedienne Marie Lloyd, "Queen of the Music Hall," and Helen Keller, who had arrived for a public lecture with her teacher and companion, Anne Sullivan. Everyone stuck in the city had to survive without heat and potable water. The waves so severely agitated Lake Erie, their source of fresh water, that they stirred up gunk thirty feet down, contaminating and clogging the pipes that delivered Cleveland's water.

Injured people who had found their way to a hospital had to take their chances with surgeons operating under candlelight and without water. Those fortunate enough to find a local saloon, however, could drink all night, since no constable was about to bother enforcing the curfew. If you found a warm building with a functioning toilet, you were wise to stay put and enjoy a pint or two.

The storm's energy finally dissipated on Tuesday, November 11, four days after it started. Once telegraph lines were restored, stories came rushing in from the rest of the Great Lakes. Even after Clevelanders had seen the storm for themselves, what they heard still boggled the imagination: Ships their city had built, supplied, and loaded had been smashed like pumpkins and sent asunder across the Great Lakes.

These reports were confirmed by pieces of ships and their contents appearing on shore. In Buffalo chunks of a floating lighthouse called *Lightship 82* washed up onto Michigan Street, including a broken section of a cabin door with a message written in crayon: "Goodbye Nellie, ship is breaking up fast. Williams."

The ships that managed to navigate back to Cleveland were covered in so much ice that the dockworkers could not identify the very ships they had loaded just a few days earlier.

For two weeks bodies surfaced on the coasts of the Great Lakes, and at least one commercial fishing boat pulled up its net to find a partially decomposed body entangled in it. On November 12, five days after the storm had started, the Port Huron (Michigan) *Times Herald* reported from Port Franks beach, at the southern end of Lake Huron: "The bodies were scattered and some of them were high on the beach while others were still lying in the water. Life belts encircled the dead men and from their drawn faces and cramped bodies it was evident that they had made a gallant fight before giving up."

There were so many wrecks and so many victims it was often impossible to determine which ship the bodies had come from. One body that washed ashore on Lake Erie was identified as a crew member from the engine room of the *Charles S. Price*, but, strangely, he was wearing a life jacket from the *Regina*, another ship that had gone down in the storm. In the days that followed more bodies from the *Price* came ashore—each one wearing a *Regina* life jacket. As far as anyone knew the two ships had not been traveling together, raising the mystery of how the men came to put on life jackets from the *Regina*. The best guess, and it's only a guess, is that the two ships collided, and the men on the *Price* had to abandon their ship. If the *Regina* took longer to sink, or if it disgorged its life jackets before doing so, then the men on the *Price* might have grabbed them as a last resort.

We can be certain that an engineer on the *Price*, Milton Smith, was right to have misgivings before his ship left Cleveland that weekend. When Smith told the chief engineer he wanted to skip this trip, his boss begged him to reconsider, but Smith refused, and took himself off the payroll. The decision cost Smith a few bucks, but saved his life. As the only surviving crewman on the ship, however, it fell to him to identify the bodies as they surfaced on the beach and arrived at the morgues—the bureau of lost souls—his last, dreadful duty for his former shipmates.

Many scribes, politicians, and ship owners would blame the Weather Bureau for failing to predict and warn the sailors of the full effects of the storm. They demanded investigations and reforms, including the advent of an intermediary caution, the "gale warning."

But the *Cleveland Press* editorial writers pointed to the greed of the ship owners; "The November dividend has been paid, in the coin of human life and suffering."

It must be said, however, that many of the captains were just as eager to pocket the bonuses their companies offered for delivering their cargo in November—a temptation that would endure for decades.

BECAUSE OF THE intensity and duration of the "White Hurricane," it is impossible to ascertain its final toll. But the best estimates tell us the juggernaut wiped out a staggering nineteen ships, with 254 people aboard.

The Lake Carriers' Association (LCA), which has spoken for Great Lakes commercial shipowners since 1880, issued a statement soon afterward: "No lake master can recall in all his experience a storm of such unprecedented violence with such rapid changes in the direction of the wind and its gusts of such fearful speed. Storms ordinarily of that velocity do not last over four or five hours, but this storm raged for sixteen hours continuously at an average velocity of sixty miles per hour, with frequent spurts of seventy and over. . . . The testimony of masters [captains] is that the waves were at least 35 feet high and followed each other in quick succession. . . . It may be centuries before such a combination of forces may be experienced again."

The LCA estimated that the total value of the ships stranded and destroyed, plus their cargo, added up to $4,782,900—or $148 million in today's dollars. That figure doesn't include the loss of human lives. For those, the LCA sent a total of $18,245.60 to the grieving families. That worked out to $72 for each husband, father, and son who died on the lakes that week—less than a month's wage. The stinginess of the ship companies toward survivors would become a familiar feature of future shipwrecks and their aftermath.

They called it the Storm of the Century. But the 1913 "White Hurricane" would hold that title for only sixty-two years and three days, until November 10, 1975—just enough time for the painful lessons of 1913 to be forgotten.

II

THE REWARDS

The Iron Rush Is On

GIVEN THE INCREDIBLE DANGERS OF SAILING THE Great Lakes, why do it?

When a reporter asked gangster Willie Sutton why he robbed banks, he allegedly replied, "Because that's where the money is."

The Great Lakes region is home to vast supplies of lumber, grain, limestone, copper, and iron; the world's best soil and climate for farming; and, of course, the world's biggest lakes, which connect to the Mississippi, Missouri, Ohio, and St. Lawrence rivers—and from there, the world's distant markets.

The region's Native Americans thrived on these assets for thousands of years. When the French stumbled upon the Great Lakes in the 1600s they recognized the potential of the fur trade, but even they grossly underestimated the magnitude. To maximize their haul the French built sturdy thirty- to forty-foot canoes, each of which could hold as many as sixteen rugged "voyageurs," and more than a thousand beaver pelts. In the 1800s, at the peak of the fur trade when beaver hats were all the rage in Europe, traders sold millions of beaver pelts every year, until the original beaver population, estimated between 200 and 400 million, was almost extinct.

In the late 1700s Great Lakes farmers discovered they could grow wheat and corn in such abundance that they couldn't sell everything they harvested. Their bountiful output depressed prices so much that it didn't pay for farmers to transport their commodities to the East Coast, let alone overseas. Before the Erie Canal and train travel, a pack animal could carry a maximum of 250 pounds and needed ten days to get from Fort Detroit to Cleveland, and twenty more to get to Albany. So Great Lakes farmers turned their grain into whiskey, which was cheaper to transport and far more profitable to sell—facts that soon led to the

Whiskey Rebellion of the 1790s, pitting the farmers against the new nation's tax collectors.

The Erie Canal was first proposed in the 1780s, but it wasn't until 1817 that New York governor DeWitt Clinton finally secured the financing for it. The canal created a nonstop waterway running 363 miles from Buffalo to Albany, including thirty-four locks to tame 565 feet of elevation.

It came with a daunting price tag: $7.1 million in 1817, or about $155 million today. Although Clinton's critics called the project "Clinton's Folly," his foes were quickly silenced when the canal cut transportation costs by an astounding 95 percent. The canal became so popular its tolls paid off the state's construction debt *in the first year*. After hauling in $122 million in tolls by 1882, the canal abolished tolls altogether. The Erie Canal also gave its Atlantic terminus, New York City, a huge economic boost over Boston and Philadelphia, a gap its rivals never closed.

But perhaps the canal's biggest beneficiaries were Midwest farmers and their customers. Once farmers could get their crops to the East Coast, they could sell them anywhere in the world. Today the U.S. still exports twice as much food as Germany, the world's second-biggest food exporter, but it started two centuries ago with the Erie Canal.

IN THE LATE 1800s, when the fur trade slowed due to overhunting, a few realized that the profits they could accrue from chopping down the region's spectacular virgin forests, where centuries-old white pine trees could run two hundred feet tall, far surpassed what they were making peddling pelts. The northern country's short summers create tight tree rings, which produce some of the strongest wood in the world. Michigan's Upper Peninsula still makes the world's best basketball floors, purchased by the Olympics, the NBA, and the NCAA for their finals.

One hundred fifty years ago the lumber industry produced some forty millionaires in the modest town of Muskegon, Michigan, alone. The lumber barons of that era, according to author Jerry Dennis, "earned far more than all the gold found by all the miners in the California Gold Rush."

But even greater fortunes—more than three times greater than what the 1849 Gold Rush would produce—were made after Douglass Houghton, a physician, businessman, and geology professor at the nascent University of Michigan, discovered *boulders* of pure copper in the Keweenaw Peninsula in 1841, and more underground. Three years later these finds launched the nation's first mineral rush, preceding the Gold Rush by five years. Copper wasn't as glamorous as gold, but it proved to be the best mineral to channel the nation's newest technology: electricity. From the Civil War to 1900, Michigan's Upper Peninsula produced 70 percent of the nation's copper.

The town of Calumet accounted for more than half the state's total, and supported ten trains a day to Milwaukee, Chicago, and Detroit; streetcars that ran every fifteen minutes; twenty newspapers in four languages; plus seven theaters and a gorgeously ornate opera house that attracted luminaries like John Philip Sousa and the actress Sarah Bernhardt. Civic leaders could also boast thirty churches, thirty schools, and sixty bars—ratios that suited the locals' lifestyle.

In 1913, in the midst of this unprecedented prosperity, the copper miners went on a strike that lasted nine months and culminated in disaster. On Christmas Eve the strikers and their families gathered to keep their spirits up at Calumet's Seventh Street Italian Hall. It had a saloon and an A&P store on the first floor and a spacious banquet room on the second, with a stage at one end. A crowd arrived for a holiday party it hoped would provide a little cheer during hard times.

The party was in full swing when somebody yelled, "Fire!" The alarm was false, but the resulting panic was real.

Because it was still commonplace for homes and buildings to burn to the ground within minutes, incinerating whoever was trapped inside, cooler heads could not prevail. The entire crowd ran to escape, but with only a pair of doors at one end of the hall, both of which opened inward, the more people pushed, the harder it became to open them. The screaming and shoving didn't stop until nine men, eleven women, and fifty-three children had been crushed, suffocated, or both. The Calumet Town Hall served as a morgue for seventy-three casualties.

"The union blamed the [mining] company for yelling, 'Fire!' and vice versa," local historian William John Foster said, "but to this day no one knows for sure."

The tragedy inspired a well-known limitation on free speech: It is illegal to yell "Fire!" in a crowded theater.

With the strike unresolved the copper companies left for Arizona and Bolivia, while Houghton County lost an average of ten thousand people every decade until it leveled off at about thirty-three thousand in 1970—a third of what it used to be.

"I saw it go up," Foster said, "and I saw it go down."

THE COPPER RUSH didn't last, but the infrastructure it built did. The trains, docks, and towns, plus the armies of immigrants and geologists it attracted—many trained at the Michigan College of Mines (now Michigan Tech), founded in 1885 to support the copper industry—readily converted to the discovery, production, and transportation of iron ore, which proved to be a more durable resource than copper.

The Lake Superior region is home to eight sprawling iron ranges spanning Minnesota, Wisconsin, Michigan's Upper Peninsula, and Ontario, with names like Cuyuna, Mesabi, and Vermillion in Minnesota; Gogebic in Wisconsin; and Marquette, Menominee, and Iron River in Michigan. At their peak those ranges could support as many as seven mines each.

The Mesabi Iron Range remains the best-known of the batch, and still pumps out iron from six active mines. This 110-mile strip runs along the Laurentian Divide, the horizontal version of the Continental Divide. When water hits the Laurentian Divide it runs north to the Arctic Ocean or south to the Gulf of Mexico.

This motherlode had gone largely untapped, however, until John D. Rockefeller bought his brother Frank's Mesabi mining company in 1897. Where Frank had failed, John D.—who once said, "Don't be afraid to give up the good to go for the great"—sensed a fortune to be made. He pumped a jaw-dropping $40 million ($1.5 billion today) into the mines and trains needed to send iron ore to the docks in Duluth, Minnesota. Then he improved shipping through the Great Lakes to Cleveland, headquarters of Rockefeller's Standard Oil, then built another train line to Pittsburgh's steel mills, thereby establishing a vertical monopoly.

The Iron Rush was on.

The men who worked on the Iron Range were tough, plain talking, and hardworking. Bob Dylan, raised in Hibbing, Minnesota, a town smack in the middle of the Mesabi Range that has recorded freezing temperatures every month of the year, once told a magazine interviewer: "I'm from someplace called the Iron Range. My brains and my feelings come from there." Dylan's honest, spare songs reflect the spirit of the range.

The Iron Range is pocked with small, self-sufficient mining towns, with so many miles between them that locals will help any stranger they find in a roadside ditch, to make sure they don't freeze to death. It gets so cold on the range, rubber hockey pucks shatter like porcelain. During World War II a broadcaster trying to describe how cold it was along the Russian front said simply, "Minnesotans would understand," and left it at that.

Thanks to Rockefeller's transformation of the Iron Range, miners became so common in the region they inspired the University of Wisconsin to pick the badger for its mascot. Contrary to popular belief Wisconsin's teams were named not for the rodents native to the area, but for the iron miners, who earned the nickname by spending their winters living in caves like badgers to stay warm.

With iron ore pouring out from Lake Superior's shores, mills popped up in Gary, Detroit, Cleveland, and Pittsburgh. There they added carbon to the iron to make steel, which is more malleable, durable, and rust resistant, perfect for making I beams and cars.

IN 1900 CHICAGO was already the country's second-biggest city, home to 1.7 million people, while Detroit had fewer than 300,000, ranking it a distant thirteenth. But that changed on December 13, 1913, arguably the most important day in Detroit history, when Henry Ford announced his five-dollar-a-day wage for anyone who wanted to work for it, regardless of their religion, race, or creed—a bold move at the time.

"Henry Ford, monster that he was," says Detroit native and author Daniel Okrent, "he did amazing things for the Blacks from the south. He hired them, first of all, when many wouldn't, and he helped them build up equity in their homes," something few African Americans could do elsewhere.

That simple stroke launched Detroit from the minors to the major leagues, more than doubling the city's population that decade alone. From 1900 to 1930, Detroit's population exploded from 300,000 to 1.6 million—one of the fastest-growing cities in American history. The bigger Detroit grew, the greater the demand for iron ore.

The vast scale of the Great Lakes' natural resources gave the United States an almost insurmountable advantage, and contributed to the mindboggling size of everything involved in Great Lakes shipping at its peak: the world's largest iron docks, which rise eighty feet and stretch a half mile into the water; the biggest industrial cities; and the most productive factories. Henry Ford's two-mile-long River Rouge factory, easily accessible for Great Lakes freighters, converted raw materials at one end into brand new automobiles at the other, to the tune of four thousand cars a day—and that was in the 1920s.

But when the high-grade iron ore started running out after World War II, the factories on the Great Lakes needed to find more to keep the machines running. They would get it from an unlikely source.

THE IRON RANGE produced so much high-grade iron ore in the late 1800s and early 1900s that the mining companies thought nothing of tossing aside a byproduct called taconite, a sedimentary rock composed of roughly one-third iron, that runs throughout the range. But once they had exhausted the reserves of high-grade ore, mining companies dusted off the work of a University of Minnesota math professor named Edward W. Davis.

Born in Indiana in 1888 and educated at Purdue University, as soon as Davis took his post at the University of Minnesota in 1912 he became obsessed with taconite. Over the next four decades Professor Davis—whose short white hair, round glasses, and clean-shaven countenance made him look more like a garden-variety accountant than the world-class scientist he was—kept working diligently, certain he was onto something important. He earned nineteen patents pertaining to taconite, including how to crush the unusually hard rock, separate the iron from the rock with magnets, and purify the bits into rust-colored, pebble-size pellets, which are also called taconite.

After World War II, when necessity forced the titans of industry to reconsider the low-grade, lowly regarded taconite, they discovered the good professor's work and quickly became his biggest devotees. In much the same way fracking reinvigorated the United States' petroleum industry after it had extracted all the easy deposits, Davis's taconite patents essentially created a new supply of iron from the old one.

TACONITE ALSO SOLVED some of the problems that shipping companies faced when transporting raw iron ore, which consists of chunks of iron stuck in clumps of hard dirt, with everything that goes with it, including impurities and moisture. It's dirty, pungent, and hard to load and unload because the piles of raw iron ore can freeze together and stick to a ship's steel hull. That can make a ship list—tilt to one side or the other—so the captain either has to stop the loading process to turn the ship around and load the other side of the holds to balance it out, or sail with the list all the way to the next port—assuming the ship makes it.

Davis's taconite pellets, however, are already purified, and don't freeze or clump, which allows crews to easily load and unload in any weather, any time of year. The pellets can be shipped by train or even conveyor belt to the docks, where they drop down through gigantic chutes atop the dock, straight to the ship's cargo holds without clogging them. Inside the ship the pellets easily roll off the sides of the cargo holds and form a nice big pyramid in the center of the hold, exactly where the crew wants it for balance. Loading taconite is as easy as pouring cereal from the box to the bowl. It's also more efficient to unload, transport by train, and ship to the steel mills at the bottom of the Great Lakes, where it's simpler to smelt, too.

Taconite created such a boom that in the early 1950s a town sprang up just to handle the material: Taconite Harbor, Minnesota, about eighty miles up the Lake Superior coast from Duluth. In between sits Silver Bay, Minnesota, where the Reserve Mining Company named its taconite pelletizer in honor of Professor Edward W. Davis.

But taconite comes with one odd characteristic: Because it's two-thirds clay, a porous material, it can absorb up to 7 percent of its weight in water, and four times that can get trapped between the pellets when it's piled high. Still, taconite's many pluses far outweigh its drawbacks.

It's not a stretch to say taconite revolutionized American heavy manufacturing as dramatically as the cotton gin transformed Southern farming, and its impact on the American economy was just as profound. America's postwar boom would not have been possible without humble Professor Davis's innovation, and the ships and sailors needed to transport it.

The Apex of the American Century

FROM THE DAY THE NEW YORK STOCK MARKET CRASHED on Black Monday, October 28, 1929, through Sunday, September 2, 1945, when the Japanese formally surrendered to General Douglas MacArthur to end World War II, the U.S. economy had been bottled up for sixteen solid years—but American industry was far from idle.

After American automobile factories produced three million vehicles in 1941, they transformed virtually overnight to wartime production. The automakers reduced their car production to a trickle of 139 vehicles over the next four years, so they could pump out all the machines the military needed in unprecedented volumes.

The speed of the shift belies its complexity. Building one fifty-six-thousand-pound B-24 Liberator bomber required some 1,550,000 parts, a thousand times more than a typical car's 1,500 parts. Despite the magnitude of the production process, Ford Motor Company's Willow Run plant alone produced one B-24 Liberator every hour, twenty-four hours a day, for years.

It was one thing for the rest of the world to read about America's impressive automotive production, and quite another to see it converted to thousands upon thousands of American tanks, ships, and bombers up close as they overwhelmed the Axis powers in Europe and Asia. By war's end the Allies alone had shot 43 billion rounds of bullets, fired 22 billion pounds of shells, and dropped 5.4 billion pounds of bombs. This prolific output of military might left German, Italian, and Japanese cities, factories, and homes in piles of smoke and rubble, while Great Britain, France, and other European Allies suffered the war's punishments almost as much.

The awe the "arsenal of democracy" inspired lasted long after the war ended. When there were no other major economies left standing to fulfill the pent-up consumer demand, no region was better positioned to pounce on this opportunity than the Great Lakes. The same factories that had produced B-24 Liberators and more were again rapidly retooled to produce cars, refrigerators, and toasters, plus the I beams, cinder blocks, and cement to build more factories to produce those things.

The bigger the base, the higher the pyramid. After World War II the Iron Range established the base of the American economy, upon which taconite, then shipping, steel mills, and finally automotive factories reached heights the world had never seen before.

In 1958, the same year the *Edmund Fitzgerald* was christened, General Motors stood atop the list of Fortune 500 companies with almost $11 billion in revenues and $844 million in profits. No other company in the world came close. Exxon ranked a distant second, followed by Ford Motor Company, U.S. Steel (which operated the world's largest mill in Gary, Indiana), General Electric, and Chrysler Corporation. Rounding out the top one hundred were seventeen oil companies, seven steel companies, and four tire manufacturers. In all, thirty-seven of the nation's top one hundred companies, more than a third, revolved around Detroit.

"I've never seen one industry so completely dominated by one region as automotive was by Detroit after World War II," says David Cole, the former director of the University of Michigan's Transportation Research Institute, and the son of Edward Cole, president of General Motors from 1967 to 1974. "As a kid growing up in Michigan, we took it for granted. Heck, the main concern at GM was not the competition, but the lack of it. They were afraid General Motors was getting so big the government was going to break it up."

Instead, General Motors decided to do the job itself, dividing its kingdom into near-autonomous divisions—Chevrolet, Pontiac, Buick, Oldsmobile, and Cadillac—which protected GM from the government's antitrust lawsuits. When the world's biggest corporation had to go out of its way to look smaller, at great expense, it shows just how powerful it really was.

The automakers depended on the Iron Range and the Great Lakes freighters to provide millions of tons of taconite for the steel mills and factories in Chicago, Gary, Detroit, Toledo, Cleveland, and Pittsburgh—cities collectively known as the "Workshop of the World."

"People rarely talk about it," Cole says. "Most probably aren't aware of it. But the auto industry was always defined by the materials that go into it. You can talk about technology and innovation, but without economically efficient access to the basic materials, you can't play the game. Iron was the centerpiece, which they shipped pretty cheaply on the lakes to make steel. We had it, and the rest of the world didn't. That's how the Big Three did it."

The combination of natural resources, cheap shipping, and American know-how was enough to move the epicenter of global industry from Europe to the United States, and kick the "American century" into full swing.

Where the jobs go, so go the people. By 1960 five of the nation's seven most populous states surrounded the Great Lakes: New York, Pennsylvania, Illinois, Ohio, and Michigan. Only supersized California and Texas stood outside the Great Lakes' orbit, and Indiana, Wisconsin, and Minnesota weren't far behind.

The Great Lakes could also claim four of the nation's eleven biggest cities: Chicago, Detroit, Cleveland, and Milwaukee. Even Rochester, New York, and Toledo, Ohio, were among the nation's forty biggest cities, outranking Miami and Tampa. Erie, Pennsylvania, stood taller than Kansas City; Gary eclipsed Nashville; and more people lived and worked in Flint, Michigan, than in Austin, Texas.

For three decades following World War II the Great Lakes hummed with all the power and prestige Silicon Valley enjoys today.

THE CAR WAS king, and the city that made those cars was the capital of that kingdom, the peak of the pyramid, and by some measures the wealthiest city in the world.

Compared to its industrial-city peers, Detroit was a reasonably clean place to live. Pittsburgh's steel mills generated so much smog they turned the street lights on during the day; Cleveland was called "the mistake on the lake" as far back as the sixties, when the Cuyahoga River burned fourteen times over a few years; and Chicago's stockyards were so pungent in the summer that wealthy families like the Hemingways escaped to their second homes in northern Michigan. Detroit's factories, meanwhile, were relatively easy on the city itself.

During Detroit's halcyon days the Motor City gave its citizens the 2,000-seat Orchestra Hall (1919), the 2,700-seat Detroit Opera House (1922), and the 5,000-seat Fox Theater (1928), all magnificent settings to showcase the best the arts had to offer.

The industry's world headquarters were elegant works of art in their own right: The General Motors building, the Fisher Building, the Belle Isle Casino, the homes of *The Detroit News* and *The Detroit Free Press*, and the Detroit Police headquarters were all designed by Henry Ford's favorite architect, Albert Kahn. With only a seventh-grade German education, the color-blind Kahn produced more than two thousand structures in his celebrated career, including the Detroit Golf Club, the Detroit Athletic Club, the Grosse Pointe Country Club, and the University of Michigan's most iconic buildings—plus the Stalingrad Tractor Factory that served as the fortress the Soviets used to turn back the Nazi invasion.

Kahn did not simply put up brutish blocks of stone or concrete, but created elegant corporate castles featuring foyers with soaring vaulted ceilings, carved mahogany staircases, intricate tile mosaics, forty varieties of marble, and stunning stained-glass windows.

The city's wealth fueled championships, world-class schools, and a unifying civic pride. The Detroit Tigers won the World Series in 1935 and 1945; in 1957 the Detroit Lions won their third NFL title of the decade; and the Red Wings (whose logo is a car wheel with a wing springing from its hub) claimed four Stanley Cups from 1950 to 1955. Led by future Hall of Famers Gordie Howe, Ted Lindsay, and Alex Delvecchio, sports writers nicknamed them "the Production Line" as a nod to Michigan's famously efficient car factories. What Detroiters of the time remember clearly, however, is how the city's teams were embraced by the entire city, Protestants and Catholics, Blacks and whites, Jews and gentiles.

The Detroit Public Schools were among the best in the country, the libraries and museums first-rate, and parents wouldn't think twice about letting their children walk or bus to those places by themselves.

"Of course I came to learn how segregated the city was," says Detroit native Daniel Okrent, "and how that impacted others. But for us, it was a wonderful place to grow up, and the city was utterly safe. Utterly."

A treasured pastime old-timers still wax about: going downtown to the thirty-two-story J. L. Hudson's department store, the world's tallest at 410 feet. Hudson's had fifty-one passenger elevators, a world-record 705 fitting rooms, a dining service that prepared sixteen thousand meals a day, and three transformers that could power a city of twenty thousand people. The store's two hundred departments advertised "600,000 items from 16,000 vendors from 40 countries," and included expansive sectors devoted to everything from fine foods to hardware to stamp and coin collecting. If you couldn't go to Hudson's, Hudson's green delivery trucks would come to you, stopping at many Detroit homes several times a week, just as UPS and Amazon do today.

But Detroiters were well aware that their favorite teams, stores, schools, libraries, museums, and safe, prosperous neighborhoods were made possible by one industry: automobiles. Cars weren't merely a livelihood, but a shared passion, and the debut of the new models was an eagerly awaited annual event. Car dealerships of every make lined Livernois Avenue between Six Mile and Seven Mile Roads, each with windows that ran from floor to ceiling. In early September each year they soaped the windows up from the inside so people couldn't see in. Then they would move the new models in undetected, and on the appointed day wash the soap off their showroom windows to let people gawk at their latest creations.

A former Lincoln-Mercury line worker named Berry Gordy Jr. applied Henry Ford's principles to music to create the "Motown sound." Starting in 1959 in a modest home that Gordy ambitiously called Hitsville U.S.A., by 1966 Motown employed 450 staffers who ran Motown's musical assembly line, with one room filled with songwriters, another with singing coaches, then choreographers, wardrobe and makeup artists, and even a coach for "grooming, poise, and social graces."

Newly signed artists would go from one room to the next, until they sang, danced, looked, and acted like Motown stars—a pop music factory that produced the Four Tops, the Temptations, the Jackson 5, Diana Ross and the Supremes, Gladys Knight and the Pips, Smokey Robinson and the Miracles, Marvin Gaye, and Stevie Wonder, just to name a few.

Thanks partly to strong unions, factory workers in Detroit could buy good homes, a family car, and a modest cabin on Lake Huron, the Great Lakes' less expensive "Sunrise Side." On Sundays the auto employees would proudly wear their logo pins on their lapels to let their fellow church congregants know they worked at Chrysler, "for Ford's," or "up at the Buick" in Flint.

By 1963 the State of Michigan funded fifteen universities spread across both peninsulas, and they were growing as fast as the auto industry that supported them. Michigan State University alone expanded from 6,000 students in 1941 to 40,000 by 1969, making it one of the nation's largest. With so many high-quality, low-tuition schools nearby, for just a few hundred bucks the miners, farmers, factory workers, and Great Lakes sailors could send their children to college, a luxury they could hardly have imagined for themselves a couple decades before.

They were truly living the American Dream, and Detroit was the hub of it all.

III

TO BUILD A BETTER BOAT

Mr. Fitzgerald's Dream

If Detroit was the beating heart of the world's most robust economy, Great Lakes shipping served as the circulatory system.

When it comes to hauling goods, trains are roughly twice as efficient as trucks, but ships are almost three times more efficient than trains and six times more efficient than trucks. The difference between ships and trucks, therefore, is not 6 percent or 60 percent—margins any corporation would covet—but 600 percent, an astronomical savings.

Shipping entails far less friction and traffic, and accommodates much more volume. A flatbed truck can haul two large steel coils; a train car can carry up to five; but a typical barge can hold two hundred, and an average-sized freighter like the *Harvest Spirit*, at 448 feet, can take six hundred. These benefits don't take into account the billions of tax dollars Americans pour every year into building, maintaining, and rebuilding the roads. Nobody ever had to pave the Great Lakes. For all these reasons shipping has been the most efficient form of transportation the world has seen since humans built their first boats—and it's never been close.

For those who wanted to make a splash in the Great Lakes' booming postwar economy, the challenge was simple: build a better boat.

In 1857, four years before the Civil War began, a few local businessmen in tiny Janesville, Wisconsin, near the Illinois border, started the Mutual Life Insurance Company, then moved it two years later to Milwaukee.

That same year a train that derailed between Fond du Lac, Wisconsin, and Chicago cost fourteen lives, including two insured by the nascent company. The victims' policies were worth twice the firm's assets, which would have put the company into bankruptcy. When the president and treasurer paid the families out of their own pockets, they saved the company.

Their decision was the right one, but also the smart one. What else does an insurance company have to sell but trust? The relationship is not complicated: Clients pay the company a little now, and the company promises to pay much more later if the worst happens. Break that faith, and no one would do business with them again.

The company rebounded and grew—fast. Just six years later, in 1865, it expanded nationwide and changed its name to Northwestern Mutual Life Insurance (NMI), which now produces annual revenues of $31 billion.

That a company like Northwestern Mutual commissioned the *Edmund Fitzgerald* in 1957 might seem strange. NMI had never owned a ship in its century-long history, and why should it? Insurance and shipping are not the same industries.

But the relationship between NMI and Great Lakes shipping was actually organic, perhaps even inevitable. In the 1900s NMI started investing in minerals along the Iron Range, and insured the freighters that carried those goods, too, many of which were based in Milwaukee.

Edmund Fitzgerald, who had been named NMI's president in 1947, had shipping in his blood. Fitzgerald's grandfather and five great-uncles had all served as captains on the Great Lakes, and his father, a famous shipbuilder, had risen to president of Milwaukee's largest shipyard. So when Edmund Fitzgerald suggested to the NMI board in 1957 that building a freighter would be a good investment, it hardly seemed far-fetched, and the board agreed.

The only point of contention between the board and Fitzgerald, who was widely admired as an unassuming, kind leader, was the ship's name: Fitzgerald insisted that the company *not* name it after him, and repeatedly refused when the proposal came up in meetings. The board members ultimately conspired to create an excuse to get Fitzgerald out of the meeting room long enough for them to vote on the name behind his back, and unanimously decided to name the ship the *Edmund Fitzgerald.*

Fitzgerald's reluctance might be explained by his innate humility, but perhaps also because he knew, as someone who had been raised in one of

Milwaukee's foremost shipping families and who had insured those ships for decades, that ships not only could sink, but often did. Having to pay out the huge claims when the worst happened was one thing; having your name forever attached to that shipwreck was quite another.

But Fitzgerald also knew that everything in life carried risk, and calculating those risks was his specialty. The surest way to reduce that risk and expand its rewards would be to build the best possible ship. And so President Fitzgerald insisted on one clear if daunting specification: that the *Edmund Fitzgerald* be the best ship on the Great Lakes.

To make Fitzgerald's dream a reality Northwestern Mutual paid $8.4 million to Great Lakes Engineering Works (GLEW) of River Rouge, Michigan (not to be confused with the Rouge River, which runs through it), to build the ideal Great Lakes freighter. But what did that mean?

A Great Lakes freighter needs to perform three central tasks:

- It must carry enormous amounts of cargo;
- It must navigate the world's biggest lakes in all kinds of weather;
- It must fit through the Soo Locks.

These requirements make for a very incongruous triathlon: load millions of pounds of taconite; navigate 350 miles across Lake Superior in heavy seas; then squeeze through a long, narrow lock that runs eight hundred by eighty feet.

Like their peers, the *Fitzgerald*'s naval architects understood balancing these three conflicting demands would be impossible. Instead, they focused on the same two criteria naval architects had favored since the Iron Range had been discovered: They would design the ship to carry as much cargo as possible, while still ensuring it could pass through the Soo Locks. Like virtually all the ship designers before them, they gave far less consideration to the ship's ability to handle the Great Lakes on their toughest days.

This approach produces very oddly shaped ships, perfectly conceived to maximize profits, but poorly designed for smooth sailing in rough waters: too flat on the bottom to avoid rolling in heavy seas, so low to the water they are easily buried by big waves, and so long and thin they risk cracking in between the waves when fully loaded.

Saltwater freighters, in contrast, rarely run as long as the lakers from the *Fitzgerald*'s era, and can be twice as wide, and twice as deep. All this makes them more stable and safer in heavy seas and less apt to "roll" in the troughs, with greater longitudinal strength, too.

To compensate for their absurdly long, narrow hulls, lakers are built to be more limber than salties, which allows them to bend in the big waves, but not break. But this, too, comes with a price: The more a long ship flexes, the harder it is to handle—and eventually, enough bending back and forth can create weak spots.

In fairness to the GLEW naval architects, these basic concepts were nothing new to the Great Lakes. The *Fitzgerald*'s dimensions echoed the canoes the French-Canadian voyageurs had built two centuries before, and for the same reason: They needed to haul huge loads—up to eight thousand pounds of trade goods going out, and eight thousand pounds of pelts coming back, all in one canoe—through tight passages, such as rivers and rapids, and still handle Lake Superior. The famously sturdy canoes typically ran thirty-six feet long and only six feet wide, with sufficient room for twelve to fourteen paddlers, and enough equipment to last for weeks, plus the piles of furs they captured along the way.

But these canoes featured two vital differences from Great Lakes freighters: The canoes were not constructed to be flexible, and their ratio of length to width was 6:1. The *Fitzgerald*'s designers created a 10:1 ratio, which is far less stable in a storm.

Shipbuilders had been making lakers long, thin, and shallow since the State Lock opened at the Soo in 1855. When they started making ships out of steel in the 1890s, they also moved the pilothouse to the bow of the ship and kept the engine in the stern, with the largest possible cargo holds stretched between them.

"Great Lakes ships are not as deep as salties, because the lakers sail in shallower water," former GLMA superintendent John Tanner explains. While the Great Lakes themselves are usually very deep, the Soo Locks and the St. Marys River are not. "You only make money hauling cargo, as much as you can, and you want to reload as fast as you can. So they made the freighters as long as possible, too, and open on top so they can load and unload them efficiently. That's why they look like big, open canoes—shallow, long, and easy to get the cargo in and out. But that also makes them weaker, by design.

"That usually doesn't matter, until you're in a storm. Then it matters a lot."

THE SHIPPING COMPANIES had been making these kinds of trade-offs for decades, but no one had taken these concepts to such extremes until 1957.

To fulfill its mission the GLEW engineers first had to determine what the limits were. The Army Corps of Engineers had mandated that no ship could pass through the MacArthur Lock in Sault Ste. Marie that was longer than 730 feet, wider than 75 feet, or drafted more than 29.5 feet. That same year, 1957, the United States and Canada had begun digging out the St. Lawrence Seaway, whose measurements could accommodate ships no longer than 729 feet.

So that's exactly how the GLEW engineers designed the *Fitz*, right down to the last inch: 729 feet long by 75 feet wide. Depending on the time of year, when fully loaded the *Fitz* would be allowed to draft between 27 feet, 1.25 inches in midsummer, and a more conservative 24 feet, 2.75 inches in winter (November 1 through March 31). That meant, of the *Fitzgerald*'s 39 feet of height, when hauling taconite all but 11 feet, 10.75 inches to 14 feet, 9.25 inches would be underwater. Building the ship exactly one foot shorter than the specifications for the MacArthur Lock would allow the *Edmund Fitzgerald*'s operators to take her up the St. Lawrence Seaway, which was an unlikely trip for a laker, but if scaling back one foot kept the option open, why not?

More than 80 percent of the *Fitzgerald*'s 729 feet were devoted to its three cavernous cargo holds, with its pilothouse in the bow and its engine seven hundred feet behind it in the stern. This made the *Fitzgerald*'s three cargo holds the best in class—that was the whole point, after all—allowing the freighter to carry twenty-one thousand long tons of taconite pellets, or fifty-two million pounds. That's the same weight as seventeen thousand midsize automobiles, enough to pack the parking lot at a football stadium, with five thousand cars left over—all on one ship.

It's hard to appreciate just how peculiar these dimensions are until you see a Great Lakes freighter for yourself. Like a giraffe's neck, which natural selection has extended to bizarre lengths, a Great Lakes freighter's enormous cargo holds look ludicrously long compared to its width. The ship's 10:1 length-to-width ratio is roughly the same dimensions as an old wooden ruler. No designer would ever concoct such a ship if proportionality were a concern, but aesthetics were never a priority.

The *Edmund Fitzgerald* would not only be the largest ship the Great Lakes had ever seen, but with her 7,500-horsepower Westinghouse steam turbine engine, she would be able to sail at sixteen miles per hour, making her one of the faster freighters on the Great Lakes, too.

Few endeavors have bound time so mercilessly to money as Great Lakes shipping did at its peak. And no vessel had been more perfectly designed to maximize those elements than the *Edmund Fitzgerald.*

By determining the absolute limits of Great Lakes shipbuilding, and pushing the *Fitzgerald* right up to those lines, Great Lakes Engineering Works had created a ship built to do exactly what President Edmund Fitzgerald had dreamed it would: shatter every shipping record on the Great Lakes, and make unprecedented profits doing so.

Like most Great Lakes freighters, the *Edmund Fitzgerald* was built to last a century.

Calculating for Safety

THE *FITZGERALD'S* ARCHITECTS WENT ALL OUT ON the ship's dimensions, engine, and other performance features, but they made cooler calculations on safety. Even their budget wasn't without limits, after all, and there were fewer safety regulations in 1958.

The Great Lakes Engineering Works outfitted the *Fitzgerald* with many of the latest safety advances, including window de-icers, short and long radar, and a radio direction finder—which puts out a signal to the ship's next destination's lighthouse, which bounces it back to the ship so the captain can determine the proper course—plus powerful ballast pumps to suck out any water that might get into the ballast tanks. The *Fitzgerald*'s four main electric pumps were designed to pull out an impressive seven thousand gallons of water in a minute, with two auxiliary pumps ready to mop up the rest at two thousand gallons per minute. But all six were built into hold number 3, in the stern. The architects assumed any unwanted water in the other two holds would run to number 3, like water running to the drain of a bathtub. But if a deluge of water invaded the *Fitzgerald*'s holds while she was carrying twenty thousand long tons or more of taconite, the individual pebbles would absorb up to 7 percent of their weight in water, and the thirty-foot-high piles would hide another 20 percent among them—which would be hard to see, let alone extract. If that happened, even the ship's best-in-class pumps would be rendered largely useless.

The *Fitzgerald*'s architects did not include any automated system to alert the crew if water invaded the cargo holds, such as cargo-hold sounding tubes, although those were not legally required. So if water seeped into the cargo holds, whether through the hatches on top or a damaged hull below, the crew probably wouldn't know it.

To avoid forcing the crew to walk the length of the ship on a heaving, slippery, and occasionally icy deck, the architects created two "tunnels," one on each side, which were basically long, narrow hallways located right below the deck that ran the entire length of the ship—a godsend in a storm. These were not made for the claustrophobic, but then the claustrophobic probably wouldn't be working on a Great Lakes freighter in the first place.

If the ship's safeguards failed to keep the *Fitzgerald* afloat, the crew could take refuge in one of two fifty-man lifeboats, or one of two twenty-five-man life rafts, one stationed on the bow, the other on the stern. The rafts were designed to release from the deck automatically, then inflate once they hit the surface of the water. The architects also provided eighty-three life preservers, and twenty-four thirty-inch ring life buoys, twelve with water lights to help with night rescue. That may seem like overkill for a twenty-nine-man crew, but after enough tragedies, the shipbuilders had learned that sailors on a ship going down might have access to only one lifeboat or raft—if they were lucky. Surprisingly, Coast Guard regulations did not require life raft training, or even the ability to swim.

ONE FEATURE FEW talked about, and fewer ever saw, was the ship's ballast tanks. The *Fitzgerald* was "double-hulled," meaning it was built with a shell within a shell, like the classic Russian matryoshka, or wooden nesting dolls.

The "first ship," if you will, carried everything a ship carries, including the crew and the cargo; the "second ship" was a larger shell containing the first ship. The gap between the two hulls, which ran up to about six feet, formed the ballast tanks. The crew kept the tanks empty for added buoyancy when the *Fitzgerald* was fully loaded, but after the ship dropped off her cargo in Detroit or Toledo, the crew would turn on the pumps to fill the ballast tanks with lake water to lower the ship's center of gravity, which improved its balance and stability for the three-day ride back to Minnesota.

Without ballast water the ship would be "double-empty"—with nothing in the cargo holds or the tanks—and therefore too light, riding so high that only six feet of the thirty-nine-foot-high boat would be underwater. At that level, the 19.5-foot-wide propeller would barely touch the water, giving the ship virtually no power and little control over its direction, which would probably burn out the engine in the process.

The *Fitzgerald*'s U-shaped "second shell" was divided into fourteen ballast tanks, seven on each side, which together ran the length of the ship. Even with the ballast tanks full, the *Fitzgerald* would ride significantly higher when empty on the way back. Seasoned sailors could tell immediately when she was "running light."

While these tanks represented another safety feature, they carried a potential danger, too: If the ship was fully loaded and one or more of the fourteen empty ballast tanks was damaged and filled with water, the *Fitzgerald* would sit too low, and become more susceptible to getting buried by a wave or capsizing. Worse, if the invading water filled more ballast tanks on one side than the other, it would create a strong list and make the ship harder to steer, or even keep afloat, especially in rough seas. But the odds of these various mishaps occurring, and all at once, seemed so long that there is no record of anyone connected to the ship expressing concerns over the possibility.

Some omissions were harder to understand, creating problems that were easier to predict. Easy example: "The binoculars they provided were so weak you wouldn't even buy them for your own use," former GLMA superintendent John Tanner says. "But that's what happens when bean counters control things."

For some reason the Coast Guard and the American Bureau of Shipping did not require ships in 1958 (or even in 1975) to be equipped with electronic sounding gear or depth gauges (sometimes called fathometers). Without such instruments the crew would have to determine the water's depth by using a "hand lead," which was nothing more than a ten-inch weight tied to the end of a string. A crew member would toss the weight over the bow, then count the number of knots in the rope that disappeared, disregarding the effect waves or currents would have on the string, the same way sailors had been measuring depth for centuries—not the most scientific method.

Doing so near Toledo's docks on a calm day would be one thing, and take only a minute or two. But how the ship's architects figured anyone onboard could perform this task in the midst of fifteen- or twenty-foot waves is a mystery—and even if they could, what would such data be worth? Without sounding gear or depth gauges, in big waves crews would simply have to guess how much water they were riding on.

"So how would you know if the water's deep enough?" former *Arthur M. Anderson* second engineer Rick Barthuli asks. "Well, did you hit ground? No? Then it's deep enough. On these ships, that's the only way you knew. So a captain had better know what he's doing."

Even with a skilled captain, angry seas and poor visibility make estimating the depth an imprecise art, at best, and some of their charts (which is what Great Lakes sailors call maps) were more accurate than others. Where Lake Superior runs one thousand feet deep or more, it hardly matters. But when a captain must navigate around Lake Superior's Six Fathom Shoal—a fathom is six feet, so the name indicates the shoal is only thirty-six feet deep, though it actually can run as little as eleven—and Caribou Island in Lake Superior's northeast corner, knowing the exact depth can be a matter of life and death.

THE CONSTRUCTION OF the ship started on Wednesday, August 7, 1957, when Great Lakes Engineering Works brought together hundreds of machinists, pipefitters, welders, and crane operators, and laid down the first keel plate for "Hull 301," as the *Fitzgerald* was known until she launched.

Typical of the millions of Americans who left Southern farming for Michigan manufacturing in the mid-1900s, the Nesbitt family moved from Morehead, Kentucky, to Detroit in 1955, when their second of three sons, Paul, was just five years old.

"You may have read about the Appalachian migrants moving north and living two families to a house, while saving enough money to have their own house," Paul, seventy-seven, says. "Well, I lived it. My parents moved to Detroit to have a better future for their three sons."

Paul's father, Grover Nesbitt, found a good job as a welder for Great Lakes Steel at Zug Island, right off the Detroit River. The union job offered better pay, benefits, and job security than farming ever could—until the steel mills went on strike. Because Nesbitt's union had no unemployment insurance or strike funds, even a short strike was devastating.

With a wife and three young children depending on Grover for food and shelter, he went looking for a new job with a strong sense of urgency.

"It was simply survival," Paul says. "I didn't realize until I was grown up the pressure my parents must have felt."

Paul's parents never discussed their troubles with their children, and their boys didn't know enough to ask.

Grover's persistence paid off when GLEW hired him to be a welder on Hull 301. It didn't take long for Grover to realize he had found more than a paycheck to keep his family clothed and fed, as great a relief as that was in itself. He had been selected to work on something everyone already knew was going to be special, the greatest ship on the Great Lakes. Grover came home after finishing his shifts dirty and tired, but proud. He felt good about what he was doing, and eager to share it with his family.

"THE BIG THING about Great Lakes shipping is, we're pretty slow to take to changes, and we're usually behind the curve," says University of Michigan naval architect Brendan Falkowski. "But that's not a bad thing. That means everything has been tested and proven before we adopt new technologies."

But the *Fitzgerald* was an exception to this rule, too. Unlike most ships, which were built entirely on site, the GLEW architects decided to try a new system with Hull 301: building the ship's body in three prefabricated sections elsewhere, then shipping them to GLEW, where they were carefully lowered onto the hull's bottom plates.

They then went a step farther, employing a new hybrid method of welding and riveting the sections together. Recent innovations had made welding faster and cheaper than riveting; because rivets are heavier than welds, and also require a joiner plate over each one, welding also reduced the ship's final weight by some 1.2 million pounds. This in turn would allow the ship to take on more cargo and go faster. Thus, this approach saved time and money in both the construction and operation of the ship, while the designers were confident the final product would be just as good, if not better, than relying on rivets only.

The Hull 301 architects were about a decade ahead of the competition, which would not make welding the primary method of Great Lakes ship construction until the late 1960s. In 1957, riveting still ruled—but not at GLEW. That also meant that Hull 301, by being such an early adopter of several innovations, would be sailing on systems that had not been thoroughly tested before launching.

Buildings, bridges, and boats are all built to bend, but how much bending is acceptable?

ABOUT TEN MILES east of Hull 301's construction site in River Rouge sits Mariners' Church in downtown Detroit, right on the city's first main street, Jefferson Avenue. Founded in 1842 as an independent Anglican church to serve sailors and their families, the church's importance had grown with the industry. In 1957, eight years before the Reverend Richard Ingalls Sr. would become the rector at Mariners', he already had a keen interest in the ships that floated up and down the Detroit River every day, as did his nine-year-old son, Richard Jr.

Four months into the new ship's construction a family friend of the Ingalls named Howard Varian, who worked as a naval architect at GLEW, invited them to take a private tour of the ship. At dusk on a windy November day the three walked among the ribs of the awesome hull, like Jonah in the belly of the big whale.

"We climbed down into the hull on a ladder and I almost panicked," Richard Jr. says. "I couldn't see the bottom of the ladder and it was like climbing into an abyss. It was a great emptiness. The wind was blowing hard out of the northwest that night. The ship was audibly creaking and groaning in the wind. Mr. Varian explained to us that the ships were designed to flex in rough weather.

"I remember imagining what it might be like to ride out a storm on a ship like this."

Fifteen years later, in 1972, Craig Silliven served on the *Fitzgerald* as a green cadet fresh from the Great Lakes Maritime Academy. Sailing on Lake Huron one day they neared the Blue Water Bridge, a graceful cantilevered structure that connects Port Huron, Michigan, to Sarnia, Ontario.

When Silliven and Captain Ernest McSorley were walking from the bow to the stern to get lunch in the galley, they knew it was too rough to walk the seven hundred feet on deck. So they took one of the two tunnels built just under the deck that rode along both sides of the ship. At one point McSorley stopped and turned around to look back at the tunnel heading toward the bow.

"We were watching that thing flex so much that the bow would go down, out of sight, then come back up," Silliven says. "McSorley told me, 'I've been on a lot of ships, and this is the limberest boat I've ever been on.'"

The architects had made the *Fitzgerald* flexible so it could take on the biggest loads in the worst seas, bounce back, and keep going. Whether their decision to construct the *Fitzgerald* out of three modular sections, and swap rivets for welds, which break more easily than rivets, ended up making the *Fitzgerald* more flexible than they intended is impossible to say. The engineers weren't on the ship to experience what McSorley and Silliven had seen that day.

"They say it was made to do that, but it still gets you," Silliven says. "When you see it flex like that, you think twice."

"The Happiest Day of My Father's Life"

June 7, 1958

When Great Lakes Engineering Works completed Hull 301, Northwestern Mutual could savor the certainty that they had done exactly what they had set out to do: create the finest freighter on the Great Lakes, the very best of the three hundred ships then crisscrossing those waters.

For the christening of the SS *Edmund Fitzgerald*, NMI went all out. President Edmund Fitzgerald invited the public to join the launch ceremony on Saturday, June 7, 1958, at the GLEW dock on the Detroit River. Fitzgerald's staff also sent embossed invitations to hundreds of Northwestern executives, dignitaries, clients, and friends to fill fifty-eight tables for the private reception to follow. The recipients eagerly accepted, many making the seven-hour drive from Milwaukee to Detroit.

The launch attracted an impressive fifteen thousand spectators, more than the Detroit Tigers averaged per game that season. But then the Tigers were on their way to a perfectly mediocre 77–77 record that year, including a 4–3 loss to the Senators in Washington that day, while GLEW could offer, as *The Detroit News* announced, "the largest and longest ship ever conceived on the Great Lakes, and perhaps the largest that will ever be built on the inland seas."

It helped that Saturday, June 7, provided perfect weather. A veritable flotilla of 250 recreational boats—many of them Michigan-made Chris-Crafts, with their distinctive white hulls and chocolate-brown mahogany decks—flying American flags from wooden poles off their sterns, bobbed in the waters nearby for a closer look.

The crowd of parents, children, and other history seekers walked briskly between the hulking workshops of rusted corrugated steel, some of them covered in ivy, to secure a spot to see the festivities. The girls and women wore skirts or dresses, while the boys and men sported white dress shirts, slacks, and dress shoes—no T-shirts, jeans, or tennis shoes among them. Beefy shipbuilders wearing clean white T-shirts and sturdy work pants patrolled the rope to make sure everyone stayed behind it, but didn't seem to care when hundreds climbed the roofs for a better vantage point.

They all wanted a clear view of the grandstand, a glorified tree fort built for the occasion atop a two-story building, just a few feet from the bow. It featured a new red-white-and-blue wooden staircase running up from the dock, patriotic bunting on the roof and the fort itself, and red, white, and blue banners flying from the corners.

But the biggest structure on the GLEW grounds, by far, was the *Edmund Fitzgerald* itself, which sat on the pier, waiting to be launched. Atop the pilothouse flew its signature V-shaped pennant with a white field, blue trim, and red capital letters reading *EDMUND FITZGERALD.*

THE NESBITT FAMILY, led by Grover, the welder who was grateful to get a job working on the *Fitzgerald*, joined the crowd.

"Dad was very proud of his work there," his son Paul recalls, "and our family was happy to attend the launching of the ship."

It was a big day for the entire Nesbitt family, with Paul, now eight, squeezing in between his two brothers, eleven and three, to take in the proceedings.

"What I remember are the crowds," he says. "We were able to see between some buildings and observed, albeit from afar, the attempted christening when the bottle wouldn't break. Then the wait . . . and wait . . . until the ship was finally launched."

When Edmund Fitzgerald's wife, Elizabeth, perched on the grandstand like a high-society mother at her daughter's wedding, tried to christen the ship with a magnum of champagne, her first two attempts failed to break the bottle—considered a bad omen among superstitious sailors—but her third attempt shattered on the bow, and the crowd cheered.

Fred Hollister worked as a machinist on Hull 301 from start to finish. On June 7, 1958, he and twenty others had the unenviable job of crawling underneath the fifteen-million-pound ship to drive gigantic wedges between her keel and the huge wooden blocks she rested on.

"It was a strange feeling," Hollister said. "We were underneath the hull for about ten minutes and we knew our instructions. When the whistle blew, we drove the wedges!"

But it would take them thirty-six minutes to jam the wedges far enough under the ship's belly to get the steel whale to budge.

"When she moved the first inch," Hollister recalled, "I couldn't believe it was moving!"

One inch quickly led to another until the freighter heaved off the sloped wooden ties into the water at 12:34 p.m., dragging much of the wood with it into the river. The *Fitzgerald*'s baptism produced a mighty splash, a wave big enough to douse many of the well-wishers on the far side of the inlet, and a thunderous ovation from the expectant crowd—and then another splash, as the ship rocked back and forth until she banged into the opposite pier, hard.

The Detroit News called it "the biggest object ever dropped into fresh water."

Another witness described the experience as "one of those moments in life that you do not forget."

Amid the raucous cheering, cameras clicking by the thousands and helicopters buzzing overhead, few noticed a tragedy in their midst. Fifty-eight-year-old Jennings Frazier of Toledo, Ohio, was so alarmed by the size of the wave the launch generated—much bigger than the spectators expected—that he had a heart attack, and died on the spot.

Once the ship settled into her new home, workers appeared at her bow. The people below yelled and waved, and the workers waved back, as if they had just returned from World War II.

"Dad went home happy," Paul Nesbitt says. "We all did."

Grover's dreams for his family ultimately came true, too. All three boys would graduate from Detroit's elite Cass Tech High School, then college, with two going on to earn graduate degrees—considerable achievements for three men who started life as poor Appalachian farm boys.

The day was just as satisfying for Edmund Fitzgerald himself. His son Edmund Bacon Fitzgerald later recalled, "The day the ship was launched was probably the happiest day of my father's life."

Edmund Fitzgerald retired two years later, a deeply contented man.

IV

"IF WE MAKE IT 'TIL DAYLIGHT . . ."

(The SS *Carl D. Bradley*)

November 17, 1958

JUST 163 DAYS AFTER THE *EDMUND FITZGERALD*'S LAUNCH ushered in a golden era of Great Lakes shipping, and fifty-four days after the *Fitz* set a record for the largest load ever carried through the Soo Locks on her very first trip, the SS *Carl D. Bradley*—the *Fitzgerald* of her time when she was christened thirty-one years earlier—was fighting for her life.

As much as Milwaukee, Detroit, and Toledo adored the *Edmund Fitzgerald*, perhaps no town in the history of the Great Lakes loved a ship more than Rogers City, Michigan, loved the SS *Carl D. Bradley*.

Named for the president of Rogers City's Michigan Limestone, the *Bradley* launched on July 28, 1927. Bradley's wife christened the ship, the Rogers City high school band played, and the townspeople cheered. And as well they should have: Their livelihoods depended on limestone and shipping, and the *Bradley* was big enough to boost both by itself.

At a record-breaking 639 feet, the *Bradley* held the title for longest freighter on the Great Lakes for twenty-two years, until it was surpassed by the *Wilfred Sykes* in 1949. At the launching Bradley himself proclaimed that his eponymous ship was "the last word in freighter construction."

Even in the *Bradley*'s thirty-first year, twenty-three of the thirty-five men on board still hailed from Rogers City, and those who didn't often moved there after marrying the sisters and daughters of fellow crewmen.

For years the *Bradley* set and reset Great Lakes shipping records. But as some of her sailors knew, the *Bradley* was built with structural flaws that the Great Lakes were bound to expose one day, and exploit.

ON NOVEMBER 17, 1958—sixteen days after the Mackinac Bridge (the "Mighty Mack") opened to connect Michigan's Upper and Lower Peninsulas—the *Bradley* dropped off her load of crushed limestone in Gary, Indiana, then headed up to Green Bay, where she was scheduled to spend the winter having her cargo hold and bulkheads replaced. But on the *Bradley*'s trip back up Lake Michigan, the U.S. Steel subsidiary that operated the ship tacked on a last-minute trip back to Calcite, right next to Rogers City, to pick up one last load of limestone, a key ingredient for turning iron into steel.

A southwestern storm earlier that week had already dropped a record six inches of snow in Tucson, Arizona, of all places. Back on Lake Michigan winds had picked up to sixty-five miles per hour that afternoon, but the *Bradley* crew was still not overly concerned until 5:35 p.m., when they heard a loud thud, followed by a second, as loud as the first—sounds no sailor wants to hear.

Twenty-six-year-old deckhand Frank Mays, married with a newborn back in Rogers City, was smoking cigarettes with a crewmate near the bow when they heard the terrible noises. Mays looked back toward the stern—but he couldn't see it. The stern had started breaking off.

Captain Roland Bryan sent the call out: Stop engines, grab life jackets, and abandon ship. First Mate Elmer Fleming got on the radio, shouted "Mayday!" and gave the ship's position to anyone who might pick up the call, just before the ship's power lines snapped.

The *Bradley* had two lifeboats in the stern and one life raft in the bow. The crew in the stern couldn't get either lifeboat free, however, because one was entangled in cables and the other dangled at an angle that made it impossible to launch or board. At the other end Mays ran to the bow and frantically worked to untie the life raft and the oars.

When Mays looked back, he recalled, "I could see John Fogelsonger running toward the stern. . . . Then, as if it were paper, the huge steel plates of the deck began to tear apart somewhere near the tenth hatch on the port side. . . . The tear quickly ripped across the deck. As the gash began to grow, I saw John run toward the crack and leap into the air. I didn't see him land. He just disappeared between the two parts of the ship."

Mays didn't have time to absorb the surreal scene he had just witnessed. Seconds after Fogelsonger vanished a huge wave struck the *Bradley*, causing the bow to twist violently to the port side. That launched the raft Mays had just climbed aboard twenty feet into the air. It landed perpendicular to the water, right on one of its pontoon ends.

But "amazingly," Mays recalls, "I stayed with it."

Just as surprising given the conditions, which now included darkness, first mate Elmer Fleming and fellow deckhands Gary Strezelecki and Dennis Meredith were able to find Mays's raft and climb aboard. The four of them watched in stunned silence while the *Bradley* plunged into the dark water. Then the ship's boiler exploded, sending up bright flames and smoke.

"With the lights of the stern gone, the darkness was total," Mays wrote.

Because Fleming was the most senior officer, he assumed command of the raft. He lit two flares and tucked the third in his jacket to keep it dry. When a German cargo ship called the *Christian Sartori* came closer, with its red (port) light showing, the men assumed they were about to be saved.

As the ship passed within one hundred yards of the life raft, Fleming reached for the third flare and tried desperately to light it, but it had already become too wet. They watched helplessly as the ship's green starboard light, indicating the *Sartori* had turned around, faded into the distance.

THE FOUR MEN on the life raft faced fierce winds and colossal waves, with no plan for saving themselves beyond simply surviving as long as possible. They relied on each other to get through the longest night of their lives.

"The cold November wind cut through my wet clothing like a knife," Mays wrote in his memoir. He had to endure "uncontrollable shivering accompanied by knife-like piercing pain from my cramping muscles. I knew that I dare not sleep. Summoning what strength I had left, I hung on."

Mays estimated the waves ran about thirty feet tall, with each occasional forty-footer convincing the four that this one might be the end of them. When an even taller wave hit the raft it knocked everyone off, requiring each man to muster whatever resolve remained to swim to the raft and pull himself back on. All four somehow managed to do just that. The raft had no handles, so they had to cling to the wooden slats on the raft's floor.

"Our hands grow numb as we grip the small slats of wood that make up the deck," Mays wrote. "Time has lost all meaning. The night is black as coal, and we get little warning before the monster waves hit us. I've never felt so cold and helpless."

When another wave flipped their raft over again they all managed to make it back once more, but each effort took a toll. After the waves turned them over a third time, they found the fourth crewman, Dennis Meredith, floating face down. When Mays and Fleming reached down to lift Meredith's head, they saw that his eyes were completely white. They let go of their crewmate, who was quickly swallowed by Lake Michigan.

Three remained.

At Mays's lowest point, with freezing-cold waves crashing down on them, no ship in sight, and many long hours to go before they would be visible to rescue crews, he found himself thinking, "If we make it 'til daylight, we will be found." Lying on the floor of the raft, shivering while clinging to the wooden slats, May focused on his brothers, his parents, and his wife and baby boy waiting for him at home. He repeated his new mantra to himself throughout that long night: "If we make it 'til daylight . . ."

When daylight finally hinted its arrival on the horizon, Mays and Fleming saw their crewmate Gary Strezelecki, in the corner of the raft, foaming at the corners of his mouth, delirious. When he crawled to the edge of the raft to jump over and end his suffering, Mays and Fleming fought to keep him back. Strezelecki finally broke free, dived into the water and started to swim, but soon slipped below the surface, and was gone.

Daylight still hadn't fully arrived, there was still no ship in sight, and the energy and hope of the remaining two men, Mays and Fleming, were draining fast. Just when they, too, were contemplating their surrender, a U.S. Coast Guard cutter called the *Sundew* came within sight, spotted the raft, and lowered a rope to the two frozen survivors.

"We tried to grab but couldn't," Mays writes. "We hadn't realized that, in our weakened condition, we couldn't even lift our arms."

With the waves still crashing around them, bumping the mismatched vessels against each other, two *Sundew* crewmen tied ropes around their waists and dropped into the raft, in a dangerous and brave maneuver. If the *Sundew* rolled toward the raft—which could happen very easily in such waters—the two crewmen and the two Coasties would be pinned and crushed.

But the Coasties executed their bold plan to perfection, and all four were hauled up onto the *Sundew*, safe at last.

"They were in bad shape, with their faces all swollen," *Sundew* hospital corpsman Warren Toussaint reported. "They were in a kind of daze at first. They had that blank look, like they're asking, 'Am I really saved?'"

The two survivors would need several weeks in their hospital beds to recover. Except for their miraculous rescue the news from the *Bradley* was tragic, and particularly so for Rogers City. The town's St. Ignatius Church, built to resemble a ship, had a capacity of 1,200, but the funeral of the twenty-one local men who died drew 2,000, with 800 standing, and another 400 paying their respects in the school gym, where the service was piped in.

The story attracted national attention, including a photo of the funeral in *Life* magazine. A relief effort, the Bradley Fund, grew to $154,000 (or $1.7 million today) in just six weeks.

Shortly after the hospital released Mays, a U.S. Steel representative visited him, and gave him a check for $300 to cover personal losses. While Mays steadfastly maintained that the *Bradley* had broken in half—he had seen it with his own eyes—U.S. Steel just as adamantly denied it, probably to avoid paying losses to the families for a ship that clearly should not have been out in those conditions, and perhaps in any conditions.

Mays naturally had no desire to board another ship, so he took a job with U.S. Steel as a clerical worker, but a year later the company ordered him to return to one of their ships. Mays was convinced it was U.S. Steel's way of firing him without actually firing him.

Years later Mays and a friend attempted to find the *Bradley*, and discovered the ship in two pieces on the lake floor. This vindicated Mays's earlier testimony refuting U.S. Steel's theory, but the company wasn't moved to do anything more for Mays or the victims' families.

Though filled with anger for several years, Mays ultimately let go his battle with U.S. Steel. He learned to savor life with his wife and two children, and their travels to sixty-two countries.

"Take my advice," he wrote, "life is a precious gift and should be enjoyed to the fullest."

The sailors on the *Edmund Fitzgerald* certainly knew the story of the *Bradley*, and some probably lost friends on the ship. Over meals, card games, and beers, they would pass the tale on to their younger shipmates, so they would know it too—their way of reminding themselves that what they did for a living wasn't just a job, and it certainly wasn't a game.

V

PRIDE OF THE AMERICAN SIDE

The Queen of the Great Lakes

THE *EDMUND FITZGERALD* FULFILLED ALL THE ASPIRAtions its creators hoped it would achieve, and more: Beyond being the biggest and best, its many admirers deemed it the most luxurious freighter on the Great Lakes.

That phrase might seem oxymoronic until you hear from those who experienced it firsthand. To outfit the *Fitzgerald*, Northwestern Mutual hired Detroit's legendary downtown department store, J. L. Hudson, which thrived during the automakers' salad days. When it came to the *Edmund Fitzgerald*'s interior, NMI told Hudson's to spare no expense, and Hudson's dutifully obeyed its client's command.

The captain's pilothouse featured top-end navigational equipment and a chart room—normally a no-nonsense space devoted solely to storing and viewing charts—with exquisite trim and spectacular views.

In 1958 carpeting and air-conditioning were considered luxuries in homes and cars, and virtually unheard of in factories. Likewise, televisions were still sufficiently rare that motels that had them saw fit to brag about this feature on roadside signs. The *Fitz* was ahead of them all, with carpeting, air-conditioning, and TVs throughout the living quarters.

The captain's quarters had its own bath, toilet, adjoining office, and a large living room and bedroom. The rest of the officers were given their own private rooms, and the designers treated the crew, too, with two spacious recreation rooms, one at the bow and the other in the stern, with televisions, libraries, and writing desks. At every level in the chain of command, from the captain to the deckhands, the engineers to the oilers, each crew member could be certain that no one at their rank had better accommodations on the Great Lakes.

The purpose of all this was not to indulge employees, but to attract the very best crewmen at every position. When you weigh the cost of NMI's onetime expenditure against the gains realized by recruiting men who were the equal of the ship itself to work twenty-four hours a day, 275 days a year, for generations to come, Northwestern's spending on the quarters was not a lavish waste but a very shrewd wager, which earned a robust return on investment.

GLEW AND HUDSON'S didn't just build best-in-class quarters; they also invented a new level of luxury with two large guest rooms to host up to six VIP passengers. Those staterooms featured deep pile carpeting, tiled bathrooms, and "stately drapes over the portholes," plus a glassed-in observation lounge where guests could sit in leather swivel chairs and look out onto the ship itself and the vastness of the Great Lakes all around her.

"Magnificent," one reporter opined, "certainly the equal of anything then available on commercial ocean liners."

But why should a company eager to shatter industry records for cargo and profits spend extravagantly to host VIPs?

The *Fitzgerald*'s owners knew that even the industry's most impressive ship and crew couldn't leave port without customers willing to pay for their services. The ship's clients were high-powered executives and their spouses who had already sampled many of the world's delights, and would surely enjoy more. Cunard would launch the *Queen Elizabeth II* ocean liner in 1969, and these were the kind of people who would purchase berths on that famed ship's inaugural cruise.

But even the upper crust had never experienced anything like this: one of only two four-star rooms on the greatest, most productive freighter the Great Lakes had ever seen, an opportunity so rare you couldn't buy it at any price. If the good people at Northwestern Mutual, and Oglebay Norton's Columbia Transportation Division, which leased and operated the ship, thought you were worthy of one of the two berths offered just thirty times a year (they spared passengers trips in the cold springs and rough autumns), then you would be granted an experience none of your peers had ever enjoyed, one worth bragging about when you returned to your country club. The *Fitzgerald* crew even provided Polaroid pictures for their guests for that very purpose.

"The layout and accommodations of the *Edmund Fitzgerald* make veteran lake sailors whistle in amazement," *The Detroit Times* wrote in September of 1958, the *Fitzgerald*'s third month on the lakes. "She's painted the same red with buff trimming as the other Columbia freighters, but that's where the similarities end."

Seen in this light, the *Fitzgerald*'s luxurious amenities weren't extravagances. They were the best available bait for crew and clients alike, and they worked exceedingly well. Once again, Northwestern Mutual had invested very wisely.

"They'd ask the honchos, 'How'd you like to go on a boat ride?'" says former *Fitzgerald* cadet Craig Silliven. "Well, who says no to that?"

INVARIABLY THE FIRST thing people who sailed on the *Fitzgerald* mentioned was not the size, the speed, or the sophistication of the great ship, but the meals.

"The galley is fantastic," *The Detroit Times* oozed about the unusually large kitchen and dining areas, then breathlessly listed all the features the *Fitzgerald* had that very few American kitchens, even commercial ones, could boast at the time. "It is completely stainless steel and cooking is done with bottled gas. There are electric freezers, electric dish washers, electric cake mixers, electric meat saws, electric potato peelers, and a main storage freezer that must hold a ton of meat."

VIP guests woke up in their state rooms to the smell of fresh coffee being brewed just for them, plus donuts and pastries right out of the oven. That did not count as breakfast, however, which the ship served at 8 a.m. in the dining room, where anyone onboard—VIPs, officers, and crewmen—could request eggs, pancakes, French toast, or omelets to order. Lunch arrived at noon, and was usually something simple but hearty like hot soup and a warm sandwich.

But dinner at 6 p.m. was when the cooks showcased their skills, and could include baked red snapper, New York strip steak, prime rib, and Cornish game hen under glass with wild rice. On each five-day round trip the captain would schedule one special candlelight dinner for the VIPs featuring a "surf and turf" of lobster and filet mignon or prime rib, and a special punch served by mess-jacketed stewards. The captain himself would arrive in full uniform at the head of the table, ready to answer questions and regale his guests with tales of maritime adventures.

Through the sixties right up to 1975, the galley was ruled by George H. "Big Red" Burgner, so nicknamed simply because he was a big guy with red hair. He charmed guests with his ready wit and delighted them with the meals out of his kitchen, which inspired the most entries in the ships' guest log.

As *Toledo Blade* reporter George Braatz wrote in his 1970 feature story, after spending a week in the VIP quarters with his parents, the *Fitzgerald*'s "George H. (Red) Burgner is not the most famous man on the Great Lakes, but he may have had the most tributes written about him."

A rider from Crete, Illinois, wrote a poem for Burgner:

And Red, bless his soul,
A bundle of laughs and heart of gold
Who has fed us with gourmet meals galore
So that we will all have to be rolled ashore.

Another VIP guest from Washington, DC, wrote:

When death's dark door I ferry o'er,
A day that surely shall come,
From heaven itself, I'll ask no more
Than an Edmund Fitzgerald welcome.

When Tom Walton served as a porter on the *Fitzgerald*, his duties included serving the VIPs. He recalls that "the passengers always complimented the food—and I mean, *always*. And they were right: The food was outstanding, the presentation was first-rate, and I hate to say it, but we cooked so much that the uneaten food we had to throw out at the end of the night was outstanding, too. Let's just say the seagulls knew where we were, and they ate very well!

"Crew and passengers would eat simultaneously, then I'd sit down to eat last, eat all I could, and give the rest to the seagulls. I put on ten pounds that season."

Even people on shore with no particular connection to the ship were so taken by the Mighty *Fitz* that they tracked her travels and crowded near her whenever they could. The tourists collected at the docks in Toledo, the shoreline of the Detroit River, and under the Bluewater Bridge, where Lake Huron funnels into the St. Clair River, just to see the great ship.

But the best place to see the freighters, by far, is the Soo Locks, where the ships have to slow down and get in line. In the *Fitzgerald*'s day American and Canadian newspapers printed lists of which ships were coming through which ports and when, news that also ran at noon on radio station WSOO. Any hotel clerk, restaurant hostess, or bartender worth their salt working near the locks could tell you off the top of their heads which ships would arrive that day, and when.

The tourists loaded their kids into their Oldsmobile Vista Cruisers, Ford Country Squires, and Chrysler Town & Countrys and hustled to beat the traffic to find a parking space. The parents grabbed their binoculars and Kodak cameras while their kids ran to get a spot on the viewing platform, which stood just a few feet back from the MacArthur Lock. When the ships approached, the fans responded as if the ships were parade floats.

For people living in either the American or Canadian Sault Ste. Marie, the ships were so familiar "it was almost like seeing a member of your extended family," says Roger LeLievre, who grew up on the American side. "'There's the *Ryerson*. There's the *Cliffs Victory*. There's the *Fitz*!' It was always called the *Fitz*."

The *Fitz* was always the fans' favorite. At 729 feet she was as long as a seventy-three-story skyscraper on its side—the height of the tallest building in Detroit's Renaissance Center complex—a rare enough sight by itself. The deckhands repainted the SS *Edmund Fitzgerald* every season and would touch her up before she went through the Soo Locks again. She was the star attraction, her various captains and crews knew it, and they made sure she didn't disappoint the folks who might get only one chance to see her. Because the Soo Locks require tourists to make a special trip, even a rainy day didn't diminish the crowds very much. They came.

"Everywhere we went we were a tourist attraction," says Tom Walton, the former porter. "Standing on that ship, when hundreds were taking photos, you couldn't help but feel a bit like a rockstar. We *loved* being on the *Fitzgerald*. Out on the lakes, when we'd pass other ships, the other crews would all come out on deck and wave at the guys they knew on the *Fitz*.

"You could *see* the pride of the crew."

By that measure alone, the money Northwestern Mutual had poured into televisions, air-conditioning, and recreation rooms for the crew had paid off handsomely. The *Fitz* had succeeded in attracting the top crewmen, and getting their best efforts.

IN 1966 CAPTAIN Newman Larson turned over the *Edmund Fitzgerald*'s pilothouse to Peter "the Commodore" Pulcer, who added a bit of showbiz to the ship's repertoire.

When the *Fitzgerald* sailed through Detroit, Port Huron, or the Soo Locks, Pulcer loved to get on the boat's loudspeakers and tell the story of the *Fitzgerald*, where she'd been, what she was carrying, where she was going, and what records she was setting. He also liked to play Mozart's famous marches, provide updates on the Detroit Tigers games, and in late fall play Christmas classics. The tourists ate it all up and nicknamed him "the DJ captain."

When the *Fitz* sailed past the Nicolet Campgrounds, about four miles downstream from the Soo Locks, Captain Pulcer would get on the loudspeaker and announce, "Wake up, campers! Rise and shine!" In July Pulcer would walk out onto the deck dressed like Santa Claus and bellow, "Ho ho ho!" to the kids screaming from the platform.

"He put on a hell of a show," Sault native LeLievre says, "and people loved it. When Lightfoot sang, 'She was the pride of the American side,' he nailed it, right there. She was the Big *Fitz*, the Mighty *Fitz*. And everyone knew her.

"She was simply the best—and that's before anything happened."

AFTER THE *FITZGERALD*'S spectacular launch, Northwestern Mutual had almost nothing to do with the ship's operations beyond taking its share of the profits and occasionally inviting VIPs aboard for a free cruise around the Great Lakes. NMI handed over the *Fitzgerald*'s wheel to Oglebay Norton, which started in 1851 as an iron ore brokerage. It managed Rockefeller's Lake Superior Consolidated Iron Mines, and in 1921 formed a fleet of its own ships under the banner of the Columbia Transportation Company, which also leased other ships. When NMI retained Oglebay Norton's services, Columbia took over, installing Columbia's trademark gold *C* on a red star on the *Fitzgerald*'s stack to stamp it as one of its own.

Columbia was responsible for hiring, training, and retaining the *Edmund Fitzgerald*'s captain and crew, soliciting clients, and setting the ship's schedule for the season. So once the *Fitzgerald* entered the water, as far as Columbia was concerned, it was full speed ahead.

A captain in a costume could thrill the crowds, but the Columbia corporate chieftains in Cleveland only cared about results. The *Fitzgerald* delivered those, too.

Officials have been keeping shipping records on the Great Lakes since 1887, and not for sport, but commerce. Yes, ego and bragging rights have always played a part in Great Lakes shipping, but profit is the point.

The authoritative annual "Statistical Report of Lake Commerce Passing through St. Marys Falls Canal, Sault Ste. Marie, Michigan" tracks such categories as "largest single cargo" for one trip and "greatest amount of freight carried" for the season. In 1958, the *Fitzgerald*'s first season, she set the record for the largest single cargo, of 22,509 long tons. The next year, 1959, she broke her own record by carrying 22,943 long tons, or 45,886,000 pounds—about 130 Statues of Liberty, on a single trip—enough taconite to build 7,000 cars *per shipload*.

But with three hundred ships on the Great Lakes all trying to set records, a challenger was never far away. In the *Edmund Fitzgerald*'s case, the competition came first from her sister ship, the *Arthur B. Homer*, which launched in 1960, just two years after the *Fitzgerald*. In the *Homer*'s very first season she broke the *Fitzgerald*'s record haul for a single trip, but the *Fitzgerald* still topped her own record for the season and finished first again in 1961.

In 1962 and 1963 the steamer *Edward L. Ryerson* (aka "Fast *Eddie*"), a 730-foot freighter built by Columbia rival Inland Steel, took the season hauling crown, the first time the *Fitzgerald* failed to win in her first five years. But the *Fitz* charged right back to become the first Great Lakes vessel to carry more than 1 million gross tons of ore through the Soo Locks in a season, and kept the crown in 1965 and 1966. After the *Ryerson* claimed the season shipping crown in 1967, *Fitzgerald* snatched it back in 1968, breaking her old record with 1.2 million gross tons through the Soo Locks, and kept it up through 1969, 1970, and 1971, showing no decline as she aged.

Each time an upstart came after the SS *Edmund Fitzgerald*, the *Fitz* delivered her best—and when the *Fitz* was at her best, no ship was better.

"Whenever the *Fitz* broke a record," recalls LeLievre, "they'd fly their *Edmund Fitzgerald* pennant. We saw that pennant a lot. In 1968 the *Fitz* was the first boat to carry more than thirty thousand [long] tons through the Soo Locks. It was a big deal at the time."

In fact, on July 16, 1968, the *Fitz* carried 30,260 long tons through the Soo Locks, shattering her own record, which she had set just the week before.

After she launched in 1958, the *Edmund Fitzgerald* claimed eleven of the first fourteen crowns she could win for the greatest amount of cargo hauled in a single shipping season. Of the three titles lakers compete for—the fastest single run, the largest single run, and the most tons delivered in a season—the latter means the most to the companies because that number determines their profits. It also is most valued by the captains, because it determines their bonuses.

But it is also most coveted by the crews because that title is the heavyweight crown, awarded to the most productive ship on the Great Lakes. For them it's a point of pride.

"She was a legend on the lakes," Tom Walton says, "setting tonnage records virtually every shipping season. She was big and she was fast. Not for nothing was the *Fitzgerald* nicknamed 'the Toledo Express.'"

Cheating the Plimsoll Line

EVEN DURING THE *FITZGERALD*'S SPECTACULAR INAUGURAL season, the *Bradley* tragedy that same year had to give the *Fitzgerald* crew pause.

But for the Columbia executives who leased the *Fitzgerald*, the *Bradley* didn't alter their calculus of Great Lakes shipping. Success was clearly defined by profit, and that required technology, skill, and luck. The men who bet with their lives worked onboard; those who bet with their pocketbooks worked on shore.

EACH TIME THE *Fitzgerald* tied up in Minnesota or Superior, Wisconsin, dockworkers poured tons of taconite pellets from the train cars above down the dock chutes into the *Fitzgerald*'s commodious cargo holds, a process that is so loud that a mere four years working on the ships can cost a crewman 20 percent of his hearing. As the taconite piled on, the *Fitzgerald* sank lower and lower in the water until it reached the "Plimsoll line," named for British politician Samuel Plimsoll.

Born in 1824 in Bristol, a port city in southwest England, Plimsoll dropped out of school to work at a brewery, rising to manager before trying his luck as a coal merchant. When he failed at that he had to take refuge in a flop house, where he became sympathetic to the plight of the poor and vowed to help them after he got back on his feet.

Plimsoll sported a high forehead, a furrowed brow, tiny wire spectacles, and a thick, flowing beard that seemed to set his face in a permanent frown—the perfect countenance for a Dickensian reformer. Plimsoll found his cause protesting the "coffin ships" so common in the mid-1800s: overloaded, unsafe cargo ships that sent many sailors to a watery grave.

Instead of improving the safety of their ships the owners took advantage of a new growth industry, insurance, by taking out large policies on their hazardous ships in a cynical bet against the lives of their helpless crews.

Determined to change this deadly practice, Plimsoll got his chance when Derby voters elected him to Parliament in 1867, but his attempts to pass a law regulating safe loading limits were repeatedly foiled by the members of Parliament who profited from the shipping industry. Undeterred, Plimsoll published a popular book on the subject, which drew the public to his side. Reenergized, he persisted until he shamed enough of his fellow MPs to pass the Merchant Shipping Act, which required ship owners to paint a line on the side of their vessels to indicate how far down a ship could sit in the water after loading and still sail safely. To this day that stripe is called the Plimsoll line.

Plimsoll gained a powerful ally when Lloyd's of London refused to cover the damages for any ship that wrecked, beached, or sank that had pushed past the Plimsoll line. That effectively flipped the insurance equation, making such disasters a total loss for the owner, not the insurer, which finally got the ship owners' attention. The Plimsoll line is now the law of virtually every seafaring nation.

"Cheat on this," former Great Lakes engineer John Hayes says, "and captains can go off in cuffs."

But the risk of losing their jobs, their licenses, and even their lives didn't stop Great Lakes captains and crews from trying to shave a bit off the Plimsoll line whenever they could, and some company fleets were particularly notorious for cutting corners.

For decades the Plimsoll line has been painted and welded onto a ship's midsection, on both the port and starboard sides. Shipping companies also paint a vertical list of numbers at the ship's bow, stern, and midsection on both sides, so anyone can readily see how many feet of the ship's hull are above water, a gap known as "freeboard."

One way to cheat the Plimsoll line: If the stern is sitting too low, instead of lightening the load, a clever first mate will order the engineer on duty to burn some fuel. Since the engine and fuel bunkers are located in the stern, this can bring the end up enough to appear compliant. A watchman can also move the hatch crane—which runs up and down the deck to remove the hatch covers—to the other end of the ship and gain a little extra freeboard on whichever end needs it.

The sailors devised other means to steal a few inches. In Silver Bay, Minnesota, the Reserve Mining company turned raw iron ore into taconite pellets right next door to the dock. From there they poured the pellets fresh from the furnace, which could run up to 150 degrees, into a stockpile, then used conveyor belts to drop it straight into a ship's holds. Dumping five hundred million hot pellets of taconite into the cargo holds can make an entire ship as pliable as a noodle. That causes the ship to sag in the middle, which drops the Plimsoll line in the middle of the ship below the water line. When this happened the first mate would call for the deckhands to hose down the deck with always-cold Lake Superior water, which made the entire ship contract, and the sag disappear. Voila, you've beaten the Plimsoll line.

That same technique worked just as well on a ship that had warmed up crossing one of the big lakes under the summer sun. The hatches would get so hot the deckhands couldn't touch them without burning their hands. While the *Fitzgerald* cruised down the ever-narrowing St. Marys River on her way to the Soo Locks, the deckhands would water down the deck, which took the sag out and made her compliant by the time she got to the locks themselves, where officials would record the ship's suddenly acceptable Plimsoll line.

If they needed to steal a little more freeboard an engineer could ask his crew to drain some potable water from the tanks holding thousands of gallons right before reaching the Soo Locks, then fill the freshwater tanks back up as soon as they got through.

All these tricks can bring a ship up an inch or two, at most. That might sound like a lot of work for such small rewards until you consider the dimensions of the *Fitzgerald*'s cargo holds, which create this brain-bending fact: If the *Fitzgerald* crew could cheat the Plimsoll line by *a single inch*, that allowed them to carry an additional one hundred twenty long tons of taconite. Do that forty-five times a season, and you've moved an additional 12,096,000 pounds of taconite, which made the company executives happy, and won the captain a nice bonus.

But all this comes with a trade-off, as Samuel Plimsoll himself could have told you. Every additional inch a ship drops into the water obviously brings it that much closer to sinking, or dropping low enough to be swamped by a monster wave, or plowing so deeply into a big wave that it can't come back, or cracking in half between two big waves.

But these possible perils all represent graduated risks, akin to going two miles over the speed limit—and then two miles more. At exactly what point is the reward not worth the additional risk? For the shipping companies, that question was easily answered.

"For many years they gave out an award for extra cargo," says retired engineer John Hayes. "One more train car of taconite, and the company will practically give the captain the Order of Lenin."

Given how such incredibly small margins on the Plimsoll line could produce such prodigious gains, especially when multiplied by forty to fifty round trips each shipping season, the executives at Columbia Transportation must have been thrilled when the American Bureau of Shipping (ABS), working with the Coast Guard, reduced everyone's required freeboard in 1969, and again in 1971, and *again* in 1973. For the *Fitzgerald*, that meant the original requirement of 14 feet, 9.25 inches of freeboard when sailing in November had been reduced to 11 feet, 6 inches—a total drop of 39.25 inches, or more than a yard, in just a few years. Other ships were granted similarly liberal ratios.

That translated to 4,710 additional long tons of taconite per trip, every trip, all season. Multiplied by fifty trips a season, that gave the company an additional 235,500 long tons of taconite a year, or 471 million pounds, the equivalent of two Nimitz-class aircraft carriers. In other words, after Great Lakes crews had spent years conspiring to nickel and dime their way to a hundred or more tons of forbidden taconite each trip, suddenly the government was all but ordering them to back the Brinks truck right up to the loading dock and take all they wanted.

But this raises a question no one bothered to ask at the time: If the Coast Guard watched everyone's Plimsoll line like a hawk in 1968, convinced that shaving so much as an inch off a vessel's 14 feet, 9 inches of federally mandated freeboard would imperil the ship and crew, why did the ABS and the Coast Guard suddenly decide by 1973 that whacking 39.25 inches off the top wouldn't make any difference whatsoever?

The answer was obvious, even if no one dared say it out loud: Industry lobbyists had successfully persuaded the federal regulators that the crews had been right all along to sneak a few more tons of cargo here and there. Those extra tons hadn't added much risk, they could claim, and even with most of the three hundred ships on the Great Lakes cheating the Plimsoll line on a daily basis, only a handful had gone down in the previous two decades, and wouldn't they have sunk anyway?

Each time the ABS lowered the Plimsoll line in 1969, 1971, and 1973, nothing particularly bad had happened, with no freighters sinking since the *Morrell* in 1966, so they could fairly conclude that lowering the standards had no effect on safety and that they must have been wise to do so. The rewards were fantastic, with season shipping records falling for the entire industry each year they lowered the line. What was the downside? Everyone was winning.

Alexis de Tocqueville noticed this American phenomenon almost two hundred years ago. "As one digs deeper into the national character of the Americans," he wrote, "one sees that they have sought the value of everything in this world only in the answer to this single question: how much money will it bring in?"

The combination of greed and hubris had proven very potent, indeed. So irresistible, in fact, that even after the industry's guardians had given the shipping companies more freeboard than they could have imagined just a few years earlier, the captains and crews kept cheating the *new* limit for an inch or two here or there, just as they had before, and the companies kept rewarding them for doing so.

If the looser freeboard regulations had demonstrated anything, it was that "more" was never enough.

Once the *Edmund Fitzgerald* loaded taconite at one of the western ports of Lake Superior, she would set off for the 350-mile trip across the big lake to the Soo Locks, then down the St. Marys River to Lake Huron, followed by the St. Clair River, Lake St. Clair, and the Detroit River, and would most often stop to unload at either Detroit's Zug Island or continue a few more hours down Lake Erie to drop in Toledo.

The trip usually took about three days, depending on weather and traffic. When the *Fitzgerald* pulled into Toledo fully loaded, she rode very low, with 28 of the *Fitzgerald*'s 39.5 feet underwater. At that level the *Fitzgerald* tested the limits of the western Lake Erie shipping channel, which accommodates a depth of only thirty feet or so, and significantly less in some places.

"We ran so low that you could almost stick a fist in the water by reaching over the side," says Tom Walton, who served as a porter on the *Fitzgerald* in 1963 before becoming an editor and columnist with the *Toledo Blade*. "An exaggeration, yes, but there was not a lot of freeboard when we had a belly full of iron ore."

It's worth noting that Walton served on the *Fitzgerald* ten years before the Coast Guard and the American Bureau of Shipping dropped her Plimsoll line another 39.25 inches. If Walton was exaggerating when he said he could stick his fist in the water in 1963, it was a much smaller stretch by 1973.

The Summer of '63

IN 1963 TOM WALTON RECEIVED A GOLDEN TICKET TO sail on the *Edmund Fitzgerald* for one magical summer. He got it thanks to his dad and uncle, who both worked for Columbia Transportation and served at different times on the *Fitz*.

Walton's uncle is listed in the official rolls as Ralph Walton, but everyone called him by his middle name, Grant. Born in 1917, Grant Walton, a big, beefy man with a childlike smile, was four years older than his younger brother, Wade. The brothers grew up with three older siblings during the Great Depression in Sycamore, a tiny farm town in north-central Ohio. Both were eager to get off the farm, with its long hours, lonely chores, and back-breaking labor just to scratch out a few bucks, if any. But how?

As soon as Grant learned he could hop on a Great Lakes freighter and earn decent money, he dropped out of tenth grade at the peak of the Great Depression to take his chances. When Wade got to tenth grade he followed Grant to the docks. Neither man would ever finish high school, but they did what so many men did during the Great Depression: They learned their jobs on the job.

Grant settled into a long career as an oiler, the engineers' assistant who oils everything that needs to be oiled, takes down all the readings of the engine's many instruments every hour to make sure it's all running smoothly, and does just about anything else the engineers ask. The working conditions were occasionally cramped, often hot, and almost always tiring, but Grant liked his work and was well regarded.

Wade had higher aspirations. During his off-hours on the ships, instead of sleeping, playing cards, or shooting the breeze over a few beers, Wade pored over dry, complicated manuals and textbooks to teach himself marine engineering. He learned it all well enough to pass the rigorous series of exams that cover physics, chemical engineering, electrical engineering, and more to earn his license as a third assistant engineer, then second engineer, first engineer, and finally chief engineer—as high as it goes on a ship short of captain. Wade taught himself all those things to become one of the top engineers on the Great Lakes.

"He had a young family, and he was determined to succeed for them," Tom Walton says. "I always admired Dad for that, even though I barely got to see him, except during the brief offseason."

After Wade married Edna Ballreich, they had four sons and moved to Oregon, Ohio, just a few miles from the Toledo docks, so the family could see Wade more often on his short stops during the shipping season.

"Great Lakes sailors are a special breed," Tom Walton says. "They love what they're doing, and they're good at it. My dad was a good man, but during the whole offseason, when the lakes were frozen, he was restless, irritable. He didn't know what to do with himself. He couldn't wait for fit out, to get back on the ship and put that engine back together again. My dad was simply not meant to be on land, and my uncle Grant was the same way."

Both Grant and Wade were fortunate enough to sail on several Columbia Transportation ships, including the *Armco*, which ranked just a notch below the *Fitzgerald*. In different seasons each brother would serve on the *Fitzgerald* itself, which both considered the greatest honor of their long careers.

Like Wade, Grant maintained the ships that were hibernating in Toledo during the winter, and enjoyed giving his sons and nephews tours of the ships he was working on. Grant's son Alan followed his father into shipping, but of Wade's four sons, only his oldest, Tom, ever served on a ship, and only for one summer at that.

"None of us wanted a life on the lakes, because we saw how hard it was to have a family," says Tom. "If you're the son of a sailor, the phrase 'Wait until your dad gets home!' loses its luster when you realize your mom is working with a calendar, not a watch. You probably would not see your dad again for months—and who could remember the sins of four boys that long?"

All four of Wade and Edna's boys graduated from Oregon Clay High

School. Tom enrolled at Bowling Green University in Ohio and two brothers went straight to work, while the youngest brother went to college to become an accountant.

"I don't know how our mom did it," Tom marvels. "She raised us all, and nobody's in prison. I think you have to call that success."

IN THE SPRING of 1963 Tom Walton was a sophomore at Bowling Green, studying political science and journalism, and had put his name on a list of potential summer workers for Columbia. When they told him, "If we need you, we'll call you," he assumed he would never get on a ship, and put it out of his mind.

Then one morning in May, when Walton was working at the student paper, *The BG News*, he received a call from Columbia: Someone on one of their ships had to leave unexpectedly, and the position of porter was his—but only if he could pack and get on the ship in Toledo by 5 p.m. that day. Great Lakes freighters don't wait for anyone, and certainly not rookie porters.

Walton had to do some quick calculating. He had about six hours to pawn off his various responsibilities at the student newspaper, drop his classes, drive thirty minutes to his parents' home, pack whatever he needed for the summer, and get to the docks—basically overhauling his summer plans, and potentially his life, in an afternoon. Could he do it all in six hours? And even if he could, would it be worth it?

The tipping point: The ship in question was the SS *Edmund Fitzgerald*. That sealed the deal. Walton was no sailor like his dad or uncle, but he had heard enough about the *Fitz* to know that working on it would make for an unforgettable summer.

"I'll take it," Walton told the dispatcher. He made hasty arrangements with his editors and professors, dashed home, packed, and climbed onboard the *Fitzgerald* by 3 p.m. He'd made it.

As one of only two porters on board, Walton's list of duties was long, and kept him running fourteen hours a day. Among other tasks, porters made certain that the VIP passengers never had to carry their bags or wait for deck chairs whenever they wanted them. The porters also helped in the kitchen, served three meals a day in white jackets to the officers and guests, and darted to the staterooms before the guests could return from breakfast to make their beds, lay out fresh towels, and fill the bowls with popcorn and peanuts—a naval concierge, if you will, right down to preparing the VIPs' desserts, delivering booze, filling ice buckets, and emptying ashtrays.

No sooner had Walton dropped his duffel bag off in his shared cabin than the cooks put their new snot-nosed college kid to work peeling a large bag of fresh onions. It had the desired effect: When Walton finished that task, he started serving his first meal with red eyes and tears running down his face.

Walton took it with good grace, knowing he was being hazed as the new kid, one whose dad had sailed with his new crewmates before. In fact, Walton suspects his father might have put them up to it, so there was no point in complaining. After he passed his initiation, the veterans treated the newbie quite well.

Walton was delighted to be onboard the *Fitzgerald* and made no attempt to hide it. A day or two after boarding the *Fitz*, Walton leaned over the bow of the ship, stretched his arms, closed his eyes, and imagined he was flying. If the folks in the pilothouse saw him do it, they kept it to themselves.

"Who knows?" Walton says. "Maybe they all did the same thing. The *Fitz* inspired that kind of almost reverent excitement.

"It was a wonderful time in my life. I had my first real job. I was making my father proud. And I was earning pretty good money working fourteen-hour days, seven days a week. Really, it was a dream."

Thanks to the tours his dad and uncle had given him on the older Columbia ships docked in Toledo, Tom had a good feel for freighters, and therefore appreciated what the *Fitzgerald* had to offer.

"On the *Fitzgerald*, everything seemed to *shine*," he says. "It just gleamed! I remember the majesty of it."

After the food, guests remarked most often on the cleanliness of the ship. "The taconite pellets hauled by the vessel are dirty," one reporter wrote, "but the ship is kept nearly spotless by the crew."

When Walton delivered coffee to the guys in the engine room in the stern, he was impressed by the "harmony of noises, everything humming and turning, doing its job. The *Fitz* ran smooth as silk."

Every day Walton provided the VIPs in the staterooms pure white hand towels with red stitching on the bottom, "*Edmund Fitzgerald*," in script—a touch of class the guests must have appreciated, because those hand towels seemed to disappear with impressive regularity. The company was wise enough not to charge their VIPs for the missing hand towels, since the whole point of pampering their business partners was to grow their attachment to the ship. The cost of a stitched hand towel or two was easily covered by a contract to deliver another twenty-six thousand long tons of taconite.

THE *FITZGERALD*'S MISSION wasn't merely to wow fancy guests, of course, and it certainly wasn't to amuse summer workers from nearby universities, but to move millions of pounds of taconite once a week. It was a working ship, and the ship didn't let you forget it.

Walton shared a room with the second cook—two bunks, two small dressers, and one bathroom—located in the stern, just above the engine room. Because their cabin shared a wall with the smokestack, during the summer their cabin could reach a brutal one hundred degrees or more—air-conditioners be damned. When it got that hot Walton couldn't touch the metal frame of his bunk without burning himself, so he had to step over the frame to get to the mattress, then settle in for a long night of sweating.

Sweltering nights were better than foggy ones, however, since the foghorn blasted every twenty seconds, loud enough to stir the dead.

"It could be heard for miles, so you can assume I heard it just fine thirty feet above my head," Walton says. "But you know, even that I consider a positive memory."

WALTON'S FAVORITE RECOLLECTIONS focus on his father. While Tom served on the *Fitzgerald*, Wade was working as the chief engineer on the *Middletown*, another Columbia ship. When the *Fitzgerald* was going upbound back to Minnesota, riding light, it often passed the *Middletown* going downbound. When the *Middletown* was half a mile away, which was as close as the ships would get, Tom Walton would go on deck with his binoculars and wave to his dad, who also had binoculars and waved back.

"That was pretty cool," Walton says, visibly warmed by the memories.

About halfway through Walton's magical summer, "a wonderful thing happened," Tom recalls: *Columbia* transferred his father to become the chief engineer on the *Fitz*—the second-highest job in the fleet, next to being the *Fitzgerald*'s captain.

"But you know how I looked at it?" Walton says, with a grin. "In terms of length of service aboard the *Fitzgerald*, *I* was the senior member of the Walton family on that crew, not my dad."

As soon as Walton's father boarded the *Fitzgerald*, he went to look for his oldest son. When he found Tom mopping the galley, Wade tromped reddish-brown taconite dust all over the freshly mopped floor.

"Get out of my galley!" Tom shouted. His father smiled from ear to ear, but respectfully backed away. "I'm sure it was the only time in maritime history that a lowly porter told off the chief engineer and lived to work another day."

Having his father on board had other perks, too. The chief engineer's quarters were second only to the captain's, a veritable hotel suite complete with its own television, a true luxury in 1963. Getting channels still required the ship to be in port or near shore, but when they could get a station or two, it felt like heaven. Wade pulled rank to pick the shows, usually the *Beverly Hillbillies* or *Dick Van Dyke*, but Tom didn't complain.

"That was fine with me," he says. "I was the envy of the other guys in the galley crew."

Despite the dangers, especially during rough water, "I was never afraid on the *Fitzgerald*," Walton says. "I figured it was engineered to withstand anything. Some things I only thought of after the fact, but they might have mattered."

Every day Walton would take the towels and linens from the VIP staterooms in the bow all the way back to the washing machines in the stern. In good weather he'd make the trip on the deck, but when the weather turned wet, windy, or wavy, he'd take one of the two tunnels just underneath the deck.

That's where Walton would notice the same phenomenon Captain McSorley and his young cadet, Craig Silliven, talked about: Even in five-foot waves, Walton noted, "a couple of the lamps at the far end of the tunnel would actually disappear from view *laterally*, for a few seconds, as the ship bent. Then they would reappear. That boat also rocked side to side, way more than I was comfortable with as a rookie. As you can imagine, this did not inspire confidence in a young sailor that his ship was sound.

"I remember thinking to myself, 'Is this normal?' Didn't seem like it to me. But I was told that such movement was normal, like a skyscraper yielding a little in high winds.

"I accepted the explanation, but years later, I wondered if it was supposed to bend that much."

VI

THIRTY-EIGHT HOURS IN A RAFT

(THE SS *DANIEL J. MORRELL*)

TOM WALTON'S CONCERNS WERE NOT IRRATIONAL. Just two years after his splendid summer of '63 on the *Fitzgerald*, another laker found itself in serious trouble.

Like the *Bradley*, the *Cedarville* was built in 1927, and many of her crew came from Rogers City. Owned by U.S. Steel, she was named for a port in Michigan's Upper Peninsula where she frequently loaded limestone that she delivered to the company's furnaces in Gary, Indiana.

In 1964 U.S. Steel appointed Elmer Fleming to captain the *Cedarville*. Fleming had served as first mate on the *Bradley*, and survived the ship's sinking with Frank Mays. One *Cedarville* crew member described Fleming as a "real nervous person," but standing on a ship that cracked in half can do that to a man. Fleming boarded the *Cedarville* on March 27, 1964, with some heavy weather swirling about—and walked right back off a few minutes later, never to board another ship again.

The next year, on May 7, 1965, the *Cedarville* pulled out of Calcite, the limestone quarry and dock that adjoin Rogers City, with 14,411 long tons of limestone headed for Gary, Indiana—and nothing but fog ahead, the weather captains feared the most. Two ships had already grounded near the Soo Locks and another had crashed into a lighthouse.

Cedarville captain Martin Joppich faced the usual bad choices: be a sitting duck, bobbing up and down waiting for another ship to run into her, or sail into the fog and risk being the rammer, instead of the rammed. Joppich decided to keep the *Cedarville* humming along at a brisk 12.3 miles per hour, violating one of the first rules of seamanship: *Whenever conditions turn bad, the best and easiest decision to make is to slow down.* Joppich did not know that the captain of a nearby salty, the Norwegian *Topdalsfjord*, had just made the same decision, going faster than he should have been in thick fog.

As the *Cedarville* approached the busy, tight, and turbulent Straits of Mackinac, which runs right under the Mackinac Bridge, the fog thickened, obscuring the seven-year-old Mackinac Bridge itself and everything underneath it, including ships trying to navigate around its piers. It wasn't long before a deck watchman on the *Cedarville* spotted the *Topdalsfjord*'s bow suddenly emerging from the fog, far too big and too close, and yelled, "There she is!"

The wheelsman turned hard to port, but the *Topdalsfjord*'s bow, built for breaking ice, hit the *Cedarville*'s left side. The visible damage seemed superficial—broken railings and deck plates—but under the water line the *Topdalsfjord*'s bow tore a huge hole in the *Cedarville*'s hull, and water rushed in.

Like too many stoic and stubborn Great Lakes captains, Joppich turned down the German-owned *Weissenburg*'s offer to rescue his men right then and there, instead trying to get his wounded ship to shore four miles away. But when the *Cedarville* started to sink, Joppich stopped the engines, called Mayday on the radio, and told his crew to man their lifeboats. Less than half an hour after the collision, at 10:25 a.m., the *Cedarville* finally rolled onto its starboard side and sank. Of the thirty-five crewmen, twenty-five were saved by the *Weissenburg* nearby, but ten went down with the ship.

The *Cedarville* was the second-largest ship ever to be lost on the Great Lakes, behind only the *Bradley*. But within a decade the *Cedarville*'s rank would slip to fourth.

AT THE SAME time the *Cedarville* sank, the SS *Daniel J. Morrell* was plying the same waters. Dennis Hale, a twenty-six-year-old watchman on the 603-foot freighter, had endured a horrible childhood. After his mother died giving birth to him in Cleveland, he and his three older siblings were taken by various relatives until their father returned from serving in World War II. What should have been a blessing quickly revealed itself to be a curse. Dennis broke free of his father's physical abuse by running away, but still managed to earn a high school diploma, then joined the military.

After Hale earned an honorable discharge, he met his wife and they had two daughters, raising them in Ashtabula, Ohio, a major port on Lake Erie. When Hale got a berth on the *Morrell*, which had launched in 1906, it seemed like the pieces were starting to click.

"The *Morrell* soon became my home and the men aboard her my family," he wrote. "For the first time in my life, I felt I really belonged."

But with more than five decades of hard sailing behind her, the *Morrell* was showing signs of stress and strain. During one offseason the company that owned the *Morrell*, Bethlehem Transportation Company, a subsidiary of Bethlehem Steel in Pennsylvania, paid Hale to make a mark on any leaking rivets and welds. He circled between 250 and 500 weak points, but he never knew if Bethlehem made any repairs.

Near the end of Hale's third season, 1966, the *Morrell* was going downbound back to Lake Erie for the winter. But when another ship in Bethlehem's fleet broke down, the company asked the *Morrell* to dump its cargo in Buffalo then go back up to Taconite Harbor, Minnesota, to pick up an extra load of taconite and deliver it to the lower Great Lakes ports before ending her season for good.

ON MONDAY NIGHT, November 28, 1966, Lake Huron was choppy, and snow started to fall—not unusual for November. But even after being warned worse conditions were coming, the *Morrell* refused to take shelter.

Hale went to sleep at about 10 p.m., while winds whipped up to sixty miles per hour and the waves crested at twenty feet. Around 2 a.m. Hale woke up to a loud bang and then another one, then watched his books fly off the shelves. He reached to turn on the light, but there was no power. Then the ship's alarm, which ran on battery power, rang out.

Hale was wearing only boxer shorts, so he grabbed a life jacket and fumbled in the dark to find his wool peacoat, then ran for the life raft.

Hale felt no fear, but "my calm was soon shattered when, while looking aft over my left shoulder, I saw the inch-thick steel decking start to tear apart from starboard to port. The tearing was accompanied by huge sparks and steam rushing from severed lines. The ship made a sound like a dying prehistoric beast, creating a scene that will be with me for the rest of my life."

Before anyone abandoned ship, Captain Arthur L. Crawley had told some of the sailors the failed electrical system made transmitting an SOS call impossible, and no one was expecting to see the ship until it arrived in Taconite Harbor, Minnesota, before noon on Wednesday, November 30—about thirty-four very long hours away.

Eight minutes after the ship's alarm first sounded the *Morrell*'s bow tore off and sank, taking fourteen men down with it. While the others scrambled to find life jackets, watchman Norm Bragg, who had survived the SS *Henry Steinbrenner* sinking in Lake Superior in 1953, which claimed seventeen lives, calmly helped his crewmates and gave them advice. Then he told them, "It's been good to know you," and went down with the ship.

Hale had little choice but to jump into Lake Huron, whose waters were only a few degrees above freezing. Once Hale overcame the shock of the water, he was able to find the life raft only because it had a carbide lamp that automatically activated when it hit the water—a recent innovation. Hale found two fellow deckhands already on board, John Cleary and Art Stojek. They hauled Hale in then took in another man swimming toward the raft, Charles "Fuzzy" Fosbender, one of the *Morrell*'s wheelsmen.

They had a seaworthy raft and each other, but not much else. The waves grew bigger, and started to break over the raft.

"For hours we clung to the storm-tossed raft," Hale recalled. "The worst part was when a wave would pass over us followed by the frigid wind and stinging spray. I can still hear the screams of the others as the wind struck their wave-drenched bodies. I screamed too, and prayed enough for a lifetime."

Hale woke up at dawn on Tuesday, November 29, to discover that Cleary and Stojek had died overnight. Fuzzy Fosbender seemed fine at first glance, until he coughed, and died on the spot. Later investigators would determine that Fosbender's upper body had been crushed, and his shoulders broken.

By the time Fosbender died, Hale had been clutching the raft for fourteen hours. He decided not to push his dead comrades overboard—partly out of respect, and also because he simply didn't have the strength. In Hale's weakened state, it was probably a good thing he didn't know that it would be at least another twenty hours before someone in Taconite might notice that the *Morrell* hadn't arrived.

Hale somehow made it through another night, and most of the next day, Wednesday, November 30. A little after noon that day, when the

Morrell was supposed to have arrived at Taconite Harbor, the Coast Guard dispatched ships and aircraft to find the ship, or perhaps just survivors.

Around 4 p.m., Hale noticed something different about the seagulls that had been circling the raft overhead for much of the day.

"They made a loud 'whopping' sound," Hale says, "and as I struggled to focus my blurry eyes, the seagulls materialized into the beautiful sight of two U.S. Coast Guard helicopters circling above me."

Hale had been on the raft for thirty-eight hours, the last twenty-four in the company of three dead friends. He was in horrible shape, but he was alive.

The Coast Guard rescuers took him to the hospital in Harbor Beach, near the tip of Michigan's "thumb." Representatives from Bethlehem Transportation soon appeared, and asked if he had his seaman's papers—an odd question to put to a man who had just spent thirty-eight hours in a raft wearing nothing more than a peacoat, a lifejacket, and a pair of boxer shorts.

Hale asked, "Where do you think I would have put them, up my ass?"

Hale would achieve an almost-complete physical recovery except for his frostbitten feet, which would require multiple operations.

Hale's mental health also suffered, resulting in drug addiction, three divorces, and years of therapy. But he eventually became a skilled machinist—working only on land—and successfully sued Bethlehem Steel for an undisclosed amount. He was pleased to see the company also forced to pay settlements to the families of his fellow crewmen.

LONG AFTER HALE'S rescue, the *Morrell*'s sinking underscored the need for more thorough ship inspections and a better tracking system to prevent another ship from sinking undetected for a day and a half. The various authorities followed these reforms for a while, including requiring ships to call in their positions on a regular basis, but the routine faded away like so many New Year's resolutions, along with better inspections. The only reform that lasted was the rule requiring ships to be equipped with rafts that inflated automatically. A comfortable complacency soon returned to the shipping industry.

The devastating fate of the *Morrell*—her bow stuck in one towering wave and her stern in another, her hull sagging so severely that she snapped in two—would also leave a lasting impression on the shipping community. That haunting image would be hard for those who investigated future wrecks to remove from their minds.

But the sinking of the *Bradley* and the *Morrell* served as reminders that even after a freighter founders, resilient survivors may still be out there, praying to see a rescuer on the horizon.

VII

THE CAPTAIN

NOVEMBER OF 1971 MARKED THE END OF THE *EDMUND Fitzgerald*'s hegemony over the Great Lakes.

The industry's insatiable hunger for bigger locks to accommodate bigger ships to make bigger profits demanded the extension of the Soo's Poe Lock, originally built in 1896, to 1,200 feet in 1968, and the construction of Bethlehem Steel's thousand-foot-long ship *Stewart J. Cort* in 1972.

Where *Fitzgerald* broke her own season haul record in 1971 with 1.3 million long tons, in the *Cort*'s very first shipping season the next year she carried 2.1 million long tons—62 percent more than the *Fitzgerald*'s highest mark.

The new game was over before it started.

NOVEMBER 1971 ALSO marked the close of Captain Peter P. Pulcer's six-year term at the *Fitzgerald*'s helm. To replace the "Santa Claus Captain," Columbia promoted a very different kind of leader, Ernest McSorley, for the 1972 season.

McSorley had less ego than most captains, but he still had his pride. If the *Fitzgerald* could no longer dominate the record books, McSorley's competitive instincts found new targets: breaking the *Fitzgerald*'s own records, year after year; making record profits for the company; and burnishing the *Fitzgerald*'s reputation among fans and other crews as the best ship on the Great Lakes. McSorley had no intention of letting the *Fitz* lose her stellar status, or his own, on his watch.

"Columbia was one of the big boys, and the *Fitz*, that was their flagship," former *Arthur M. Anderson* second engineer Rick Barthuli explains. "Moving cargo, a million tons a year, that was their goal—and they hit it. I never met McSorley, never worked for him, but I can tell you McSorley didn't get to be the *Fitzgerald*'s captain by accident. Anyone knows that. Your reputation gets around pretty fast on the lakes, and I never heard a bad word. But he was a gunner, for sure."

Nobody needed to tell Ernest McSorley how dangerous the Great

Lakes were. He'd started sailing on them when he was just eighteen, and by the time he assumed command of the *Edmund Fitzgerald*, he was widely considered the best captain on the Great Lakes—and a particularly skilled navigator in rough weather.

Born on September 29, 1912, in Spencerville, Ontario, near Ottawa, McSorley was eleven when his family moved to Ogdensburg, New York, right on the St. Lawrence Seaway—a good place to catch the boat bug.

He boarded his first ship in 1930 as a deckhand, the lowest-ranking crewman, and needed just thirteen years to climb all the way to captain of the Columbia steamer SS *Carrollton*. At just thirty-one years old, McSorley was the youngest master on the Great Lakes. He would captain eight more ships of increasing size and importance before he reached the pinnacle of his profession in 1972, at age fifty-nine, when Columbia tapped him to lead the *Edmund Fitzgerald*.

If being a Great Lakes captain were an Olympic pentathlon consisting of five events, McSorley would probably win piloting, racing, recruiting, and leading his crew, and finish high enough in the fifth event, VIP relations, that no other Great Lakes captain could challenge him for the top spot on the podium.

Unlike Pulcer, who reveled in entertaining the crowds the *Fitzgerald* attracted all over the Great Lakes, McSorley hadn't become the *Fitzgerald*'s captain on the strength of his schtick, but because of his uncommon skill at the helm, his poise under pressure, and his ability to deliver cargo faster than his peers. While McSorley could engage the VIPs on board, too, and appeared comfortable doing so, he wouldn't leave the pilothouse or man the megaphone unless the job required it. Under McSorley's leadership there would be no Detroit Tiger baseball updates, no Mozart music, and no Santa Claus costumes. He had been hired to do a job, and he intended to do it well.

But, says Craig "Red Dog" Silliven, who served as a GLMA cadet in 1972, during McSorley's first season at the *Fitzgerald*'s helm, "McSorley didn't get that boat because he was a jerk. He was a very good schmoozer with all the corporate passengers, and he knew how to do it without being a phony."

Quiet but not shy, McSorley had the in-your-bones self-assurance required of all captains, but without the arrogance and anger that often accompanied it. His straightforward, selfless demeanor earned him the loyalty of his crew, something that is not willed through authority, but earned through character. Perhaps the best evidence we have: When McSorley rose in the ranks from ship to ship, ten in all, his crew members at both ends of the vessel repeatedly followed him, straight up to the *Fitzgerald*.

But only those onboard knew *how* McSorley cultivated his crew's fidelity. Craig Silliven was one of the few.

Late in the summer of 1972 the *Fitzgerald* made its weekly stop in Toledo to unload. Because the docks there still used the aging Hulett cranes to extract the taconite from the *Fitzgerald*'s holds, most of the crew could enjoy about fourteen hours of liberty while the Huletts did their job. As was McSorley's custom, he ate dinner at Mancy's, Toledo's best steakhouse since 1921, then visited his wife, Nellie, recovering from a serious illness at Lake Park Nursing Care Center, before retiring at their house in Ottawa Hills, considered one of the nicest Toledo suburbs.

Before lunch the next day Silliven's parents drove ninety minutes from their home in Hillsdale, Michigan, to take him to Tony Packo's, a Hungarian hot dog and sandwich joint made famous by the TV series *M*A*S*H*. On their drive back to the dock, however, they found themselves stuck at a railroad crossing, watching one of the endless freight trains the *Fitzgerald* had just loaded rolling slowly in front of their car. As they sat stewing they heard the telltale short whistle of the *Fitzgerald*, warning everyone that the *Fitz* was about to leave the dock.

"Oh man, was that stressful!" Silliven says. "Trust me, that ship doesn't wait for *anyone*, let alone some cadet, and I knew it. I was about to get left behind and written up—not good for a newbie on probation. No captain could hold a ship up for a missing crewman without getting in trouble with the company himself. The corporate bean counters watched everything."

They didn't take roll on Great Lakes freighters, because the ship did: if you were onboard when it left port, you were on time—and if you weren't, you weren't. Before cellphones the captain usually didn't know where a missing crewman might be, what was holding him up, or how long he would take to get there. How the AWOL sailor might catch up to the ship downstream was his problem, not the captain's.

Fortunately for Silliven he had been assigned to the pilothouse, so McSorley at least would have noticed his new cadet was missing.

"Well, he must've taken a shine to me," Silliven says, "because instead of using the engines to push out to sea, like usual, they used the winches to crawl slowly down the dock."

"Using the winches" meant the deckhands would roll out hundreds of feet of cable from the ship's winches on deck, pull the ends down to the dock, and tie them up to a deadhead (which looks like a fire hydrant) near the ship. Then they would let the winches pull the cable in, which drew the ship toward the deadhead like a climber scaling a mountain. When the ship reached the deadhead, the deckhands would untie that cable and loop it around the next deadhead farther down the dock, then repeat the process. That way the ship inched all the way down the dock, as slowly as it could, while still moving forward.

But this maneuver was not routine, and could be ordered only by the captain.

"That was pretty clever," Silliven says. "McSorley didn't set off the bean counters, because the ship had officially left the loading dock, and they're moving. But he still gave me a chance to catch the ship."

Back in the Sillivens' car they were relieved to see the freight train's caboose pass in front of them and the crossing gates lift, so they were finally free to speed their son to the dock.

"When the crew saw me running up to the ship," Silliven says, "they all yelled, 'There he is! Come on—get on!'"

McSorley had also ordered his crew to keep the ladder out at the bow, another unconventional move, so Silliven could scurry up onto the ship. Once on deck, still breathing hard, Silliven turned to wave to his grateful parents on the dock below.

"I would call this very gracious of McSorley," Silliven says. "But he and I never said anything about it to each other. It would have embarrassed him, and we didn't want it getting out anyway, because that trick cost the company a little money.

"But that's why McSorley had a very good reputation with the crew. Well deserved, too."

For all McSorley's social graces toward his crew and his guests, what most defined the man was his intimate knowledge of the Great Lakes, the odds of various strategies navigating their waters, and his fearlessness in playing them.

McSorley had never hidden from the western winds—which start on the Great Plains hundreds of miles to the west and sweep across Lake Superior—by laying anchor on the eastern side of the Keweenaw Peninsula or Isle Royale, a forty-five-mile-long island that is ten times the size of Manhattan, and the only island in the United States National Park system. Isle Royale is big enough to have a lake within it, with an island on that lake, and a lake on that island. But because it is so remote, much closer to Ontario than Michigan, it is also the least visited of the National Parks, with only twenty-five thousand visitors a year. What's bad for tourism can be good for captains, who appreciated Isle Royale as one of the few places a ship could hide from storms.

Sailors call this the "lee side," which is protected from the wind. During a few treacherous storms each fall the temptation to seek shelter must have been all but overwhelming, especially when resisting that urge could be fatal, but McSorley never surrendered to it.

"McSorley had ice in his veins," says Silliven. "A great pilot, too. I was on the stern at Silver Bay once when the big boats from Cleveland Cliffs were already at the docks. Doesn't leave a lot of room. Well, Captain McSorley came in, swung it around, then slipped 729 feet of steel in a slot between the freighters with just a few extra feet, like he was parallel parking his pickup truck.

"McSorley was the best ship man I've ever seen. He was the best on the Great Lakes, that's for sure—and everyone knew it."

VIII

THE TOLEDO EXPRESS

The Best Bar in Silver Bay

Taken together, the towns of Silver Bay, Two Harbors, and Duluth, Minnesota, plus Superior, Wisconsin, comprise what sailors call "the Head of the Lakes," the western tip of all the Great Lakes. If your ship is hauling taconite, your trip will probably start at one of these ports.

At each of these towns the locals will eagerly tell you about the differences among them, but they have far more in common than not. In an interview with Oprah Winfrey, Prince said of his home state of Minnesota: "It's so cold, it keeps the bad people out."

When people up here drive to a store in the winter, they leave their keys in their trucks with the engine running, so their seat will be warm and their engine working when they return. If they sell their homes they have to hire a locksmith, because no one can find a key. They never use them.

Driving down from the Canada–Minnesota border on the picturesque Voyageur Highway, you'll come upon a twenty-eight-thousand-acre complex squeezed between the road and Lake Superior.

Called Reserve Mining in the *Fitzgerald*'s day, it's now Cleveland Cliffs Northshore Mining, one of the last factories in North America to produce taconite pellets, and a vital link in a perfect vertical monopoly. The trains bring the raw iron ore from the Iron Range straight to the pelletizer, which then funnels the finished taconite directly into the freighters sitting at the company-owned docks next door. Those ships each send tons of pellets down to the factories and mills at the bottom of the lakes.

The *Edmund Fitzgerald* docked in Silver Bay more often than anywhere else on Lake Superior, making Silver Bay its unofficial northern home.

At the intersection of the Voyageur Highway and Outer Drive they've posted a big sign that says, "Welcome to Silver Bay," with a statue of "Rocky Taconite" in front of it, consisting of one large black "taconite" pellet for his body, attached to a smaller one for his head. Rocky holds a pickaxe for mining iron ore, and wears red boots, red gloves, a hard hat, and a big smile. Since 1964 he has stood "on a boulder of taconite," the town's website says, "the ore that saved America's steel industry when we learned to extract iron from it after the pure ores in the Mesabi Range were exhausted."

The plaque on the boulder says that Rocky "honors the 'genius' of those who figured out how to change a useless rock into a valuable product." They don't mention University of Minnesota professor Edward Davis by name, but that's the genius they're talking about.

The basic layout of Silver Bay—with the factory and loading docks on the waterfront, and the town up on the hill—is repeated throughout the Great Lakes, and confirms a basic fact: for most of the nation's first two centuries the waterfronts were not designated for recreation but for industry, first and foremost. About a half mile up Outer Drive sits a cozy village of 1,876 people, slightly less than half of its peak population in 1960. Countless sailors have made this trip by foot, which they call "going up the street," since every port bar sits higher than the waterfront. They go in search of a cold beer, a pretty face, and some cash.

In the *Fitzgerald*'s time, once a month the first mate, in charge of payroll, handed the crewmen paper checks. If you think it would have been difficult for them to get their checks cashed on a Monday night in a tiny port town in 1975, before the advent of ATMs, think again.

"The bars were *more* than happy to cash your check!" says retired engineer John Hayes with a laugh. "No charge. They knew the checks were good, and they were pretty confident they'd be seeing your money again—and they were right."

Most payroll checks ran about three hundred to five hundred dollars, but some bars would cash checks as big as three or four thousand, and nobody ever went out of business doing so.

THE *FITZGERALD* CREW'S most frequent stop was the Silver Bay Municipal Liquor and Lounge. The bar's brown cinderblock wall faces the parking lot, with one glass door. Inside visitors first see the liquor store in the front, then the bar-restaurant in the back.

"The Lounge" is a sunny spot with blond wood, windows on three sides, and a U-shaped bar up front. The city itself built the bar in the early 1960s—thus the name Silver Bay Municipal Liquor and Lounge—and has remodeled it twice. But sailors who haven't seen the place in fifty years say it feels just the same. About the only difference to them is that the payphone where sailors lined up to call home has been removed. The city still owns the bar and liquor store, and the profits go toward Silver Bay's city services, particularly parks and rec.

Tom Byrnes, sixty-eight, is a lean, six-two, blond-haired guy with a gray goatee, wearing a T-shirt and jeans. He doesn't look too far removed from the wiry seventeen-year-old who used to patrol right field for the Silver Bay High School Mariners, who play just a few hundred feet from the bar on a beautiful expanse of green at the top of the town. Byrnes carries himself with the easygoing, friendly manner of a man who has worked behind a small-town bar his entire life—which he has, right there at the Lounge. Byrnes graduated from Silver Bay High School in 1975, and started working at the bar the next week, back when the drinking age was eighteen.

In those days Byrnes's classmates didn't even have to walk down the street to get a job at the Reserve Mine, because the Reserve Mine came to them. At the Mariners' high school graduation the Reserve Mining representatives set up tables in the cafeteria where the graduates could sign a contract right then and there and start working at the plant the very next day. Since the Reserve Mine was offering good money, thirteen weeks' vacation, full benefits, and job security, why go to college? Teachers with master's degrees received much less. And just like that, your life was laid out.

"I had a lot of friends who did just that," Byrnes says.

But Byrnes has never regretted skipping the plant to bartend at Silver Bay Municipal Liquor and Lounge.

"In the old days, captains would come in with their crews, buy a round, and then leave first so the guys could have their fun," he says. "Fifty years, I've only seen a couple of dipshits. Almost all the sailors were good guys who worked hard and put down as much beer as they could when they were here. But they weren't looking for trouble. One time one of them said, 'Hey, mind if we get your truck and go golfing?' I said, 'Sure. Keys are in it.' No problem.

"They *loved* this bar! And they took care of it."

Byrnes explains the unwritten code: The sailors could flirt with the local women, but if the women weren't interested the sailors had to cool it or there would be trouble. Very rarely, Byrnes reports, would someone go "over the top" by looking for a fight, or talking to a woman who wasn't there to meet sailors. If a sailor pushed it, his fellow sailors would haul him out of the bar, so Byrnes rarely had to deal with rowdies.

"But they still had to walk their buddy down the street and up that damn ladder on the dock to get back on the boat," Byrnes says. "Couldn't have been easy, some nights."

Back in 1975 Byrnes got to know the sailors on the *Fitzgerald* pretty well, too.

"We'd see those guys up here damn near every week. One of the mainstays. Everyone knew the *Fitz*. It was *the* ship. Good guys. No troublemakers. They had a very good reputation, because they policed themselves. They were just happy to get off that boat and have a beer, and didn't want to screw it up.

"You can always tell when the captain has the sailors' respect."

Sit in a Great Lakes sailors' bar long enough, and the talk will eventually turn to the *Edmund Fitzgerald*. At the Silver Bay Municipal Liquor and Lounge, the discussion invariably includes Nolan Church, a local father of five who worked at the taconite plant down the street before getting a job on the *Fitz*.

"I don't think Nolan's sons played baseball, but Nolan loved it, so he'd come down and cheer us on," Byrnes recalls of his high school days. "He'd yell things like, 'Play's at first!' And if I'm gonna be honest here, he might have had a pint in his pocket. Something brown. Not a big deal back then. Always good to see him."

Nolan Church was born on July 13, 1920, in Cass Lake, a lumber town in north-central Minnesota of about two thousand people. Now a third that size, it serves as the headquarters of the Minnesota Chippewa Tribe and the Leech Lake Band of Ojibwe.

Nolan's children never knew much about their grandparents because both died in their fifties. But they do know their dad moved to Babbitt, Minnesota, a town formed in 1944 when a taconite mine opened there. Babbitt helped create another town ten years later when they ran a rail line sixty miles east to Lake Superior and called it Silver Bay. Today, depending on which way you drive from Babbitt to Silver Bay, you'll pass towns called Happy Wanderer, Isabella, Finland, and Greenwood Junction. (Go the wrong way and you end up, appropriately enough, in Embarrass, Minnesota.)

Nolan married a nurse named Thelma Pederson, then followed the taconite trail from Babbitt to Silver Bay, where they bought a sturdy ranch home at 12 Garden Drive, and raised five children there: Ricky, Bonita (Bonnie), Debra, Marilynn, and Michael, better known as Mikey.

Sisters Bonnie Church Kellerman and Marilynn Church Peterson are still close, and once they start talking they finish each other's sentences.

"Everybody knows everyone there, and everyone helps everyone out," Marilynn says of her childhood home. That was particularly important to the Churches because their mother worked at Two Harbors Hospital thirty minutes down the coast, but never learned to drive. "Someone always had to take her—and someone always did. 'Minnesota Nice.'"

"Dad was a small guy," Bonnie says. "He wasn't short, just real small-boned, not the kind of guy looking for a fight. But if you met him, you'd never forget him. If he didn't know you, he'd make it his business to get to know you."

One fall their dad brought home one of those small organs with the numbers printed on the keys to help novices learn, and taught himself how to play. Every Christmas Eve he loved to gather his family around him while he played "Silent Night" and other favorites, and they sang along. He also painted a holiday scene each Christmas on the family's bay window, and the local kids would come by to see what he'd created that year. In the summer, when Nolan saw a crowd of kids at the local Dairy Queen, he'd stop to buy them all ice cream cones.

"He was a bullshitter for sure," Marilynn says, laughing. "But oh, he *loved* kids! That was his life."

Those kids at the Dairy Queen, now in their sixties, still talk about Nolan Church, and how he once helped a little girl crying outside the Churches' home after losing her boot in a snowbank. He dug her boot out, and gave her a reassuring pat on the head before sending her home.

Church enjoyed serving as the neighborhood barber, too, with young and old coming over to the house. He didn't have much need for a barber himself, with his receding hairline, but he'd tell his patrons not to wear hats or they'd go bald, too.

Church enjoyed many pursuits, but his day job at the taconite plant wasn't one of them. It was hot, loud, boring, and occasionally very dangerous. After decades of this work Church decided the vista from the prow of a ship had to be more interesting than the one from inside the factory. So in the spring of 1971, when he was fifty years old with a wife and five kids, Nolan Church made the bold decision to apply for his Lake Carriers' Association card, and hop on a Great Lakes freighter.

"He joined the LCA on April 24, 1971," Bonnie says. "I know that because we have it on his card. How I got in possession of that card, I have no idea."

After a few years on the lakes he earned a berth on the *Fitzgerald*, a plum assignment, and perhaps especially for a porter, whose position is a combination of waiter, concierge, and maid. Because Church knew how to cook he also served as the ship's unofficial chef's assistant, and because he knew how to cut hair he always had a steady stream of sailors only too happy to get a free haircut—but only among the older ones.

"They got paid good on the boats," Bonnie says. "And they worked hard, but Dad just loved it. It was a completely different world than what he was used to. He was always meeting different people."

Whenever the *Fitzgerald* loaded in Silver Bay, Church would bring one of his crewmates up the street to meet his family and enjoy a home-cooked meal.

"He loved it, he did," Marilynn agrees. "He told us that many times."

By 1975 Church had a big, close-knit family with six grandchildren and a seventh on the way, a few creative hobbies, a solid paycheck, and a job that he actually loved—a first for him. The *Fitz* was an uncommonly happy ship, but Church might have been the happiest man on it.

Whenever his children asked him if it was scary being out on that big lake, Church replied that McSorley ran a tight ship and all the guys knew what they were doing.

"You kids never have to worry about me," he'd say, "because the *Fitz* is the biggest ship out there, and the safest. Lake Superior doesn't have a hole big enough to fit the *Fitzgerald*!"

The happiest man on board had no fear of the lakes, or the future.

Head of the Lakes

Go back down Silver Bay's Outer Drive, turn south on the Voyageur Highway, continue past Split Rock Lighthouse—one of the most dramatic on the Great Lakes, perched on a 133-foot sheer cliff overlooking Lake Superior—and a half hour later you'll pull into Two Harbors, a town that exists solely because of iron ore. But in case any travelers aren't sure, the town sign states:

TWO HARBORS
Population 3,633

Followed by another sign that announces:

It's a big Ore-Deal!

Two Harbors's population peaked at 4,990 in 1910 and almost reached that again in the 1950s and '60s, thanks to the boom in taconite shipping.

Although twice the size of Silver Bay today, everything in Two Harbors seems tiny—the town park, the band shell, the downtown—and almost all of it is made of wood, except the two gigantic rusty docks that stretch one hundred thirty feet long and rise eighty feet above the water. Railroad tracks run above them to allow eight hundred train cars to dump tons of taconite down 112 chutes straight into the ships' cargo holds.

Up the street the town's main drag features the Moose Lodge, the Masonic Lodge, and the American Legion Post 109, the sailors' preferred port of call. It's a welcoming spot for nonmembers, too, provided they heed the sign near the door: "Please Remove Your Cap in Honor of Our Departed Comrades."

A few years ago, retired engineer John Hayes recalls, a couple twenty-somethings thought the request didn't apply to them, and stubbornly kept their baseball hats on. They had time to reconsider their decision once they were out on First Avenue again, this time on their backsides.

ANOTHER HALF HOUR down the coast sits Duluth, the Great Lakes' westernmost seaport and Lake Superior's unofficial capital, which runs steeply up the slope from the lake. Its population peaked at 107,312 in 1960, though it's still big enough—just shy of 90,000 people—to host the state's fourth-largest university, the University of Minnesota Duluth, whose hockey team has won three NCAA Division I titles. At one point, the locals are quick to tell you, Duluth had more millionaires per capita—lumber barons, taconite tycoons, and shipping magnates—than any city in the United States.

Duluth's grain elevators are among the world's largest, with Elevator A standing 185 feet above the water, big enough to hold 3.5 million bushels by itself.

"The rats were the fattest I've ever seen, big as cats," retired sailor John Hayes attests. "They knew where the food was, and they ate very well."

Duluth rests on the hillside like a miniature San Francisco, but even in August the locals don't swim in Lake Superior unless they're wearing full-body wetsuits, and then only for ten minutes to avoid triggering hypothermia. The weather weeds out all but the hardiest souls.

MICHAEL ZRONEK, A native of Solon, Ohio, right outside Cleveland, found out why for himself. After joining the Coast Guard he transferred to the USCG station in Duluth, where he worked on the USCG *Woodrush*, a 180-foot buoy tender. Zronek ran payroll and supplied the ship for its two-week trips on Lake Superior.

In May of 1975 the *Woodrush* crew had to do "man overboard" drills on Lake Superior to see how fast they could get a lost crewman back on the ship. Out of boredom Zronek volunteered. They squeezed him into an inch-thick wet suit, complete with a hood, gloves, and footies. Zronek jumped in while the *Woodrush* took a U-turn to come back to pick him up.

"I wasn't scared," he says, "just cold. Your body is trying to keep the warmth in your inner core, to keep your organs functioning, so your extremities go cold. After ten minutes I had a hard time using my arms and my hands. You get so stiff because you have no circulation in your limbs. By the time they got me after about fifteen minutes, I couldn't move my hands or my feet, or even feel them. Well, that's what happens to you, no matter who you are.

"Could you last ten minutes in Lake Superior *without* a wet suit?" he asks. "I don't think so."

But Zronek also recalls his days as a firefighter executing rescues on small lakes. When the victims were frozen, the firefighters always said, "You're not dead until you're *warm* and dead." Even when no pulse is detected, sometimes the cold can preserve a victim for hours, who might then come back to life as they warm up.

When Zronek got out of the water that day, frozen stiff, he had no idea he would put that knowledge to use six months later.

PATRICK LABADIE MOVED from Detroit to Duluth in 1972 to run the Canal Park Marine Museum, right by the docks.

"That first year we were buried in forty-two inches of snow, on *Halloween*!" he says. "And the snow was still there in February. Well, welcome to Duluth."

When Labadie was running the museum, Duluth's docks were always loading at least five big lakers at one time, and sometimes ten or twelve. The tourists would wait at the piers in front of the museum for the ships to come and go, so a few hours in advance of each ship Labadie would post the shipping schedule on the museum's big board outside, and broadcast the arrivals and departures over the PA system. Once the postings caught on, the ship companies would call the museum with changes, to keep the board current.

"The people loved it!" Labadie says. "It was a beautiful location, right at the shore, so it wasn't unusual to have crowds waiting for the next ship to come in.

"One time a pretty young lady was waiting for a ship at our museum.

When it came in she said, 'Oh, here comes my fiancé!' So she went out to meet him. I thought that was really sweet.

"But three or four hours later, she was back at the museum, looking for her next 'fiancé.' I had heard some stories here and there about working women, but I'd never seen it myself before that.

"Next time I saw a woman waiting for her 'fiancé,' I was a little wiser."

DULUTH BUTTS AGAINST a state line that separates the banked cityscape of tourists, college students, and dockworkers from the city of Superior, Wisconsin, a flat industrial town one-quarter the size of Duluth. As one Wisconsin waitress said, "We make our money in Superior, and we spend it in Duluth."

But Superior, Wisconsin, knows its raison d'être: It is home to the world's largest dock, Burlington Dock No. 1 (of four), commemorated by a historical marker standing off in a swamp few can see. The rusting hulk stands eighty feet above the water, and runs 2,244 feet from shore—almost half a mile—complete with 374 huge chutes that can hold 1,435 train cars of taconite, or 64,000 long tons. That's enough to fill two one-thousand-foot-long ships at once, in just a few hours.

In 1967 Burlington Northern Santa Fe (BNSF) Railway's Allouez Taconite Facility built more than twelve miles of conveyor belts that run from the company's Allouez Taconite Facility, right over Superior's buildings and roads, straight to the chutes attached to the docks 3.5 miles away. The conveyor belts eliminated the need for train cars, and reduced the labor required to run the plant from 500 workers to 140.

The conveyor belts are completely enclosed but they still kick out enough rusty dust to cover people's houses underneath. Allouez gives each homeowner a five-hundred-dollar check every year to power wash it off.

Burlington Dock No. 1 is where the *Edmund Fitzgerald* filled its cargo holds with 26,116 long tons of taconite pellets on November 9, 1975, while some of the crew walked a half mile up the street to get their final rounds before their last scheduled trip of the season.

Between the twenty-foot-high pyramids of taconite at the Allouez yard and the four Burlington docks sits the President Bar and Liquor

Store, right across the five-lane U.S. Highway 53 from the Tipsy Beaver Bar. The President Bar and Liquor Store is split in half: The liquor store offers rows and rows *and rows* of every kind of booze you could name, and more than a few you couldn't, all displayed in military-straight formation, clean as a whistle, and brightly lit with pure white tile floors. An open doorway leads you into the President Bar, with dark carpeting, wood paneling, mood lighting, and a jukebox playing all the sailors' favorites.

"We've cashed thousands of sailors' checks over the years," says James Bolin, a President bartender in 1975 and now the owner. The bartenders have always welcomed back the sailors by name, including the *Fitzgerald* crew.

"The *Fitz* boys came up fairly often," Bolin says. "Wasn't rare."

Bolin saw most of them on the weekend of November 8 and 9, 1975, but not Eddie Bindon, forty-seven, the *Fitzgerald*'s first assistant engineer, from Fairport Harbor, Ohio. A big man with a bit of a belly, who wore the tails of his blue work shirt flapping outside his jeans, Bindon had a round, open face, the kind you trust immediately.

"It was probably Eddie's last year on the lakes," says Patrick Devine, a deckhand on the *Fitzgerald* in 1975 and a good friend of Bindon's. "He was certainly talking about it, but he had not made his decision yet."

That weekend, while Bindon's buddies were savoring their last beers of the season at the President Bar, Bindon went to Duluth to pick out a two-carat diamond ring to surprise his wife, Helen, a petite, cheery woman, for their twenty-fifth anniversary. But instead of packing it away in his duffel bag so he could give it to her in person when she picked him up in Toledo, "for some reason," says his niece, Fran Gabor, "he didn't want to take it aboard the ship."

Instead, he gave it to a friend, and asked him to make sure Helen got it.

Only Eddie Bindon knows why.

The Bottleneck

For decades the United States and much of the world have depended on the billions of dollars of cargo that pass through the Soo Locks every year. But few people have the slightest notion that their prosperity hinges on these narrow passages, or even where they are.

On a routine run under normal conditions, once the *Fitzgerald* loaded at the Head of the Lakes Captain McSorley would sail to the tip of the Keweenaw Peninsula, then run directly toward Whitefish Bay. The route resembles two sides of a squashed isosceles triangle. This first leg of the weekly trip to Toledo was as simple as Great Lakes shipping gets, and in good weather the easiest part of their journey.

If a captain's goal on Lake Superior is simply to get across the 350 miles as fast as possible, which it usually is, that line is the most efficient one to take. But even that uncomplicated path presents the potential for disaster.

When the winds are up, Superior's long fetch—the distance wind can blow in one direction without interference—pushes waves higher and steeper. Then the waves multiply by reverberating off the shores, and collide back in the middle of the lake, as in a swimming pool. This effect can produce the occasional "rogue wave," which is what sailors and scientists call a wave that's much higher and stronger than those around it. (Three in a row are called the "Three Sisters.") All of this wave activity must then squeeze into the relatively tiny opening of Whitefish Bay in the southeast corner of the lake. That's where Superior's 350-mile length and 150-mile width are suddenly reduced to a 15-mile-wide funnel.

Sailors long ago named Superior's last 100-mile stretch from Munising to Whitefish Point "the Shipwreck Coast" and "the Graveyard of the

Great Lakes." It alone has claimed two hundred ships, starting with the *Invincible* in 1816, and stolen thousands of lives.

"At the eastern end of Lake Superior," John Tanner says, "the number of ships lost is simply shocking."

Michigan's 3,288 linear miles of coastline are studded with 129 lighthouses, the most of any state, so there are plenty to look for. But because of the anxiety produced by the Graveyard of the Great Lakes, sailors agree that the lighthouse they are most eager to see is the one at Whitefish Point. Lake Superior's oldest operating lighthouse sits at the tip of "the Point," which marks the entrance to Whitefish Bay. After a day or two out at sea without being able to see either shore, while the waves are tossing your ship around like a cork, the Whitefish Point lighthouse is a very welcome sight indeed.

"If you've never looked over the big lake's black water at night to see the Whitefish Bay lighthouse at the end of a stomach-turning trip," retired engineer John Hayes says, "you could never know what a relief it is to see that bright beam staring at you, what that feels like, what that *means*.

"That lighthouse is a promise: The worst is behind you. You're going to make it. You're going to get home. To a sailor, the Whitefish Point lighthouse is the most beautiful sight on the Great Lakes. More times than I can count, I saw that lighthouse and said, 'Thank you, Jesus!'

"And then when you're going through the Soo Locks and down the St. Marys River for the next four hours, you can crawl in your bunk and sleep like a baby. Because by then, you've made it. You're safe. And you know it."

Once the *Fitzgerald* got to the Soo, two-thirds of the crew would get to rest while McSorley and a wheelsman guided her through the locks and the rest of the St. Marys River that followed.

They would be halfway home.

BEFORE THE LOCKS were built, however, the St. Marys River was not a peaceful respite in the middle of a tough trip, but the trickiest stretch of the Great Lakes. Because Lake Superior drops twenty-one feet to Lake Huron in just three-quarters of a mile, the ride was so rough the sailors didn't call it the St. Marys River, but the St. Marys Rapids, and sometimes the St. Marys Falls. You could hear the whitewater roaring four miles away.

Even the brave voyageurs didn't attempt anything that crazy. With each of their long canoes loaded with eight thousand pounds of pelts, when they approached St. Marys Falls they would pull onto the American shore and portage their canoes and their contents until they were safely below the rapids. The voyageurs blazed a pathway that is now the main drag of Sault Ste. Marie, Michigan, running right along the St. Marys River—still named, aptly enough, Portage Avenue.

That was fine for the voyageurs, but the bigger vessels couldn't portage around the falls, so they were forced to stop at the Soo. To tap into the vast resources that lay beyond St. Marys Falls, someone had to figure out a way to make it navigable.

To find the best ideas, the engineers reached back a few centuries.

The Chinese started building canals 2,300 years ago. Their works include the Grand Canal, the world's largest, which spans a thousand miles between the Yangtze River and Beijing. Their clever canals made water travel easier, safer, and faster than sailing the high seas, but they didn't solve the problem of navigating rapids.

In the tenth century Chinese engineer Qiao Weiyue created a rudimentary lock system: A ship traveling from high water to low water stops in front of a gate that functions like a temporary dam, then a gate behind the ship drops down, too, like a slow guillotine, trapping the water in that section with the ship inside it. Then the front gate operator lets water out of the holding tank through holes in the lower gate, and this slowly lowers the boat until it's at the same level as the water the ship wants to enter. Finally the front gate is lifted, and the boat floats off into the lower waterway without having to unload, portage, or risk a reckless maneuver.

The lock system allows vessels to go upstream, too, by reversing the process: letting water from above *into* the lock, until the level of the water inside the lock matches the level outside the lock, then opening the gate so the ship can sail into the upper river.

This simple idea transformed travel around the world.

The lock system solved an ancient problem by working *with* the flow of water instead of against it, but it was still hard to move the "guillotine" gates up and down, since the powerful rapids pushing against the gates quickly wore them out.

The man whose ideas solved this problem was none other than Leonardo Da Vinci. In his drawings five hundred years ago, he replaced the "guillotine" style single gate, which was still used in the 1800s, with "miter locks": two gates that come together to form a V, with the point always facing upstream. Once the open gates start leaving the canal walls to close, the water rushing downstream does the rest of the work, pushing the doors together in the middle and shutting them watertight. The water above the lock won't let the gates open again until the water inside the lock is at the same level. Once that downward pressure is relieved, the gates open easily.

In 1798, to accommodate the voyageurs' canoes, the Northwest Fur Company built a canoe lock about forty feet long and nine feet wide on the Canadian side of the St. Marys Rapids. It worked perfectly fine until the War of 1812, when the American soldiers destroyed it.

As soon as Michigan had been granted statehood in 1837, its leaders lobbied the federal government to build a durable lock system at Sault Ste. Marie to benefit the entire nation. That effort backfired when Kentucky senator Henry Clay argued that the Upper Peninsula sat "beyond the remotest settlement of the United States and digging a canal there would be like placing one on the moon."

The Senate's views changed dramatically after Douglass Houghton discovered copper in the Keweenaw. In 1852 the U.S. Congress granted the State of Michigan 750,000 acres of Upper Peninsula land, an area larger than Rhode Island, which the state held in trust for the contractor. Once the contractor successfully completed the canal, the state transferred the land to the company to sell for its payment. When the company discovered some of the parcels had copper deposits, their profits soared.

In 1853 construction started on the new lock at the Soo, which replaced guillotine-style gates with Da Vinci's miter locks.

Construction of the State Lock still required 1,700 men working twelve-hour days for twenty dollars a month through snowstorms, subzero winters, and even a cholera epidemic—but they finished the ambitious project in just two years, opening on June 18, 1855. In the State Lock's first season, ships sent an impressive 32 million pounds of cargo through it, a third of it iron ore and copper, validating Congress's decision.

The Upper Peninsula's skyrocketing output probably didn't thrill the Southern senators who first objected to the Soo Locks, however. Six years later, when the Civil War broke out, the minerals that poured out of Lake Superior through the Soo Locks fueled the Union Army's production of the warships, cannons, guns, and ammunition needed to defeat the Confederacy.

Before the Civil War one Confederate leader brazenly declared, "Cotton is king," and therefore the South could not lose.

It turned out cotton wasn't king. Iron was—but it depended on a fickle mistress: water.

AFTER THE UNION won the Civil War, increased demand for the Great Lakes' natural resources easily justified building larger and larger locks at the Soo: the 515-foot-long Wietzel Lock in 1881; the original Poe Lock, at 800-feet, in 1896; the 1,350-foot-long Davis Lock, then the largest in the world, in 1914; and its twin, the Sabin Lock, in 1919.

When World War II broke out President Franklin D. Roosevelt knew the fate of the free world rested on the Allies' ability to produce exponentially more planes, tanks, and ships to beat the Axis powers. At his urging Congress empowered the U.S. Army Corps of Engineers to build the much-deeper MacArthur Lock, named for General Douglas MacArthur, a former U.S. Army Corps of Engineers officer himself, who had risen to become supreme commander of the nation's Southwest Pacific forces during World War II.

The Army Corp of Engineers worked around the clock to finish the project in 1943. To protect the MacArthur and the other Soo Locks, the Army leaders surrounded the area with "barrage balloons," which looked like white zeppelins, with cables hanging down to catch incoming planes; they had thousands of trees cut down so the antiaircraft gunners could see enemy planes approaching; and they stationed seven thousand soldiers throughout the area, making the Soo Locks the most heavily guarded position in North America.

"If the locks went down, we would have lost the war," says Sault Ste. Marie, Michigan, native Roger LeLievre. "No locks, no steel, no arsenal of democracy. That simple."

After the war the booming economy necessitated building even larger locks.

In 1968 the corps replaced the original Poe Lock with a new Poe Lock that ran 1,200 feet long and 110 feet wide, with gates 60 feet high by 63 feet wide, weighing 220 tons each.

Today only the Poe and MacArthur take freighters. A lockage now takes about an hour to raise or lower a ship twenty-one feet.

Instead of building big electric pumps to drain those twenty-two million gallons of water out of the lock—equal to thirty-three Olympic-size swimming pools, which would take the pumps sixteen hours each time—the locks use gravity, which takes only twenty minutes, at two million gallons a minute. It works just as well filling the locks, too. To take advantage of all this natural power the Army Corps of Engineers built two hydroelectric plants nearby, with the Soo Locks requiring only 5 percent of its output to operate. The remaining 95 percent powers the eastern half of the Upper Peninsula.

During the forty-two-week shipping season the Poe Lock runs twenty-four hours a day, seven days a week, completing up to seven thousand lockages a year, or about twenty-five a day, and always free of charge. A busy ship can pass through the Soo Locks a hundred times per season, which the *Fitzgerald* commonly did during its fifty trips from the Head of the Lakes to Toledo and back.

The only major iron ore deposits left in North America are found in the Iron Range. U.S. industry moves about 46 million long tons of iron each year, worth about $500 billion. None of that iron travels by truck, and only about 5 percent moves by train, with the remaining 95 percent hauled by freighters going through the Soo Locks.

If the Poe Lock went out of order for just six months, it would cost the U.S. economy eleven million jobs.

In the mid-sixties, when the Army Corps of Engineers started building the Poe Lock, they needed so many workers that locals could get jobs there without a resume, an interview, or even a high school diploma—just two strong hands and a willingness to work. The pay was good, too, but the work was hard and hazardous. (It still is, which is why the Soo Locks got their own episode of *Dirty Jobs*, the long-running cable TV show.)

Every fifty feet or so along the Poe Lock workers have set out brightly painted yellow blocks, about a cubic foot each, with long, thick ropes attached. If someone falls in the lock the nearest worker throws the hard rubber cube in after the person in the water, who jams the cube between the ship and the side of the lock as fast as they can, so they don't get crushed—a greater threat in the locks than drowning or hypothermia.

Ships are secured at the dock by four cables, two at the bow and two at the stern. These pose their own dangers when they're pulled so tight they split or unravel, which is announced by a loud whipping sound. Workers are trained to hit the deck immediately, or else the whirring cable can decapitate them in a split second. That's happened before, too.

"You have to know what you're doing and pay attention, or you're going to be in danger, or get someone else in trouble," says Michelle Briggs, who's worked at the Soo Locks as the chief park ranger for sixteen years. "It's a real-life dangerous place."

Once the water levels inside and outside the lock have evened up, the lock gates swing open slowly and easily. The captains give a blast on the horn to let the workers know it's time to pull up the lines, so the ship can sail into open water. But while most of the crew is free to go to the galley, play cards, or retire to their cabins for some much-needed sleep, the captains are about to earn their keep, piloting their ships carefully through sixty-three miles of tight turns along the St. Marys River. If a captain makes even a tiny mistake here, their ship could get beached or banged up, which could shut down all traffic on the river for days and end their career in the captain's seat.

About fifteen miles down the St. Marys River from the Soo Locks lakers slip through a mile-and-a-half section called the Rock Cut, so named because it was cut out of solid rock to allow the big ships to pass through—but barely. Between the ships' flat keels and the floor of the rock cut, the gap is only eighteen inches. The fit is so tight that several times a day the Coast Guard at the Soo calls the harbor masters at the Head of the Lakes to let them know the *exact* water level at the Rock Cut that day, down to the inch, so the dockworkers can load the ships at the Head of the Lakes right up to the limit and still make it through the Rock Cut unscathed. But time is money, so even with the tight margins, captains will still typically go ten miles per hour, or about two-thirds of their maximum speed, through this stretch.

"You're cooking right along," says retired engineer Rick Barthuli. "So you best not fuck up. We did it twice a week, so you don't think of it as being any big deal, but I can't imagine other people doing it."

Sailing from the Soo Locks down the St. Marys River to Lake Huron takes about five hours. It's easy to see why it's one of the sailors' favorite passages on the Great Lakes: calm and smooth, perfect for eating, sleeping, or shooting the breeze with a crewmate while floating past rustic cottages and simple, well-kept homes with kids playing along the shore, like you're sneaking through the locals' backyards.

When the ship finally gets to Lake Huron the captain can go to the galley for a bite, then back to his quarters for a well-earned rest.

LIFE AT THE Soo is far less peaceful for a captain who's not following the rules because he will get in trouble with the lock master, who runs the operation. That's what happened to a man we'll call Ward Barkle, who captained the *Edwin H. Gott*.

"I did not like that man," says John Hayes, who worked under him. "He was a drunk, and an idiot. Bad combination."

The highlight of Captain Barkle's week was drinking with his buddies at the Moose Lodge back in Two Harbors. On one trip he was driving the *Gott* through a horrendous storm for just that purpose. When they got to the Soo Locks he figured he could shave fifteen minutes off the usual one-hour lockage if he pushed it.

His theory failed on two fronts. First, when a ship enters a lock, it functions like a cork in a bottle, with little wiggle room. With big ships the fit is so tight that water struggles to get around the narrow gaps between the hull and the lock walls, so captains have to go slowly to allow the water to ease its way around the boat from the bow to the stern.

If captains go too fast, they push the water in front of them against the lock gates with more pressure than the gates are designed for. That's one problem. But the stunt also leaves an insufficient amount of water behind the boat, so the propellers grind in the air and whine horribly.

"And that's just what this jackass was doing," Hayes says. "Our engines have no water, so they're rattling like a dog trying to crap out a peach pit."

Sure enough, the lock gate jammed, prompting the lock master to get on the radio with a clear message for the captain: "You ever do that to my lock again, I will tie you up on the east pier, and you will sit there until I'm goddamned good and ready."

One assumes he was referring to the ship, not the captain.

"And he would have," Hayes says. "The lock master, those are *his* locks—he has complete authority—and you forget that at your peril."

Captain Barkle got his boat through, hauled it across Superior at full speed through heavy seas, and made last call at the Moose Lodge in Two Harbors.

"But I tell you," Hayes says, "that's where the animosity between captain and crew starts. You want to go kill yourself, go ahead. Just let me off."

The Dirtiest Zip Code

THE GREAT LAKES CAN BOAST THIRTY-FIVE THOUSAND beautiful islands.

Zug Island is not one of them.

Named for Samuel Zug (1816–1889), a furniture manufacturer and ardent abolitionist, the land was purchased to build a posh manor for Zug's wife. The mansion was grand, but the land wasn't. A glorified marsh on the Detroit River, south of downtown, it was beset with dampness, occasional floods, and swarms of bugs that drove the Zugs crazy.

Once Zug admitted defeat he made out pretty well, selling the land in 1891 for $300,000, one of Detroit's largest real estate deals at the time. A series of companies bought and sold the property, but not for the mansion, which they knocked down. They coveted the land's frontage at the intersection of the Detroit and Rouge Rivers, fertile ground for factories. To increase the value they cut a canal, which Henry Ford later widened, separating Zug's plot from the mainland, thus creating a man-made island of almost one square mile.

Over the years Detroit Iron Works, National Steel, and U.S. Steel all added factories and mills to the island. For more than a century Zug Island's three docks took in taconite, coke, and other raw materials, which was why the *Edmund Fitzgerald* was headed for National Steel on Zug Island when she left Superior, Wisconsin, on November 9, 1975.

Zug Island was never pretty, but it was efficient. As soon as a ship docked, overhead cranes would pounce on its cargo holds, pulling out the taconite to be smelted in the blast furnaces right on the dock, then emptied into special train cars lined like thermos jugs. Many of these trains went directly to the automobile factories a mile or two up the rails, where they poured the liquid steel into auto part molds. The parts were then assembled into cars in Flint, Saginaw, Lansing, and Toledo.

But if a ship from Ford Motor Company's fleet hauled the taconite, it sailed right past the plants on Zug Island to go straight to Ford's famous two-mile-long River Rouge complex, where the molten taconite would go in at one end and a finished car would roll out the other.

"Dad liked to take us kids to the island to show off the huge blast furnaces," says Paul Nesbitt, whose father had worked on Zug Island before he joined the welding crew on the *Edmund Fitzgerald*, right next door. "Those things converted the iron to steel in a spectacular shower of sparks and fire coming from the crucible."

Zug Island comprised a huge, effective, and nasty machine, turning all but a small patch of the island into a dense, dirty landscape of black, brown, and purple soil. It's so grim that the Detroit Water and Sewage plant, right across the canal, actually brightens the scene up a bit.

Before the creation of the Environmental Protection Agency and the Clean Air and Clean Water Acts, the air on Zug Island was so toxic that unsuspecting visitors often convulsed with dry heaves. When workers blew their noses at the end of their shifts, the dirty discharge turned their white handkerchiefs black. Six of Michigan's ten most polluted zip codes were on or adjacent to Zug Island.

Working on the *Edmund Fitzgerald* wasn't easy, but when the sailors watched the Zug Island factory and dockworkers do their jobs, none of them ever asked to trade places.

PERHAPS THE ONLY thing more dangerous than working on Zug Island was drinking there.

Detroit's Jefferson Avenue, plotted in 1807 and named for the then-current president, now runs sixty-three miles along Michigan's east coast, from the tony suburbs of Grosse Pointe through downtown, then along the back end of Zug Island before terminating at the mouth of Lake Erie. Few roads anywhere can offer a greater range of scenery.

In the 1970s, at the dirty end of the road right next to Zug Island, East Jefferson Avenue was home to three memorable bars.

"The Honey Bee was for country alcoholics," retired engineer John Hayes says, "and the Hinky-Dink was for psychotic alcoholics."

At the Hinky-Dink, Hayes says, "when a motorcycle gang came in, that changed the mood pretty quickly. Good time to pay your tab and get back to the dock." Knife fights and gun play were common, and occasionally fatal.

The Honey Bee had steel grating on its front door and bars on its sole window. The front door was always locked, even when the bar was open. Prospective patrons had to buzz at the door to get the bartender's attention, then show their faces at the small window. The bartender would look to the window to size them up, and if he decided they weren't going to shoot someone or settle a grudge with a knife, he'd buzz the door to let them in. As the customers walked in the bartender would then lean forward and reach under the bar for his sawed-off shotgun just in case he had guessed wrong. If the bartender concluded they were safe after all, he let go of the sawed-off shotgun, straightened up, and asked what they were having: whiskey, beer, or both. No daiquiris.

At the third bar, Mel Hall's, ships would call the bartender with their estimated time of departure, then the bartender would announce to the sailors present when their ship was leaving.

"The bartenders usually knew the schedule better than the sailors did," former GLMA superintendent John Tanner says. "But not always."

Tanner recalls one visit to Mel Hall's when a call came in from a ship to the bartender. He hung up and shouted, "Ship's leaving in ten minutes!"

Guy at the bar says, "No it's not."

Bartender says, "Oh yes it is. They just called me."

Guy at the bar says, "No, it's not."

Bartender says, "Oh yeah? How do *you* know?"

"I'm the captain."

The ship did not leave in ten minutes.

Another time Tanner and some crewmates were drinking at the Hinky-Dink when a fire broke out upstairs—but no one stopped drinking.

"We only had so much time on shore," Tanner explains. "Can't waste it putting out fires. The firemen came in, put the fire out, and then stopped to have a drink too.

"We were *efficient*."

The Glass City

THE *EDMUND FITZGERALD* UNLOADED FAR MORE OFTEN in Toledo than Zug Island, for which the crew was grateful.

One reason: Unlike Zug Island, which used bridge cranes, the older docks in Toledo (and Gary and Cleveland) still used Hulett cranes, enormous iron giraffes built into the ground that reached over and into a ship's cargo holds. The Huletts would scoop out the ship's cargo then drop it into a pile on the dock, or directly into a hopper that filled train cars.

Patented in 1898 by George Hulett of Conneaut, Ohio, an hour east of Cleveland, the Huletts were as essential to the Great Lakes shipping boom as the creation of taconite pellets, and the Soo Locks themselves. Where the era's various other methods of unloading a single ship could take days, and cost about eighteen cents a ton, Hulett's crafty cranes could do the same job in five to ten hours, at only six cents a ton. This got the attention of the industrialists, who eventually had seventy-four Hulett cranes installed among the Great Lakes' major ports, plus one in New York to unload the garbage barges.

In the *Fitzgerald*'s era the Hulett cranes' gigantic buckets could grab as much as seventeen tons of taconite, or thirty-four thousand pounds—the same weight as a Greyhound bus—in a single scoop. But because the *Fitzgerald*'s holds carried fifty-eight million pounds of taconite, even the Huletts' big buckets had to reach into the holds hundreds of times to empty the ship. Emptying vessels the size of the *Fitzgerald* took about fourteen hours on a good day, about three times longer than it took the trains, conveyor belts, and chutes to load the *Fitz*. The job wasn't done until the Hulett crane lowered a full-size bulldozer into the cargo hold to pile up the last pellets, so the Hulett could scoop them out and drop them onto the dock or into a long row of waiting train cars, then pull the bulldozer back out.

But by the 1970s the Huletts' days were numbered. Naval architects started building "self-unloaders," ships that could empty themselves. Self-unloaders are built with conveyor belts running along the bottom of their cargo holds, which move the cargo to the stern of the ship. There a second conveyor belt brings the cargo up to a third conveyor belt, this one attached to a long boom that usually runs a couple hundred feet. Once the cargo reaches the boom, it swings around and pours the cargo wherever they want it.

Once they invented self-unloaders, which emptied the ships even faster and cheaper than the Huletts could, nobody wanted to buy more Huletts or even maintain the ones they already had, so companies invested as little into them as possible. By the 1970s the once-proud Huletts were breaking down on a regular basis.

For the crew members, however, the Huletts were a godsend. If the Huletts were working properly, they still gave the crew enough time to sneak out to the restaurants and bars for half a day, and if the Huletts broke down, crew members could extend what was already the longest break they would receive each week by a few more hours, or even a day.

While the Huletts unloaded a ship, a crewman called an oiler would fill the ship's empty ballast tanks with lake water for the return trip, while the rest of the crew filled their bellies with burgers and beers before putting in another two or three days back to Minnesota, riding light. Once back at the Head of the Lakes, the captain and crew would do it all over again.

The *Fitzgerald* crew also preferred Toledo over Zug Island for the simple reason that Toledo was not Zug Island. Despite Toledo's reputation today, from the crew's point of view almost everything about Toledo was better than just about anywhere else they stopped, which helps explain why a quarter of the *Fitzgerald*'s crew lived there.

In 1970 "The Glass City" was home to 383,818 people, ranking thirty-fourth in the U.S., ahead of Portland, Oregon; Oklahoma City; Miami; Saint Paul; Tampa; Sacramento; Charlotte; and Salt Lake City—all of which can now boast at least one major league franchise.

Driven by the auto industry, Fortune 500 stalwarts like Dana Corporation, Owens Corning glass, Champion Spark Plug, and Jeep all pumped money into Toledo's fabulous parks and museums, a zoo with four thousand animals, plus a state university, the University of Toledo, and its iconic stadium, the Glass Bowl, where the Rockets ran a thirty-five-game winning streak to number twelve in the nation in 1970.

Toledo's prosperity came with a catch: "If Detroit sneezes, Toledo catches cold." But so long as Detroit was booming, so was "The Glass City," which supplied the windshields for the Big Three, among other components.

"Toledo usually gets laughs," says Christine Brennan, the *USA Today* sports columnist and *Good Morning America* commentator, who grew up in Ottawa Hills, an upper-end Toledo suburb where the McSorleys lived. "You say you're from Toledo, and there's a giggle on the other end. But Toledo was a big deal. This wasn't the hinterland. Toledo was right smack dab in the middle of everything. We had the Toledo Symphony Orchestra; the Toledo Museum of Art, which is always ranked in the top ten; the Mud Hens [minor league baseball team]; the Toledo Zoo; Jeep headquarters; the glass companies; and an airport that would take you directly to Florida or New York. We almost never flew out of Detroit."

"Toledo has been made fun of forever, seems like, but when I was growing up there, it was a darling city," says Denise K. Lockie, who waited tables at Mancy's Steakhouse, Captain McSorley's favorite, in the 1970s.

A classic, old-school restaurant originally built in 1921, with wood paneling, dark timbers, and an old limestone fireplace, Mancy's provided the kind of smoke-filled rooms where shipping and manufacturing barons could dig into their steaks, then sit back and enjoy a snifter of fine cognac and a Cuban cigar, while playing kingmakers in business and politics. After a fire destroyed the original restaurant in 1973, the Mancys replicated the original, but added a second floor for private parties. Loyal customers included Teamsters union president Jimmy Hoffa and his lieutenants.

"There was an archway upstairs with no doors," says Gus Mancy, grandson of the founder. "They needed to block it off for privacy, so we found some trifolds to cover it up. Uncle George told me they brought their own girls to light their cigars and cigarettes—not our servers. Ours are conservatively clothed. Theirs were topless."

Hoffa and the Teamsters took a meeting there with the Giacalone family in the spring of 1975, one of the last times Hoffa was seen in public before he disappeared on July 30, 1975.

"Mancy's was crazy, just insane," former waitress Lockie says. "No reservations, no children allowed, no high seats. They opened the doors at 5 p.m., and filled the place immediately. If you showed up at 5:10, there would be a ninety-minute wait. People were lined up on the staircase, and standing outside waiting to get in. Never seen a scene like that in any restaurant, and I'm a foodie and well traveled. Whenever anyone in Toledo wanted to go out for a special occasion, where'd you go? You went to Mancy's."

While Lockie and other waitresses occasionally had to deal with inappropriate behavior from some male customers, with little recourse at the time, the sailors, perhaps surprisingly, were generally well-behaved.

"There were quite a few sailors who came in," Lockie says. "Mancy's was high-end, but back then you could get two pounds of king crab for thirty dollars. That's a good deal! And those guys had cash."

Like six other members of *Fitzgerald*'s crew, Captain McSorley called the Toledo area home. He and his wife, Nellie, who had three adult children from her first marriage, lived in a stately home with pillars in Ottawa Hills. Like most of his colleagues, McSorley hoped to be a better husband than the shipping life had permitted. But first, he had to see Nellie through a serious health problem, one which confined her to a wheelchair and required 24-hour health care while McSorley was on the *Fitzgerald*.

In 1971 Terry Sullivan spent the summer as a deckhand on one of Columbia's top ships, the *Armco*, which McSorley captained before he was promoted to the *Fitzgerald*.

"McSorley, I believe his wife was being treated for cancer," Sullivan says. "So whenever we unloaded in Toledo, once that bow line and aft line were secure, McSorley was on that ladder going down, and you didn't see him again until the Hulett was pulling the bulldozer out of the cargo hold and it was time for us to go. Everybody knew what was going on, but no one thought he was slacking or dodging work. He didn't cheat the ship out of a minute."

McSorley was going to check on Nellie, then stop in at Mancy's. By all accounts Captain McSorley conducted himself at the restaurant with quiet class, a perfect gentleman.

"Captain was a really good customer," Gus Mancy says, "and close to Uncle George, who ran the place. The captain would bring George fresh whitefish or pickerel that they'd caught on the ship, and have it cooked at Mancy's. George was happy to do it. The captain's daughter, Delores, she came in and got a job on her own merit, and worked here for many years. Mancy's was their spot."

Whenever McSorley envisioned his final docking in Toledo, his day-dream always ended with a celebratory dinner at Mancy's, the perfect capstone to a great career and the start of his golden years.

IX

THE SAILOR'S LIFE

Life Onboard

BACK IN THE *FITZGERALD*'S HEYDAY, SOME THREE HUNdred Great Lakes freighters transported more than one hundred million tons of cargo annually—the equivalent of 50 million cars. They hauled the cement in your basement, the steel in your car, and the food on your table. And they delivered all that in just nine months a year.

Those three hundred freighters were each run by about thirty crewmen, or a mere nine thousand sailors across the entire industry. They were as vital as they were overlooked—not only because they were so few, but because they were scattered across the Great Lakes, and home only three months of the year. That meant they couldn't join the Rotary Club or the local PTO, or coach their kids' baseball teams, so even in their hometowns they were all but invisible.

"We know the farmer, and the fisherman, and the factory worker," says John Tanner. "But no one knows the sailor."

SHIPPING CAN BE difficult and dangerous, but also boring and lonely.

Short of a child's wedding or a family funeral, the crews back then usually received no holidays, no vacations, no weekends. That was what they signed up for, that was what they did, and they did it every day for forty-two weeks a year. But everyone onboard agreed it was still better than working for the factories they served or the farms many had left as soon as they were old enough.

On every ship some crewmen couldn't wait for the season to start, while others couldn't wait for it to end. Former chief engineer John Hayes liked his work, but he still fell squarely in the latter category.

"Every spring I said goodbye to my wife and kids," says Hayes, whose best friend Tom Bentsen served on the *Fitzgerald* as an oiler. "I didn't teach any of my kids how to ride a bike. You miss a lot."

Hayes regretted not being able to be the full-time father he wanted to be, partly because he knew firsthand—as the son, grandson, and great-grandson of ship captains—the pain of being a child of a Great Lakes sailor. He never learned to play baseball, a sport he loved, because his dad was never home in the summer, and it pinched whenever he recognized his three children were missing the same things he had.

One day when Hayes was at the kitchen table reading the newspaper, his ten-year-old daughter walked in to throw some papers into the trash can.

"What was that?" Hayes asked.

"Oh, just some old papers at school," his daughter said.

"That didn't sound right," John recalls thinking, "so I went to the trash can and pulled out the papers. It said: 'Don't forget the father-daughter square dance!' I was going to be on a ship, as usual, and she knew it. That one stuck. You don't forget that."

When Hayes boarded his ship for the season—what sailors call "fitting out"—he would set up his bunk, unpack framed photos of his family, and then lay them down on the end table, face down. He would not prop them back up until there was just one week left in the season.

"I couldn't take looking at their pictures for any longer than that," he explains. "I couldn't miss them every single day. It'd kill me."

Once they were on the seas, Hayes says, "Within fourteen days, I always had a personality change. Some guys retreat to their rooms, some guys can't shut up—but the ship changes you. Whatever you are around your family, you're different on board. And then you're in for hours and hours of sheer boredom, spiked by moments of sheer terror."

Few things cheered up sailors more than getting mail from home. The sailors got theirs at certain ports, the Soo Locks, or directly from the *J. W. Westcott*, the U.S. Mail tugboat docked in Detroit. The *Westcott* is the nation's only boat with its own zip code, 48222, which every Great Lakes sailor can recite by heart. Today the fifth generation of Westcotts is running the routes, bouncing from ship to ship to deliver mail in a red, white, and blue bucket—"mail by the pail"—with a rope the sailors pull to get their reward.

But even letters from home can help only so much. Hayes recalls his first season on board, 1971, when he was a cadet and a coal passer—either of which would put you at the lowest rung on the ladder.

"I was both, so I had no friends on that ship," he says. "I thought I was lonely before I came to shore in Two Harbors. Then I walked up the street and saw all the pretty girls hanging out with their friends, and then you see what you're missing.

"On the ships we were surrounded only by each other for months, which made it easier, in a way. For half the year, that's your family—like 'em or not.

"But you have to ask yourself: *Why am I doing this?* And no one you meet on shore understands what you do, or why it matters."

FIFTY YEARS AGO entertainment options for sailors were few: reading, telling stories, playing cards, and drinking, and often in some combination thereof.

"Sailors were always pretty tough customers, but big readers," Hayes says. "I used to devour *Reader's Digest*, and loved the section Toward More Picturesque Speech. Gobbled them up. We also used to get the Coast Guard magazine, *Proceedings*, which I read every month."

Hayes would pick up his magazines and condensed books—ten different stories in a two-inch-thick book, which made for very efficient reading—while going through the Soo Locks, where a local librarian would roll a cart of books out to the boats. Before cable TV, cell phones, and laptops, the sailors were voracious readers, which explains why so many have vocabularies far beyond their educational levels, but they can switch back and forth to sailor-ese with aplomb.

Next to reading, sailors favored card playing, with poker proving to be the most effective means to separate a rookie from his hard-earned wages. After a long season's work more than a few sailors returned home empty-handed—to a very upset spouse. That's why many fathers and mentors advised the newbies to avoid the poker games altogether, and the wise ones listened.

Sailors also enjoyed cribbage and euchre, which plays like a five-card version of bridge, a distinctly Midwestern game. Popular on Big Ten campuses between classes and in factory break rooms because the workers could squeeze in a game or two during their union-protected lunch and coffee breaks, it spread to the ships.

Card playing, drinking, and storytelling often went together, and the sailors often enjoyed all three in the galley or their cabins.

"What's the difference between a fairy tale and a sea story?" Rick Barthuli asks. "The fairy tale starts, 'Once upon a time . . .' The sea story starts, 'This ain't no shit.' Otherwise, they're about the same."

The hours spent spinning yarns produced raconteurs who were amazingly good at recreating all the noises a ship can make. Such bull sessions naturally included nicknames for everyone—but as in a locker room, you didn't get to pick your own. On the *Hudson*, the GLMA training tugboat, Rick Barthuli says, "Bill Kivell picked all the nicknames, like 'Rodent,' 'Parks and Rec,' and 'Finlander.' Kivell himself was called 'Willie the Tongue.' You'd look for the thinnest part of a sailor's skin, and then you'd keep poking it."

Some stories were common to every ship. When things got quiet on one of those nights you can feel summer turn to fall, the veterans would tell the rookies about the 1913 Storm of the Century, and the more recent *Carl D. Bradley* and *Daniel J. Morrell* shipwrecks. On the *Fitzgerald*, some of the older crewmen would have known someone on both ships, and would share those stories with added reverence.

Most of the sailors' pastimes were generously supplied by "bum boats," tugboat-size craft that pulled up alongside the freighters as soon as they docked, offering all manner of snacks, beer, wine, liquor, cigarettes, playing cards, books, and magazines—including *Playboy* and the rest—in any quantities you wanted.

The tradition started with the Kaners, one of the few Jewish families in Duluth, whose business began by selling goods in packsacks to sailors onboard. The Kaners eventually bought one boat, *Kaner I*, and then a second, *Kaner II*, to deliver everything sailors wanted.

"They were good people," John Tanner says, "and provided a service everyone appreciated."

The bum boats were so popular they spread to Chicago, Detroit, and Toledo, where they served the sailors for decades.

"They didn't care what age you were," Craig Silliven says. "If you had the money, you got what you wanted—booze, smokes, whatever."

Former *Fitzgerald* deckhand Patrick Devine recalls buying a case of Olympia Beer from the bum boat in Duluth, putting it in a net, and tossing it out a porthole, then dragging it behind the ship across Lake Superior.

"Took just twenty minutes, and you'd pull out ice cold beer," he says. "You had to let it sit for a few minutes, or you'd get a beer bath. Ask me how I know! Went down very well on a hot day."

Like the sailors' bars, the bum boats didn't hesitate to cash sailors' checks, and for the same reason: They knew a lot of those crisp bills would be left with them. From a bum boat you could buy almost anything, including outdated TVs and electronics that ran on direct current (DC) power, which the older boats still used. If you were short staffed, you could even hire a helping hand through a bum boat.

"The bum boats were like a floating general store," Rick Barthuli says. "They had just about everything, and what they didn't have, they could get for you on your next time through. Some sailors never stepped foot on a dock. They just went from their ship to the bum boat to another ship."

The bum boats have since faded out, but not in the memories of those who relied on them for decades.

Some difficulties are common to all ships, whether on the ocean or the lakes. While seasoned sea dogs almost never get physically ill on a given trip, no matter how wild the waves, almost every crewman will lose their lunch at some point in their careers. Horatio Nelson himself, arguably the world's most accomplished sailor, was notoriously weak stomached. In 1804 on the HMS *Victory*, he wrote, "I am ill every time it blows hard, and nothing but my enthusiastic love for the profession keeps me one hour at sea."

John Tanner admits, "I used to give people a hard time until I was on the *Stewart J. Cort*, the first thousand-footer, out on Lake Superior.

Biggest seas I've ever seen, thirty-footers—and boom, it got me. I felt humbled that I'd given people a hard time over the years. Guess I should have kept my mouth shut.

"People think the ship just goes up or down, or one way or the other, but it goes up and down and left and right, and it rolls, and that's what gets you, that combination."

When sailors start to feel queasy, the smart ones replace their next meal with water and a few crackers.

"Anything else, you're taking your chances," Tanner says. "And you should keep looking at the horizon, which is stable, instead of the boat, which is going up and down. It boils down to your inner ear, and what you had for supper."

Even workers on a ship tied up at the dock can get seasick.

"If the ship is rolling," Tanner says, "and it's dark and hot down there, and they don't have a window to look out of, it can get to them. Once one guy gets sick, where ventilation is poor and the smell is everywhere it sets everyone else off like a string of firecrackers. But there's always one guy who won't get sick no matter what."

Even facing five-, ten-, and twenty-foot waves on a fairly regular basis, most career sailors might get seasick once or twice in their entire careers—or they consider another line of work. Landlubbers, however, usually start running for the railing when the waves reach five feet, and often less. Great Lakes ferries know they can't go out if the waves are more than that or they'll have a very unhappy boat.

The same five-footers that will make most of us sick won't make a pro blink, but they can have serious side effects for even the most steel-stomached sailor.

"Your ability to think in rough seas is distorted and compromised—almost like being sleep deprived or drunk," Tanner says. "I've been in rough seas enough, and it's a fatigued feeling, and it's hard to think sharp. Your judgment is affected over time, and these ships can go three or four days in heavy waves. You don't get the deep sleep you need, either, so you wake up groggy. It affects your performance, and your judgment."

With every decision, the weary captain and crew teeter between making a wise choice and a fatal mistake.

Winters on the Great Lakes are brutal, but summer days can get surprisingly hot. When the sun hits the thick steel decks for hours upon hours, you can cook an egg on the hatches, and it's worse down below.

"On a hot day you always put your gloves on *before* you walked down the stairs into the engine room," Rick Barthuli says. "You *do not* touch the handrail without gloves. If you do, you'll leave skin on it. You learn that once."

If it was 90 degrees outside, it could be 120 degrees in the engine room. The engine crew would sweat so much they'd leave white salt lines on their blue work T-shirts from the sweat drying. They'd counter the dehydration by drinking a gallon of water during each four-hour shift.

"Your quarters might be a hundred degrees," John Hayes says, "and there's no AC back then. Then you've got a crewman sleeping across the room, and he smells and he's snoring and farting all night. You can't sleep. Then you wake up tired, soaked in sweat, and cranky—and you have to do it all again."

And yet, even in the dead of summer, on the Great Lakes the night after a blazing hot day can turn shockingly cold.

"On July Fourth, 1967," John Tanner says, "we were sailing on the *Ernest T. Weir* in Lake Superior, painting the aft cabins—and it snowed!"

The jobs were hard, the hours long, the sacrifices many, but the pay was good.

Although many of the veterans had a love-hate relationship with their union, "it has to be said," Rick Barthuli concedes, "the pay was poor until unions grew in the 1950s. Then you could make good money, even put your kids through college."

Depending on their roles on the ship, Great Lakes sailors are members of the United Steelworkers Union, the Marine Engineers' Benevolent Association, the Seamen's International Union, or the American Maritime Officers union, while the dockworkers are protected by the Teamsters. When sailors treat the dockworkers with respect everything goes smoothly, but making an enemy on the docks tends to create problems.

"Never mess with the dockworkers," Hayes says. "If you're a pain, they can 'accidentally' spill cargo on deck and you're the one who gets to shovel it off. Lesson learned."

On the Great Lakes there's an old joke: How many Teamsters does it take to screw in a lightbulb?

Sixteen. You gotta problem with that?

And the answer is no. No, you do not.

SOME OF THE fringe benefits of sailing could not be measured, including incredibly beautiful scenery.

"If your ship is going through the St. Lawrence River," says Rick Barthuli, a grizzled vet not given to poetic statements, "you don't want to miss the Thousand Islands. And the northern lights on Lake Superior is something that has to be seen to be believed. When and where they show up, and how they bounce around, and the colors—it's always different. Most people never see them. We were doing forty-five to fifty round trips a year across the big lake. It became so common, I really didn't look after a while. It's like the Soo Locks: first time, you got to see 'em."

John Hayes recalls sailing in Lake Superior when the temperature dipped to five below zero and he looked out the porthole to see the northern lights "like I'd never seen them: a multicolored curtain, like the one behind Johnny Carson, waving back and forth, purple and orange and blue and red and green."

On the Great Lakes, and especially on Superior, the autumn leaves appear in colors and quantities not seen anywhere else due to the unequaled levels of moisture in the leaves. When the trees are in full bloom a savvy captain will come up with just about any excuse to go through the canal that cuts across the Keweenaw Peninsula for a spectacular two-hour color tour, especially if he has VIPs onboard.

The towering dunes, the deep forests, the northern lights, the fall colors, the sunsets that glow for hours, even the big cities at night are sights sailors keep with them their entire lives.

"Look, it was hard," Barthuli says of the sailing life. "And you're gone for seven or eight months a year, too. But you know, it was a fun way of life, in a lot of ways. No one could bother you out there, and you got to see so much. Better than sitting in an office, that's for damn sure.

"I never wanted to get a real job—so I stayed in sailing. No regrets."

SOME SAILORS LIKED it so much they dreaded the last day of the season.

"The lifers are the guys who never went home on the last day, or didn't have a home to go to," Hayes says. "It was like a funeral for them."

Some would spend their offseason at Cleveland's Flat Iron Bar, sleeping in the rooms two floors above. They were giddy to get back on board, but not John Hayes, who longed all season to return to his growing family for those few sweet winter months.

"There was nothing better than coming home from the last trip with a nice big bonus in your pocket. My kids would hug me and say, 'You smell like a truck!'

"I'd tell them, 'No, I smell like a paycheck.'

"You're home, and your wife and kids love it, and you've done good work. You're safe, and you're done for a few months. Life is good."

That's when the sailors would make a fire, pour their desired drink, turn on the game, sit down in their favorite chair, and savor being warm, dry, and immobile for hours at a time, in the company of the people they loved most.

LIKE SO MANY of his retired colleagues, John Hayes rarely goes out on Lake Michigan's picturesque Grand Traverse Bay, even though it's just a few miles from his home. After working twenty-three years on the Great Lakes and another twelve on the Atlantic, he's earned the right. Happily married to Helen for forty-eight years, and now with three grandchildren, he lives in a home that's neat, tidy, warm, and comfortable—but with no water in sight.

"I don't fish. I don't sail. I don't boat," Hayes says. "If I want to see water, I can turn on the faucet.

"I've seen enough water for the rest of my life, forever and ever.

"Amen."

Life on Shore

GIVEN THE LONG STRETCHES OF MONOTONY, THE occasional moments of alarm, the heat, the cold, the rain, the snow and the ice, and the waves churning the crews' stomachs and tiring their brains, it's not hard to appreciate how eagerly these long-faced sailors yearned to see the next port.

Literally seconds after they tied the ship to the dock the sailors would race down the ladder to the nearest payphone, almost always located within a hundred feet of the pier, to call home. They ran because most docks had only one payphone, and their entire crew wanted to use it. While the big trains heavy with cargo rumbled by, the sailors would stand ten deep for their chance to drop a few dimes into the phone and assure their wives and children they had arrived safely.

"You'd wait in the cold and the rain, too," John Hayes says, "and if someone took too long, they'd hear about it."

Those who didn't have to stay on the ship for their next shift would walk up the street. The shores of the five Great Lakes are home to 167 towns, but most sailors go to only a few of those ports. Their favorite bars were never part of a chain, and few were well-known outside their circle, but they all had one thing in common: They were the closest bars to the dock.

When you had only a few hours to let your hair down, you didn't have the luxury of shopping around. Besides, all these sailors wanted were a few beers, and the chance to look at someone other than the same two dozen unshaven crewmates they'd been working with all summer.

"When you're surrounded by fuel oil, diesel, exhausts, and chemical fumes for three days," John Hayes explains, "and then you sit down in a bar and a woman walks by and her perfume drifts over—yeah, you notice."

Whether way up at the Municipal Liquor and Lounge in Silver Bay, Minnesota, or down at the Flat Iron Bar in Cleveland, every sailor bar offered cheap beer and a great jukebox. A quarter would get you three songs in Chicago, Detroit, or Toledo, and five songs in Silver Bay or Superior, Wisconsin, and fifty cents got you a pack of smokes.

If the older sailors were the first ones up the street, they would line up a playlist of Loretta Lynn, Tom T. Hall, George Jones, Charley Pride, and Johnny Cash. But if the younger guys made it through the door first, they would choose from among some of the best rock 'n' roll ever recorded for their evening soundtrack.

"And I mean the Rolling Stones, Van Morrison, Creedence Clearwater Revival," Hayes says. "Solid gold."

When McSorley's *Fitzgerald* crew started pumping quarters into the jukeboxes across the Great Lakes, they could also punch in the numbers to hear emerging Michigan stars like Flint's Grand Funk Railroad ("We're an American Band"), Ann Arbor's Bob Seger ("Ramblin' Gamblin' Man"), and the Motown artists who had been crowding the charts for a decade.

"Man, Grand Funk's double album was like gold bullion," Hayes says. "'Captain, My Captain' was a favorite. So was Blues Image's 'Ride Captain Ride.'" ("Seventy-three men set sail, from the San Francisco Bay.")

John Tanner points to another common theme: "We played a lot of songs about homesickness."

The two generations couldn't agree on country versus rock 'n' roll, but they all loved one song above all the others: "Brandy (You're a Fine Girl)," which they would play a half dozen times before the night was done.

In 1970 Rutgers University student Elliot Lurie started a band called Looking Glass, which played local bars and fraternity parties. One day when Lurie was tinkering around with some chord progressions, he stumbled onto something good.

"It actually took a week or two," Lurie says. "It's pretty tight, that story. When I ran the song by the band, we all liked it. But we didn't think we had a hit."

The melody was catchy, but the story Lurie told about a waitress in a seaside bar was the hook.

There's a port on a western bay
And it serves a hundred ships a day
Lonely sailors pass the time away
And talk about their homes

There's a girl in this harbor town
And she works laying whiskey down
They say, "Brandy fetch another round"
She serves them whisky and wine

The sailors say, "Brandy, you're a fine girl
What a good wife you would be
But my life, my love, and my lady is the sea"

Lurie's knowledge of the girl, the bar, and the sailor's soul seemed so intimate, and so real, that actual sailors have long assumed Lurie must have been one too.

"People always ask," Lurie says, "but the biggest boat I'd ever been on was the Staten Island Ferry. Honestly, I just made it up. I know that's disappointing."

"Those guys might not have been sailors," says John Hayes, "but man, that song is spot-on. Spot. On. 'My life, my love, and my lady is the sea.' I worked with guys like that, who dreaded the end of the shipping season."

Lurie and his bandmates were living in a farmhouse in New Jersey when their manager called them to New York to meet with the record company. As soon as they sat down the manager told them they were about to have a number-one hit and sell a million records. The bandmembers looked at each other, speechless, then Lurie asked, "How do you know that? There's only one station in Baltimore playing it.

"He said, 'Kid, we do this for a living. When we see that happen in a big market, we know it's going to spread.'"

Sure enough, the song became a number-one hit. For decades it was the most popular song in every bar on the Great Lakes—the one song that would get the two generations to put aside their differences and literally sing together.

For *Edmund Fitzgerald* oiler Tom Bentsen, Hayes says, "it was practically his theme song."

THE SAILORS' CURFEW was set not by the captain, but the dockworkers. The second they finished loading or unloading the ship, the captain ordered the lines pulled in, and the ship pushed off, without looking back to see who might be running up to catch it. If you missed your ship you'd have to figure out how to get to the next port, and fast, then take the hit when the company docked your pay—or worse, when you had to explain to your wife and kids how you lost the family's meal ticket.

Few sailors had access to a car, and good luck finding a taxi in Alpena, Michigan, at two in the morning on a freezing night. So when their time in the bar was up they walked, always downhill, back to the docks to climb the ladder, get onboard, and do it all again.

The Milkman of Two Harbors, Minnesota

CRAIG ELLQUIST SERVED AS A DECKHAND ON THE *Edmund Fitzgerald* for the last two months of the 1974 season. He planned to return to the *Fitz* a few months later to start the 1975 season, until an unexpected offer changed his mind—and his life.

The year before, in the spring of 1974, Ellquist had graduated from Two Harbors High then joined the U.S. Air Force. But with Vietnam winding down the military's need for recruits diminished, so the Air Force gave Ellquist and his peers the option of staying in the service or going home.

Homesick, Ellquist opted to return to Two Harbors, thus ending his military career at twenty-eight days. He fell into the local business, shipping, working as a relief deckhand for crewmen who were off their boats for two to four weeks at a time, usually due to injury. Late in the season he got a longer stint on the *Edmund Fitzgerald.* Ellquist's discharge slip—all the sailors seem to save these—lays it out in black and white: On Thursday, November 28, 1974, he boarded the *Edmund Fitzgerald* as a deckhand, and worked through January 28, 1975, when the *Fitzgerald* docked in Toledo for the winter.

Ellquist did what all deckhands do: when the *Fitzgerald* was in port he helped load and unload the ship; as soon as they pushed off, he swept and hosed the thousands of stray taconite pellets off the deck, pushing them into the water (legal, back then); when the *Fitz* was out at sea he painted the ship; when they were going out he clamped the hatches, and when they were coming in he unclamped them to start the unloading process.

"They'd find work to keep you busy," Ellquist says. "You never got to lay on your bunk for four hours."

Ellquist had the four-to-eight shift, both morning and night.

"When the guy came down to wake you up for the morning shift," he says, "it was brutal."

But when they were about to dock Ellquist would try to jigger his starting time so he could put in an eight-hour shift, four hours of which would qualify for overtime at one and a half times his normal pay. Since Ellquist and his fellow deckhands were already getting $7.25 an hour, working overtime at $10.87 an hour was five times the national minimum wage of $2 an hour.

By maximizing overtime, deckhands could make $20,000 to $30,000 a season ($125,000 to $175,000 today), plus a few thousand more in bonus if they finished the season. That was strong incentive to keep sailing through the cold, rough seas of November and December. Add it all up, and a rookie deckhand could make twice America's average income. The best part: Smart sailors could take home most of what they made.

"It was easy to do, because you got nowhere to spend it!" Ellquist says—provided, that was, they avoided the poker games on board and the strip clubs in Duluth, Detroit, and Toledo, temptations that could drain a drunken sailor's pocket with impressive speed. It helped that the restaurants on shore couldn't top the one in the *Fitzgerald*'s galley that served them for free three times a day.

WHEN TWO OF a twenty-year-old man's greatest desires—good food and good money—were provided in such ample supply, being a deckhand on the *Fitzgerald* was about as good as it got for young men willing to work. But the good life came with two catches: clamps, and bad weather—and the two were not unrelated.

The *Fitzgerald* had twenty-one cargo hatches, each one measuring eleven by forty-eight feet and made of 5/16-inch-thick steel. Each hatch featured twenty-four inches of coaming around the opening—miniwalls rising two feet off the deck—on which the hatch covers rested. When in port the deck crane (attached to the ship, unlike the much larger Hulett cranes on shore) would roll over a hatch cover, which weighed fifty tons, pick it up and set it down between two hatches, leaving the hatch open so it could be loaded or unloaded, then move on to the next hatch cover.

When sailing, the three deckhands secured each hatch cover with Kestner clamps, which function like large C-clamps. These had to be tightened either by hand or with an iron bar slid into a hole at the top of the clamp, then spun to loosen or tighten. The bar was very helpful on the sticky clamps.

Clamping the hatches down (or "dogging" them) was much harder than unclamping them, and not as fun, either. When the ship neared port, the first mate would give the deckhands the order to start taking the clamps off to ensure the cargo holds were ready to unload the second they tied up at the dock. The echo of the clamps being removed reverberated throughout the ship, drawing smiles from the crew, especially the engine crew working below deck who couldn't see shore.

"Ta-lunk, ta-lunk, ta-lunk!" recalls retired engineer John Hayes. "That means we're getting into port, and all ashore who are going ashore. No better sound."

On the *Fitzgerald* each hatch had 68 clamps hanging down when not in use, waiting to be flipped up and secured. With twenty-one hatches, that totaled 1,428 hatch clamps. If the deckhands were going along at a good clip they could fasten or unfasten a clamp in about ten seconds. But even with three deckhands, that still took almost two hours of hard work—so hard that even when it was snowing, the deckhands would sweat so much that they'd take their coats off and finish the job in their T-shirts.

But during the spring and summer months, when the winds and waves were light, even pleasant, the first mate would require the deckhands to secure only two clamps on each corner of each hatch, or 168 total, instead of 1,428, and leave the rest unsecured. By reducing the deckhands' workload by 88 percent, they could get the job done in a half hour or less. So long as it was nice out, their supervisor would also let them wait until the ship had already left the dock to clamp them, which allowed the ship to leave the port that much sooner—always a plus.

"Time is money, time is money," Ellquist says, repeating the mantra beaten into his head decades ago. Professional race car drivers know that every second on the track they need to be jamming their foot down on either the accelerator or the brakes, and never coast. Likewise, a good crew is always either loading the ship, sailing, or unloading—and doing all of it as fast as they can. Everything else is a waste of time, and therefore money. Since everyone depended on them to finish before they could do their jobs, the deckhands felt the pressure.

"No breaks till you got 'er done," Ellquist recalls. "They don't want to be waiting for the deckhands—or anyone else. They always wanted to get moving, moving, moving."

But if they knew bad weather was on the way, or if it was simply later in the season, no matter the weather, "we *always* clamped down—every clamp, no skipping," Ellquist says. "We were always careful about that. They wouldn't even leave port without clampin' 'em all."

If the temperature dropped low enough to make the freshwater waves freeze when they hit the deck, the deckhands attacked the ice with hot water, steam, and sledgehammers until they could take the clamps off.

"We saw some big weather," Ellquist says. "I saw twelve-, fourteen-, maybe even sixteen-foot waves. The boat just kind of rolls with it, but I'll never forget being in that tunnel in bad weather, and holy cow did that ship move! It's not a roller coaster, but a Tilt-A-Whirl, going all directions at once. That's what gets you."

When the *Fitzgerald* smashed into and over big waves it felt as though Poseidon himself had grabbed the ship and started twisting it back and forth. Once, while painting a closet during some waves, Ellquist emerged looking purple, and lost his lunch—repeatedly.

"Probably took a good day to straighten my stomach out," he says. "Holy moly, never felt anything like that."

FOR ELLQUIST, THE *Fitzgerald*'s captain and crew ranked up there with the money and the food as the best reasons to stay onboard.

"That ship got along very well. *Very* well," he says. Of the twenty-nine crew sailing on the *Fitzgerald*'s last run, Ellquist knew eighteen of them from his stint ten months earlier. "Everyone respected everybody. Never saw anybody bickering at someone."

It helped that many of them had been working together with Captain McSorley on other Columbia ships before reuniting on the *Fitzgerald*. If the crew liked you, Ellquist says, they made sure you came back. And if they didn't . . .

"I'm pretty sure they had some kind of 'no asshole' policy," Ellquist says.

That started from the top.

"Oh, definitely, everybody respected McSorley," Ellquist says. "Good guy. It was how he treated people, always fair. So long as you did your job, he left you alone. He wasn't sitting there nickel-and-diming you on stupid stuff. He let you do your job, and if you got it done right, that's all he cared about.

"Some people become bosses and they become assholes, but that wasn't him. He didn't talk much. He'd say hi to you. He'd know your name. And he never yelled, that I saw.

"And he was good! The best, they said. At Silver Bay everyone else pivoted around in the bay so they could pull in forward to the docks, and that takes time, but not McSorley. He backed right in, no problem, and that could save forty-five minutes.

"Time is money."

Ellquist also made an unlikely friend during his time onboard.

Eugene "Red" O'Brien, a fifty-year-old wheelsman with thick red hair and freckles, stood about six feet tall. He had been sailing since he was sixteen except for four years when he worked in a Toledo windshield factory. He loved casinos and playing cards so much they nicknamed him "the Great Lakes Gambler." A few crewmen found out why they called him that the hard way.

O'Brien had a son about Ellquist's age, but rarely saw him after Red got divorced. When the *Fitzgerald* docked each week in Toledo, O'Brien's hometown, he never went home.

"I figured he must have missed his family," Ellquist says, "and I was a substitute."

One day in the galley O'Brien struck up a conversation with Ellquist, and that started their friendship. O'Brien would often take Ellquist and others to Tony Packo's in Toledo, where Ellquist would order their famous chicken paprikash, with dumplings. O'Brien always picked up the tab, he told Ellquist, because "you don't make enough to treat people."

O'Brien occasionally let Ellquist steer the ship, which was how Ellquist learned about the few-second delay between turning the wheel and the ship actually changing direction, something every wheelsman has to learn.

"Red took me under his wing," Ellquist says. "He was more like a father to me than anything. Maybe that's why he didn't let me play cards with him!"

WHEN THE 1974 season was winding down, Ellquist recalls, the buzz on the ship was about who might be hanging it up before the next season. First Mate John McCarthy and Wheelsman John Simmons, both sixty-two, and McSorley himself were "already talking about whether they were going to go one more season or not," Ellquist reports, as was his friend, Red O'Brien. "Probably a few others, too. It seemed like they were all deciding together."

When the ship docked in Toledo for the winter in January of 1975, Ellquist still wasn't sure which crewmates were going to retire, if anyone, and perhaps they weren't either. Three months later they all came back for one more season, but Ellquist is convinced that 1975 "was going to be their last season, no matter what. The *Fitz* would have needed a whole new crew in '76."

Ellquist planned on returning to the *Fitzgerald* in Toledo that March of 1975, too, but that still gave him two more months to kill before fitting out. So when Al Ruberg of Al's Dairy in Two Harbors asked him to deliver milk to the area stores, Ellquist figured it would be a good way to stay busy while making a few bucks.

But two months later, right before Ellquist was supposed to head to Toledo, Ruberg asked to meet him at Miller's Café in Two Harbors, and made his pitch: Ellquist could work for Al's Dairy, have a great summer, then return to the *Fitzgerald* in the fall.

"So I gave my notice to the first mate," Ellquist says, "and got back on the milk truck."

X

THE VETERANS

"Beat the Victory!*"*

An old sailor saw goes like this: If you have twenty-nine men on a ship, you have one captain, and twenty-eight men who think *they* should be captain.

Because everything that happens on a ship ultimately falls to the captain, they must have thick skin and a deep self-assurance to make quick, decisive calls in the pilothouse, decisions they expect others to follow—and fast. On ninety-nine trips out of a hundred, a first or even a second mate could probably land the ship. But as with airplane pilots, you pay a good captain for that hundredth run, when only the best can overcome the conditions. That's when they earn their keep.

Captains in McSorley's era knew just one mishap could end their carefully cultivated careers, so they tended to be control freaks who enforced the chain of command. They were endowed with more temper and self-importance than the average person, prone to yelling, pointing, banging their fists on the table, throwing cups of hot coffee, and worse.

Yet McSorley's crew consistently regarded him as a voice of reason, cool in a crisis, a man who rarely raised his voice, and who leaned on the chain of command only as much as needed. When he made a decision, whether his people agreed or not, they could be confident he had come to his conclusion by considering the best interest of the ship and its people, not himself, his ego, or his status. In the pressure cooker of a Great Lakes freighter, whether fighting big waves on Superior or traffic in Detroit, McSorley's rare combination of quiet confidence and quick-thinking resolve was exactly what the crew needed.

These qualities were on full display when McSorley navigated in tight quarters, but he didn't get to the top just for his skillful piloting. Most importantly, to Columbia Transportation at least, McSorley was the most reliable captain on the lakes. He rushed to deliver on time, every time.

"A lot of these captains were infamous for being go-go-go," says former GLMA superintendent John Tanner. "They're like top-tier football coaches, very aggressive, and McSorley was right up there. Whatever the weather, you knew McSorley's ship was going to go. To beat someone to the dock first captains will do all kinds of things. Sometimes, if you get there first, you can save a whole day. And McSorley had a reputation for pushing it."

Former *Fitzgerald* cadet Craig "Red Dog" Silliven recalls one trip going upbound on Lake Huron, toward the St. Marys River and the Soo Locks. It was a typically crowded day in the early seventies, with ships vying to arrive first at the gateway to the St. Marys River, located between DeTour, Michigan, and Drummond Island, at the extreme eastern tip of Michigan's Upper Peninsula. Whoever gets there first holds their position for the five-hour trip up the river to the Soo Locks, where they get to go through the locks first. Lose by a minute, you lose by an hour—or a day.

Captain McSorley knew exactly how his bosses back at Columbia's corporate headquarters in Cleveland would react to such a holdup. Finishing second was expensive in every way, and to be avoided at all costs.

On this trip Silliven remembers the *Fitzgerald* was racing the *Cliffs Victory*, one of the 534 Victory ships the U.S. Navy built between 1944 and 1946. After the war Cleveland Cliffs converted the *Victory* to commercial use, then extended her to seven hundred feet in 1957, making her the longest ship on the Great Lakes until the *Fitzgerald* debuted the next year. The *Victory* could draw on 8,500 horsepower, 1,000 more than the *Fitzgerald*, and had a top speed of twenty miles per hour, compared to the *Fitzgerald*'s sixteen miles per hour, making the *Victory* the fastest ship on the Great Lakes. But the race wasn't run on paper.

It helped that, among other factors, the *Fitzgerald* was riding light on its way back to Minnesota. But perhaps the biggest factor would be the captains in their pilothouses. The race was on, and even a few hours from DeTour the *Fitzgerald* crew knew it was going to be close.

McSorley, eyes alive and focused, stared out the pilothouse window with set jaw, and hissed to himself, "*Beat the* Victory."

"It was quiet, but you could tell he meant it," Silliven says. "That's all he had to say."

Northwestern Mutual president Edmund Fitzgerald insisted that the *Edmund Fitzgerald* be the best ship the Great Lakes had ever seen. She not only set records, she could boast the finest quarters, galley, captain, and crew. "She was simply the best," says Roger LeLievre, who took this photo, "and that was before anything happened." Here she is fully loaded in August 1975, just months before her last trip. *Courtesy of Roger LeLievre*

Designated as "Hull 301" during construction, the *Fitzgerald* featured two "tunnels" right below the deck to walk fore and aft during storms, large ballast tanks on the sides and bottom, and the biggest cargo holds the Great Lakes had ever seen. *MHSD*

Edmund did not want the ship named for him, but his board went behind his back to overturn his decision. On June 7, 1958, in front of 15,000 people in Detroit, Edmund's wife, Elizabeth Fitzgerald, needed three tries to break the bottle. Their son said, "The day the ship was launched was probably the happiest day of my father's life." *The Associated Press*

Later that summer the Fitzgeralds hosted an open house for the public and the press back in Milwaukee. The shipbuilders had achieved Fitzgerald's daunting dream: They had built the greatest ship the Great Lakes had ever seen. *GLSHS*

The *Fitzgerald*'s pilothouse featured spectacular views and a chart room described as "beautiful," with exquisite trim. Here the captain gives directions to his wheelsman, who actually steers the ship. Now imagine standing there while the ship is going up and down thirty feet every six seconds. *GLSHS*

The *Edmund Fitzgerald* was equipped with a 7,500-horsepower Westinghouse steam turbine engine, which required eleven licensed crewmen to keep it humming during the ship's forty-five round trips each season. While most ships suffered from a bitter rivalry between the deck crew above and the engine crew below, *Fitzgerald* captain Ernest McSorley and chief engineer George Holl got along very well, setting the tone for the entire ship. *GLSHS*

The *Fitzgerald* loads 26,000 long tons—58 million pounds—of taconite at Silver Bay, Minnesota, where she most frequently loaded. Filling the three huge cargo holds took about five hours. *GLSHS*

Three days after leaving Silver Bay the *Fitzgerald* would typically unload in Toledo, where the enormous Hulett cranes would take fourteen hours to pull the taconite out. "The Huletts were mesmerizing," former *Fitzgerald* deckhand Patrick Devine says. "The guys who operated those things were *amazing*. That was a ballet, truly." *GLSHS*

The Kaner family started the beloved "bum boats" in Duluth, Minnesota, and they soon spread to other Great Lakes ports, including Superior, Toledo, and Cleveland. They sold just about everything a sailor could want—snacks, alcohol, cigarettes, magazines, and DC-power television sets that could run on the ships' old systems—and they'd even cash your paychecks.

Robert Haworth Collection

ERNEST McSORLEY

Ernest McSorley, born in 1912, joined his first ship in 1930 as a deckhand and in thirteen years climbed all the way to captain, the youngest on the Great Lakes. McSorley would captain eight more ships, earning a reputation as the best on freshwater, before Columbia Transportation tapped him to lead the *Edmund Fitzgerald*. *GLSHS*

A representative from Columbia awards McSorley (left) a clock for his service. Columbia loved McSorley because he always delivered his cargo on time, no matter what the weather. *GLSHS*

McSorley married Nellie Pollock and took care of her after she became ill. Here he is pictured with a crewman's children, or possibly grandchildren, on a tour of the ship. Along with a handful of his colleagues, McSorley planned to retire at the end of the 1975 season. *GLSHS*

NOLAN CHURCH

Nolan Church liked to give neighbors and crewmates haircuts, paint Christmas scenes on their bay window at home, and play Christmas carols on the organ for his wife, Thelma, who worked as a nurse in Two Harbors, and their five children. *GLSHS*

By 1975 Church had six grandchildren (five here), with the seventh due in April of 1976. "Oh, he *loved* kids!" his daughter Marilynn says. "That was his life." *GLSHS*

Church, fifty-five in 1975, wearing the hat, had left his job at Reserve Mining in Silver Bay just a few years earlier to pursue his dream of working as a porter—a very rare move. "Dad just loved it," his daughter Bonnie says. "It was a completely different world than what he was used to." *GLSHS*

EDDIE BINDON

Eddie Bindon, forty-seven in 1975, the *Fitzgerald*'s first engineer, was considering retiring after the season. On the ship's last weekend in port he went to Duluth, Minnesota, to buy his wife, Helen, a two-carat diamond ring for their twenty-fifth anniversary. But instead of taking it on the ship to deliver it to her in person, he gave it to a friend in Duluth to send to her. *GLSHS*

Like the conductor of a world-class symphony who has to give only the slightest hand gesture to get the musicians to deliver their best, McSorley didn't need to rant or rave. With his responsive crew, his whisper was enough.

"First of all, he's the captain," Silliven says. "So what he says, goes. And second, nobody wanted to disappoint that man. Third, he knew how to maneuver. When he first went to work for Columbia they had a lot of small ships, so he would go into a lot of ports the bigger lake freighters could not go into, like the Cuyahoga, so that gave him a lot of experience in tight spaces other captains didn't have. That's where he learned to drive, and to park it. And finally, for a big ship, the *Fitz* could move!"

The race raged back and forth. When the DeTour lighthouse came into sight, both crews were urging their ships forward.

"Well, McSorley's pushing it, everyone's pushing it," Silliven says. "We get to DeTour first, by a nose, so we get our assignment [for the locks] ahead of the *Victory*. I could hear McSorley say, '*Beat 'em*!' Wasn't loud, but you knew he was mighty happy about that!"

All the qualities that made McSorley the best captain on the Great Lakes—experience, skill, judgment, leadership, and even social graces—boiled down to that one singular result: "*Beat the* Victory."

Know Your Job, Do Your Job

GAME SHOW PRODUCERS AREN'T WILD ABOUT HAVING Midwesterners as contestants, because they simply don't react. Northeasterners, Southerners, and Californians yell and jump around when their names are called, and run down the aisle to play the game. Midwesterners are more likely to walk to the front row, grab the button, and get ready to work, without comment or expression.

If chivalry was the hallmark of a proper antebellum Southern gentleman, stoicism would be the chief characteristic of a Great Lakes sailor. It might be due to the cold, the small-town backgrounds, or the fact that almost everyone who moved to the Great Lakes did so for a job, not the weather or a glamorous lifestyle. Tough and taciturn, Great Lakes sailors don't waste their words on boasting—or anything else.

The story goes that a Finnish woman in Michigan's Upper Peninsula walked down to the local paper in Negaunee to submit her husband's obituary.

"Toivo died," she told the newsman at his desk.

The reporter typed it out and waited for more, but when none came he asked, "Is that it?"

"Yes," she said.

"Well, the obituary costs twenty-five dollars for five words," the reporter said. "You still have three left."

She thought for a moment, then said, "Toivo died. Truck for sale."

Great Lakes sailors are not flatterers, either. When they describe a fellow crewman as "competent," they are not damning with faint praise but offering a sincere compliment, one they don't give out freely.

In *The Demon of Unrest*, Erik Larson's insightful narrative of America's run-up to the Civil War, he cites *The Code Duello*, a published guide to the ornate protocols a true Southern gentleman must adhere to if he aspires to attain that most valued of Southern qualities, chivalry.

Great Lakes sailors have no such code, and even if they did, they wouldn't be so presumptuous as to write it all down. Besides, it would probably take only a few lines anyway: *Know your job. Do your job. Don't quit, and don't make excuses.*

Complaining, griping, and grumbling are all fair game, especially about the weather, the company paying you, or even the union. But what they do not allow themselves to do is give up or point fingers. No, you do your job, then you turn it over to the next guy in better shape than you found it.

This ethos is the foundation for each job on a Great Lakes ship.

OPERATING THE *EDMUND FITZGERALD* required twenty-nine men filling thirteen different roles.

The organizational chart of a ship breaks down like a football team's coaching staff. Just like a head coach, Captain McSorley oversaw everything and was responsible for all of it—not just driving the ship, but managing the entire crew, and the floating factory that is a Great Lakes freighter.

The crew under him was divided into two groups, similar to offense and defense: Those working above deck, including the pilothouse, were the offense, and those working below deck, usually in the engine room at the stern, served as the defense.

Both were essential to success, but each brought different mentalities to their work. On some ships the two sides got along, and on others they didn't.

The chart looked like this:

1 Captain.

DECK CREW

3 Mates

3 Wheelsmen

3 Watchmen

3 Deckhands

ENGINE CREW

5 Engineers
3 Oilers
1 Wiper
2 Maintenance men

OTHERS

2 Porters
2 Cooks
1 Cadet

On the deck side of the team, Captain McSorley and his three mates, who served as "junior captains," worked in the pilothouse. On November 9, 1975, the roster read as follows:

DECK CREW

OFFICERS

Captain: Ernest McSorley, 63, Toledo, Ohio
First Mate: John McCarthy, 62, Bay Village, Ohio (near Cleveland)
Second Mate: James Pratt, 44, Lakewood, Ohio (Cleveland)
Third Mate: Michael Armagost, 37, Iron River, Wisconsin (Head of the Lakes)

McSorley's first mate, John McCarthy, supervised everyone working above deck; the second and third mates also functioned as Captain McSorley's understudies, and would man the pilothouse during the less hectic stretches of the Toledo Express. When they navigated the trickier waters through the Soo Locks or the St. Marys or Detroit Rivers, McSorley or McCarthy were either at the helm or on hand to oversee their work.

The first mate also handed out the paychecks, so he was not someone you wanted to rub the wrong way. In McCarthy's case, his hold over the men wasn't based on leverage but relationships: his with Captain McSorley, who trusted him completely, and the deck crew's relationship with McCarthy.

"I liked McCarthy a lot and found him very easy to work with," says Patrick Devine, who served as a deckhand on the *Fitzgerald* in the summer of 1975. "Very competent. Not a real tall man, or a big burly guy, like a lot of them. Had short gray hair, not too imposing. But he was the Energizer Bunny. When you're the first mate you gotta be, because you've got a lot of balls you're juggling."

WHEELSMEN

John Simmons, 62, Ashland, Wisconsin (Head of the Lakes)
Eugene "Red" O'Brien, 50, Toledo, Ohio
John Poviach, 59, Bradenton, Florida

When the captain or one of the mates was in the pilothouse, working with charts and binoculars to plot the ship's course, they never actually touched the wheel itself. Instead they gave their directions to one of three wheelsmen on duty, who performed the actual steering. The more smoothly they worked with each other, the better.

It's fair to assume no wheelsman worked better with Captain McSorley than Senior Wheelsman John Simmons. Born in 1913, just one year after McSorley, Simmons lived his entire life in Ashland, Wisconsin, an hour east of Duluth on Lake Superior's southern coast, a pretty harbor town that's a popular spot for local weddings and honeymoons.

It says something about the sailing life that Ashland is seven hundred miles by car from Toledo, where McSorley lived, yet the two had been best friends for half their lives. When you spend three-quarters of each year working a few feet apart, living seven hundred miles away three months a year doesn't mean much. Whenever McSorley got a promotion to captain a better ship, the first thing he did each time was ask Simmons to follow, and Simmons always said yes.

Simmons was a true professional behind the wheel, and the translations between McSorley's directions and Simmons's actions were as fluid as any on the Great Lakes. But away from work Simmons was McSorley's alter ego: a notorious jokester, prankster, and pool shark at the sailor bars. Because McSorley could never allow himself to do any of those things, he probably enjoyed living vicariously through his wheelsman's exploits.

"John Simmons was a great guy," attests Craig "Red Dog" Silliven. "A good wheelsman. He'd stay in his cage [the pilothouse], and him and [fellow wheelsman] Red O'Brien would pace back and forth. But he'd also come outside and lean on the rail to talk with me, a lowly cadet. Didn't have to do that, but he did."

Simmons loved the sailing life, but like his boss and best friend McSorley, Simmons had promised his wife, Florence, that he, too, would retire after the last run of the 1975 season, and live his remaining years with her and their two daughters, Mary and Patricia, back in Ashland.

WATCHMEN

Ransom Cundy, 53, Superior, Wisconsin
William Spengler, 59, Toledo, Ohio
Karl Peckol, 30, Ashtabula, Ohio

Next in line were three watchmen, who'd earned their able-bodied seaman (ABS) endorsement to work on a ship. They each covered two of the six four-hour shifts every day. Their duties included deck maintenance (cleaning, painting, or fixing something), standing lookout when the ship was in confined waters or reduced visibility (nighttime, fog, or snow), preparing the ship to enter port by running the hatch crane to remove the hatch covers, and helping to guide the boat in by telling the captain by walkie-talkie how much space he had to work with from one of the four compass points on the ship.

The *Fitzgerald*'s watchmen included Ransom Cundy. Born in 1922 in Houghton, Michigan, on the Keweenaw Peninsula, Cundy was the son of a copper miner. Ransom enlisted in the Marines and survived the bloody Battle of Iwo Jima, earning medals and commendations for his heroism. After the war he moved to Superior, Wisconsin, married Betty Ewen in 1946, and had two daughters, Cheryl in 1947, and Janice in 1950.

A rakish-looking man photographed in dirty overalls and a hat at a jaunty angle, with a cigarette in his hand and a sly grin suggesting pending mischief, "Handsome Ransom" spent three months working in the copper mines before escaping to a freighter. He was the rare *Fitzgerald* crewman who had worked under both Captain Pulcer and Captain

McSorley. Well-liked, with a reputation as a friend you could count on, Cundy loved to pull pranks, and didn't spare his best friend, porter Fred Beetcher, who also lived in Superior.

Surprisingly a lot of sailors couldn't swim, including Cundy, but that didn't disqualify anyone from working on the ships. There was no swimming test; it wasn't even a question on the application; and many joked that swimming only prolonged the agony of drowning. It was considered bad form even to ask a fellow crewmate if he could swim. Cundy once told his older daughter that if his ship sank, "I'd go down with the boat, because I can't even dog paddle."

Cundy's lighthearted outlook disappeared on March 30, 1974, when the estranged husband of his youngest daughter, Janice, drove up from Chicago, entered her home, and killed her and then himself, all with their three young children in the house.

"He was no longer that happy, jovial man," one biography says. "He turned into a sad and beaten man."

To avoid suffering alone, Cundy took refuge on the *Fitzgerald*. His crewmates weren't therapists but they were good company, especially Beetcher. Even though both lived in Superior, Wisconsin, if Cundy wanted to talk with Beetcher he needed to be on the *Fitz* nine months a year. By November of 1975 Cundy was a long way from peace, but the *Fitz* was the best place for him to be.

DECKHANDS

Paul Riippa, 22, Ashtabula, Ohio
Bruce Hudson, 22, North Olmsted, Ohio (Cleveland)
Mark Thomas, 21, Richmond Heights, Ohio (Cleveland)

Rounding out the deck crew, the deckhands did everything else that needed doing, including painting, cleaning, and clamping and unclamping the hatches. On the *Fitz*, this trio consisted of three men aged twenty-one or twenty-two: Paul Riippa, a former high school football player, and Bruce Hudson and his buddy Mark Thomas, who planned to go on a cross-country trip in Hudson's burgundy Dodge Challenger as soon as the *Fitzgerald* docked for the winter in Toledo.

ENGINE CREW

ENGINEERS

Chief engineer: George Holl, 60, Cabot, Pennsylvania (Pittsburgh)
First assistant: Eddie Bindon, 47, Fairport Harbor, Ohio (Cleveland)
Second assistant: Thomas Edwards, 50, Oregon, Ohio (Toledo)
Second assistant: Russell Haskell, 40, Milbury, Ohio (Toledo)
Third assistant: Oliver "Buck" Champeau, 41, Milwaukee

The engine crew, working below deck and in the stern, was led by the chief engineer, George Holl, followed by his first assistant engineer, two second assistant engineers, and a third assistant engineer—a parallel structure to the captain and his three mates. The engineers were responsible for keeping the ship's many mechanical systems running smoothly, especially the 7,500-horsepower Westinghouse engine.

For the *Fitzgerald*'s third engineer, the company hired Oliver "Buck" Champeau. Although licensed to serve as second engineer, Champeau decided working with George Holl on the *Fitzgerald* more than made up for the bump down to third engineer. Of course, being third engineer on a well-run ship has its advantages, and you are responsible for the engine for only two four-hour shifts a day.

When John Hayes finished his climb from third engineer to chief engineer on another ship, "I thought, 'Hayes, you have *arrived*! Got the big bedroom, with a queen-size bed, a bathtub, a big picture window—*gorgeous*.' Then I saw the phone in the corner, and I realized when it rings, that call's for *you*, no one else, with big problems you need to solve. That's the price you pay for all that. You're it."

To an outsider, Buck Champeau's decision to accept a demotion might have looked foolish. But Champeau had seen enough of life to know what made him happy, and to ignore the rest.

OILERS

Ralph Walton, 58, Fremont, Ohio (near Toledo)
Blaine Wilhelm, 52, Moquah, Wisconsin (Head of the Lakes)
Tom Bentsen, 22, St. Joseph, Michigan

Three oilers assisted the engineers by, simply enough, oiling everything that needed oiling, plus taking hourly readings on the boilers' pressure and temperature, and pumping ballast water in and out of the huge tanks. In calm seas taking the hourly readings was routine, but in heavy seas it was harder and more important because temperatures, pressures, and boiler water levels all grew more volatile.

If the boiler runs out of water it will melt down, and then you're stuck in the middle of the lake hoping for a tow. And yet sometimes the engineers have to choose between risking damage to the boilers to get the ship out of heavy seas as fast as possible, or making sure the boilers don't blow up. A good engineer will collaborate with the captain to make that trade-off work down to the last ounce, but the success of that decision can depend on timely, accurate information from the oilers.

The *Fitzgerald*'s three oilers were Blaine Wilhelm, who saved his change in a coffee can for his seven kids and aspired to take the engineer's test one day, despite his fears of it; Grant Walton, older brother of Wade Walton, who had served on the *Fitzgerald* back in 1963 with Wade's son Tom, a porter that summer; and Tom Bentsen, John Hayes's best friend, whom he'd asked to serve as his best man for his wedding, scheduled for the summer of 1976.

WIPER
MAINTENANCE MEN

Wiper: Gordon MacLellan, 30, Clearwater, Florida, and Presque Isle, Michigan

Special maintenance man: Joseph Mazes, 59, Ashland, Wisconsin

Maintenance man: Thomas Borgeson, 41, Duluth, Minnesota

Because all the machines on the *Fitzgerald* had to be hand lubricated, after the oilers oiled, the wiper wiped all the excess lubrication off the machines and the floor, while two maintenance men assisted just about everyone below deck. The trio also helped with painting, cleaning, and the trash, among other duties.

In the old days, before the creation of the Environmental Protection Agency in 1970 and the Clean Water Act in 1972, the wiper simply threw the ship's trash overboard. In the late sixties companies started equipping ships with incinerators to burn their trash en route, which is what they still do today.

EVERY DAY ALMOST all of these sailors worked two four-hour shifts, called "watches," which started at four, eight, and twelve o'clock, both a.m. and p.m. Whichever watch you worked in the a.m. was the watch you worked in the p.m. So if you worked 8 a.m. to noon, you'd also work 8 p.m. to midnight.

Most crewmen think the best watches on the ship are four to eight, a.m. and p.m. At those hours there's usually less work to do, "so your main job is to make coffee," Hayes says. The watches are picked by seniority, so the first mate in the pilothouse and the first assistant engineer down below almost always take the four-to-eight watches, leaving the least desirable twelve-to-four watches for the rookies.

The captain and chief engineer don't have watches because they are responsible for the entire ship, twenty-four hours a day.

THE REST

PORTERS

COOKS

CADET

Porter: Frederick Beetcher, 56, Superior, Wisconsin
Porter: Nolan Church, 55, Silver Bay, Minnesota
Steward (first cook): Robert "Bob" Rafferty, 62, Toledo, Ohio
Second cook: Allen Kalmon, 43, Washburn, Wisconsin (Head of the Lakes)
Cadet: David "Cowboy" Weiss, 21, Agoura, California (LA)

In addition to the thirteen crewmen working above deck and eleven below, the *Fitzgerald* paid four more sailors whose jobs didn't fit into either division and didn't follow the four-hour-watch schedule, either. Sticking to the football analogy, the remaining five workers could be considered special teams.

Two porters helped in the kitchen, served meals, did laundry, and distributed clean towels and sheets. One, called the "bedbug," provided hotel-level service for the officers' rooms, with new towels and bedding daily. (The rest of the crew made their own beds.) The other porter waited on the officers, VIP guests, and crewmen, and washed dishes.

On most ships the porters tended to be young, and were sometimes college kids working for the summer, like Tom Walton. But given the *Fitzgerald*'s coveted status the ship could attract Fred Beetcher, fifty-six, and Nolan Church, fifty-five, who had left his job at Reserve Mining to pursue his dream of going out to sea.

Last but far from least was the head cook, called the steward, who planned every meal for each five-day round trip, ordered the food in military-size quantities, and cooked it. The cook's assistant, called the second cook, focused mainly on baking breads, pies, cakes, and cookies, which was why he was usually covered in flour.

"The cook is the only guy on board who has his work evaluated by everyone on the ship, three times a day," Hayes notes, "and often right to his face. They tended to be very good—and thick-skinned."

The *Fitzgerald*'s longtime cook, George H. "Big Red" Burgner, who had been repeatedly praised by the VIP guests writing in the ship's journal, had turned over the *Fitz*'s gleaming galley to a young cook named Richard Bishop, who would be 28 in 1975, of Duluth. But in October 1975, due to Bishop's bleeding ulcer—which perhaps speaks to the tremendous stress of that position—Columbia, at McSorley's suggestion, replaced Bishop with Bob Rafferty, 62, an experienced boat cook who was happy to come back from retirement for a few weeks to see his old friends.

"He always said that the *Fitzgerald* was king of the lakes," his sister Mable Schwann said. "It had the biggest kitchen he had ever had, and the ship was so big, he said they'd never have any trouble."

In early November, a week before the *Fitzgerald* was scheduled to push off for its last trip of the season, Rafferty sent a postcard to his family in Toledo. "I may be home by Nov. 8," he wrote. "However, nothing is ever sure."

Starting in the 1970s, the *Fitzgerald* also supported a relatively new position, cadet, a sailor in training from the recently opened Great

Lakes Maritime Academy. In 1975 the *Fitzgerald* filled that role with David "Cowboy" Weiss, who was studying to be a first-class Great Lakes pilot and eventually a captain.

When it's all humming, from the top on down, a Great Lakes freighter is a thing of beauty, with the crew working together as harmoniously as the ship itself. Peaceful productivity was probably not the rule on Great Lakes freighters, but the *Edmund Fitzgerald* tended to be exceptional in almost every way.

Captains and Chiefs

THE FIRST POTENTIAL OBSTACLE TO A HAPPY, EFFICIENT ship is the relationship between the two officers most responsible for the vessel's performance: the captain above deck, and the chief engineer below. These two set the tone. If they get along, the ship will run like the proverbial well-oiled machine that it is. If not, as John Hayes says, "everything is going to be a tug-of-war, like a never-ending divorce that everyone else has to live through all season long. Miserable, and inefficient."

Like most ships of its time, the *Fitzgerald* featured an officers' dining room where the captain, his mates, the chief engineer and his assistant engineers ate, plus a crew's mess for everyone else. The *Fitzgerald* also had a third room for "the passengers' dining room," where the captain would host the VIPs for their candlelight dinner.

In the *Fitzgerald*'s day, the captain—universally called "the old man," no matter his age—usually sat at one end of the officers' table, and the chief engineer at the other. Some ships were so contentious that the chief engineer would refuse to eat with the captain, so the chief would wait until the captain left before walking in. Some captains, wise to the game and just as stubborn, would wait out the engineer until he was forced to join the captain.

If the ship's central relationship is dysfunctional, it's a sure bet that those working under each leader will perpetuate the problems. It doesn't help that, even on the best of ships, those above deck and those below simply think differently.

When a new class of cadets would ask John Hayes why he signed up to be an engineer, and not a captain, he would reply, "It's true the captains and mates don't get arthritis and deal with one-hundred-degree engine rooms. They're going to be able to listen to the [FM] radio their whole watch, and it's a lot more comfortable and scenic on the bridge than it is in the engine room down below. They're not going to smell like a truck, either, and when they finish their watch they can go right to their beds without taking a shower first.

"But I couldn't imagine spending eight hours a day looking through a pair of binoculars, pacing back and forth in that wheelhouse like a tiger in a zoo cage, talking with some moron wheelsman who I can't stand, or trying to ignore him.

"I'll take the engine room over that—every time. Down there I'm working, and I can be productive, and be my own boss to a much greater degree."

As a rule, the crew working above deck doesn't want to switch with the crew below deck and vice versa, much like how people who work in sales don't want to work in service, and service people don't want to work in sales. The jobs aren't the same, and neither are the people who do them.

Patrick Devine started out as a wiper in the engine room of the *Armco*, then switched to deckhand on the *Fitzgerald*, so he saw both sides.

"It always seemed like the guys working with the engine were more cerebral, and more introverted. They liked fixing things. Guys on the deck were more extroverted. They liked talking.

"Everybody on board had their own story about how they got there. A ship, even a good one like the *Fitz*, is sort of like the Island of Misfit Toys. Some were going toward something they always wanted to do. Others had troubles they were running away from. Maybe some were both."

Most ships in the seventies fostered a robust rivalry between the deck and engine crews. As late as the 1970s some captains would insist that everyone else walk on the port side of the deck, so the captains could have the starboard side entirely to themselves. The chief engineer might return the favor by telling his people not to go forward of the eighteenth hatch, to avoid associating with "those rope chokers," the captain's deckhands.

"On a ship, there are two kinds of people," retired engineer Rick Barthuli says, "those who break things, and those who fix things. We fix things."

But if a captain is too afraid to break things he won't get very far, and if the engineers don't have anything to fix, they'll be out of work.

As Tolstoy once wrote, "Happy families are all alike; every unhappy family is unhappy in its own way."

So it is with ships. There are a thousand ways to render a crew dysfunctional, but only a few ways to get it right. On a well-run ship the captain and chief engineer talk often, and if they're not good friends, they at least have a mutual respect their subordinates can sense and follow.

"The captain is like the pitcher on a baseball team, and the engineer is like the catcher," Hayes says. "The pitcher sees the catcher and the batter, but the catcher sees everything behind the pitcher, the whole field. A good chief engineer can see just about everything that's happening on the ship. He can make the captain's life a lot easier if the captain includes him, asks questions, trusts him. Or the chief can make the captain's life miserable. But the captains often don't ask what's really happening, and that's what starts the trouble."

To illustrate his point, Hayes recalls a tug-of-war between the captain and chief engineer years ago on the *Raymond Reiss*. When the captain called down to Hayes's boss, chief engineer Norman Janusiewicz, Hayes says, "Captain says, 'More power!' Norman listens to the captain's request, and says, 'Sure,' hangs up, lights his cigar, opens his newspaper, and turns to me. 'Watch this, kid.' He just sits there, smoking and reading for a minute, then calls back and tells the captain he made some adjustments. 'Try it now,' he says.

"Captain responds, 'Yes, definitely better! Can you give it a little more?'

"'Let me see,' the chief replies. Then he hangs up, takes a couple more puffs, reads a little longer, calls back, and asks, 'Any better?'

"'Yes, you've got it! Thanks!' the captain says.

"The chief hangs up, looks over, and says, 'Learn something, kid?'"

Hayes had: The captain will probably believe what the engineer tells him, and the engineer ultimately has to do what's best for the ship.

ON THE *FITZGERALD* Captain McSorley established a decidedly different culture, one the rest of the crew picked up on. McSorley included even the newly minted GLMA cadets, whom most captains despised as know-nothing college kids and treated them accordingly.

When cadet Craig "Red Dog" Silliven first boarded the *Fitz* he was hesitant to knock on the door of the pilothouse, but Captain McSorley waved him right in.

"When I introduced myself to Captain McSorley, he said, 'Yeah, we've got the Irish Mafia on this one: O'Brien, McCarthy, McSorley. Silliven, you'll fit right in.' For a greenhorn like me, from the academy no less, that was music. Never forgot it. McSorley was a hell of a captain, and just a very personable, good guy."

Thanks to Captain McSorley's welcome, everyone else did the same—or almost all of them. As much as Silliven remembers the kindness of Captain McSorley, wheelsmen John Simmons, and Eugene "Red" O'Brien, he can't forget the rude welcome he received from the third wheelsman at the time.

"He was a jerk," Silliven says. "I don't know any other way to put it. He told us, 'Don't talk to me. Don't even walk behind me.' He was nasty, and he hated cadets. He asked the cook what he could eat so he could fart the worst farts, because he thought if he kept that up he could get me to leave the wheelhouse. Let's just say his demeanor was— Well, he was a bit of an asshole. And not just a bit."

But once Captain McSorley got the measure of the third wheelsman, and saw that the cadets were proving to be capable, coachable sailors, McSorley got the third wheelsman off the *Fitzgerald* and onto another ship, where he would become someone else's problem.

Three years later, in 1975, when Great Lakes Maritime Academy professor John Tanner boarded the *Fitzgerald* twice that season to check on another GLMA cadet, David "Cowboy" Weiss of California, the cranky third wheelsman was long gone, and harmony ruled the ship. Neither happened by chance.

"You hop on enough ships you learn to pick up a vibe pretty fast," Tanner says. "I would visit thirty ships a season, so you learn to get a sense. And 1975 wasn't my first season, either. When things aren't right, you feel the tension quickly, even though you're not sure where it's coming from or why—but you can't *wait* to get off that ship. A lot of the time when the ship feels good, it's not because of the ship itself. They might not have the best vessel, or even close. But whatever feeling you get, it always starts with the captain. *Always.*

"Because Captain McSorley was setting the proper tone for the ship, I didn't sense any of that negative tension on the *Fitzgerald*. Everything seemed quite calm, no drama, *low key*.

"The *Fitz* was as good as it gets."

Daddy's Girl

Oliver "Buck" Champeau came into the world in 1934 in Sturgeon Bay, Wisconsin, a small shipping town on Door Peninsula, which protects Green Bay. His parents named him for his father, and his grandfather, who lost a thumb in World War I. Buck was proud of them, his daughter Debbie says, but not of his given name.

"I'm not sure why," Debbie says. "He never talked about it, but he certainly didn't *look* like an Oliver. He was a big guy, and you didn't mess with him. Everyone called him Buck—except me! When I called him Buck one time, he said, 'No! I am your dad. You do not call me Buck.'"

A picture taken of Champeau in the engine room of a ship he served on before the *Fitzgerald* shows a short, powerful man wearing a white V-neck T-shirt over a hard, round belly. His forearms look like the barrels of two hefty baseball bats, with a dark Marine tattoo on his left arm. Champeau's head is shaped like a horseshoe: a full, round face with a well-groomed flattop above. His clear, open eyes and slight grin come off as friendly, not cynical. In short he looks like the kind of guy who could be a great friend, or a bad enemy. The choice was yours.

In that picture Champeau was probably in his late thirties but he looks older, perhaps because his life had been anything but easy. When he was just thirteen years old his father died, but even Buck's daughter doesn't know how.

"Dad never talked about it," Debbie says.

With no life insurance settlement or other money to speak of, and five children to feed, their mother took in sewing, laundry, and other small jobs, but still couldn't make ends meet. Buck, the oldest, didn't have to be told what to do. He dropped out of eighth grade and took every odd job he could get, the kind of sacrifice his generation so often made without much thought.

In 1953, when Champeau was eighteen, he joined the Marine Corps and fought in Korea. When his buddies went to the bars Champeau stayed behind so he could send every dollar back to his mother. After receiving an honorable discharge he returned to Sturgeon Bay to help his mother and younger siblings.

"His family values, the love he felt for his brothers and his sisters, that's what drove him," Debbie says. "He was the protector of them all, his whole life."

Champeau married Eileen Egan at St. Michael's Catholic Church in downtown Milwaukee. Eileen gave birth to their only child, Debbie, in 1958. When Debbie was in grade school Buck enrolled in the Milwaukee Area Technical College to get his engineering license, and later rose to second engineer. But in 1975 he accepted a position as third engineer on the *Fitzgerald*.

"He took the demotion," Debbie explains, "because the *Fitz* already had a second engineer, and Dad was very proud to be on the *Fitz*."

Buck Champeau felt like he had finally made it. He was providing his family with plenty to eat, nice clothes to wear, a solid house, and even tuition for Debbie to attend St. Pius XI High School, education being his highest priority—all the things he lacked as a kid.

"Dad was a big guy, and oh yes, very handsome, with a great sense of humor," Debbie says. "He had a big, jolly laugh that filled the room. He'd tease everybody. He was always doing some kind of trick with a coin to my cousins, or had tons of candy to hand out. Family was everything to him."

Champeau loved being an engineer and teaching the trade to others, but he didn't like being on the ship itself, away from his daughter.

"He was full of love, full of joy, and always glad to be with me," she says. "There was a piece of him that was lonely when he had to go. That had to be hard. But he never complained about anything. Not once. He didn't share his stories from the ship, or talk about being afraid. I really didn't understand what he did on the ship until after he was gone. For sailors' kids, your dad being away for months, then popping back home, it's normal."

After Buck would fit out in March he'd send Debbie presents from his travels: a big bunny with a basket full of candy eggs for Easter, and more for Christmas and her birthday. He'd send postcards, too, with just a few lines: "This is where I am. I miss you! Love, Dad."

Then he'd be home for three months, then gone again for nine.

Buck cared about his daughter's grades and expected her to attend college—a possibility he didn't dare dream of when he was a kid. When he made it home after the long shipping season he liked to drive to St. Pius, unannounced, and surprise Debbie while she was cleaning the chalkboards.

When her father was serving on the *Edmund Fitzgerald* in the spring of 1975 Debbie sent a letter to the ship before her junior prom, telling him she had found the perfect prom dress. It cost $79.99, she wrote—a lot of money for a blue-collar family. The fancy matching shoes cost another $29.99, and she also wanted to get her hair done by a professional stylist. When Buck called her from one of the dock payphones, Debbie pleaded that she just couldn't go to the prom without the dress and matching shoes. After he asked her some questions about her date Buck agreed to send her the money, but insisted that she be home by eleven.

"And I *was* home by eleven—that time!" she says. "My mom was flashing the porch light for me to come in."

When Debbie sent her father pictures of her in her fancy dress, shoes, and hairstyle, he beamed.

"I was Daddy's girl, but he made me that way!" she says. "He made me feel very special and very much loved."

Not long after the junior prom Debbie begged her dad for a car, and once again Buck relented. He found a used navy Rambler with a black interior, automatic transmission, and manual steering, and wrote down a list of rules. After explaining that he had already changed the oil and battery and given the car a tune-up, he underscored: "Nobody drives this car except you. Only Earl's Garage is to work on your car; and if I find these rules have NOT been followed you will never get another car from me again."

"Dad never yelled at me, but he didn't have to," Debbie says. "He never laid a finger on me, but he was not a man you wanted to disappoint."

They often took the two-hour drive to Sturgeon Bay together to see his family, or to go to his cabin on Clark's Lake. He would put his arm around her in the days before people wore seatbelts, and he would read the signs of towns with Native American names—Milwaukee, Sheboygan, Manitowoc—and translate them, and stop along the way for fresh blueberries to eat all the way up north.

Buck loved to visit his mother and siblings, and often told his brother Jack, who was serving in Vietnam, "If anything happens to you over there, I will bring you home."

During the offseason Buck would often drive by the Milwaukee Rescue Mission, which helped men who were down on their luck. He knew a lot of the men standing against the building by name, and would ask who wanted to work on his cabin in exchange for fair pay, food, and a nice place to stay for a night or two. One man named Caput most often accepted Buck's offer.

But Buck could be tough, too, especially if it involved his daughter. When Debbie brought a boyfriend, Jack, to the family Thanksgiving at Buck's brother's home in Port Washington, Wisconsin, the young couple drove together in her Rambler. On the way back, when she blew out the transmission, Jack yelled, "How stupid can you be?"

After she pulled over she saw her dad's Oldsmobile right behind her. Buck grabbed Jack out of his daughter's Rambler, took him behind the car, and did the talking. Jack returned to the passenger seat white as a ghost. His relationship with Debbie ended that night.

"Dad could be a teddy bear, but he was a tough one," Debbie says. "You didn't mess with family, and if you were family, he'd protect you at any cost."

A Coffee Can Full of Coins

BLAINE WILHELM, A FIFTY-TWO-YEAR-OLD OILER ON the *Fitzgerald*, kept an old blue Maxwell House coffee can—"Good to the last drop!"—by his bunk bed. When he returned to his room with change in his pockets he'd empty it all into the can, with a satisfying rattle. He thought of his children each time he did it, his tithing to keep his children close at heart.

One of eight children himself, Wilhelm fought for the Navy in World War II and Korea, earning an honorable discharge as a first-class fireman.

A few years after returning home he boarded an iron ore freighter called the *Reserve*, as an oiler. He married Lorraine Ida Clark, the youngest of ten children from Ashland, Wisconsin, and together they raised seven children in Moquah, ten miles inland.

Their sixth child, Heidi, born in 1963, says of her parents, "They were both lookers, and friendly sorts. I don't think Dad met too many people he didn't like."

Wilhelm was a bit bowlegged—a common trait among career sailors, who learn to keep their balance on a rolling deck—with a wide stance and a low center of gravity. On the ship he read Zane Grey westerns, always popular on board, and thought about his family, especially when his ship came in range of Ashland.

While working on the *Reserve* Wilhelm met Frank Kobasic, a fellow oiler, who lived in Escanaba, Michigan, on the Upper Peninsula's southern shore. Now seventy-nine, Kobasic recalls Wilhelm as "a good, hard-working man, a real meat-and-potatoes kinda guy. Nothing precious about him. Not afraid to get dirty. He had really good workingman's hands—rough, like sandpaper."

When their watches ended at the same time, Wilhelm and Kobasic would sit in their cabin and "shoot the shit until the wee hours. Nothing in particular. Wonderful, wonderful man. A good family man. We became real good friends."

One morning, when Wilhelm said to Kobasic, "Right about now my kids should be getting on the bus," Kobasic could tell how much he missed them.

Kobasic regarded Wilhelm as a first-rate mechanic, but couldn't persuade him to take the test to move up from oiler to engineer. Wilhelm confessed he had already tried to get his engineering license but he always got anxious taking tests, and failed it, which pained him.

In 1973 Columbia Transportation hired Wilhelm to work on the *Fitzgerald* as the ship's second oiler behind Grant Walton. Wilhelm called Kobasic with the news, ecstatic.

"The guys on the *Fitz* prided themselves on breaking records," Kobasic says. "They'd say, 'Next time put a little more on it.' And they'd load another hundred tons or two of taconite, and break another record. Blaine was proud to be on the *Fitz*."

Wilhelm's new post didn't make leaving home any easier for him or his family. But he was one of the rare sailors who insisted on taking a couple weeks off every summer, a costly habit, so he could take his kids to nearby Long Lake and give them the same warm summer memories he had from childhood.

"At school my friends would always ask, 'Where's your dad?'" Heidi recalls. "I'd say, 'My dad is on a ship. Your dad is on a farm.' That's just the way it was.

"When Dad got home he'd dump the coffee can on the table—nine months' worth of change!—and split it with all the kids. I think he saved every penny. I must've gotten a few bucks out of it each time, which was great back when candy bars only cost a dime. That was the *best*."

In 1975 Blaine was only fifty-two years old, but he had already set up a comfortable retirement from eleven years with the Navy and twenty with Columbia. But first, he told his family, he wanted to overcome his lifelong fear of tests to earn his engineering license. He had been bolstering his fragile confidence year by year, and he and Kobasic thought that with a little homework he could pass it, once and for all.

Wilhelm also had a granddaughter on the way, his first, due on

November 14, 1975. He figured that when he retired in a few years his daughter Candace, stationed at the Air Force base in Dover, Delaware, could bring his granddaughter back home and he would have plenty of time to teach her how to play catch, ride a bike, and drive a car, and even take her to a national park—all of the things he couldn't do with his seven children. He would be home, and this time for good.

XI

THE ROOKIES

The Academy

Of the *Edmund Fitzgerald*'s twenty-nine crewmen the median age was fifty, with six men in their forties and fifteen men in their fifties and sixties—more than half—led by Captain McSorley himself at sixty-three, one of ten crewmen born in the 1910s. At the other end were a half dozen young bucks between twenty and twenty-two, all born between 1952 and 1955, in the heart of the baby boom.

Twenty-nine men does not a demographic make, but even within that small crew you could detect the same generational fault lines that were splitting the country.

The twenty-one oldest were essentially of the same generation of patriotic, stoic men. Having been hardened by the Great Depression and World War II, they had grown up accustomed to doing without, didn't expect sympathy for it, and felt grateful to have secured union jobs that provided their families everything they needed, if not everything they wanted. That was no small achievement for men who'd been raised in small, blue-collar towns by fathers who had often struggled to find work, and mothers who had to scrimp to make ends meet.

These crewmen had not only avoided the soup lines, they had managed to escape the farms, the factories, and the mines, too—the places where most of their neighbors now worked—for adventurous if demanding careers on the gorgeous Great Lakes.

Almost all of the fifteen crewmen who had been old enough to serve had fought in World War II, and five other crewmen had served in the Korean War or the early years of Vietnam.

The young guns, on the other hand, had grown up in a country where they could afford to take steady work and solid paychecks for granted. While they were no strangers to hard work, they expected more from life than just a fair wage, a small home, a car in the garage, and a chicken in the pot. They wanted to have some fun, too. None of them had served in the military, or planned to—and that was no accident. They had all graduated from high school between 1970 and 1973, prime years for being drafted into a war that had already started going badly.

Craig "Red Dog" Silliven is now a seventy-four-year-old man with more belly than hair, but in the summer of 1972 he was a fresh-faced cadet out of the Great Lakes Maritime Academy with a thick red mane and a flat stomach. He boarded the *Fitzgerald* in 1972, not long after McSorley had assumed the helm.

Silliven grew up in a small town called Hillsdale in south-central Michigan, home to Hillsdale College, now a nationally known incubator of conservative thought. Hillsdale County is one of the state's most rural, poor, and landlocked counties, yet Silliven decided the sea life was for him.

"What attracted me to the lakes?" he asks. "That's easy: the Vietnam War."

You'd have a hard time explaining this to a twenty-year-old today, since the U.S. military has been a volunteer force since 1973, but when Silliven finished high school in 1969 the Selective Service conducted a lottery on national TV to determine who would get drafted. After printing each day of the year on a strip of paper and putting each one inside its own plastic capsule, which looked like Ping-Pong balls, they would spin them around, then pull one out—with families anxiously watching the proceedings. The date selected determined the order in which young men would be drafted. The closer your birthday was to the one they picked, the greater your chances of going into combat.

In the draft's first year, Silliven's number was forty-six—dangerously low. He knew he'd get drafted if he didn't figure out a plan B, and quick. So Silliven enrolled in the brand-new Great Lakes Maritime Academy in Traverse City, Michigan.

His parents were not just relieved but thrilled, since they were both boat nuts willing to drive a few hours to see their son and his ship whenever they docked on Lake Erie, especially when Craig was assigned to the

Edmund Fitzgerald in 1972. Each time his dad visited the *Fitz*, usually in Toledo, he would try to stow away for the next trip, but his son always managed to kick him out before they pushed off.

Silliven's first stroke of luck was the creation of the GLMA itself—and just in time.

"You need an act of Congress to start a maritime academy, and that means the stars have to align," former GLMA professor and superintendent John Tanner says. "To get that, you need a team of leaders to push for it, including your governor, a U.S. congressman, a U.S. senator—and not just any congressman or senator, but people with pull—plus a few other federal units, and the Coast Guard. If you're missing any one of those pieces, it's not going to work. That's why there were only five maritime academies in the country opened before us, and none since."

The other maritime academies are located on the coasts of Maine, Massachusetts, New York, Texas, and California, and all those states except Maine were more populous and powerful than Michigan, even then. The political leaders spearheading Michigan's effort to create one, as part of Northwestern Michigan College (NMC) in Traverse City, located at the base of Grand Traverse Bay on Lake Michigan, also had to surmount a common problem: explaining to their fellow politicians around the country just how big the Great Lakes really are, and how much the rest of the country depends on them.

After the federal government gave its final approval in 1969 the Great Lakes Maritime Academy opened its doors at NMC, but to call it a modest affair would be giving it too much credit. When the academy started the classroom buildings included a cannery, a walk-in freezer, and the former Traverse City Brewery. The academy held labor relations classes in Jack's 7-11 Bar across the street. (No relation to 7-Eleven.)

In the middle of class, when then-professor John Tanner would turn his back to the students to write on the chalkboard, the cadets would see the sales rep for Blatz beer walking outside and yell, "Blatz man!" because they knew he would buy the first round at Jack's 7-11. By the time Tanner turned back the students were gone, right out the windows. Tanner naturally preferred they remain in class, but he knew the cadets would need some of that chutzpah if they were going to make it at sea.

"If you're going to have a maritime academy, and the cadets are any good, they're going to walk with a swagger, like jocks on campus," Tanner says. "So there was a little friction with the rest of the school sometimes."

That swagger occasionally found unexpected outlets, including domination of the intramural leagues.

"I don't know if we were better athletes than the rest," former cadet Rick Barthuli says, "but we were definitely tougher—and more violent. We'd get crowds for softball, *softball*, because even the city folks knew there was gonna be blood. We didn't do anything halfway. Everything was full blast."

But, Tanner says, if you're training future sailors, "Those are the people you have to have. The academics on campus go at a slower, quieter pace, but that's not going to work on the Great Lakes. You won't make it a week."

The academy's early application pool might have been a mixed bag, but the ones who survived meteorology, navigation, and engineering, followed by arduous apprenticeships on Great Lakes freighters, proved to be knowledgeable, gritty, and durable. Most of them would enjoy long and distinguished careers on the Great Lakes, with some overseas, and hundreds of them rose to become captains and chief engineers. Today the academy has a first-rate training ship, the *State of Michigan*, three other vessels, its own rebuilt dock, and an impressive new building overlooking it all.

"When you look at what we had to do to get the academy through those early years," Tanner says, "it's kind of amazing it became what it is today."

The California Cowboy

OF THE *FITZGERALD*'S TWENTY-NINE CREW MEMBERS, nine hailed from the Head of the Lakes, seven from the Toledo area, and seven more from Cleveland and its suburbs. The remaining six were scattered: Milwaukee, Wisconsin; Michigan; Pennsylvania; Florida; and exactly one from California, David "Cowboy" Weiss.

Aaron and Selma Weiss had their hands full raising four boys in Los Angeles County's Agoura Hills, but their third son, David, probably cost them more gray hairs than the other three combined. David was eager to leave LA, where he'd gotten in some kind of minor trouble, now lost to history. Weiss also had a strained relationship with his father, common for his generation, which provided another motive to move away.

Weiss wore a full beard, big brown sunglasses, and a white cowboy hat, thus earning him the nickname "Cowboy" Weiss—an unusual moniker for a Jewish kid from LA. Right when LA's magnetic powers were at their strongest, drawing thousands from the Midwest every year, Weiss went the opposite direction, enrolling in the still-unproven maritime academy in Traverse City, 2,317 miles away, sight unseen. But once Weiss got to Traverse City in 1973 he fell in love with the town, the area, and Grand Traverse Bay's clean turquoise waters, reminiscent of the Bahamas.

"David, he was a character," says Tanner, who taught Weiss cargo stowage and piloting, and supervised his apprenticeship. "How do I say this politely? Like a lot of cadets, he'd try to talk you into this and that, but there was nothing sinister about it. He wasn't trying to get away with anything, just playing the angles."

Former GLMA cadet John Hayes recalls attending a local road rally in nearby Antrim County and seeing Weiss sitting in the back of a pickup truck playing his guitar.

"Apparently, that's the kind of thing he'd do," Hayes says. "Just met Cowboy once, but he made an impression. A classic California cool dude, something we hadn't seen before. By all accounts a good guy."

IN JUNE OF 1974 Cindy LoCicero, an attractive girl with long blond hair, had just finished her junior year at Benzie Central High School in Benzonia, a tourist town on Crystal Lake forty-five minutes southwest of Traverse City, and was looking forward to another fun summer.

One afternoon LoCicero and her best friend, Teresa Revnell, prepared to camp at a site on Lake Ann. LoCicero drove her navy-blue Volkswagen Beetle to a small grocery store for supplies, and as they walked toward the store LoCicero saw a young man in a cowboy hat parked in a yellow muscle car, "bebopping to the music," she says. She mimicked him in a playful way, "and he noticed."

After LoCicero and her friend finished their shopping they happened to walk out at the same time David Weiss's friend did. When LoCicero and her friend drove off Weiss followed them in his car, and then parked two campsites down from the women. The two men pulled out a speaker and started blasting some Neil Young, perhaps as a mating call.

It worked. LoCicero told her friend, "Let's go over and meet 'em." The four campers talked for an hour, and then Weiss asked for LoCicero's phone number.

"He didn't call me until three weeks later!" LoCicero says. "When he finally did he said, 'Do you remember me?' I said, 'Sure.'"

Weiss asked her out for a movie, but she explained that her dad had to approve of anyone she dated, so he'd have to come over and meet him first. While it seems odd to us, even scandalous, for a twenty-year-old man to date a high school senior, it didn't raise eyebrows in 1974, even with LoCicero's parents. When Weiss arrived LoCicero's father pretended to be sleeping on the couch, so David chatted with her mother.

"He could talk!" LoCicero says. "He was telling my mom that he wanted to make a million dollars before he was twenty-five. Finally she said, 'Take her. Good bye!' "

They had just gotten into his car when he turned and asked her, "Can I kiss those ruby lips?" He did, then asked, "You're not really going to make me take you to the movies, are you?"

"Well, yeah," she said. "When I get home I'll have to tell Dad about the movie. He'll have questions."

At the State Theater on Front Street, Traverse City's main drag, she says, "he put his arm around me, and kept whispering in my ear. He was funny. There was an older couple behind us, and I kept thinking, 'I hope they can't hear us!' "

After the movie they went back to Weiss's place, a rental house just a few blocks away. Weiss had a sophisticated telescope, and loved looking at the stars at night. In northern Michigan, especially fifty years ago, you could see the stars more clearly than almost anywhere else—a virtual impossibility in Southern California.

They both liked Neil Young, so he played *Harvest*, with hits like "Old Man" and "Heart of Gold," until it was time to take her home. LoCicero didn't have a curfew but her folks expected her to be home at a reasonable time, and she was. That in itself was a minor miracle, because as she soon discovered, "David was late to absolutely *everything*."

She also learned Weiss had been "a troubled child growing up," LoCicero says, "and he got into some issues in California, I know that, but I don't know what they were. But when he got to the academy, he just *loved* it."

Weiss fell in love with Cindy LoCicero, too, and seemed to be homing in on what he really wanted out of life. Weiss told her he wanted to have lots of kids, but she wasn't even thinking about children yet, so they took a break.

That fall of 1974 Weiss made another unconventional choice, moving thirty miles up the coast of the Leelenau Peninsula, Michigan's "pinky," to Northport. It was there that his phone rang near Christmas time, and when he picked up he heard Cindy's voice on the other end.

"I told him I was kind of having second thoughts," she says, "and wanted to be with him."

Weiss returned from winter break in LA with a necklace. He hadn't decided if he was going to give it to her, because he wasn't sure if they were going to be a couple, but ultimately decided to present it to her in the hopes that they would.

"Then that spring," she says, "he got on the *Fitzgerald*."

WHEN THE TIME came for Weiss to fit out on the *Fitzgerald*, GLMA professor John Tanner spotted Weiss in his trademark cowboy hat standing on the side of the road in Acme, just outside of Traverse City, where M-31 meets M-72. Weiss, carrying only his duffel bag and guitar case, was trying to hitchhike to Toledo to catch the *Fitzgerald*. Tanner pulled over and gave his student a ride to Grayling, about an hour to the east.

Along the way Weiss told Tanner that in California the landscape was always dry and brown, but in Michigan it was lush and green, which he much preferred.

"He used those words, 'lush and green,'" Tanner says. "That stayed with me. I always thought maybe he was saying more than that: that the old David was back in California, dry and brown, but he could see a bright future, lush and green, in this new place. He was starting a new life, and he was really looking forward to it."

Weiss boarded the *Fitzgerald* a couple days later. If ever there was a cadet who represented the younger generation, it was David "Cowboy" Weiss.

"The generational conflict was ripe," Tanner says. "The senior sailors saw it all as boom-boom-boom—do this, do that, and do it all just because I said so. In the military, that works. And of course the younger people were questioning everything, but when they did, the response from the older guys was 'How dare you ask!'"

Because the academy's early cadets had suffered high dropout rates during their apprenticeships, in July of 1975 Tanner made the rounds to check on all his cadets onboard. After hopping on the *Fitzgerald* in Silver Bay, Tanner was chatting with the first mate, John McCarthy, when McCarthy pulled him aside to tell him about David "Cowboy" Weiss.

"McCarthy wasn't upset," Tanner says. "He was soft-spoken, a very gentle guy. But he figured, as David's supervisor, I should know."

McCarthy told him that a few weeks earlier a steel executive VIP on board asked Weiss the seemingly innocuous question "How are you getting along?"

"I'm okay," Weiss told him, "but these old guys, I don't know about them." Weiss proceeded to list everything he thought they were doing wrong, he questioned their intelligence, and he asserted that he could do it all better.

"It's not hard to see how this happens," Tanner says. "Before you've done anything you think, *This looks easy. Anyone can do it.* It's amazing how smart you are in your twenties. Well, you knew it was going to be a problem."

Weiss had broken a few unwritten rules all at once: Cadets don't run the ship; if you have a problem, you bring it to your superior officer, not one of their VIP clients; and if you're confronted about crossing the line, you apologize, keep your head down, and make sure you don't do it again. Weiss had whiffed on all three points of protocol. When his tales out of school inevitably got back to his older crewmates, they gave him a predictably chilly reception. It was a big ship, but there weren't many places to hide.

After talking with McCarthy, Tanner met with Weiss, who asked Tanner to transfer him to another ship. To do so Weiss would have had to trade places with another cadet. Tanner already had someone in mind, but the more Tanner thought about it, the more convinced he became that swapping ships was not the right thing to do.

There were only three hundred big ships on the Great Lakes, with just thirty or so crew per ship. That's a small club. Tanner believed if David didn't clean up his mess on the *Fitzgerald*, it would get around to other ships, and dog him the rest of his career.

"It wasn't the biggest mistake anyone ever made," Tanner says, "but no one needs to start their career like that."

Tanner had to weigh another consideration, too. In 1975 the maritime academy was just six years old, and still trying to prove itself. Many captains considered the cadets a waste of their time, and treated them so badly—one telling his cadet to keep his feet stuck to the floor, and his mouth shut—they washed out when they shouldn't have.

"But not on the *Fitz*," Tanner says. "Captain McSorley and McCarthy, those guys were all very good to Cowboy and the other cadets we'd put on the ship, too, like [Craig "Red Dog"] Silliven. If we couldn't make this right on the *Fitzgerald*, where could we? It wouldn't be good for anyone."

After mulling over Weiss's request, Tanner told him, "Look, you've been running your mouth, but guess what? You're staying. You need to work it through and get back in their good graces, because there are only so many ships on the Great Lakes, and you're on the best one there is, with the best officers.

"So get back on board. Work hard and keep your head down and show 'em you belong. You can fix it. You'll be okay."

Weiss looked at his professor, thought about it, then nodded and returned to his work on the *Edmund Fitzgerald*.

The Best Man

"TO ME, SHIPPING HAS ALWAYS BEEN A STORY OF fathers and sons," John Hayes says. "The sons either want to be like their fathers, or get as far away from them as possible—and sometimes both."

Hayes clearly fell into the former category. His father, grandfather, and great-grandfather were all licensed sea captains, the eldest in Ireland and the next two on the Great Lakes. In the spring of 1970 John Hayes was among the first cadets to enroll at the Great Lakes Maritime Academy, fully intending to become the family's fourth-generation captain. But his plans changed his first day on campus.

"When we were all pretending we knew what we were doing, I met Tom Bentsen," Hayes says. "We had little in common. He was an engineering cadet, and favored Budweiser. I was a deck cadet [on the captain track] who liked Stroh's," Detroit's "Bohemian-style" fire-brewed beer.

Also unlike Hayes, Bentsen wanted to get as far as possible from his father. Harold Bentsen had flown a B-17 in World War II before becoming an executive for Whirlpool in St. Joseph, Michigan, on lower Lake Michigan.

"Tom was very devoted to his mother," Hayes says, "and later, when his parents divorced, he sided with her."

Bentsen found the escape hatch he was looking for when the GLMA opened its doors, promising adventure far from his father's workaday lifestyle in St. Joe's.

Bentsen carried only 148 pounds on his six-foot frame. But he sported long hair, high-top leather boots, and a long leather duster, like the coats gunslingers wore in Western movies.

"He had a full beard, while I hardly shaved and still had my high school braces," Hayes says. "Tom wasn't that good-looking, but he *projected*. He had an air about him which earned him respect above his weight class. He walked into the room and the girls would swoon. The more he ignored women in the bar when they said hi, the more they came around. Go figure. He wasn't *like* the Fonz. He *was* the Fonz," Hayes adds, referencing a character on the popular sitcom *Happy Days*, which debuted in January of 1974. "I became his Richie Cunningham—and not willingly, either, but that's how it went."

By the end of the cadets' first summer at the academy they had to declare a study program, which would determine whether they would spend their careers above deck in the pilothouse or below deck in the engine room. When Bentsen elected to pursue the engineering track, Hayes decided to switch programs and join his friend, "much to my father's great displeasure," Hayes admits.

When Hayes successfully completed the academy's engineering coursework, his year apprenticing on a ship, and a week of difficult U.S. Coast Guard exams needed to earn his engineer's license, he called his father with the great news. His father sarcastically asked if he got his engineer's license as a consolation prize for failing the mate's license exam, the first step to becoming a captain. But bolstered by Bentsen's self-assurance, Hayes ignored his father's barbs and stuck with his new plan.

IN THE WINTER of 1971, when Bentsen's ship docked in Buffalo to unload taconite, he recalled that Hayes was also in Buffalo for three days working on a grain ship and would be staying at his folks' home in town. With twelve hours to kill Bentsen hoped to see his GLMA friend, so he left a message with Hayes's parents, asking Hayes to pick him up at a dumpy bar on Chippewa Street.

While the jukebox blasted hits like the Guess Who's "American Woman," Three Dog Night's "Mama Told Me (Not to Come)," and the Temptations' "Get Ready," Bentsen managed to stir the interest of the few women in the bar, then beat a local hustler at pool. But his evening came to an abrupt end when he reached down to take the money he'd won and the local hustler pulled a gun, with clear instructions to leave the money on the table.

Luckily for Bentsen, Hayes had gotten the message from his parents, and at that exact moment happened to pull up in front of the bar in his mom's 1965 Pontiac Star Chief. Hayes couldn't find a parking spot so he double-parked, stayed in the car, and honked for Bentsen to come out.

Bentsen came out of the bar, all right—running, and praying that Hayes was the driver doing the honking. Bentsen jumped in Hayes's car and yelled, "Go! *Now*!" right as the hustler charged out of the door, shooting at them. Hayes's mom's Pontiac Star Chief was just fast enough for the two to escape unharmed.

Bentsen had two sides, the first seeming "hell-bent on being the baddest dude on the block," Hayes says. Bentsen's mouth wrote checks his skinny physique couldn't back, but "he became invulnerable once the drinking began."

On Bentsen's other side, he played the bass with the Traverse Symphony Orchestra—something he confessed only to Hayes, swearing him to secrecy. Over time Hayes noticed that Bentsen, though quite a ladies' man, never allowed any of them to get close to him.

"I became convinced that he was on a trip to a dark place," Hayes says. "He had a fatalistic streak a mile wide that would come out from time to time. He loved the song 'Brandy,' about a loner at sea. That song truly defined his view of life."

ON JANUARY 8, 1973, at the Shadowland Bar in downtown Traverse City, Hayes and Bentsen hit the ground running to make sure they were rolling when the clock struck midnight, and Bentsen turned twenty-one.

"But at twenty-two hundred hours that night," Hayes says, "I met Helen Filip."

Bentsen had just started his last semester at the academy, but his grades soon mysteriously started falling off. With his degree just a few months in front of him, Bentsen dropped out, then shipped out on the *William P. Snyder, Jr.* as an oiler, a position he could have gotten without putting in three hard years at the academy.

The next two winters Bentsen and Hayes rented a series of apartments together in Traverse City. One night Bentsen told Hayes that if he ever left Helen, he would love to date her. That led to some hot words, verging on a fist fight, until Bentsen backed off, and they repaired their friendship.

"Tom didn't seem to 'get it' until he met Cindy Gagnier, a lovely young lady," Hayes says. "They became very close."

So close, in fact, that the two would soon get engaged. It appeared Bentsen had found at least one piece of life's puzzle.

IN MARCH OF 1975 Hayes and some classmates formed the Great Lakes Maritime Academy Alumni Association. Although the GLMAAA's rules allowed Bentsen to join, when Hayes conducted their first meeting in an academy classroom Bentsen sat out in the hallway alone, as if punishing himself. He told Hayes he would join once he had earned his engineer's license the hard way, on a Great Lakes ship, without the help of the academy—the way the World War II vets had done it.

That spring Bentsen invited Hayes and Helen to meet him for breakfast at Traverse City's Gaslight Restaurant, where he surprised the young couple with an Easter card.

"That was very out of character for Tom, maybe a sign of maturity," Hayes says. "He was thinking of others. Then he gave us the good news that he would be getting on the *Edmund Fitzgerald* in April. He was really happy to be fitting out."

Bentsen liked working on the *Fitzgerald*, and told Hayes that Captain McSorley had put together a first-rate crew of highly skilled, good guys. Bentsen managed to wangle a little vacation time in August of 1975 to spend a week in Traverse City with Hayes, Helen, and Bentsen's new girlfriend, Cindy Gagnier. For the first time in their five-year friendship, Hayes thought Bentsen was genuinely happy.

IN SEPTEMBER OF 1975 Hayes sent a letter from his boat, the ST *Crapo* (pronounced *CRAY-po*), a freighter based in Alpena, Michigan, to the post office at the Soo Locks so Bentsen could pick it up when the

Fitzgerald came through. Hayes wrote that he was going to marry Helen, and he wanted Bentsen to be his best man.

"Tom sent me back a letter filled with colorful metaphors," Hayes says, "pointing out that I hadn't yet asked for his permission to marry her. But he accepted my invitation, and I think he was pretty happy about it."

Hayes picked a wedding date that fit neatly into a narrow gap in both the *Crapo*'s and *Fitzgerald*'s tight schedules: Saturday, August 21, 1976.

The Deckhand

Bruce Hudson wore his hair long, his sideburns down his cheeks, and the uniform of his generation—blue jeans, a T-shirt, and a flannel shirt—plus lots of orange and black, the colors of North Olmsted High School.

"Bruce had lots of school spirit," his cousin Pam Woodman Wittig says.

In the fall of 1974, after Hudson had dropped out of Ohio State to become a deckhand on the *Ashland*, a friend of his, Paulie Spence, told Hudson that he was going to meet some girls at Toledo's Woodville Mall, and he should come along. Hudson didn't need too much persuading.

The two girls, Cindy Reynolds and Cyndi George, were juniors at Oregon High School, right outside Toledo, and friends of Paulie's from the neighborhood. Cindy Reynolds's father had worked as a mechanical engineer before he decided to leave the field altogether to become a commercial fisherman, pulling in walleye and perch out of Lake Erie.

Cindy grew up on the water. She was a cute, perky, seventeen-year-old blonde who waited tables at the Bay Shore Supper Club, just down the road from the docks.

Reynolds recalls talking with her friend at the mall "when here comes Paulie, and he had Bruce with him, and we were giggling. 'Who's that? Ohhhhh he's cute!' He had dark curly hair, big brown eyes, and a big smile.

"He was very pleasant. I said it right then to my friend: 'He's a really nice guy! And he's *funny*.' He was *always* funny. He could make you laugh about anything. And me and him just hit it off. Something just clicked as soon as we saw each other."

A week or two later Reynolds and George finally got up the nerve to go to Spence's house, and were happy to discover Hudson was still renting a room there, along with Paulie's brother Farrell, another sailor. Hudson, Paulie, and the girls went to McDonald's, where Reynolds didn't order anything because she was still too self-conscious to eat in front of Hudson.

"He was so cute and so nice and so well-mannered," she says.

But when they said goodnight he didn't ask for her number, so she didn't know if she would ever see him again. "No cell phones or Facebook or email back then. He was going back on the *Ashland* anyway, so you just never knew."

When she was working at the supper club a few weeks later, Hudson showed up at the back door of the kitchen, unannounced, and asked a coworker if Cindy Reynolds was working that night. When Cindy appeared at the door Hudson got right to the point: "Hey, I'm in town! What time do you get off?"

Hudson waited at Spence's house for a couple hours until she joined them. Hudson needed some new work clothes before he got back on the ship, so the two went to KMart. Before the night was over they had exchanged phone numbers, and agreed to see each other again when Hudson was back in town. Each time Hudson returned they'd run some errands for him, go see some friends, then go to the Ponderosa, a popular steakhouse chain, which became their spot.

After a few weeks of dating Cindy felt she needed to bring him home to meet her dad, "because that's the right thing to do. And Bruce wanted to. But Bruce was the first boy I ever brought home, and my dad was pretty strict, so I wasn't sure how this was going to go. Bruce was twenty-one, and I was about to be eighteen. I was a nervous wreck."

She didn't need to be. Bruce and her dad proved to be kindred spirits, talking about fishing and boats nonstop for hours. Instead of feeling anxious, Cindy felt neglected. She wanted to shout, "Hey, I'm right here!"

At the end of the night the two men shook hands, and it was done. Bruce said, "Hey, your dad is a pretty nice guy!"

One less thing to worry about.

Before the shipping season ended Hudson suffered a gastrointestinal issue on the *Ashland*. Cindy visited him when he was spending a few days at the hospital back in North Olmsted and met Bruce's parents, Oddis and Ruth Hudson.

Ruth later told Cindy that when she first met her, she thought Cindy was too young for her son, "because he knows better."

Cindy replied, "'Well, it takes two!' I knew what I was doing, and an age gap like that wasn't uncommon back then."

Cindy also met Bruce's German shepherd, Kelly, and saw immediately how much Bruce loved that dog.

Ruth, for her part, knew her son was in deep with Cindy. "I'm warning you, Bruce: She's gonna get you!" Ruth worried about her only child when he was on the ship, too, and kept a hairbrush with Bruce's hair, just in case it was needed one day for identification. But even Ruth Hudson didn't know everything.

THE *ASHLAND* FINISHED the 1974 shipping season in Toledo, where she docked for the winter. Hudson stayed on board as the "ship keep," a deckhand who keeps an eye on the boat during the offseason. When Cindy wasn't waiting tables she would invite a couple girlfriends to join her on the ship, which required climbing a twenty-foot rope ladder at night in the middle of winter.

No problem. Cindy Reynolds wasn't a "high heels kinda girl," and would never invite anyone aboard who was. Cindy and her friends often stole some of the peanut M&Ms the captain had stored away.

"We used to run that ship," Reynolds says. "Not a bad bachelor pad—not bad at all. We were just two kids who hit it off and acted crazy and had fun and enjoyed our time. We did a lot for the time we had together.

"Bruce would say *please* and *thank you* and open the door for you. Regular homegrown manners, the kind that few boys had then—and no boys have now! His mama taught him right, and I wasn't surprised he was an Eagle Scout."

But she learned Bruce had a wild side, too. For Bruce's twenty-first birthday, September 10, 1974, Reynolds bought him some *MAD* magazines to read on the ship and a "big purple skull bong," she says. Bruce enjoyed both presents.

When Cindy teased him about having a girl in every port, he told her he rarely got off the ship because he preferred staying on board to get overtime.

"He was making good money, *really* good money," Reynolds says, "and he had money in the bank. He was smart about it."

Hudson did have one indulgence, however, common to his generation: a muscle car, an extravagance suddenly available to a generation with money to burn.

America's booming economy had made possible something the previous generation could hardly imagine: a second car, and a two-car garage to house them both. Those novelties created a third innovation: a car designed not for hauling the family or commuting to work, but strictly for fun.

Ford debuted its eye-popping Mustang on April 17 at the 1964 New York World's Fair's "Wonder Rotunda"—arguably the last World's Fair the world actually noticed. The car and its creator, Lee Iacocca, were featured in an oil painting on the cover of *Time* magazine, back when that was an event in itself, too. One ad featured a red, a white, and a blue model of the car surrounded by good-looking blond men and brunette women on a California beach with surfboards. To say that it had captured the imagination of the baby boomers is to understate the case considerably. It practically defined their hopes and dreams: young, attractive, impractical, fun, and exciting.

But the Mustang was merely the start of this trend, which led to the creation of "muscle cars": "Drop a big engine into an otherwise pedestrian car," former *Motor Trend* columnist Daniel Charles Ross says, "pump up a big advertising campaign, and start a revolution."

Bruce Hudson procured one of the exemplars of this trend: a gleaming burgundy 1974 Dodge Challenger.

"He was very proud of that car," says Cindy Reynolds. Hudson washed and waxed it often, and kept it at the docks in Toledo so he could jump in his prized possession every time the *Fitz* tied up.

The older generation of parents and bosses could satisfy their own impractical desires for previously unseen levels of luxury with the Chrysler Imperial, the Buick Riviera, and the Lincoln-Mercury, all striving to achieve the prestige of the one and only Cadillac, perhaps the only American product whose very name became synonymous with the highest standards of quality. For the men working on Great Lakes freighters, America's car craze meant two things: They needed to continue to feed the insatiable factories in Detroit with taconite and other raw materials, which appeared to give them job security for the foreseeable future; and when they finished their season each fall, with their robust wages a muscle car or land yacht was now within reach.

Like the boomers' affinity for rock 'n' roll and long hair, however, their passion for muscle cars made their parents uneasy. It took Cindy Reynolds an hour and ten minutes to drive from Toledo to the Hudsons' house in Olmsted. In front of his mom, Bruce teased Cindy for being a slow poke, boasting that he could easily make the same trip in his Challenger in under an hour.

"I don't want to hear that!" Ruth protested, since it took her ninety minutes to cover those same miles, driving very carefully.

Bruce often told Cindy, "My mom worries about me too much." But as the mother of an only child, one with a bit of a wild streak, it was easy to understand Ruth's apprehension.

HUDSON STILL PLANNED to return to Ohio State one day and earn his degree, but he liked sailing and the money it offered well enough to stick with it for at least one more season. In the spring of 1975 Columbia Transportation upgraded Hudson to the *Edmund Fitzgerald*.

"I never heard a bad word from Bruce about the *Fitzgerald*," Bruce's cousin Pam says. "They treated him well, and he really loved it. It seemed like this might be a career for him."

Bruce made friends on the *Fitz*, including fellow deckhand Mark Thomas, a twenty-one-year-old from Richmond Heights, Ohio, another Cleveland suburb. The tall, skinny Hudson and his shorter, stockier sidekick planned to take Hudson's muscle car on a cross-country trip once the *Fitzgerald* docked in Toledo for the winter.

But Hudson still had Cindy on his mind, and kept writing her letters from the SS *Edmund Fitzgerald*.

"They were sweet letters, about what he was doing on the boat, his duties, his travels," Reynolds says. "He'd write, 'We should go here someday,' 'We should go there someday.'"

Reynolds always wrote him back, and Hudson was very happy to get her letters at the Soo Locks and the *Westcott* mailboat in Detroit. Hudson often wrote Reynolds little poems, this one lifted from David Bowie's "Space Oddity." It's a song about an astronaut, but seems to apply almost as well to a deckhand on the *Edmund Fitzgerald*.

For here I am floating 'round my tin can.
Far above the moon
Planet earth is blue
And there's nothing I can do.

Bruce also wrote regularly to his mom. In one letter he ribbed her, "Oh mom, don't worry. If I go down with the ship, the world is going to know about it. It's going to be a big deal."

Only a twenty-one-year-old sailor could think that might be reassuring to a mother of an only child. But Bruce Hudson was young, in love, and invincible.

IN LATE JUNE 1975, Hudson hurt his back working on the *Fitzgerald* and had to leave the ship for a couple months to recuperate. While the union put a substitute on the ship in his place Hudson went back and forth between his parents' home in North Olmsted and his apartment in Toledo, and continued dating Cindy Reynolds. They no longer had an empty ship for a bachelor pad, but they made good use of his rented room at Paulie Spence's place. During those happy weeks Hudson told Cindy of his plans to go on a month-long West Coast road trip with his fellow deckhand, Mark Thomas.

She told him that was a really cool idea—one more reason Bruce Hudson thought Cindy Reynolds might be someone special, someone he wanted to keep seeing when he returned from the road trip out West.

Ruth Hudson's warnings were prescient: that girl had gotten him.

The Replacement

PATRICK DEVINE WAS NOT YOUR AVERAGE DECKHAND. Born in 1955, Devine grew up in the old West End of Toledo, among the mansions built by shipping and manufacturing magnates. The barons had left, however, and now their castles were being converted into apartments, or bought by large families like the Devines. When Patrick was five he already had three siblings, and would get two more—a full load for any parents.

Their father, Andy Devine, had graduated from Milwaukee's Marquette University law school and become a highly respected politician, and then a judge, leading Lucas County's juvenile court for almost two decades. A loyal Democrat, "he always had a great relationship with the local Republican leaders. He was open to their ideas, and they were open to his. They all just wanted to get things done for the next generation."

Few Great Lakes deckhands had a father who'd gone to college, let alone become a judge, but Patrick's father had always loved boats, too. When Andy was a law student, instead of clerking in the summers he worked on a car ferry running across Lake Michigan, and relished the experience.

Patrick was a decent student, but his real talent was business. He would get up at 5 a.m., pick up a stack of newspapers, bike down to the Jeep assembly plant right when the overnight shift got out at 7 a.m., and sell them all by 7:15. He started buying up paper routes, too, delivering one edition right after school and another, the "blue streak," in the early evening.

"I was a natural entrepreneur, but that was not something to be admired in our family," he says. "What my parents did admire was service to others."

Devine and his father often disagreed, but they shared a love of politics, sports, current events, and shipping. On summer Sundays after church Patrick's father and grandfather would take Patrick and his two younger brothers down to the two coal docks owned by the Chesapeake and Ohio (C&O) and Baltimore & Ohio (B&O) Railroads to watch the big ships load.

"I was completely taken by the lake freighters, everything about them," Patrick says. He liked to see the train cars and chutes load coal onto the ships, but he *loved* to see the Hulett cranes unload iron ore.

"The Huletts, boy, they were mesmerizing. The timing—wow! You'd see three Huletts working at once on the same ship. The arm reaches out, the bucket goes down and scoops out the iron, then it pulls back and dumps it into a hopper, which funnels the iron into a rail car. The guys who operated those things were *amazing*. That was a ballet, truly. I was *hooked*. That's what got me on the ships."

In the summer of 1973, just before Patrick followed in his father's footsteps by enrolling at Marquette University, he hopped on his first laker. Some fantasies are better left to the imagination, but not this one. Devine loved it from the start.

"I thought it was pretty epic!" he says with a laugh. "But it was intimidating, too—my first job, with all these mean-looking lake freighter guys."

All the more reason Patrick appreciated his boss on the *Armco*, forty-five-year-old first assistant engineer Eddie Bindon. (Devine and Bindon would meet again two summers later on the *Fitzgerald*.) After working the next summer on other ships, Devine managed to flunk out of Marquette in the fall semester of his sophomore year.

"Needless to say, my dad wasn't too happy with me."

Shortly after Devine returned to Toledo that winter he went down to the union hall on the first day you could register for relief jobs, right when it opened up at 7 a.m., which put him very high on the list of workers to be called when jobs opened up.

Devine started that season, 1975, on the *Crispen Oglebay*, where his quarters were right above the engine. In the summertime it got so hot he'd take his pillow and a blanket and sleep on the upper deck.

"I slept like a baby," he says.

One day in June 1975 Devine got the call every Great Lakes sailor wanted: The *Edmund Fitzgerald* had an opening.

"The call was all no-nonsense," Devine says. "They ask, 'Do you want the job—yes or no?' You've got to decide right then and there. And if you don't, they call the next guy. But I already knew how good the *Fitz* was."

When Devine accepted on the spot, they told him he had two hours to get on the ship before it left Toledo. No problem. Devine was already packed, and ready to go.

ONCE ON THE *Fitzgerald* Devine learned he was replacing Bruce Hudson, who was out with a bad back.

"After a few weeks I came to believe Bruce Hudson wasn't coming back and the job was mine," Devine says, "and I *wanted* it to be mine. It was a good job! I knew what I had."

Devine took over the same list of chores Hudson and Craig Ellquist, who was now working as a milkman in Two Harbors, had performed before him: hosing the deck, painting when the ship was out in calm, open waters, and constantly cleaning something.

"You were always busy," Devine says. "They made sure of that."

During the summer of 1975 the *Fitzgerald* deckhands and watchmen were given an especially unpleasant task: cleaning out the "inner bottoms," the ballast tanks that lined the bottom of the ship.

"You talk about a nasty job!" Devine says. "You would crawl in the tanks with a hose to wash out the sediment, the mud. It smelled like a stagnant swamp or a sewer. You'd come out soaking wet, smelling like that. It was dark, too. Once we were downbound on the open waters that summer, that's all we did."

One task didn't change: clamping and unclamping the hatches.

"They all worked," he says, "but some clamps worked better than others. The ones we used the least got the stickiest, especially when some dipshit got paint on the threads. They had to be tight, but you weren't supposed to tighten them super tight, because you had to get them off."

Because they clamped only the corners of the hatches in good weather, most of the clamps would go all season without being used until the fall, when the weather turned. The corner clamps worked best, because they got the most use. But any hint of rough weather, Devine says, and they would clamp the centers, too. If it was going to be really rough, especially in the fall, they would clamp them all.

Just about everything else seemed unique to the *Fitzgerald*. In Devine's shipping career he would work on ten ships in all. But, he maintains, "The *Fitz* was different. A different environment, altogether. The sleeping quarters were the best I ever had. They were newer, they were bigger, they were better maintained, they were cooler. The *Fitz* was just *better*."

Like seemingly everyone else who'd been on the *Fitzgerald*, Devine puts the galley at the top of the list.

"Best food of any ship I was on, by far," he says. "For breakfast they'd make you anything, on the spot."

For lunch they would get something simple but hardy, like soups, casseroles, stews, and "shit on a shingle," dried, chipped beef and gravy on white bread. For dinner they would occasionally get lobster thermidor, and every Saturday night was steak night.

"They'd feed you as much as you wanted," Devine says. "You could always get seconds. They encouraged eating. They were smart. They wanted to fatten you up to make sure you could work."

Each shipping season Devine gained ten pounds the first month, and thirty pounds over the summer.

"It was mostly muscle," Devine says, "but I'd lose it each off-season when you're just not eating or working as much."

BUT THE BIGGEST contrast between Devine's ten other ships and the *Fitzgerald*, he says, was the men onboard.

"The *Fitz* was an elite crew. There was no doubt about that. There were no slouches, let's put it that way. Those guys were the best.

"There were hardly any weirdos, either, and there can be a lot of weirdos on ships—and this was the seventies! Now this may be the perspective of a college kid, but on the other ships you learned how to keep to yourself. Do your job. Go back to your room. Go to the mess when you want to eat, but don't talk too much.

"But on the *Fitz*, it wasn't like that. It was a really good bunch of guys.

Easy to make friends. You're on what's considered the best boat on the lakes, so everyone worked to stay on it."

The list of good guys included his fellow deckhands Mark Thomas, Bruce Hudson's future road trip buddy, and Paul Riippa, Devine's cabin-mate. Devine wasn't as close to Mark Thomas as he was with Riippa, "but Mark was a good guy, and we made a good team," Devine says. "You're thrown together, and some guys you hit it off with, and other guys you don't. But we never had any fights. Paul Riippa and I became very close. A very religious guy. Kind, generous, hard-working, funny."

Devine owned a cassette of the Moody Blues album *Days of Future Passed*, which included their hits "Tuesday Afternoon" and "Nights in White Satin."

"Paul loved that tape," Devine says. "He played it on our little cassette player more than I wanted to hear it!"

The *Fitzgerald*'s culture started with Captain McSorley. Devine was impressed by McSorley's piloting abilities, the high standards he'd instilled, and the team he'd built, but he didn't feel comfortable around him.

"I didn't dislike him, but I feared he didn't like me. Nothing he said or did. He wasn't mean, just not a talker. My memory of him is he was just all business."

When Devine came aboard in June he had long hair and wasn't particularly big or strong. Devine surmises that the "old man" might not have been too happy to see a skinny hippie college kid on his crew.

"But I'm only guessing," he says. "I don't know what it was about McSorley, exactly, but he intimidated me, so I just stayed out of his way."

One night, however, Devine could not avoid him. After Devine got talked into playing in a late-night poker game in the officers' dining room, Captain McSorley himself showed up and asked to be dealt in. Devine wasn't a frequent poker player, so it surprised him and probably everyone else when he kept pulling in the big pots. Unexpectedly up a few bucks, Devine decided he'd better go back to his cabin while he was still ahead.

But as soon as he stood up McSorley said, with a wry grin, "Sit back down, son. You're not done yet."

Devine recalls, with a chuckle, "He and the others apparently objected to my early departure with their money. I just didn't know any better."

Everyone laughed, but Devine, unsure whether McSorley was kidding or not, sat back down. Over the course of the next hour Devine figures he probably ended up giving half of it back, but he still had a few big bills in his pocket. When Devine finally stood up again, McSorley said, "Have a good night," his way of giving Devine permission to go—but Devine wisely avoided playing cards with the captain, or anyone else, again.

Devine holds a special place in his heart for Eddie Bindon, the *Fitzgerald*'s first assistant engineer, from Fairport Harbor, Ohio, outside of Cleveland.

The two had first met two years earlier on the *Armco*, when Devine was working below deck as a wiper, the engine room equivalent of a deckhand, and Bindon took the time to show Devine the ropes. Although the two had little in common—Devine was a young bachelor, Bindon had been happily married for almost twenty-five years—they became good friends.

When Devine boarded the *Fitzgerald* two years later, in 1975, he was pleasantly surprised to discover Bindon had been promoted to Columbia's flagship. Although they would no longer be working directly together on the *Fitzgerald* now that Devine was a deckhand, Bindon never bought into the enforced division on most ships between the deck crew and the engine crew, which often forbade such "cross-friendships." The fact that Devine was a young deckhand and Bindon a high-ranking engineer meant nothing to Bindon, either, and the two picked up where they'd left off.

"He liked me," Devine says. "He was my protector. He made sure I stayed out of trouble, and nobody bothered me. Never lost his temper, very focused, very hard working, but he was such a gentle soul, always giving me advice, telling me how things worked, looking out for me. What can I say? Eddie was just a really good guy."

Bindon was only forty-seven but he had been on the lakes for more than two decades, and was talking about hanging it up—and he wasn't alone.

"Seemed like everyone knew 1975 was McSorley's last year," Devine says. "Word was he was trying to break his own load record that season, then retire. We ran heavy all year long, the whole time I was on—beyond the Plimsoll line."

While locking through the Soo one time, Devine looked down to see just how low the ship was sitting in the water. "I remember thinking, *They're going to bust us this time, for sure*. But nothing ever happened."

On another trip Devine remembers passing through the Soo Locks and going downbound through the St. Marys River. He was at the stern and could see mud churning up, something he had never seen before, nor after. He wasn't sure if the river was low or the *Fitzgerald* was running heavy, or possibly both.

"Whatever it was, we were pushing it," he says. "The *Fitz* ran lower than any boat I ever worked on."

In early September, 1975, the *Fitzgerald* was making a rare trip to unload in Ashtabula, Ohio, which happened to be the hometown of Devine's fellow deckhand Paul Riippa. Just an hour before the ship reached port First Mate John McCarthy came to their cabin.

"You're getting off," McCarthy told Devine. "Hudson is coming back. Time to pack up."

It was all done by the rules, but Devine wasn't happy about it.

"McCarthy was a good guy. I liked him a lot. But I was surprised, and furious! I planned to put in for winter work on the *Fitz* in Toledo that year."

"Take it up with the union," McCarthy told Devine. "Take it up with the company."

Devine left to tie up the ship—he still had a job to do—then walked back to his quarters, where Paul Riippa watched Devine stuff his things into his duffel bag. Everything, that was, except Devine's Moody Blues cassette that Riippa liked so much. Devine handed it to Riippa, who looked at the tape, looked Devine in the eye, and thanked him for it. They shook hands, then Devine went to say goodbye to Eddie Bindon, and climb down the *Fitzgerald*'s ladder for the last time.

Just minutes after Patrick Devine got off the *Edmund Fitzgerald*, Bruce Hudson eagerly climbed back on. The two would never meet.

Replacing the Replacement

SHORTLY AFTER HUDSON REPLACED HIS REPLACEMENT, his life took a dramatic turn.

Back in Oregon, Ohio, his girlfriend, Cindy Reynolds, came home from school one day in September and took a pregnancy test. She didn't think the odds were very high, but it came up a clear, bright positive.

"I was shocked," she says. "I really couldn't believe it—but it happened."

She cried, but she kept it to herself, she kept going to school every day, and she kept waiting tables at the Supper Club every night. She knew she had to tell Bruce, but even that was not a simple task because she was still living with her parents, they had only so many phones, and Hudson was on the *Fitzgerald*, with no phone. She would have to wait for him to call her.

A few agonizing days later Hudson finally called her one night, most likely from the Silver Bay Municipal Liquor and Lounge. Reynolds had to take the call on her family's dining room phone, surrounded by her parents and siblings.

"I couldn't say a whole lot with my parents in the room," she says, "so I had to be clever about it."

"I've got some news!" she told Hudson, cheerfully.

"What is it?" Hudson asked.

"Guess!"

"You got your own apartment?"

"No, guess again!"

"You're pregnant?" he asked.

"*Yep*! That's it!"

"*What*?"

Hudson was not expecting that one, but he quickly regained his composure.

"That's fine, that's fine," he said, reassuring himself as much as her. "We'll get an apartment together."

Hudson's response brought Cindy great relief.

"He was raised right," she says. "He was going to stay with me. I felt good about that, but I was still scared to death."

The only other person Cindy Reynolds told was her best friend, Cyndi George. Reynolds didn't even go to a doctor, for fear her parents might find out.

In a later phone call Hudson admitted to Cindy that he still wanted to go on the cross-country road trip with fellow deckhand Mark Thomas, and asked her about it. He was greatly pleased to hear her say she still thought it was a fine idea. She wasn't due until June, after all, and she knew Bruce and Mark had been dreaming of their trip for a long time.

"That's what everyone our age did back then," Reynolds says, "go West, pick up some Coors in Colorado, and see LA."

So there it was. Hudson knew that, in a couple months, as soon as the *Fitzgerald* finished her season in Toledo, he and Thomas would get in Hudson's Challenger to embark on their epic road trip, and that when they returned, Hudson and Cindy Reynolds would get an apartment in Toledo and start a family. It was all laid out before him.

Bruce Hudson had just started the biggest year of his life.

XII

LUNCH WITH THE CAPTAIN

MARILYN FRERICKS PACKED HER HUSBAND DON'S lunch for work every day in a gray pail. A dented Stanley Thermos—the old kind sealed with a cork, not a screw-on cap—full of hot, black coffee took up the top half of the lunch pail, leaving the bottom for a sandwich of baloney and cheese, or hard salami, cheese, and butter, plus some fruit and carrots.

When Don wasn't feeling well he'd still go to work, so Marilyn would fill the Thermos not with coffee but some homemade chicken soup. If he wasn't on a diet she'd throw in a bag of chips, but not the little bags they sell at gas stations. She'd buy the big, cheaper bag of chips, and put some in a little plastic sandwich bag each day. With a family of five living off Don's paychecks, they had to save money wherever they could.

Don Frericks had grown up on his family's farm in southern Minnesota, left school with an eighth-grade education, and served in the Korean War. In 1956 he found a job at Reserve Mining in Silver Bay, then got married in 1958, and had three kids. Frericks often fixed small engines out of his garage for some side money, and in his spare time he passed his GED.

"Dad was great at maintenance," his son Doug says. "He could take anything apart and put it back together."

Eventually Reserve Mining put Frericks in charge of the yards and the docks, the powerhouse, and the pelletizer, which made the taconite pebbles. The machine pulverized raw iron ore into powder, then combined the iron with clay to form taconite pellets by the millions. The second the pellets were finished they were loaded directly onto a ship at Reserve Mining's dock.

"Those were hot loads," former engineer John Hayes says. "That was miserable work in the summer. The steam!"

The work took its toll. Don's brother suffered a heart attack in the break room and died, but Don seemed built for it. At six two and 225 pounds, he had fingers as thick as thumbs. It was his job to make sure the ships got loaded properly and quickly. If something went wrong, Frericks fixed it.

"The quicker it got fixed, the quicker Captain McSorley could leave," Don's son Doug says. "So the captain and Dad had a bond."

Don worked the factory's first shift, 7 a.m. to 3 p.m. "Seven to threes," Doug says. "And Dad was home every day by 3:13. You could set your watch by it."

Sometimes when Don came home Marilyn would open her husband's lunch box and say, "You didn't eat anything!"

"Ah, I had lunch with McSorley," Don would say. "The *Fitz* was in today."

By 1975 Ernest McSorley and Don Frericks had been friends for a decade, and would have lunch whenever the *Fitzgerald* came to Silver Bay, usually once a week. They always had lunch, not dinner, due to Frericks's seven-to-three shift, and they always ate on the ship because McSorley never left the boat, even in port, and the *Fitzgerald*'s food couldn't be beat. While Frericks and McSorley caught up over lunch, the *Fitzgerald*'s off-duty crew members would walk "up the street" with empty backpacks to the Silver Bay Municipal Liquor and Lounge to have a few cold ones, then stuff their packs with more for the road.

"They stuck out like a sore thumb at the bar," Doug Frericks says. "You had the locals and the boat guys. And the boat guys always had money to spend."

Doug Frericks, who was fourteen in 1975, got the clear impression from his father's stories that McSorley's crew knew that it was a privilege, not a right, to get off the boat and go "up the street." If they embarrassed themselves or their ship, that right would be quickly revoked.

"If you did what you were told to do, and you didn't create any problems, McSorley had no issues with you," Doug Frericks says. "As my dad described him, McSorley was quiet but friendly, and a hard charger in the pilothouse.

"You know, there are certain things that you remember, that just stick out, even years later. My dad told me that if he had to pick a boat to be on in bad weather, it would be the *Fitz*, because the *Fitz* was the best boat, and it had the best captain in rough weather: Ernest McSorley."

SOMETHING ELSE IN that conversation sticks out, too. Both McSorley and Don Frericks knew the *Fitzgerald* would be laying up for the offseason sometime in November, but why? Lakers usually ran to mid-January, going as long as they could before ice clogged the Soo Locks. That was exactly what the *Fitzgerald* had done the previous season, when Craig Ellquist had gotten off with the others on January 28, 1975.

A ship might cut the season short to undergo its routine five-year inspection by the U.S. Coast Guard and American Bureau of Shipping (ABS), but the *Fitzgerald* had already checked that box the year before, in the spring of 1974, and she wouldn't require another full inspection until 1979.

But there was another possible reason for the *Fitzgerald* to stop sailing in November of 1975. By laker standards the *Fitzgerald* was still young at eighteen years, but she had already completed 748 round trips from the Head of the Lakes to Detroit or Toledo, and logged more than a million miles, the equivalent of forty-four trips around the world. She had suffered her share of dings along the way, too, running aground in 1969, colliding with another ship in 1970, and striking a wall at the Soo Locks in 1970, 1973, and 1974. Nothing unusual by shipping standards, but they start to add up.

On October 31, 1975—perhaps as a follow-up to the more thorough five-year inspection of 1974—the USCG and ABS gave the *Edmund Fitzgerald* a cursory, one-day inspection in Toledo. On Coast Guard Form CG-835, inspectors noted any deficiencies that might not be urgent but that the company promised to fix after the season, things like cracks in the hatch covers, which are very common. In this case, the USCG and ABS reported several hatch covers did not seal completely, which would allow some water to get in. While not deeming them urgent, the Coast Guard ordered Columbia Transportation to complete repairs before the 1976 shipping season.

So why would Columbia decide to bring the *Fitzgerald* into Toledo for repairs on November 12, 1975, and forego two full months of the shipping season? With the *Fitzgerald*'s records missing we can't be certain, but the best guess might be this: As much as Columbia's executives wanted to make money, they wanted to save it, too. By starting the *Fitzgerald*'s repairs two months before the other three hundred ships on the Great Lakes came in for their inspections and repairs, Columbia could enjoy easy access to normally scarce resources, including a dry dock, a team of welders and other tradesmen, and their tools, all of which could push repairs in January to a million dollars ($6 million today) or more. It's also possible Columbia believed the *Fitzgerald* needed more repairs than the USCG report required.

"It's much cheaper to get your ship in early, when it's not busy, than in January, when everyone wants in," former GLMA superintendent John Tanner says. "You get a better rate on the dry dock, the high-end equipment, and the specialists who do the work. None of it's cheap."

Whatever Columbia's motives, we can be reasonably certain the *Fitzgerald* was expected to layup in Toledo after the ship left Superior on November 9, based on a number of sources repeating the information; Bob Rafferty's postcard back to his family in Toledo ("I may be home by Nov. 8. However, nothing is ever sure."); and several people who clearly recall their friends and family on the *Fitzgerald* telling them they would be home in November, not January. This includes Cindy Reynolds, pregnant with Bruce Hudson's child, who probably had more incentive to assiduously follow the *Fitzgerald*'s schedule than anyone.

Craig Ellquist had opted to postpone his second season as a deckhand on the *Fitzgerald* that year to deliver milk in Two Harbors, but he stayed in touch with his former crewmates throughout the 1975 season. During their frequent trips to Silver Bay he would join them at the Municipal Lounge or on the ship itself.

"Everyone was saying the same thing," he recalls. The November 9–12 run "was their last trip of the year, because it was going in for repairs. I was planning to go down to Superior [Wisconsin, on November 9] to see them before they pushed off."

At about the same time, most likely the week before, Captain McSorley and Don Frericks had lunch again on the *Fitzgerald*, docked as always right next to Reserve Mining.

"The season was winding down," Doug Frericks recalls. "So my dad asked McSorley if the *Fitz* was done for the year." Don Frericks knew the *Fitzgerald* was expected to end the season in Toledo very soon.

"No, we've gotta make one more run," McSorley told him.

Both men knew the companies gave their boats a quota of cargo each season. Once a ship met its quota, any cargo delivered beyond that put a nice bonus in the pockets of the captain. As usual, the *Fitz* had already made her quota, so one more run would simply drive McSorley's bonus up another notch or two, which naturally played into his decision to push it one more week.

"I don't think McSorley was a greedy man," Doug Frericks says. "I don't think he'd tack on trips just for a few bucks, especially in November."

But, McSorley told Don Frericks that day, his wife, Nellie, was sick and she needed more medical care, and possibly an operation.

"McSorley had figured that last run would cover the cost of it," Doug Frericks says. "I got all this from my dad."

McSorley added that, to pick up that last load of taconite the following week, the *Fitzgerald* would dock in Superior, Wisconsin, about sixty miles down Lake Superior's western coastline from Silver Bay.

"So my dad said, 'See you next year.' He remembered that.

"And that was the last time they talked."

XIII

ONE LAST RUN

(November 8–10, 1975)

An Unseasonably Warm Day

Saturday, November 8, 1975
Superior, Wisconsin

THE *EDMUND FITZGERALD* MOST OFTEN LOADED IN Silver Bay, Minnesota. But perhaps because McSorley apparently added one more trip to the schedule, this time she docked in Superior, Wisconsin, at Burlington Dock No. 1.

Captain McSorley still knew the Superior docks well, and once at sea the rest of the trip would be even more familiar to him than the ship he would be leading into the Great Lakes. In the course of McSorley's forty-five years at sea he had made this three-day trip, up or down, more than a thousand times. Every inch of the route that lay ahead of him he had committed to memory.

From Sunday afternoon to Monday afternoon, November 10, he and his crew would drive the *Fitzgerald* the full 350-mile-length of Lake Superior to reach the relative calm of Whitefish Bay. McSorley would guide the *Fitzgerald* through the Soo Locks and St. Marys River for the last time of his long and storied career, then drop down into Lake Huron and chug another 350 miles south to Detroit's Zug Island, where the ship would arrive at the National Steel dock sometime after noon on Tuesday, November 11.

There the dockworkers would take fourteen or so hours to unload the *Fitzgerald*'s five hundred million taconite pellets, and form them into huge piles on the dock. While they unloaded the cargo some of the *Fitzgerald* crew would make quick calls home, then take their chances at one of the bars on Jefferson, just across the canal: the Hinky-Dink, the Honey Bee, or Mel Hall's.

On Wednesday morning, November 12, Captain McSorley would lead his crew through the last sixty miles of his career to the C&O pellet dock in Toledo. Blaine Wilhelm would be packing his bag, careful to secure the Maxwell House can of change he'd saved all season long, a small but heavy fortune he couldn't wait to bring home to his kids back in Moquah, Wisconsin.

Because the *Fitz* would have unloaded at Zug Island, she would be riding light to Toledo, carrying only ballast water.

Once they tied up in Toledo the crew members would hustle down the ladder to the payphone to call their families, this time to share the brief but reassuring message to their wives, children, parents, and girlfriends that they had made it through another strenuous season, and would soon be home for five long winter months. The nine crewmen who lived in the Toledo area would either be met by their loved ones, or jump in their cars waiting at the dock. But more than a few of the locals would join their out-of-town friends for one last night at the Harbor Light, a brick box with no windows but plenty of cheap Stroh's Bohemian-style fire-brewed beer and a juke box with vinyl 45s of everything from Hank Williams to Motown to Michigan's own Bob Seger—and, of course, "Brandy," which they would belt out together several more times that night, while toasting each other on another great season.

Buck Champeau's Oldsmobile would be waiting for him at the Toledo docks, ready for the drive around Chicago to Milwaukee, where he would give his seventeen-year-old daughter Debbie, now a senior at St. Pius XI, a big, season-ending hug, and a few souvenirs from his latest stops on the Great Lakes.

Tom Bentsen and David "Cowboy" Weiss would call their Traverse City girlfriends, Cindy Gagnier and Cindy LoCicero, respectively. Since Weiss would be turning twenty-two years old on Thursday, November 13, the day they returned to Traverse City, that would be cause for celebration, too. On the five-hour drive back Bentsen and Weiss could daydream about hitting their favorite haunts with their GLMA classmates, and rekindling their budding romances with their hometown sweethearts. Both had gotten through some bumpy years, but now the road ahead seemed clear, and they were both as settled as they had been in years, maybe ever.

Deckhands Bruce Hudson and Mark Thomas—who shared the laborious job of securing the clamps with Paul Riippa on each of the ship's twenty-one hatches every trip—would be running to Hudson's gleaming burgundy 1974 Dodge Challenger to embark on their long-awaited road trip before Hudson came home to assume his new duties with Cindy Reynolds as young parents.

But before the crew started their various celebrations, they would stop to salute and cheer their captain, Ernest McSorley, who would take his time getting down from the ladder for once—a noted contrast to his usual brisk exit to see his wife, Nellie, in the few hours they had. This time, he could revel in the knowledge that he had all the time in the world, an entire future just for Nellie and himself. He would drive directly to her facility, then to Mancy's for a long-anticipated celebration, and once Nellie was well again, back to their handsome home in Ottawa Hills—this time, for good.

Home is the sailor, home from the sea,
And the hunter home from the hills.

McSorley would finally be able to give Nellie the undivided attention she deserved, and the care she needed. Thanks to the bonus from this last, extra trip, he would have the money to do so.

The *Fitzgerald* would then hibernate in Toledo, where she would undergo her scheduled repairs. At just eighteen years old her best years were still ahead of her, and a half dozen or so lucky sailors would get the privilege of replacing the *Fitzgerald* veterans who would be retiring with McSorley.

When the crew members boarded the *Fitzgerald* in Superior, Wisconsin, they would know that all of this, everything they had been working for all season long—and for some of them, decades—was now just three days and 784 miles away. They were that close.

THE PLAN FOR this last trip was as simple and routine as walking to the mailbox, but things started going awry before they even set out.

Just a few hours into Saturday, November 8, a familiar Arctic front called the Alberta Clipper—a fast-moving, low-moisture system that pushes cold air down to the States—had started running across Western Canada toward the east. Nothing surprising about that, especially in November. But there was also a low-pressure system starting to spin over Southern California and move northeast, which *was* unusual.

"Warm weather, no snow on the ground, and then these two weather masses come right at Lake Superior," former GLMA superintendent Tanner says, grimacing. "That's going to be something to see."

But none of the crew members in Superior, Wisconsin, knew about those systems, and they probably wouldn't have cared, in any case. They expected some wind and waves this late in the season, the weather that day was beautiful, and their thoughts had already turned to home. While the dockworkers at Burlington Dock No. 1 poured taconite into the *Edmund Fitzgerald*'s cargo holds, some of the crewmen trekked up the street to the President Bar and Pay Less Liquors, where the beer flowed as freely as "Brandy" wafted from the jukebox. Craig Ellquist, the former deckhand who had traded clamping hatches on the *Fitzgerald* to deliver milk in Two Harbors, planned to reunite with his former crewmates in Superior, but he got tied up back home and couldn't make the ninety-minute round trip after all. No problem, he figured. He'd see them again when they fitted out in April of 1976, and maybe by then he'd be working on the ship once more.

First assistant engineer Eddie Bindon slipped off to Duluth to pick out a two-carat diamond ring for his wife, Helen, as a twenty-fifth anniversary present. Bindon, who had no siblings and no children, had also been thinking about retiring after this season, so this ring represented his pledge to spend the rest of his years with Helen. But at some point between the purchase and the time Bindon returned to the ship, instead of pocketing the gift to deliver to Helen himself, he entrusted the ring to a friend in Duluth, who promised to make sure Helen got it.

Nolan Church, the happiest man onboard, had also made other plans. Weeks earlier Church had asked his children to promise to join him and his wife for a big night in Duluth that Saturday, November 8.

This was not easy when four of their five children were married and out of the house, with six grandchildren, and a seventh due the following April. Marilynn lived with her husband in Two Harbors, with no children yet. Middle sister Debbie also had a home in Two Harbors, with her husband and two children and a third on the way. Bonnie had moved to Rockford, a Minneapolis suburb, with her husband and two kids. Their oldest son lived out east, and their youngest was still at home.

"Dad wanted all the girls to come meet him," Bonnie says. "He was *so* insistent that we do this, so we did it, just us three girls and our mother."

Nolan took the Church women out shopping at the Miller Hill Mall in Duluth, and told each of them to pick out something special.

"He bought me a nice sweater, a beige cardigan," Marilynn says. "Deb got a pair of shoes. Dad got a big cowboy hat for himself—and he's the one who always said, 'Don't wear hats because they make you bald!'"

They enjoyed a good dinner at the Chinese Lantern, one of Duluth's fancier restaurants, and talked about the offseason ahead.

James Bolin was bartending that night at the President Bar and Pay Less Liquors. He cashed a few checks for some of the *Fitzgerald* crew, their next-to-last checks for the season, putting a few hundred-dollar bills in their pockets, enough to cover their drinks, their final celebration in Toledo, and their trips home for the winter, with plenty left over. Bolin recalls the crew members kept it going until he closed the bar at 1 a.m.

About the same time, the low-pressure system in the Southwest was gaining strength as it traveled through Arizona and New Mexico, then drifted north and east. But it was literally not on anyone's radar in the Great Lakes, where the weather couldn't have been nicer.

Blissfully unaware of the trouble gathering steam thousands of miles away, the *Fitzgerald* sailors laughed and stumbled their way back down the street in the dark. They successfully scaled the thirty-foot ladder to get back on deck, found their cabins, and settled into their bunks for their last night on shore that season, secure in the belief that in just a few days they would be sleeping in their own beds, in their own homes.

Sunday, November 9, 1975
Superior, Wisconsin

By Sunday morning the low-pressure system out of California had made it to Kansas, picking up warm moisture by the tons along the way, but the National Weather Service (NWS) predicted only a "typical November storm," which would pass "just under" Lake Superior by Monday night, November 10, around 7 p.m. The Alberta Clipper, meanwhile, was cutting a straight line across the American border with dry cold air, heading straight for the upper portion of Lake Superior.

But if you woke up in Superior, Wisconsin, that morning to another unseasonably warm, sunny day with temperatures sneaking into the seventies—almost unheard of on Lake Superior in late autumn—even the NWS's tepid forecast sounded implausible. Any thoughts of the dangers that might lie ahead were easily eclipsed by the clear skies, the wonderfully warm day, and the shared dream of finishing the grueling shipping season just three days later.

For a Great Lakes sailor, November 9, 1975, was as good as it gets.

AFTER NOLAN CHURCH, the organ-playing baseball fan who became a porter at age fifty, enjoyed a great evening shopping and dining with his wife and three daughters in Duluth, they dropped him off at Burlington Dock No. 1.

"Right before Dad got on the ship," Marilynn says, "he gave his new cowboy hat to us and told us to keep it in good hands. And then we said goodbye."

Nolan climbed the ladder, stepped on the deck, then turned to wave to his family, and they waved back.

While Burlington dockworkers loaded taconite onto the *Fitzgerald*, they simultaneously filled the cargo holds of the SS *Wilfred Sykes*, a 678-foot freighter that had been the biggest on the lakes when it launched in 1949. The *Sykes* was scheduled to leave Superior a couple hours after the *Fitzgerald*.

With a little more time to kill, a few *Fitzgerald* crew members returned to the President Bar and Pay Less Liquors for last rounds. They couldn't linger long, however. As bartender James Bolin recalls, the dockworkers finished the load in about four and a half hours, about as fast as it could be done.

The loading speed was all the more impressive because the dockworkers had filled the *Fitzgerald*'s belly with 26,112 long tons of taconite—far from the staggering amounts the new thousand-footers were carrying, but a fitting finale to McSorley's celebrated career. The load that day was almost 4,000 long tons more than the 22,509 the *Fitzgerald* needed to set the Great Lakes record on its very first run just seventeen years earlier, a testament to the extra 39.25 inches the Coast Guard had allowed the *Fitzgerald* to sink in the water since 1973—plus the crew's ability to cheat a few more inches on the Plimsoll line. This was such a common practice it would have been more remarkable if the crew had *not* cheated on the Plimsoll Line. Even the crew's families knew about it.

"They were overweight because they wanted to break their own record," says Blaine Wilhelm's daughter, Heidi Brabon. "So they cheated."

But what was unusual, according to former *Fitzgerald* deckhand Terry Sullivan, was that she was carrying a full load so late in the season, when even the USCG rules start scaling back the limits. While the *Fitzgerald* might not have been cheating by much, on the grand scale, when you combine those extra inches, plus the 39.25 inches the Coast Guard had already granted the *Fitzgerald* two years earlier, and the fact that all ships were supposed to scale back their loads for the rougher fall weather, any reasonable analysis can draw only one conclusion: The *Fitzgerald* had loaded thousands of tons more than what her architects had designed her to carry.

By 2:15 p.m. that Sunday the last pebbles of taconite had settled into the ship's three massive cargo holds, while the *Fitzgerald* took on more than fifty thousand gallons of No. 6 fuel oil.

The deckhands cast off the lines, the watchmen started the winches to pull the cables in, and then the deckhands climbed back up the ladder onto the deck. Captain McSorley directed his best friend, Wheelsman John Simmons, to steer the *Edmund Fitzgerald* out of the port, toward Lake Superior.

PATRICK LABADIE WAS finishing his fourth season as director of the Canal Park Marine Museum in Duluth, where he loved to watch the lakers from his perch. He'd observed the freighters come and go thousands of times, and posted their arrivals and departures on the big board outside the museum for the tourists. But something about November 9 felt different, even at the time.

When Labadie heard the scanner transmission announce the *Fitzgerald*'s departure from Superior, he strolled over to the board to mark her passage even though there were "pretty darn few" visitors that day.

"The *Fitzgerald* was no longer the biggest," Labadie says, "but she was still the most popular ship on the Great Lakes—and I don't think it was close."

Although Labadie had never been aboard the *Fitzgerald*—his favorite ship, too—he assumed he'd get his chance someday, but there was no rush. The ship was just eighteen years old.

Labadie climbed the stairs to the second-floor windows of the museum, which provided a sweeping view across the harbor where he could watch the *Fitzgerald* make its way out to the open seas.

The water was calm and the sky was clear, with nothing to suggest conditions would change any time soon. Yet something told Labadie not to look away, to keep watching, to pay attention. To pay respect. He couldn't place the source of this impulse, but he felt it strongly, and he obeyed it.

The *Fitzgerald* slowly pivoted into the five-hundred-foot-wide Superior Entry Channel, then glided between Minnesota Point and Wisconsin Point—the two slender arms of land reaching out from each state, nearly touching in the water. After the *Fitz* slipped out of the safety of their embrace, Labadie watched her cruise out into Lake Superior until she was finally out of sight. Then he turned back to the museum to post the departure information on the big board:

Edmund Fitzgerald
Departure 2:15 p.m., 11/9/75
Destination: Toledo
ETA: 11/12/75

Labadie would be one of the last people on land to see the *Edmund Fitzgerald.*

Fitzgerald's Cousin

JUST THIRTY MILES UP THE VOYAGEUR HIGHWAY FROM Burlington Dock No. 1, the *Arthur M. Anderson* loaded taconite in Two Harbors for its own trip down the Great Lakes.

Although not a sister ship of the *Edmund Fitzgerald*, the *Anderson* had to be considered a close cousin. Named for Arthur Marvin Anderson, a former director of U.S. Steel, she launched in Lorain, Ohio, in 1952, six years before the *Fitzgerald*. The *Anderson* stretched 647 feet until the winter of 1975, when U.S. Steel extended the *Anderson* to 767 feet, 38 feet longer than the *Fitzgerald*. She would never surpass the *Fitzgerald* in popularity—no freighter could—but she had the respect of everyone who mattered, including the crew of the *Fitz* itself.

While the *Anderson* took on its load of taconite, half the crew went up the street to the American Legion Post 109. But unlike the *Fitzgerald* crew, the men on the *Anderson* weren't toasting their last trip of the season. When the *Fitzgerald* docked in Toledo the *Anderson* would be on its way to the U.S. Steel complex in Gary, Indiana, and would keep working until January's ice finally ended their season.

Like the *Fitzgerald*, the *Anderson* was a "high seniority vessel." Because so many sailors wanted to work on the *Anderson*, only those with the highest seniority could get on. As a result, the *Anderson*'s crew was close to the *Fitzgerald*'s in terms of experience and skill.

"People knew what they were doing," says former *Anderson* second engineer Rick Barthuli. "Everybody was extremely professional on the *Anderson*, like the *Fitz*. It was a serious crew."

But there was one key difference: the captains. While Ernest McSorley had earned the respect of his crew and beyond, *Anderson* captain Jesse

"Bernie" Cooper did not enjoy the same universal admiration. Cooper brought considerable skill and confidence, but some thought he suffered from too much of the latter.

"Everyone tends to glorify Cooper," says Barthuli. "I'm not sure why. I've had a shortlist of captains I liked, maybe three or four out of fifty, and Cooper's not on that list. I know some [on the ship] who liked him, but not many. Look, some people are born to suck up. That's who liked him. And some people are born not to. That's who didn't."

What bothered Barthuli most was Cooper's ego, which Barthuli believes was too big, "even by captain standards."

Barthuli acknowledges that, unlike many of Cooper's peers in the captain class, he was never outwardly dismissive to the newly minted academy cadets like Barthuli. Further, Cooper was "competent and took his job seriously," Barthuli says. "I'll give him that. Good boat handler. On the lakes that's important, because you've got to get from dock to dock and not hit shit! Some guys can't do that. Maybe a lot of guys can't do that. Cooper could."

But Barthuli was troubled by Cooper's tendency to take unnecessary risks.

"One of his sayings was, 'You don't haul a million tons of iron ore a year by laying on the hook' [dropping the anchor]. True enough. You're paid to go. If you spend time hiding from bad weather, no good. Taking chances and making money, that was his job. You don't move the boat, you won't be a Great Lakes captain very long. But he took some chances with other people's lives that were a bit much. Sometimes the seas were so bad the risk didn't seem worth the reward, even for the company."

Still, Barthuli concludes, "Cooper delivered come hell or high water, so the company loved him. And the *Anderson* is still running today, so I guess he might have been right?"

Cooper was also wise enough to establish a productive partnership with his chief engineer, Jim Boyle. Short and stout like an Olympic weightlifter, even in his sixties Boyle exuded raw power. Hailing from North Dakota, he had followed the trains from his family's farm to the grain docks in Duluth, and from there to the freighters.

"Common story," Barthuli says with a grin. "Once they see the lights of Duluth, how you gonna keep 'em down on the farm? But Boyle knew what he was doing, and he was fair. Can't ask for more."

One indication of the respect Boyle had earned: Every now and then Captain Cooper let Boyle bring his wife on a trip. Called Queen Isabelle by the crew, she was a kindly reminder of their moms at home, and they treated her accordingly.

Boyle, likewise, had a strong working relationship with his top report, First Engineer Harry Ashcroft, a tall, thin, distinguished-looking middle-aged man who still possessed a full head of medium-brown hair. The crew teased him for having a perm (this was the seventies), but sailors know that if you're not getting teased about something, you're probably on the outs. Ashcroft had grown up in the port city of Conneaut, Ohio, on the Pennsylvania border, and started as a wiper, the lowest rank on the engine side, then worked his way up to one of the best positions on the Great Lakes.

"Ashcroft was an excellent engineer," Barthuli attests, "the only one I ever knew who had a nuclear license. He was a damn good teacher, too. I was stupid and had a lot to learn, and Ashcroft was better with the cadets than most."

Ashcroft was that rare sailor who enjoyed Broadway plays and piano concerts, and he didn't try to hide it.

"He was someone who had a little bit of class," Barthuli says. "Definitely his own man, in a tough era to be one."

Ashcroft's independence extended to his personal life.

"Let's just say he was *out*," Barthuli says. "He wasn't making any statement, but there aren't many secrets on a steamboat. Everyone knew he was gay, and he didn't seem to care. He didn't hide it, but he was not flamboyant, and he didn't make it anyone else's business, either. Never messed with anyone on the ship, so far as I know—and as a young cadet with no power, I would have been a prime target.

"He probably had his boyfriends up the street. I really don't know. It was a live-and-let-live atmosphere on the ship, for the most part. There were some people who didn't like him because he was gay, and some guys who didn't care. Probably most."

The combination of Ashcroft's competence and independence seemed to make him immune to Captain Cooper's occasional attempts to intimidate.

"Ashcroft was not afraid of Cooper," Barthuli says. "Even Cooper had enough respect for Ashcroft that he wasn't going to mess with him, either."

Ashcroft's quiet confidence would soon pay off in ways Barthuli and his fellow crewmates could never have anticipated on that sunny Sunday afternoon.

Sunday, November 9. 2:15 p.m.

As the *Fitzgerald* made her way out of Superior Bay, McSorley took in the familiar sights of the Wisconsin Point lighthouse to the east and the Superior North Entry Lighthouse to the west, now fading behind him one last time.

Once the *Fitzgerald* entered the vast expanse of Lake Superior, McSorley ordered the *Fitz* up to her full speed of 16.3 miles per hour. At that rate the *Fitzgerald* would need two hours to pass Two Harbors, around the same time the *Anderson* was expected to leave that port.

As DUSK DESCENDED on this fantastic fall Sunday, the Coast Guard's 180-foot-long buoy tender *Woodrush* passed the *Fitzgerald* on its way back to its home port of Duluth. The *Woodrush* crew, who'd just spent a couple weeks on Lake Superior retrieving a hundred directional buoys before the ice froze them in place, were headed for a well-earned break.

Woodrush crewman Michael Zronek remembers the day well.

"It was maybe seventy, seventy-five degrees," he says. "We didn't even have jackets on. Up there, that's almost unheard of in November. It felt good to come into port in weather like that."

Back in Duluth the crew would catch up on maintaining the *Woodrush*, prepare for ice-breaking duties in December, and enjoy a little time off. When in port the *Woodrush* crew operated on a three-shift rotation, with each shift working twenty-four hours followed by forty-eight hours off, similar to a firehouse schedule. But for the next day, Monday, November 10, the captain had granted everyone liberty—a rare full day off for all shifts, which meant they could get a pizza, go bowling, or just stay home, drink some beers with their fellow Coasties, and watch the Monday Night Football game.

"Going ashore when you've been rolling for two weeks," Zronek says, "getting back on terra firma—man, there's something to be said for that."

On such a wonderful evening they would never have guessed that their long-awaited liberty would be cut short.

Taking the Long Way

Sunday, November 9. 5:00 p.m.

A FEW MINUTES BEFORE THE SUN SET AT 5:15 P.M. THE *Arthur M. Anderson* pushed off from Two Harbors. The slightly faster *Fitzgerald* soon caught up to the *Anderson* off the southeast shore of Isle Royale, the forty-five-mile-long U.S. national park.

Due to their ships' comparable capabilities, and their own competitive instincts, both captains knew their ships would be getting to the Soo Locks at about the same time. But at the start of the trip the two ships were more allies than adversaries, pairing up to navigate Lake Superior together.

That afternoon the National Weather Service had posted a "gale warning," a level of caution the NWS had created after the 1913 Storm of the Century showed it needed intermediary warnings, not just hurricane alerts. A gale warning predicts winds blowing thirty-nine to fifty-four miles per hour. But the NWS projected the wind would barely reach the gale range, which meant about forty miles per hour.

McSorley and Cooper knew better than to take any November storm lightly, but with the waves running only three to six feet, it was nothing to make either captain change his plans to take the most direct route across Lake Superior: a straight shot from the Head of the Lakes to the tip of Michigan's Keweenaw Peninsula, then southeast to Whitefish Bay. That was what both men knew best, having followed that path almost every time they traversed Lake Superior.

Later, Patrick Devine, the *Fitzgerald* deckhand whom Bruce Hudson had replaced that September, would look over the weather forecasts for

Lake Superior that night and wonder why McSorley and the other captains had sailed at all.

"My theory is they knew a storm was coming," Devine reflects, "but they were rolling the dice, figuring they could outrun it."

They had before. By dinnertime McSorley's innate aggressiveness returned, pushing the *Fitzgerald* a little ahead of the *Anderson*. But Dudley J. Paquette, captain of the *Wilfred Sykes*, sensed trouble.

After Paquette pulled the *Sykes* out of Burlington Dock No. 1 two hours behind the *Fitzgerald*, Paquette began to suspect even the NWS gale warning underestimated the coming storm, and he also believed that it would cross Lake Superior, not slide below it. Paquette, considered one of the era's best forecasters in the captain class, knew taking the usual southern route would expose ships to the big lake's brutal 350-mile fetch, where high winds can churn across the lake's entire length to multiply the size of the waves on the eastern side.

Instead of the straighter, faster line, therefore, Paquette opted for the longer, better-sheltered course called the northern route. This would send the *Sykes* closer to Isle Royale and Superior's western shore to provide greater protection from the winds sweeping across the plains, then almost straight east across the northern half of Lake Superior all the way to the lake's eastern coast, then south to Whitefish Bay.

When Captain Paquette told the crew members in the pilothouse his decision, they warned him that if the storm didn't arrive as he was predicting, he would catch hell from the company office in Chicago for taking the long way to the Soo Locks—about fourteen hours longer, in fact. Paquette knew they were right, but he was so convinced a bigger storm was coming that he was willing to risk being chewed out by corporate headquarters.

The *Sykes* would be taking the northern route.

Paquette's ship was sailing close enough to the *Fitzgerald* and *Anderson* that he could overhear several conversations between McSorley and Cooper on the marine band radio. He was not surprised to hear McSorley, already ahead of the *Anderson*, tell Cooper that he would be taking the faster, straighter southern route, and Cooper agreed to do the same.

Sunday, November 9. 7:00 p.m.

By 7 p.m. the National Weather Service noticed the storm system that started out of California had reached Iowa, and was gaining speed. It issued a gale warning for all of Lake Superior, correcting its earlier prediction that the storm would slip just below the big lake. Now, the NWS meteorologists said, the storm would cut diagonally across Lake Superior, producing waves from five to ten feet. That might not sound like much, but because the *Fitzgerald* had only 11.5 feet of freeboard, ten-foot waves wouldn't give the ship much margin for error.

If McSorley's first idea was to outrun the storm, five hours of sailing on increasingly choppy seas, a few conversations with Captain Cooper, and a revised NWS forecast all made McSorley think better of it. After talking again, both McSorley and Cooper decided to take the northern route after all.

Besides, this was McSorley's last run. While he still had his competitive pride he also knew that, unlike Captain Paquette, he was unlikely to incur the wrath of the corporate bean counters no matter when the *Fitzgerald* delivered her taconite to Zug Island. And even if he did, what could it matter? He'd be home, for good.

Taking the northern route was a prudent choice, befitting a seasoned captain facing harsh conditions. But the decision to take the safer path was not without consequence. Sailing the northern route would commit the captains to running along three sides of Lake Superior: the western shore, the northern shore, and then a hard turn south down the eastern shore to Whitefish Bay. That last leg would leave their ships completely unprotected from the full force of the lake's fury, with the biggest waves on the lake hitting their ships for hours—and broadside at that, which would make their vessels roll side to side in the troughs the entire way south—which would be unpleasant at best, and dangerous at worst.

By Sunday evening both captains knew they faced a "pay me now or pay me later" dilemma: contend with the winds and waves coming up behind their ships right away, or take shelter along the Canadian shores in relative comfort before bracing for the worst on the final southern stretch. By going north, they were taking out a loan their ships would have to pay later.

The decision also came embedded with a hidden risk: While both captains took the southern route almost fifty times a season, or one hundred trips if counting both directions, they followed the northern route only a few times each year, if that. Neither Craig Ellquist, who had worked as a deckhand on the *Fitzgerald* during the worst months of 1974–75, nor Patrick Devine, who served on the *Fitzgerald* in the summer of 1975, can recall McSorley taking the northern route on a single trip during their time onboard.

"Never," Devine says. "It had to be a real humdinger of a storm to go that way."

"It took a lot longer," Ellquist adds, "and we weren't out for joyrides."

In fact, November 9 was probably the first time all season that McSorley had opted for the alternate path, which captains pursued only under extreme conditions. Once McSorley directed his ship to sail north, the comforting familiarity he felt pulling out of the Head of the Lakes, past markers he'd seen thousands of times, would leave him, and be replaced with winds, islands, and shoals he saw only once or twice each season, at most.

Because the northern path would also take about fourteen hours longer than the *Fitzgerald*'s usual route, it could give other threats time to grow. Both captains nonetheless opted for the northern route, knowing it was one of the few cards they had to play.

By taking the longer but ostensibly safer route, McSorley had made a rare decision to play it safe—or at least safer than his usual course of action. If McSorley was simply trying to beat the *Anderson* to the Soo Locks, he would have taken the lower route and saved fourteen hours, waves be damned. Perhaps a few years earlier he would have done just that, maybe even a few weeks earlier. But not on this day, and not on his last trip.

The first crucial decision had been made, and both captains knew there would be no turning back.

FOR THE CREWS on both ships, the route less taken sent a clear signal.

"There's always talk in the galley about whatever's going on," says *Anderson* engineer Barthuli, who maintained his ship's bilge pump, bow thruster, and other equipment. As soon as he clocked out he would go straight to the galley to catch the first half of the dinner hour, which ran from 4:30 to 5:30 each evening.

"It'd been a nice day, but once we saw we were heading north, instead of straight for the Keweenaw, we knew it was going to be shitty. When the wind's blowing out of the west, you stay along the north shore because that's going to be calm no matter what. That's the whole point of going that way, to avoid the worst of it. So just the fact that we're running on the north shore tells us it's gonna blow. Cooper never would have gone that way otherwise."

The new route meant the trip to the Soo Locks would stretch from a typical thirty-hour journey into a grueling forty-four hours through heavy seas. The crews ate quietly, steeling themselves for what might lie ahead.

They already knew this much: It wasn't going to be another ordinary crossing.

Pent-Up Fury

Monday, November 10. 1:00 a.m.

When Sunday night tripped into Monday morning, the captains still out on Lake Superior—including McSorley, Cooper, and Paquette, now all running together on the northern route, and just south of Isle Royale—understood the smooth sailing was behind them. They accepted November's heavy weather as part of the job, but the intensifying wind and waves were starting to make them wonder exactly how much trouble might be headed their way.

At 1 a.m. the *Edmund Fitzgerald* reported steady winds at forty miles per hour, with gusts reaching sixty miles per hour, and waves cresting above ten feet.

"We were still in the lee of the Canadian shore," says Barthuli, who was on the *Anderson* that night, sailing alongside the *Fitzgerald*. "You need to be about twenty miles off the coast before the wind really starts to build, and we were tucked in closer than that. So whatever was happening farther out on Lake Superior, we weren't seeing the worst of it. Ten-footers? It ain't fun, but nothing unusual."

That's why *Sykes* captain Paquette was "stunned" to hear McSorley, whose reputation for skill, speed, and nerve was known to all, announce his intention to ease the *Fitzgerald*'s engines.

"We're going to try for some lee from Isle Royale," McSorley told the *Sykes*. "You're walking away from us anyway. I can't stay with you."

Instead of racing the *Sykes*, the *Fitzgerald* slipped in behind the *Anderson*, content to follow for a while. Still, it's hard not to view McSorley's oscillating decisions—first to sail straight across the southern route, then to take the longer northern route; to pass the *Anderson*, then to slow down behind it—as a sign that he was out of his element, uncomfortable juggling his conflicting desires.

That's at least how *Sykes* captain Paquette interpreted it.

"No captain ever reveals very much on the radio," Paquette said, "and what [McSorley] said wouldn't mean a helluva lot to most people. But I just had a feeling that something wasn't right when I heard that."

For his part, Paquette had seen enough to conclude even the northern route wouldn't be safe enough, instead opting to take the *Sykes* into safe harbor for the night in Thunder Bay, Ontario, on the western side of Isle Royale.

Up to this point the three captains were communicating directly with each other—not with first or second mates filling in so the captains could get some food or rest. If any of the captains had left their pilothouses, it couldn't have been for long, another sign that the masters were taking the growing threats seriously.

But this too came with a cost: The captains had already put in a long day, a longer one had just started, and fatigue was starting to build.

LATE SUNDAY NIGHT the National Weather Service revised its forecast again, now predicting that waves Monday morning would reach ten to fifteen feet high. At 2 a.m. the NWS escalated its gale warning to a storm warning, reserved for winds expected to reach fifty-five to seventy-three miles per hour—strong enough to tear off roofs, uproot large trees, and knock over people attempting to walk outside.

But the reality on the water was already starting to outpace the NWS's forecasts. Winds on Lake Superior had already surged past fifty-eight miles per hour, and were still accelerating. The storm was gaining power like a boulder thundering down a steep hill.

"So now you've got two air masses on either side—and that's the key," says John Tanner, who taught climate classes at the Great Lakes Maritime Academy, referring to the southwestern storm and the Alberta Clipper both headed for the middle of Lake Superior. "When they collide they're going to push up on each other, like two sides of a mountain, and when transitions like that happen fast, it generates a lot of wind. When you've got wind, you've got waves."

Rick Barthuli provides the perspective of a second engineer on the *Anderson* that night: "When two fronts come together, it all just turns to shit. Choppy, wild, *confused* seas."

At 3 a.m. Captain McSorley's impatience got the better of him. Whether it was fueled by pressure from the company—stated or assumed—the hope of outrunning the storm, his desire to finish first, or simply his eagerness to reach Toledo for the last time and call it a career, McSorley ordered the *Fitzgerald*'s engines back up to full speed. He had returned to his aggressive roots, exactly what he'd been trained to do for three decades at the helm.

"We were within a boat length of each other on the first day, all day—and we were *racing*!'" Barthuli says. "Through a storm! It's so often an ego game between the companies and the captains and crews. Guess who wins? The company, of course."

Yet, unbeknownst to both captains, even as the *Fitzgerald* started separating from the *Anderson*, the two storm systems were now barreling full speed toward Lake Superior.

THERE WAS A lot the captains didn't know—and worse, they didn't know what they didn't know.

Although the NWS was doing its best with what they had, and the captains on Superior that night seemed to put aside their competitive instincts long enough to share information about the weather freely, the heart of the southwestern storm was doing an unusually good job of sneaking up on Whitefish Bay. Instead of running diagonally across the lake, as McSorley, Cooper, and even the NWS expected it to do, the worst of the storm actually hugged the southern coast of the lake, running low and fast, and gathering force with every mile.

But the NWS and the captains did not know this, because either the ships sailing along the Graveyard of the Great Lakes that night were not reporting the conditions—perhaps because they were already too busy fighting for their lives—or more likely, there were simply no freighters on the southern coast that night, because they had stayed in port or taken the northern route.

Years later David Schwab, an oceanographer with the National Oceanic and Atmospheric Administration's Great Lakes Environmental Research Laboratory, who had also worked on projects at the University of Michigan and Michigan Tech, created a computer model of the storm coming up from the southwest that closely matched reports from the ships on Lake Superior that day. Schwab's model confirmed what McSorley, Cooper, and other captains did not know that night: A powerful pocket of the storm was racing west to east, from the Keweenaw Peninsula toward Whitefish Bay.

Firsthand accounts from Marquette, Michigan, where the southwestern storm's epicenter passed, seem to confirm Schwab's model.

PAT SCHUTTE GREW up in Rochester, Michigan, a Detroit suburb, and enrolled at Northern Michigan University in Marquette in 1982. When he first moved into his dorm, therefore, the stories of November 10, 1975, were still fresh.

When powerful storms rolled in—and there were plenty during Schutte's years at NMU—students and locals alike would rush down to Lake Superior's edge to witness the spectacle.

"Gargantuan waves crashed hard into the shoreline, sending up enormous sprays," Schutte says. "It was like something you'd expect in the Pacific Northwest. It was always epic. One storm in particular, a nuclear nor'easter in January, hit so hard it actually washed massive rocks—we're talking *boulders*, the size of beach balls—across Lake Shore Boulevard. If you hit them with your truck, you'd be wrecked—or stuck on top of the rock."

Yet those fierce winter blizzards couldn't compare to the legendary storm of '75. For an assignment in Schutte's investigative journalism class, his professor, Dr. Gerald Waite, encouraged him to interview a longtime Marquette resident who lived in a big log cabin on the shore, where he had witnessed the storm firsthand.

When Schutte arrived unannounced, an elderly man invited him onto the porch, then disappeared momentarily before returning with a photo album and two bottles of Stroh's. The man thumbed through the album, pointing out photos of the storm's aftermath.

"The shore looked like the scene from *Apocalypse Now* where the beach is strafed with napalm," Schutte says. "Trees and even some buildings were leveled, but his sturdy log house survived."

Then the man closed the album and led Schutte to the edge of his property. Standing where dune grass gave way to beach sand, he gestured toward Picnic Rock, a formation Schutte knew well. He had swum many times to the rocky outcrop of an island, which stands just a few hundred feet from the shore and sixteen feet above the water. He and his buddies had occasionally dared to cliff dive off the backside of the rocks. They weren't scared of diving sixteen feet off a rock but of freezing in the famously cold water, so they always wore wet suits, and made it quick.

The old man fell quiet, took a swig of his beer, pointed to Picnic Rock, and said, with his voice trembling, "Those waves, on November 10, 1975, went right over that." The man estimated the waves, in order to roll completely over the rock formation, had to be about twenty-five feet high. That wasn't white spray, either, he explained, but thick green waves of solid water, the kind that can bury boats.

"Think of that," Schutte says. "twenty-five-foot waves, at the *shoreline*, on a freshwater lake. Now think of what was going through the minds of the twenty-nine men on the SS *Edmund Fitzgerald* that day."

Schutte's source may not have been a scientist or a sailor, but he was a rare eyewitness. Years later the data Professor Schwab and his team produced would corroborate the old man's account. Their models showed the storm that had started in California had run along Lake Superior's southern coast directly toward Whitefish Bay—the very haven the *Fitzgerald*'s crew was longing to reach.

Like a catcher guarding home plate, the center of the southwestern storm was moving into perfect position to block the *Fitzgerald*'s path to safety. Because the *Fitzgerald* had taken the long way, adding fourteen hours to the trip, the storm would get there first, and would be waiting for the ship's arrival.

Dreaming of Home

Monday, November 10. 6:31 a.m.

WHEN DAWN BROKE THE WORLD LOOKED A LITTLE better for the captain and crew of the *Edmund Fitzgerald.*

The *Fitz* was still running parallel to the Isle Royale coast, about fifteen miles south of the island and thirty-five miles north of Copper Harbor, Michigan, at the tip of the Keweenaw Peninsula. If McSorley had taken the southern route, the *Fitz* would have been hugging the crown of the Keweenaw about ten miles off land.

The storm hadn't let up, but it hadn't gotten any worse for the *Fitzgerald*, either. Crew members could take some solace in the fact that they had handled storms like this before. No doubt the veterans, especially the half dozen who were just a few days from retiring, joked about finishing their careers with a grand finale.

At 7 a.m., right on schedule, a *Fitzgerald* mate sent out the required weather report to the NWS in Cleveland, listing winds reaching forty miles per hour, "overcast skies, visibility at two to five miles in a continuous moderate rain, a temperature of 41 degrees (F), and waves of ten feet."

The crew member followed up with another routine assignment, the "normal radio call" at 7:20 a.m. to Columbia's home office, also in Cleveland. Due to the weather and McSorley's decision to take the northern route, they had to inform their superiors that their estimated time of arrival at the Soo Locks was now "indefinite"—the medicine McSorley had to take. Based on McSorley's conversations with Cooper, both captains had clearly concluded that the conditions, while demanding, didn't warrant pulling off to find safe harbor, as the *Sykes*'s Captain Paquette had done. If they just kept going, McSorley surely figured, they would get there. The only question was when.

On the positive side, the crew member calling in to Columbia could assure headquarters that captain and crew were pushing the *Fitzgerald* at full speed—probably faster than anyone else on the lake that day.

John Tanner, the former superintendent of the Great Lakes Maritime Academy, which had two students aboard the *Fitzgerald*, the oiler Tom Bentsen and Cadet David "Cowboy" Weiss, has thought about that day for many years.

"If the *Fitzgerald* had reached a port, any port, nothing would have happened, and you'd never have heard about November 10 or the *Edmund Fitzgerald*," he reflects. "I've seen thirty-foot waves on Lake Superior, and it gets ugly fast. Bad things start happening. It's never just one thing that sinks a ship; it's a series of events, like dominoes. And if you don't stop the chain, they can start tumbling fast."

The simplest step to stop the chain is slowing down—a lesson the wreck of the *Cedarville*, sailing too fast in dense fog near the Mackinac Bridge, had reconfirmed just ten years earlier.

"Running the right speed is critical," Tanner says. "You want to slow down to synchronize with the waves if you can, instead of fighting against them. But the pressure to get there first often takes over. They all think, 'Well, if that other ship can do it, then I can do it too.' So they keep plowing through."

Any driver's ed teacher could tell you the same thing: When traffic shows signs of collapsing into chaos, the most important action a driver can take is hitting the brakes. Reducing speed gives you more control, and even if an accident occurs, the risk of serious damage is much lower.

But without knowing much, if anything, about the heart of the storm coming up from the southwest, the *Fitzgerald* pushed ahead at full speed, lengthening the gap between herself and the *Anderson*, and driving ever deeper into the unfolding maelstrom.

THE VETERANS ONBOARD wouldn't have been too concerned. They expected some waves whenever they pushed off in November, and ten- to fifteen-footers were nothing they hadn't handled before.

The young bucks, on the other hand, were already in the biggest storm of their lives. If one of them was going to get sick, this was as good a time as any—and if one deckhand lost it at the fence rail in front of the others or, worse, down below, the odds were good his young mates would soon follow. But it wouldn't count for much, beyond some ribbing from the veterans.

Otherwise the rookies probably tried to ignore the waves, but that isn't the right approach for moving around a ship. If you don't take into account the waves, going up or down the almost-vertical ladders—always with two hands on the rails—can become twice as hard: If you are trying to go up when the ship is going up, or go down when the ship is going down, you will be fighting the forces working against you at every step.

But the veterans knew how to work *with* the waves. When they wanted to climb up, they'd wait for the ship to go down, and vice versa—and that's how they let the waves do the work for them, allowing them to float up and down the stairs as if they were escalators going their way, in something closer to zero gravity.

If the *Fitz*'s rookies were smart they would have cut back on their breakfast, too, but the veterans with stronger stomachs would have dug in to the myriad delights Bob Rafferty, a favored veteran subbing for the last three weeks of the season, and second cook Allen Kalmon were cooking up. They would be telling stories about all the storms they'd already been in, and talk about all their old friends onboard who were about to retire as soon as the ship docked in Toledo.

While they chowed down on Rafferty's omelets, pancakes, and more, Buck Champeau knew his daughter Debbie was driving herself in the used Rambler he bought her to St. Pious XI in Milwaukee.

Blaine Wilhelm would have already dropped his change from the *Fitz*'s stop in Superior, Wisconsin, the day before into his blue Maxwell House coffee can, now brimming from a full season on the lakes. In just two days he'd be enjoying one of his favorite rituals: gathering his kids around their kitchen table back in Moquah, Wisconsin, and dumping the full can of coins out to let the kids divvy it up. He might have even been thinking that, with a longer offseason than usual coming up, it could be the perfect time to study with his buddy Frank Kobasic to pass that engineer's test once and for all.

Nolan Church, the fifty-five-year-old porter, would have been hustling up and down the ship despite the waves, wisely using the tunnels instead of the deck, picking up dirty towels and delivering clean ones—the last batch of the season. He'd be thinking about his wife and three daughters, and their wonderful trip to Duluth that weekend. He wasn't worried. Like he'd repeatedly told his son Ricky, "The *Fitz* is the biggest ship out there, and the safest. Lake Superior doesn't have a hole big enough to fit the *Fitzgerald*!" Church was probably thinking this trip would be the perfect story to tell his six grandkids once he got home, then he could sit down at the organ and play some singalong Christmas songs to make sure they weren't too scared.

The young bucks would be busy, queasy, and eager to get to Toledo, then back to their girlfriends. David Weiss planned to call Cindy LoCicero as soon as they landed, and tell her that he'd be back up at his place in Northport by Thursday at the latest so they could celebrate his twenty-second birthday that night. Because he'd left his troubles behind in California, found a new paradise in Northern Michigan on his own, stayed on the *Fitzgerald* as Professor Tanner had advised him to restore his good name, and even managed to find a sweet girlfriend along the way, his life had never been better, and his twenty-second year seemed destined to be his favorite.

Tom Bentsen, for perhaps the first time in his life, would have had just one woman on his mind, Cindy Gagnier—the only one he'd met who could give him a run for his money, and make him forget the others. He had a lot to look forward to: getting back to his apartment in Traverse City, which he shared with John Hayes; comparing notes on this storm, since Hayes was going through it on the *Crapo* sailing back to Alpena that night; then going out on a double date with Hayes and his fiancé, Helen, to talk about the couple's wedding the following summer. Bentsen and his fiance, Gagnier, hadn't yet set a date, but he was prepared to serve as Hayes's best man. And who knows? He might even return to the Great Lakes Maritime Academy to complete his last semester and earn his degree. But no rush. He was making good money, and there would be time for everything else. All he had to do was get through this storm without losing his lunch. The winter would be easy.

Bruce Hudson's horizon looked a little different than it had when he'd returned to the *Fitzgerald* in September to replace his replacement, Patrick Devine. With Hudson's girlfriend, Cindy Reynolds, now pregnant back in Toledo and the two planning to move in together to raise the baby, Hudson knew a good portion of his future had already been laid out for him. But Cindy, God bless her, had okayed his cross-country trip with fellow deckhand Mark Thomas, and that was going to be a blast—maybe even more so now, knowing that it could be his last hurrah as a footloose young man. But he'd been salting away his paychecks, and could even return to Ohio State whenever he wanted. They could sort all that out in the long winter ahead. He and Thomas just needed to get into Hudson's Dodge Challenger and hit the road.

SHORTLY AFTER THE *Fitzgerald* radioed Columbia's home office Monday morning, she altered her trajectory across the lake by lowering her sights slightly from the little town of Marathon, Ontario, home to a few thousand people and a pulp mill, to a ghost town called Pukaskwa Depot, where the Pukaskwa River meets the eastern shore of Lake Superior. This was routine on the northern route, creating a line that would guide the *Fitzgerald* almost due east to Lake Superior's eastern coast.

The waves were now coming up directly behind the *Fitzgerald* in what sailors call a "following sea"—literally, a sea that follows the ships, with waves coming right up on the stern to give the ship a little extra boost. But a following sea also makes steering a challenge, like a car getting pushed from behind on icy roads.

When the *Fitz* neared Pukaskwa Depot, McSorley turned the *Fitzgerald* to starboard, a slow turn ninety degrees south, to start the third leg of the northern route—and the hardest.

Hard Turn South

Monday, November 10. 9:53 a.m.

TWO HOURS LATER THE *ANDERSON* FOLLOWED THE *Fitzgerald*'s lead and changed course too, turning slightly to due east, straight for the eastern shore of Lake Superior on the northern, Canadian side. Then at 11 a.m. the *Anderson* also made the sharp turn to the southeast, but unlike the *Fitzgerald*, which had sailed much closer to the Pukaskwa Depot on Superior's east coast before turning south, the *Anderson* made the turn about twenty-five miles earlier. By cutting the corners off *Fitzgerald*'s route, the slower *Anderson* cleverly took the "inside track" to keep the *Fitzgerald* in sight.

Now that the *Fitzgerald* was heading south toward Whitefish Point, the big waves coming across the full fetch of Lake Superior started hitting her broadside, the worst possible angle, because those waves roll the ship from starboard to port, then back again, every few seconds. With the *Fitzgerald*'s long, flat bottom, and all but nonexistent keel, she was perfectly designed to slip through the Soo Locks and St. Marys "rock cut" with no room to spare, and just as poorly designed to handle the big, broadside waves that were now coming after her.

Not long after both ships made the turn they were about to face another well-known adversary: the abrupt arrival of winter.

Conditions on the Great Lakes can change quickly and dramatically, and it's hard to predict the exact moment when they might turn dire. That was particularly true in the seventies, when sailors had to rely on more rudimentary technology to track the weather, and more fallible communications to receive timely weather reports. But even back then every-

GRANT AND WADE WALTON

The fourth of five children born on an Ohio farm, Grant Walton (left) and his younger brother, Wade, were desperate for a different life, and they found it on the Great Lakes. Grant dropped out of tenth grade to become an oiler, while Wade taught himself how to pass the engineer's tests. Wade's oldest son, Tom, also served on the *Fitzgerald* one summer, but only Grant was still on the *Fitz* in 1975. *Courtesy of the Walton Family*

BUCK CHAMPEAU

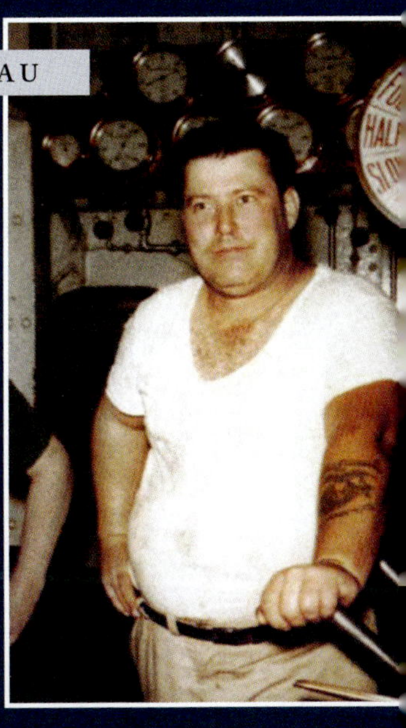

The oldest of five children, Buck Champeau was thirteen when their father died. Buck left school to help support the family, then joined the Marines, fought in Korea, and became an engineer on the Great Lakes. He accepted a demotion to third engineer to work on the *Fitz* because it was that special. He loved to dote on his only daughter, Debbie, buying her a special prom dress and a used Rambler. *GLSHS*

BLAINE WILHELM

Every day Blaine Wilhelm, a fifty-two-year-old oiler on the *Fitzgerald*, emptied his change into an old blue Maxwell House coffee can by his bunk bed. When he got home at the end of the season, he would spill the change on the table for his seven children. He loved to read, here with wife Ida, but he feared taking the test to become an engineer. *Courtesy of the Wilhelm Family*

With mom and dad, 1964. *Courtesy of the Hudson Family*

Ruth and Oddis Hudson had only one child, Bruce, born in 1953. He played trombone in his high school band, achieved the rank of Eagle Scout, and enrolled at Ohio State to study forestry. But he left school to become a deckhand and loved working on the *Fitzgerald*. *Courtesy of the Hudson Family*

Bruce Hudson (left) and fellow deckhand Mark Thomas (right and inset) planned to take Hudson's Dodge Challenger on a road trip to California after the *Fitzgerald* ended the 1975 shipping season in Toledo. Hudson vowed to then return to his pregnant girlfriend in Toledo and raise their child together. *Courtesy of the Hudson Family*

With the money he was making on the Great Lakes Hudson bought a 1974 Dodge Challenger, on which he stuck a Columbia Transportation sticker, the same logo that appeared on the side of the *Fitzgerald*'s stack. He was proud to work on the *Fitz*. *Courtesy of YouTube/History Mystery Man*

TOM BENTSEN

Tom Bentsen, with the red beard, was tall and skinny but carried himself with such confidence that women swooned. He dropped out of the Great Lakes Maritime Academy to become an oiler on the *Fitzgerald*, but still hoped to earn his engineer's license. His best friend John Hayes, in the sweater vest, had none of Bentsen's confidence, but excelled at the academy. He asked Bentsen to be his best man for his wedding in 1976. *GLSHS*

DAVID "COWBOY" WEISS

The third of four boys, David "Cowboy" Weiss seemed like a lost soul in Southern California, then he discovered northern Michigan and the Great Lakes Maritime Academy. He loved it all, and seemed to have found his passion—plus a girlfriend in the area who loved him back. *GLSHS*

Superior, Wisconsin's Burlington Dock No. 1, on the far right, was the world's biggest dock. The Allouez Steel Company sends tons of taconite via the overhead conveyor belt that runs 3.5 miles from its plant, straight down the dock's enormous chutes and into the ships' cargo holds. The *Fitzgerald* crewmen would walk a half mile "up the street" to the President Bar and Pay Less Liquors, where they had their last beers on November 9 before leaving the dock the next afternoon. *Roger LeLievre Collection*

ARTHUR M. ANDERSON

Gordon Lightfoot, an experienced recreational sailor, had been working on his ballad for months before he finally played it with his band. Incredibly, that first take proved the best and has played on the radio for decades. Lightfoot grew very close to the families, whom he always invited backstage. Here he's in the kitchen of the crews' quarters at Whitefish Point, talking with Aunt Ruth Hudson on her deathbed back in South Carolina, on November 9, 2015. It would be her last phone call. *GLSHS*

To honor their loved ones, the families of the victims decided to retrieve the bell, clean it up, and display it at the Great Lakes Shipwreck Museum at Whitefish Point, just seventeen miles from where the *Fitzgerald* lies today. *Roger LeLievre*

Aunt Ruth was determined to do everything in her power to ensure her only son, Bruce, would not be forgotten. Here she sits on the beach at Whitefish Point, gazing out at her son's final resting place. *Courtesy of the Hudson Family*

The SS *Edmund Fitzgerald* was built to last a hundred years, but now lies 530 feet beneath the surface of Lake Superior. *GLSHS*

one knew this basic truth: *The later winter comes, the angrier it arrives.* In November of 1975, summer left the stage much later than usual—and that spelled trouble.

"Every major storm on the Great Lakes, it's that same scenario," says former GLMA superintendent John Tanner. "Once you have snow on the Great Lakes, it calms things down. The snow moderates the weather.

"But what happens when you have a very mild fall is that winter gets held up. There's no snow. The day before the *Fitz* left Wisconsin was very warm, unseasonably warm. But right behind it was winter, piling up, ready to drop, like water behind a dam that's about to break.

"And when it does, *watch out*."

"For *Fitzgerald*'s storm," Michigan Technological University professor Guy Meadows adds, "the air-sea temperature difference was huge. This made the waves twice as big as forecast. Today we take that factor into account."

But not in 1975. Leading up to the *Fitzgerald*'s departure from Superior, Wisconsin, that Sunday, Lake Superior's water stood at forty-four degrees, unusually warm for a lake that often freezes in January, while the air temperature had been hitting seventy. Once the air temperature began to fall, it dropped fast, and then the cold air ushered in by the Alberta Clipper started pulling the warm water up—and now you've got serious trouble.

With the limited forecasting and communication systems available to Great Lakes crews in 1975, the men aboard the *Fitzgerald* were privy to only a few pieces of the picture, and had little sense that two storm systems were about to collide overhead. While the forecast had warned of worsening conditions, the information wasn't communicated clearly, strongly, or quickly enough to stop the *Fitzgerald* and other ships from setting out.

"It was November, and in November, stuff happens," says former *Fitzgerald* porter turned *Toledo Blade* columnist Tom Walton, whose uncle Grant served on the *Fitzgerald* in 1975. "Some of the ships get off the lakes to miss the storms. Some crewmen take early vacations to avoid it. But those guys on the *Fitz* wanted to go, so the *Fitz* goes."

Monday, November 10. 1:00 p.m.

After making the hard turn south the *Fitzgerald* had eleven miles to go before reaching Michipicoten Island—a seventeen-mile-long stretch of land that's left uninhabited during the cold months.

Now, with only a half dozen hours remaining before the *Fitzgerald* would reach the safety of Whitefish Bay, McSorley and his crew felt a cautious optimism. Every Great Lakes sailor knew the drill: just keep going, stay alert, trust your training and experience, and avoid unnecessary risks. In their years on Superior this approach had always carried them through, even on the roughest days. The first leg of the trip had been anything but smooth, but the *Fitzgerald* was holding strong, and leading the way—its customary position.

But now the debt that they had incurred by taking the long way to avoid the fetch across the middle of the great lake had come due. This third and final leg of the trip, almost straight south, would have the two ships running along Lake Superior's eastern shore, like swimming down the far wall of a pool. On this stretch they would catch the full force of the wind and waves that had been sweeping across Lake Superior, building size and strength for 350 miles, ensuring that the waves would be at their wildest and meanest precisely where these two ships were headed: Whitefish Bay.

Monday, November 10. 1:40 p.m.

After the *Fitzgerald* passed Michipicoten Island, she had twenty-five miles to go before reaching tiny Caribou Island, a tricky little spot of land with the dangerous Six Fathom Shoal in front of it, a patch that should always be avoided at all costs.

At this point McSorley radioed Cooper and mentioned that the *Fitzgerald* was "rolling some." For a freighter, "rolling" more than usual in the troughs of the broadside waves is a troubling sign, which raises questions about the extent and causes of the side-to-side motion. This confession also marked McSorley's first public admission that anything on the *Fitzgerald* was less than ideal—unusual for any Great Lakes captain, and exceedingly rare for the taciturn and competitive McSorley—which suggests that the ship's rolling was probably a significant issue.

With the toughest stretch ahead, the *Fitzgerald* picked a bad time to start rolling. At 1:50 p.m. the *Anderson* reported that winds had picked back up to fifty-eight miles per hour. The respite the two ships had enjoyed in the lee of the Canadian coast before turning south was over.

"We get to the northeast corner of Superior, and it's rough, but we're okay," remembers Barthuli, who was on the *Anderson* that night. "It doesn't turn to super shit immediately, because you have to get farther away from the land to get really beat up. You have so much cover from the coast, the size of the storm barely matters. But once we make the turn down the east coast and lose the lee of the land, about twenty miles out, we're just getting our asses kicked."

Barthuli recalls the disorientation he experienced that day while working below deck in the engine room, without a clear view of the waves crashing against the ship—a recipe for seasickness.

"If you're only looking around your engine room, the rolling and rocking back and forth doesn't make sense," he says. "The same room that was sitting perfectly still at the dock is now going up and down, back and forth. When your mind and eyes are in conflict, you get sick."

To stave off seasickness, Barthuli knew to look out the porthole whenever possible and focus on the horizon, but even that worked only so well.

"After a couple hours, you usually get used to it. It becomes 'So what?' But this storm—this was different. I'd never been in anything like it. You look out the portholes, and the main deck's six feet underwater half the time. When you're down, you're only seeing the top of the hatch crane [attached to the deck] sticking out of the water. Yeah, you're in some shit."

The expanding waves increased the ships' rolling and sent both vessels up and down and back and forth, which will strain any ship's basic mechanics. Each time a ship rises over a wave crest, the propeller lifts partially out of the water, spinning too fast in open air before plunging back into the lake and grinding down.

"The solution is simple," Barthuli explains. "Keep the screw [propeller] in the water. And you do that by checking the speed, slowing down, keeping it steady. It all goes smoother that way, and you don't break things."

While the crews fought to adjust to the conditions, each mile pulled them deeper into the two storm systems' relentless grip—but only the *Fitzgerald* was going full speed.

"We were about the same-sized ships," Barthuli adds. "We could go about the same speed. We were never more than a boat length apart on the first day, but by the middle of the second day, they're eight miles ahead, then sixteen. What happened?"

Barthuli knows the answer—because he witnessed it.

Sensing that their problems were multiplying, and that Captain Cooper had no intention of slowing down, the *Anderson*'s first engineer, Harry Ashcroft, came up with a simple solution—one that echoed the lesson John Hayes had learned watching his chief engineer, Norman Janusiewicz, handle their captain on the *Raymond Reiss* years earlier by ignoring his pleas for more speed. Barthuli was about to see that lesson put to use at arguably the most important moment of his life, and that of his fellow crewmates.

Unlike a car, in which speed is controlled by stepping on or letting off the gas pedal, the freighters' enormous engines—7,000 horsepower on the *Anderson* and 7,500 on the *Fitzgerald*—were complex systems which provided more than one way to adjust the speed.

"It's not a lawnmower or a go-cart," Barthuli explains. "Moving the throttle back and forth puts a lot of wear and tear on the steam valve. The valves don't like it. The throttle fluid erodes, too, which wears things out over time—or sometimes just by the next port—and it's expensive. So we don't usually mess with the throttle unless we're leaving or entering port, and speeding up or slowing down for good."

Instead, the engineers preferred turning on or off a number of nozzles, the spigots that direct steam into the turbines that propel the ship. Both the *Anderson* and *Fitzgerald* had twenty nozzles, arranged in specific groupings. Ten were housed in a large silver box, about the size of a small shed. If the ship was sailing, those ten nozzles were always in use, while the remaining nozzles could be activated in groups of six, three, and one. The various permutations allowed the engineers to vary power levels from ten to twenty nozzles, without touching the throttle and putting undue stress on the machinery. By opening or closing these groups of nozzles, the engineers could fine-tune their speed, all while sparing the system from overuse.

While they could open all twenty nozzles, "that's not efficient," Barthuli says. "You burn a lot more fuel that way, and you don't gain much. It might be worth it to the captain, but not to the chief, who has a fuel budget he has to watch, too. And if it's rough out there and you're pressing that hard, you risk screwing other things up.

"Seventeen nozzles is full power—more than enough."

When Barthuli's shift ended on Monday, November 10, he stayed in the engine room, sensing the worst was far from over.

"You'd think, *The ship's only going fifteen miles per hour, what's the problem?*" Barthuli explained. "Well, you've got thirty thousand tons of momentum riding on ten-foot waves, and it's hard to control. The water's slippery; the brakes aren't great. And now going too fast is a problem."

While the storm was hammering both ships, First Engineer Harry Ashcroft descended into the *Anderson*'s engine room, with a purpose. His crew knew the *Fitzgerald* was already miles ahead of them, and now passing Michipicoten Island, with no signs of slowing down on her way toward tiny Caribou Island and beyond.

Ashcroft didn't care. He calmly instructed Barthuli to dial back from seventeen to fourteen nozzles. But such was Ashcroft's confidence that he made these bold decisions without notifying Captain Cooper, or even his boss, the chief engineer.

"Harry looked right at us when he did it," Barthuli recalls. "To make sure we got the point."

Before long Captain Cooper noticed the *Anderson* was losing even more ground to the *Fitzgerald*, so he called down to the engine room.

"Cooper ain't happy," Barthuli says. "He's having a hemorrhage because he's losing the race! He's not thinking about survival. He's deathly afraid of losing a couple hours waiting behind the *Fitz* at the Soo. But the *Fitz* was going to Detroit. We're going to Gary. So it don't amount to nothing! But that's not how captains think."

Cooper demanded more power, shouting at Ashcroft, "You'll give me what I ask for!"

But Barthuli already knew the unspoken rule from John Hayes's story: *The captain gets what the engineer gives him.*

Harry Ashcroft knew it, too, and wasn't about to flinch.

"Will do, Cap," he replied, and ended the call. Then he looked straight at Barthuli again, without saying a word, to make sure he was paying attention. Ashcroft then said nothing to any of the engine crew, he changed nothing, and he walked back to his office.

A few minutes later, Ashcroft called Cooper back.

"Better?"

"Yeah, better," Cooper said.

Ashcroft hung up the phone, then gave Barthuli an inscrutable grin worthy of the *Mona Lisa*.

"Now, that's hanging it out there pretty far," Barthuli says. "Harry just disobeyed a direct order, with witnesses. If the captain figures out Harry's slowing her down against his orders, Harry'll be out for a week without pay. Maybe fired. Captain might even have you up on charges.

"That's a high price to pay, but what I learned that night is: *You gotta be willing to pay it.* Because if you do the smart thing you'll live to see another day. So will the crew. And so will the captain—even though he won't know why, and he'll probably think it's because of something *he* did.

"Harry might have saved my life," Barthuli adds, then thinks a bit more on it. "Probably did."

No one knows what Captain McSorley and the *Fitzgerald*'s engineers discussed that day, if anything. In another cruel irony, it's possible that the very respect and affection McSorley's men had for him would have made them less likely to push back on a request for more power, or to flat out ignore him, as Harry Ashcroft had done with Captain Cooper.

We know only this: The *Fitzgerald* ran past Michipicoten Island, then headed right for Six Fathom Shoal and Caribou Island, at full speed.

Crossing Caribou Island

Monday, November 10. 2:45–3:30 p.m.

THE TWO CAPTAINS KNEW THEY WERE STUCK IN A storm to remember, but they had no idea how much more would be coming after them—or from where.

According to Professor David Schwab's computer model, by 3 p.m. that Monday the average waves along Lake Superior's southern coast had built up to fifteen feet, and they were growing fast as the storm coming up from the southwest roared past Marquette and Munising toward Whitefish Point.

While the system out of the southwest carried warm, wet air across the southern shore of Lake Superior, the Alberta Clipper delivered a cold, dry front across the north—and the two were about to crash into each other with catastrophic consequences.

At 2:45 p.m., winter finally broke through right over the two ships, and with a vengeance. Suddenly heavy winds and thick snowflakes were flying around their pilothouses, severely reducing visibility—the greatest fear of a Great Lakes captain—while the cold air started freezing the water splashing on the windows and deck.

The *Fitzgerald* was now roughly fifteen miles ahead of the *Anderson*, or about an hour. Captain Cooper could still track the *Fitz* on radar and communicate by radio, but once the snow started flying no one on the *Anderson* could see the *Fitzgerald* any longer.

Normally there was no downside to being the lead ship, a position the *Fitzgerald* had worn well throughout her life. But leading this particular race came with a toll. While the *Fitzgerald* might win the competition to the Soo Locks, to do so she would also have to be the first to encounter every hazard ahead. The lake's waves, expanding across 350 miles of fetch and hitting the ships broadside, were the *Fitzgerald*'s to experience first. As she made her way south down the Canadian coast, and the protection of the lee receded mile by mile, the growing waves caused her to roll side to side with increasing violence.

THE TIMING OF winter's arrival was particularly cruel, striking just as the *Fitzgerald* was executing a "two-island slalom": first steering west and south around Michipicoten Island, then veering east past the treacherous Six Fathom Shoal, which lurks right off the northern tip of tiny Caribou Island. Navigating this area requires clarity and precision—two elements the *Fitzgerald* now lacked.

Lake Superior, which reaches a depth of 1,332 feet and averages 500 feet, is home to four hundred islands, each of which comes with its own hazards. But the area around Caribou Island might be the most dangerous on the entire lake.

Six Fathom Shoal is far more treacherous than it sounds. Six fathoms equals thirty-six feet, which in itself would make it perilous to sail over even in calm waters for a ship like the *Fitzgerald*, which stood thirty-nine feet tall and drafted twenty-seven and a half feet fully loaded in normal conditions—and these were far from normal conditions.

Six Fathom Shoal runs about two and a half miles long north to south, and despite its name in some places it's a mere eleven feet below the surface, just a foot more than the deep end of a backyard pool—not the kind of waters the heavily loaded *Fitzgerald* should have been attempting.

South of Six Fathom Shoal lies Caribou Island, which itself is no bargain. Spanning only 1.5 by 3.5 miles, and sitting just 3 miles north of the invisible Canadian borderline, Caribou Island is an unwelcoming little pile of dirt. A former hunting preserve abandoned decades before, the island has no infrastructure or trails, and is noted mainly for its insect-infested swamps. There is little incentive for a recreational boater or nature lover to stop here, and plenty of reasons not to.

For a freighter, getting anywhere near Six Fathom Shoal and Caribou Island is pointless at best, and reckless at worst. The island is so small it's simultaneously easy to avoid, and hard to see—offering only risk, and no reward. The only sensible response is to steer as clear from the shoals and Caribou Island as possible.

For a sea captain, Caribou Island's only redeeming feature was a lighthouse, but judging distance at night was notoriously tricky.

"You can see the light, but is it twenty miles out or ten?" Barthuli asks. "That night, I was doing 'gangway door' navigating: open the gangway door and take a look. It's crude, but sometimes it's all you've got. And that day you just couldn't tell."

BECAUSE MCSORLEY SO rarely took the northern route, he was also not nearly as familiar with the charts that covered the area. The large, detailed paper charts, about the size of a desktop, that he and his crew laid out to study in the chart room, were all they had back then to navigate that route.

The chart for Six Fathom Shoal and Caribou Island that McSorley used on this trip, the *1973 U.S. Lake Survey Chart No. 9*, sounded a lot more current and accurate than it actually was. The chart's fine print warned: "For data concerning Canadian areas, Canadian authorities have been consulted." The U.S. map, in other words, relied on the Canadian 1973 navigational chart—and it turns out the Canadian 1973 navigational chart had been based on Canadian surveys conducted in 1916 and 1919.

How much difference could that make? In 1976 the Canadian Hydrographic Service surveyed Six Fathom Shoal and found that it actually ran about one mile farther east than indicated by the chart McSorley was using. The U.S. National Transportation Safety Board (NTSB) later concluded that the *1973 U.S. Lake Survey Chart No. 9* was not accurate enough to present Six Fathom Shoal "even as a hazard," let alone the lethal one that it is.

That's trouble enough, but passing these obstacles would have been even harder if McSorley and his team had not been using Chart No. 9, as flawed as it was, in the first place. That may sound to land dwellers like an impossible mistake to make, but not to Great Lakes captains.

"When you approach Caribou Island, you use a detailed chart showing Six Fathom Shoal and other shallow points," explains longtime Great Lakes captain Tom Wiater, who is now the president of Central Marine

Logistics, which owns the *Edward L. Ryerson* and operates the *Wilfred Sykes*. "Once you're past those hazards, you switch to a larger-scale chart that shows Whitefish Point and Whitefish Bay, but Caribou Island disappears on that chart and so does Six Fathom Shoal."

In 1975, without GPS, if a captain operating in fifteen-foot waves and a blinding snowstorm through unfamiliar waters thought he'd already passed tiny Caribou Island, or wasn't near it, he might switch to the next chart too early, and thereby lose track of potential dangers the previous chart marked on the lakebed below.

"McSorley was a serious captain with lots of experience," Wiater says. "But after twenty-four hours with no sleep and the ship taking a beating, it's possible he, or a crewman, mistakenly switched charts too soon. That would explain a lot."

Wiater alludes to another possible factor: More than twenty hours of heavy, rolling waves had begun to affect McSorley's ability to think clearly, as it would for anyone.

"It's cumulative," says former engineer John Hayes. "After twenty hours of constantly going up and down, and left and right, your decision-making erodes, just like it would if you rode a roller coaster for twenty hours. Doesn't matter who you are. It gets to you."

The Navy's research on motion fatigue (as opposed to motion sickness) has found the effects so tangible that they can accurately predict the percentage of crewmen who will become effectively dysfunctional after each hour of turbulent seas.

"After too many waves," Michigan Tech professor Guy Meadows says, "anyone can become useless, like being drunk."

It's impossible to know exactly where the *Fitzgerald* sailed that day, but the *Anderson*'s Captain Cooper reported to authorities later that week that he and his wheelsman watched their radar screen in horror as the gray blip on a black background, representing the *Fitzgerald*, seemed to run directly over Six Fathom Shoal, then slip too closely down the east side of Caribou Island. (Cooper would later back off this claim by raising another possibility—that McSorley "either had a stress fracture or he bottomed out"—but he later repeated his original statement on video.)

"The *Fitz* took a different route than we did," Rick Barthuli says, "cutting much closer to Caribou Island—so close, she probably had to go over the shoals. That's dangerous any time, and more dangerous in a storm.

"Why the hell do you go across the shoals? Why do you even *come close*? It's a big lake. Not hard to avoid. I can only think: *Speed*! McSorley wanted to beat the *Anderson*. He's still racing. He's *still racing*!"

In fairness, Barthuli says, it wouldn't have taken much to cross over the shoals by mistake, too. "Good ol' navigational error," he says. "They had a kind of rudimentary GPS, but nothing like what they have now—just a weak version of it. Radar was what they depended on more than anything."

The radars didn't show depth, however, only surface objects. So Caribou Island would have appeared on *Fitzgerald*'s radar, but Six Fathom Shoal would not.

So why didn't Captain Cooper, seeing this scary scene unfold on the *Anderson*'s radar, get McSorley's attention and advise him to steer farther from Six Fathom Shoal and Caribou Island?

"On the one hand, a captain doesn't want to tell another captain how to run his ship," explains John Tanner. "It's part of the professional courtesy built into their roles, especially back then. But on the other hand, you'd think if Cooper knew McSorley was running too close to Six Fathom Shoal, he'd say *something*—'Hey, you're too close! Slow down and back off!' But there's no record of anyone communicating with McSorley. No warning."

Captain Tom Wiater confirms this. When the men on the *Anderson* watched the *Fitzgerald* run over the shoals, Wiater says, "it sounds like Cooper gave McSorley the 'silent dude' treatment. You watch a fellow captain make a mistake, but no one wants to tell another captain what to do, so they just go silent."

If the *Fitzgerald* did cross Six Fathom Shoal, it likely would have bottomed out, slamming thousands of tons of steel and taconite against sandstone bedrock at full force. The fact that McSorley never mentioned this in his radio conversations with Cooper might suggest it never happened—or it might simply reflect the unspoken code among captains: *Never admit your mistakes or your ship's problems to another captain, especially over an open transmission anyone can pick up.*

"Look, you gotta understand," Barthuli explained, "you don't put shit on the radio if you don't have to. Pride, ego, competitive edge—you want to win the race. And that radio's basically a party line. Once it's out there, it's out there for everyone to hear, and now you've given your rival your playbook. Even on the engineering side, you keep as much to yourself as you can. That's an ingrained habit for a pro like McSorley. You're just not gonna ask for help or tell them everything that's happening.

"Later that same night, some big waves hit our starboard lifeboat on the *Anderson* and crushed it flat. Think we told anyone about that? Of course not. Why would we?"

Seasoned sailors also maintain that, as hard as it is for landlubbers to believe, even running fully loaded at full speed the *Fitzgerald*'s crew would have been hard pressed to tell the difference between the concussive pounding of massive waves and the impact of bottoming out on the sandstone seabed.

"The guys down below wouldn't have even known they hit the shoals," Barthuli surmises, "because it would've felt about the same as plowing through a wave—just shudders and shakes, like a train pileup, over and over again. And the *Fitz* went another fifteen miles after that, so they probably would've figured, if they felt it at all, whatever that was must've been nothing to worry about."

Whatever happened during the *Edmund Fitzgerald*'s tight pass around Caribou Island, she sailed on, full speed ahead.

Cooper might not have said anything to McSorley, but he didn't hesitate to direct his wheelsman to make sure they didn't make the same mistake. The *Anderson* proceeded to go out of her way to avoid Six Fathom Shoal and Caribou Island. The extra time that route required seemed to be a small price, indeed.

Checking Down

Monday, November 10. 3:30 p.m.

WHEN THE *ARTHUR M. ANDERSON*'S FIRST MATE, Morgan Clark, entered the ship's pilothouse for his watch, he reported winds of fifty miles per hour. Bad, but still manageable.

All the *Anderson* had to do now was cover the remaining sixty miles, rocky as they were, to Whitefish Bay. But the *Anderson* was having problems of her own.

"By the time we were near Caribou," Cooper later said, "we were beginning to take considerable water on deck with a following sea, and by the time we were clear of [Caribou Island] the seas were coming across our entire deck. It was in this area when we had damage to our starboard lifeboat [crushed by waves]. . . . I estimated that occasionally we had a sea up to twenty-five feet. We did not know about the lifeboat until we arrived in shelter as no one was permitted on deck."

Cooper's difficulties were quickly put in perspective when Captain McSorley radioed Cooper at 3:30 p.m.

"*Anderson*, this is the *Fitzgerald*," McSorley said. "I have sustained some topside damage. I have a fence rail laid down, two vents lost or damaged, and a list. I'm checking down."

McSorley was asking Cooper to catch up to the *Fitzgerald*. Cooper agreed without hesitation, and McSorley knew Cooper's word was good. McSorley might have been racing to the Soo Locks, but they were veteran captains who scrupulously followed the unwritten code of the sea: *You look out for each other until everyone reaches safe harbor.*

When McSorley said, "I'm checking down," he was telling Cooper that the *Fitzgerald* was closing some nozzles to slow down from sixteen miles per hour to twelve or thirteen. With that, the race was officially over.

This moment marked McSorley's third departure from his aggressive instincts: first, opting to take the longer northern route across Lake Superior; then dropping behind the *Anderson* for several hours Sunday; and now slowing down to wait for the *Anderson* to catch up.

For McSorley, asking Cooper to catch up and guide the *Fitzgerald* home was no small concession. It implied that, possibly for the first time in McSorley's sterling career, he now doubted his ability to get his ship into port alone. Survival had officially overtaken speed as McSorley's paramount objective.

As with all McSorley's decisions, twenty-eight men and their families depended on him to make the best ones—but that pressure was nothing new. His response to it was, however. Throughout this journey McSorley's decision-making would alternate like a toggle switch between his usual boldness and a newfound caution, but each choice would be laced with its own risks. In a painful twist, McSorley's uncharacteristic restraint on this voyage would at times lead the *Fitzgerald* into greater peril than his usual hard-charging approach might have.

McSorley conveyed his problems in the calm, cool cadence all Great Lakes captains used, akin to airplane pilots soothing their passengers during turbulence. The Coast Guard investigation reported that none of the *Anderson* crew who listened to McSorley's call "felt that it indicated any real concern about the welfare of [the] *Fitzgerald*."

McSorley's nonchalant tone might have tempted the listeners on the *Anderson* to dismiss the issues he mentioned as insignificant, but they were anything but. Some of the problems he was confessing suggested far greater damage, and the severity of others was bound to get worse over time.

What exactly had happened to the *Fitzgerald*, and how threatening was it?

We may never fully know what occurred when the *Fitzgerald* passed Six Fathom Shoal, if anything, but McSorley's message offers some clues.

The "topside damage" McSorley mentioned—the broken fence, the damaged ballast tank vents, and now a list—indicated a range of potential problems, some more serious than others, but each with the possibility of compounding.

The *Fitzgerald*'s architects equipped the ship with fourteen ballast tanks, seven on each side of the keel. Each tank had two vents, for a total of twenty-eight, which ran from the ballast tanks through the tunnels up to the deck. These vents, positioned along the deck's edge between the cable fence and the hatches, stood about a foot tall—the perfect height to catch an inattentive crew member's shin while walking to the galley—and each one was capped with a mushroom-shape cover designed to keep water from pouring down the pipe into the ballast tanks below.

But now, with at least two vent covers either damaged or torn off, each wave could flow directly down the vents and into the ballast tanks. Because the *Fitzgerald* was riding fully loaded, the ballast tanks were empty. The vents weren't particularly large, however, only about eight inches to a foot in diameter, and thus a few damaged or missing covers could send only so much water into the ship, not nearly enough to threaten its stability.

The most likely culprit behind the torn vent covers was the raw force of the waves, which intensified steadily throughout Monday afternoon. The damaged vents, therefore, were more a symptom than a cause of the *Fitzgerald*'s problems.

The fence being ripped off the deck, however, raised more troubling questions.

The fence consisted of three steel cables, each a half inch thick, that ran ten inches apart horizontally, and outlined the entire deck. The cables looped through holes drilled into flat steel posts that were about three feet tall, two inches wide, and half an inch thick. The posts were bolted into the deck every few feet. The cables were set close enough to each other to keep adults from being swept off the deck, though sailors could easily go *over* the three-foot-high fence, especially in a storm.

When McSorley told the *Anderson*, "I have a fence rail laid down," he meant more than he said. While a missing fence certainly made the already-hazardous deck more dangerous, especially in a snowstorm, a damaged fence by itself wasn't catastrophic. Thanks to the tunnels that ran the length of the ship on both sides, just below the deck, anyone who needed to walk from one end of the ship to the other would have no trouble doing so. Besides, in a storm the crew should have been taking the tunnels anyway. That's what the tunnels were for. So a fence being ripped out wouldn't have mattered much the rest of the way to Whitefish Bay, and once in port, the crew could have readily repaired it.

But the fallen fence railing is more significant for what it might tell us about the potential causes of the damage. Yes, it's possible that the violent seas could have taken out the fence posts, but they were designed to let water pass through with little resistance. Waves rarely take out cable fences, so it's reasonable to consider other causes.

One possibility is "hogging" (the opposite of sagging), in which the center of a ship is lifted by a huge wave while its bow and stern are drawn downward by the their own immense, unsupported weight. Unlike sagging, which causes the fence cables to slacken, hogging pulls the cables downward with the weight of both ends of the ship. When a fully loaded ship weighing seventy-five million pounds hogs, the stress can easily snap half-inch cables and pop fence posts out of their holds.

The ship could also have hogged if the *Fitzgerald* had bottomed out at Six Fathom Shoal, particularly if the middle of the hull hit the bedrock; such an impact would have been more than enough to snap the cables and fence posts, just as surely as hogging from a wave would have.

The second possibility could be related to the most worrisome issue McSorley mentioned, almost in passing: the *Fitzgerald*'s list, or tilt.

A Great Lakes freighter can suffer a list for a number of reasons, including ice freezing unevenly on the deck. But since the snow had just started on Superior, it's very unlikely enough ice had accumulated on the *Fitzgerald*'s deck to cause it to list significantly.

Another way to create a list is to take on tons of water. If the damaged but small ballast vents could not have admitted water in catastrophically large quantities, an open gangway door or cargo hatch, or a damaged ballast tank at the bottom of the ship, could have done the job. If so, it would be even worse news that the water was entering unevenly, which would exacerbate the list over time.

If the ship was taking on water, how was it getting in?

The simplest way for water to enter the *Fitzgerald* would be through one of the oval-shaped steel doors installed by the dozens throughout the ship. When properly secured these doors were watertight, locked on both sides with three latches, known as "dogs." However, if even one of these doors had been left unsecured—a common enough oversight—or if a wave dislodged it, the three-by-six-foot opening would allow tons of water to flow into the holds. Worse, the force of the water coming in could make shutting the door nearly impossible. But given the severity of the storm, First Mate McCarthy almost certainly would have made sure the crew was extra vigilant in dogging all the doors well before the worst of it arrived.

A greater threat would be the twenty-one cargo hatches that dominated the *Fitzgerald*'s 729-foot deck. To fully seal them, deckhands Bruce Hudson, Mark Thomas, and Paul Riippa had to secure 68 Kestner clamps per hatch, totaling 1,428 clamps—a taxing task on a good day. If they had clamped only the corners, as they did during calm summer trips, or if the relentless waves knocked enough clamps loose, a major wave could have torn off a hatch cover or two and the amount of water then rushing into the cargo holds would have quickly overwhelmed the ship. This scenario—unsecured or damaged cargo hatches—would later become the Coast Guard's primary theory.

But there was another devastating possibility: Water might have come up through the bottom of *Fitzgerald*'s steel hull, which was almost an inch thick and weighed forty pounds per square foot. Not easy to crack, but if the *Fitzgerald* had scraped an underwater rock formation or one of the lakebed's countless wrecks, or smashed against the sandstone bedrock of Six Fathom Shoal, that could have allowed water to rush in by the tons.

If such a collision compromised enough ballast tanks on both sides of the keel, and fore and aft, the *Fitzgerald* would become evenly weighted down with water. This wouldn't create a list, but so much water coming in would surely sink the ship. But if the impact breached only a few of the fourteen ballast tanks on the starboard side, the uneven flooding would create a list that McSorley's four ballast pumps—powerful as they were—would be helpless to overcome.

Worse, once water got inside the cargo hold, it would be virtually impossible to get it out, because the *Fitzgerald* was carrying taconite, which is two-thirds clay. When wet, each pellet absorbs enough water to increase its weight up to 7 percent, or four million pounds, while the thirty-foot-high piles of taconite would hide another fifteen million pounds of water between the pellets, rendering the pumping system all but useless. The water would be coming in faster than the pumps could get it out in any case.

As a result, if water was coming into the *Fitzgerald*, the crew would not have known it. Veteran sailors also maintain that if the *Fitz* was taking on water, the effect would have been sufficiently gradual that it's possible that few if anyone onboard would have noticed it, minute by minute.

HOWEVER THE WATER got in, the *Fitzgerald*'s list was a serious problem, one that would only get worse until the crew could get into port and take action to fix it. For such a heavy ship, a slight list would make steering difficult, even in calm waters—and these were far from calm waters. Listing also pushed the *Fitzgerald* deeper into the water, especially at the bow, and in greater danger of being pinned down and sunk by one of the bigger broadside waves.

That, in turn, increased the danger of the *Fitzgerald* capsizing, since it would already be tipping heavily to one side; and because it was becoming heavier and more sluggish by the minute, it would also be more vulnerable to getting crushed or cracked by a rogue fifty-foot wave, like a wounded animal limping before its predators.

For all the *Fitzgerald*'s mounting troubles, the mere fact that McSorley could make the call confirmed that at least one critical component on the ship remained intact: the pilothouse. That was no small bright spot, as it would take only one well-aimed forty- or fifty-foot rogue wave to smash through the pilothouse windows and send tons of freezing water into the ship. Such a breach could flood the bridge in short order and take out McSorley, his wheelsman, and everyone else in the pilothouse—an Achilles' heel all the big freighters shared.

But exactly what was causing the list, McSorley didn't say. That he was using only two of the *Fitzgerald*'s six bilge pumps, adding that "everything appears all right," suggests he might not have known himself. Whatever the source, if water was entering the *Fitzgerald* in quantities large enough to make the seventy-five-million pound ship list, it's unlikely the culprit was something as minor as a couple damaged vent covers—and just as unlikely that whatever the breach was, it could have been stopped before the *Fitzgerald* found safe harbor.

If McSorley had concluded that enough water was entering his ship to create a pronounced list, he would have grasped that he, his crew, and his ship's ever-declining buoyancy were now in a race against not the *Anderson*, but time itself; and that the longer McSorley waited for the *Anderson* to catch up, the more water his ship would take on, the more pronounced the list would get, and the deeper the ship would sink into each successive wave.

Unbeknownst to McSorley, the *Fitzgerald* was also engaged in another race, this one with the center of the southwestern storm, which was marching along Superior's southern border and headed straight for a rendezvous with the *Fitzgerald* near Whitefish Point.

When McSorley told Cooper he was going to "check down," he was doing the right thing—*based on what he knew*. But that decision would give two possible threats a head start: the water that was likely flooding into his ship by the tons, and the center of the storm rushing to the entrance of Whitefish Bay.

Of the countless trips McSorley could have played it safe, when he finally traded confidence for caution, it might have been at the exact wrong time.

"The Worst Seas I've Ever Been In"

Monday, November 10. 4:00 p.m.

When the Alberta Clipper delivered the snowstorm at 2:45, it naturally hampered visibility—a big enough problem in itself. By 4 p.m., it turned vicious. A fierce wind blew thick, wet gobs of snow sideways, creating an opaque white shield in front of the pilothouse.

Captain Cooper, now running an hour behind the *Fitzgerald*, later reported waves "up to twenty-five feet" when the *Anderson* neared Caribou Island.

Since the *Fitzgerald* was now about twenty-five miles and an hour and forty minutes beyond the coordinates whence the *Anderson* had made that report—that much closer to the safety of Whitefish Bay, but also the storm's epicenter—the waves the *Fitzgerald* was now experiencing were probably worse than the twenty-five-footers the *Anderson* had reported. Because the *Fitzgerald* had only 11.5 feet of freeboard, and probably less by the hour due to its compounding problems, those waves would be more than enough to wash green water—entire waves, not just the spray—over the *Fitzgerald*'s deck.

The combination of the snowstorm, the rising waves, and a slowly sinking vessel threatened to turn the waves running across the *Fitzgerald* into layers of ice, which would add tons of weight to a ship that couldn't afford to sink any lower.

Every ship has a center of gravity, which pushes down on the ship, and a center of buoyancy, which pushes up. Naval architects and engineers work hard to get this balance just right, whether a ship is fully loaded or sailing light. The tension between these two forces is the key to what's called a "righting moment" (or RM)—the point at which a rolling or tilting ship begins to return to an upright position. John Hayes likens it to those little plastic birds that dip their beaks in water and then, after a long pause, start to rise again. That's what a "righting moment" looks like.

"I've been on tankers taking on hundreds of tons of water, maybe thousands, as waves sweep over the deck," Hayes says. "That's the 'green water'—the solid wave under the white foam, and that's what does the heavy damage. Think about how six inches of water flooding your basement can crack a four-inch-thick cement floor."

The pressure waves put on a ship is many times greater. A wave that is thirty feet tall by sixty feet wide carries about 400 tons of water, or 800,000 pounds—heavier than three locomotive engines. Now imagine that much water crashing onto the deck and burying the ship every eight to ten seconds.

"You feel like there's no way it can take that—it's just too much," Hayes says. "Then you watch the ship slowly lift itself out, exactly like it's supposed to, with tons of water cascading off both sides. It's mesmerizing. You wonder: *How did they design it to do that?*"

When a ship's centers of gravity and buoyancy are balanced, the ship is stable and sound. This allows the ship to recover from each roll smoothly, without snapping back too quickly—like an anvil suddenly crashing down on the opposite end of a seesaw—or too slowly, which feels sluggish, and scary.

"But ice throws all those calculations off," Hayes says. "Any captain will tell you that when ice builds up on deck, you get top-heavy, and stability starts to fail. It's too likely to roll to the side, and then it takes too long to roll back."

Ice can also push the nose of the ship down, a phenomenon called "pitching," which makes the ship dive lower and deeper into each wave, so the bow takes progressively longer after each wave to resurface. If, while all this is happening, a wave at the back of the ship lifts the stern, that will push the ship's nose down even further—similar to how the "human wheelbarrow" picnic game works: The higher the "wheelbarrow's" legs are lifted, the more likely their head will end up driving into the ground.

When a ship's bow is plowing ten feet under the wave in front, and its stern is being lifted by a second wave coming up behind it, that leaves the ship's midsection in the air, unsupported, and in danger of sagging—and that can cause the ship to crack, especially with a few extra tons of ice pushing down on it.

Short of cracking, these combined factors would have made the *Fitzgerald*—already listing to starboard—significantly harder to steer.

For all the unknowns, this is virtually certain: If the *Fitzgerald*'s captain and crew could have voted at that moment to give back the additional tons of taconite the Coast Guard had permitted in exchange for 39.25 inches of freeboard, the verdict would have been unanimous.

Monday, November 10. 4:10 p.m.

In addition to the roughest storm anyone onboard had ever seen, many of the man-made devices McSorley and his crew relied on starting failing them, often at the worst possible moment.

At 4:10 p.m. Captain McSorley radioed Captain Cooper on the *Anderson* with more bad news: The *Fitzgerald*'s short- and long-range radars were both out of commission. For the remainder of the journey McSorley would be sailing without any electronic means to determine where they were or where they were going.

But this raises the question: *When* did the *Fitzgerald*'s radars fail? Before McSorley navigated Six Fathom Shoal and Caribou Island, or after? If it was the former, that would help explain why the *Fitzgerald*, with nothing to gain, might have sailed right over Six Fathom Shoal and run far too close to Caribou Island.

In addition to the *Fitzgerald*'s mechanical failures piling up, the odds of human error were increasing with each mile, too. We can't say how much McSorley's navigational abilities were compromised by the snowstorm, the encroaching darkness, losing both radars, using an outdated chart or even the wrong chart, his relative lack of familiarity with the northern route, and the mental fog getting thicker from sleep deprivation and motion fatigue, but some combination of these factored into this final leg.

In the same conversation, McSorley reiterated to Cooper that he would continue to slow down until the *Anderson* had cut the *Fitzgerald*'s lead from about fifteen miles to ten, then rely on the *Anderson*'s radar and directions to guide the *Fitzgerald* safely into Whitefish Bay.

Monday, November 10. 4:39 p.m.

The bad news was as relentless as the waves.

At 4:39 p.m. McSorley contacted the U.S. Coast Guard station in Grand Marais, Michigan, on Lake Superior's south shore, to ask whether the station's lighthouse and navigation beacon—which bounced the *Fitzgerald*'s radio signal back to the pilothouse to show the captain where to steer—were operational. The Coast Guard replied that high winds had knocked both systems out. Neither would provide any help that night.

Through remote controls based at its Sault Ste. Marie station, the Coast Guard made several attempts to restore the Whitefish Point lighthouse—the one every Great Lakes sailor longed to see—which sits roughly fifty miles east of Grand Marais. Their efforts appeared to pay off when the lighthouse started working again around 5 p.m., but a few minutes later the lighthouse went black once more, and its radio signal fell silent. Two hours later, at 7:05 p.m., the Coast Guard's Group Soo, based in Sault Ste. Marie, issued a safety broadcast notifying vessels of the outage.

Monday, November 10. 5:01 p.m.

With no operational radar on deck, and no lights or radio beacons on shore to guide her, the *Fitzgerald* radioed the *Anderson* for a position report. The *Anderson*'s first mate, Morgan Clark, had just returned from the galley and answered the call. At 5:01 p.m. Clark informed the *Fitzgerald* that she was now fifteen miles ahead of the *Anderson* and thirty-five miles from Whitefish Point. That meant the *Fitzgerald*'s refuge was about two and a half to three hours away, depending on her speed, but perhaps four or more if she continued to wait for the *Anderson* to catch up.

Despite the *Fitzgerald*'s onslaught of problems, Whitefish Bay still seemed to be very much within reach.

Sometime between 5 and 5:30 p.m., McSorley attempted to radio nearby ships to confirm the Grand Marais USCG station's report that the Whitefish Bay lighthouse had fallen dark and silent. Cedric Woodard, the captain of a Swedish ship called the *Avafors*, responded.

> WOODARD: *Fitzgerald*, this is the *Avafors*. I have the Whitefish light[house] now in sight but am still receiving no beacon. Over.

The radio beacon was out, but the light was on. This marked a small but significant piece of good news for McSorley, the first he had heard all day. He could be excused for believing the legendary lighthouse might just be enough to guide the *Fitzgerald* home.

> MCSORLEY: I'm very glad to hear it.

But Woodard's report would prove false. McSorley soon learned that the oldest operating lighthouse on Lake Superior was still dark after all. With the snowstorm now creating a near-total whiteout, the *Fitzgerald*'s radars dead, and the Whitefish Bay lighthouse invisible, McSorley was effectively sailing blind, as though he and his crew had traveled back in time to 1848—the year before the Whitefish Point lighthouse first opened—when a captain's only means of escaping a severe storm were his wits, luck, and prayer.

The next exchange between Woodward and McSorley hints at something else.

> WOODARD: The wind is really howling down here. What are the conditions where you are?
>
> MCSORLEY: [undiscernible shouts overheard] *Don't let nobody on deck!*

The reasons for McSorley's urgent order are at once obvious, and mysterious: With bigger and bigger waves washing overboard, the boat heaving up and down twenty-five feet and more, the cold air threatening to turn water into ice on deck, and the ship's cable fence knocked out, anyone who actually dared to step out onto the deck could be swept away and swallowed by the lake in an instant.

But what's not clear is *why* McSorley would have to shout that command in the first place. What made it necessary to bark this order—something McSorley almost never did, by all accounts—when any member of his crew would have already understood the folly of setting foot on deck? Why would a crew member venture out in such conditions?

Years later a potential answer would arise when a team of videographers searched the floor of Lake Superior and noted a small but revealing detail: They found the *Fitzgerald*'s forward winch to have 120 feet of its one-inch-thick cable pulled out.

Like most ships in its class the *Fitzgerald* had three winches fore, and three winches aft. These were basically large spools, about four feet high and four feet wide, with three hundred to five hundred feet of one-inch steel cable coiled around the drum. When the *Fitzgerald* was in port, a deck officer or watchman would push the lever to let the cable out so a deckhand could use it to tie the ship up to the dock. When they were ready to push off, he'd pull the lever to pull the cable back in. Simple stuff.

Tom Wiater, a licensed captain who now owns the *Ryerson*, which had been one of the *Fitzgerald*'s top competitors, asserts: "These winches don't release by accident. They're fixed. Not even the worst storm could make them let go of the cable accidentally."

So why would anyone want to unspool 120 feet of cable in the middle of a horrible storm? The most plausible reason might be this: The *Fitzgerald*'s deck had already begun to crack, and the crew, in a desperate attempt to tie the ship together, had let out the cable to loop it around timberheads on both sides of the splitting deck.

"It's a very seafaring solution," Wiater explains. "People have done it before, sometimes with success. But to try something like that, you have to have a seasoned mate, one who's seen it done."

The veterans on the *Fitzgerald* had probably heard about previous crews' desperate attempts to keep their ships together, and the veterans on the *Fitzgerald* might have known how to do it.

While there are still more questions than answers, Wiater's theory would explain two things: Why the cable had been unwound, and why

McSorley interrupted his call to Woodard to shout, *"Don't let nobody on deck!"* If any crew members had been on deck to attempt the maneuver, McSorley's command would have sent them scurrying back to safety, abandoning the attempt.

"So maybe that's where the idea dies," Wiater speculates. "But one hundred twenty feet of cable? Someone made that call. And it had to be a veteran mate making that decision, not a deckhand. If that's true, then we have a clue: The ship was already coming apart before it went down, and the men on board knew it."

Another clue: Investigators found one of the pilothouse doors latched open.

"Those doors don't latch themselves," John Tanner says. "Sometimes you latch it open for ventilation on a hot day. But to latch it open like that when you're rolling in heavy seas? Never seen that. The only reason to do that is if they were supervising the deck crew."

Taken together, McSorley's shouted command, the released cable, and the door latched open all raise the odds that at least some crewmen knew their ship was cracking, and were taking measures, however risky, to keep it together—before McSorley abruptly stopped the operation. These three clues do not offer conclusive proof for this theory, but add weight to it.

WOODARD: What's that, *Fitzgerald*? Unclear. Over.

Realizing the mounting gravity of his situation, McSorley set aside the seasoned captain's stoic façade. With the *Fitzgerald* taking on water, battered by relentless waves, and possibly coming apart at the seams, McSorley knew he needed to inform Captain Woodard of the severity of both the weather and the state of his ship. In McSorley's forty-five years on the Great Lakes he had seen just about everything—but never all this, and certainly not all at once.

MCSORLEY: I have a bad list, lost both radars. And am taking heavy seas over the deck. One of the worst seas I've ever been in.

WOODARD: If I'm correct, you have two radars.

MCSORLEY: They're both gone.

Although McSorley couldn't be accused of downplaying the situation, his captain's pride still held back a measure of truth: This wasn't merely "one of the worst seas" he'd faced—it was the worst he'd ever seen, by far, and it was likely the worst anyone had seen on the Great Lakes since at least 1913. In fact, the wind and waves reported on November 10, 1975, both exceeded those of 1913. *This* was the storm of the century, and McSorley had sailed right into it.

How McSorley framed his ship's troubles also reveals something. Two hours earlier, when he had first mentioned his problems to Cooper, he referenced the ship's listing almost in passing, at the very end, after emphasizing the topside damage, the fence being "laid down," and "two vents lost or damaged." Now, sometime after 5 p.m., McSorley led with the list, describing it as "bad"—a simple adjective that a veteran like McSorley wouldn't use lightly. The list must have worsened since he last spoke with Cooper, as lists will do, and McSorley now seemed to consider that his primary concern.

While the *Fitzgerald* waited for the *Anderson* to catch up, the water flooding into the *Fitzgerald* wasn't waiting for anyone.

"Never Saw That Before, or Since"

IF YOU ASK THE PEOPLE WHO WORKED FOR DECADES AT the Mackinac Bridge—which is about eighty miles south of Whitefish Bay—what the roughest night they ever saw on the Great Lakes was, they won't hesitate: November 10, 1975.

Despite the steel grating in the bridge's middle section that allows wind to flow through, on that night eighty-five-mile-per-hour winds caused its hard surface to roll up and down in sickening ten-foot waves, as though the concrete and steel were rubber and the gods were playing "crack the whip." Perhaps more unsettling, the storm also made the bridge sway thirty-five feet side to side, like a snake slithering through the grass. Architect David B. Steinman had designed the bridge to do all these things, but it had never been tested like that before.

For one of the few times in the Mackinac Bridge's history, they closed the bridge that night.

Monday, November 10. 6:00 p.m.

Captain Cooper recalled that around 6 p.m. that night the *Arthur M. Anderson* was sailing about fifteen miles southeast of Caribou Island. Once she had left the tiny island's protective lee, she got hit broadside with a series of waves twenty-five feet or higher.

With the *Fitzgerald* still ahead of the *Anderson*, the *Fitz* had no place to hide. It was a mathematical certainty that those same waves, and more, would find the *Fitzgerald*, if they hadn't already.

After Rick Barthuli witnessed the *Anderson*'s first engineer Harry Ashcroft check down the engine from seventeen to fourteen nozzles, against the express orders of Captain Cooper, then lie to Cooper about it, Barthuli went back up to his quarters. His cabin was considered a good one because it was a little farther from the engine than the others, and therefore not quite as hot. With no air-conditioning on the *Anderson*, that mattered. But on November 10, 1975, the heat was not Barthuli's main concern.

"That night, all the windows are closed shut," he says. "It's snowing sideways. Looking out the window from my room, you could tell she was taking a beating, but it was coming from the stern. The waves were chasing us, pushing us.

"I think I saw twenty-five- to thirty-foot waves, biggest I've ever seen, but you really can't tell. You're in them! You could see the top of the waves getting blown off by the wind—like they were mountain ranges being strip-mined—so you couldn't tell how tall they were. But it was one hell of a night, I can tell you that. No one out that night can ever forget that one."

ON THE *FITZGERALD* the discomfort and inconvenience the waves delivered at breakfast had been replaced by graver concerns by dinner. With twenty-five-foot waves and more, nobody onboard was walking anywhere they didn't have to, and certainly not on the deck. The tunnels were the only option.

What's it like being on a ship in thirty-foot waves?

Imagine standing in your kitchen at home, and your house suddenly rises thirty feet, then eight seconds later it falls thirty feet—and it keeps going like that for hours. Then it starts rolling back and forth, too, and then tilts to the left in a sickening list.

In such conditions all but the most important tasks are suspended. Laundry, maintenance, painting—all postponed. But some jobs become more important, including the engineers' and oilers', who must monitor the engine and other equipment more carefully because now it's all under duress, and more apt to fail at the worst possible time. Despite working on a ship going up and down thirty feet every few seconds, they still had to check the levels and measurements on all their machines, and more frequently, too, to ensure the machines didn't run dry, burn out, and leave them all stranded in the middle of Lake Superior.

The men in the pilothouse weren't taking any time off either, but doing everything they could to help Captain McSorley get through this mess.

"I think there's a good chance the *Fitzgerald* crew was more scared than the *Anderson*'s," Barthuli says. "Because they already have the list, they know they have some damage somewhere. The ship is not intact, but they're still basing their mindset on their career experiences. We've always made it, right? So we'll make it this time."

No doubt that's exactly what the veterans were telling the rookies on board. Panicking was not an option. Whatever thoughts the crew might have had—about returning to their families, their girlfriends, or their muscle car waiting at the Toledo dock—they would likely have kept those to themselves, and tried to focus on the horizon and keep their lunches down.

"In that stuff, you're not gonna sleep anyway," Barthuli says. "I saw two gigantic waves, but how big, it's hard to judge when you're in that kind of crap. You don't stop to pull a tape measure out. You can't tell much."

But Barthuli could tell that one of their two lifeboats, the one on the starboard side, had been flattened like a beer can.

"Crushed flat by the waves," Barthuli says. "Those things are made of solid steel, not aluminum. Never saw that before, or since. There was no fixing it."

THANKS TO RECENT research, scientists have been able to calculate what conditions were like that night.

Michigan Tech's Guy Meadows measures "significant wave height" by taking the tallest third of the waves and averaging them. Significant wave height closely mirrors what our eyes see and our brains take in, to assess the waves that could do the most damage.

But there's more to it. "When you're out in a major storm," Meadows says, "the Rayleigh distribution tells us one in a thousand waves will be 1.9 times bigger than the significant wave height. One in five thousand will be 2.15 times bigger, and one in ten thousand waves will be 2.23 times the significant wave heights.

"So if you're out there on Lake Superior for twenty hours, where the waves are coming every six to eight seconds apart, you're going to see nine thousand to twelve thousand waves. And that means you're going to see at least one wave *twice as big* as the significant wave height you're seeing on a regular basis."

That's what's called a rogue wave.

"So if you're already facing twenty-five-footers," Meadows continues, "that means you're going to see some forty-footers, a few fifty-footers, and maybe a sixty-footer out there somewhere coming your way. So when you hear the sailors talk about thirty-footers on Lake Superior that night, and a rogue wave twice as big, those aren't stories. That's what the data tell us was happening. We know that now, and we see it in our buoy data."

The *Fitzgerald*'s crew was not only seeing twenty-five-footers coming at them throughout the afternoon, which were already ten feet bigger than any waves most of the sailors had seen in their long careers; according to Meadows's data and the Rayleigh distribution, they would have seen forty-seven-foot waves ten times, fifty-four-foot waves two or three times, and possibly even a sixty-footer or two—the height of a six-story building.

This is when the *Fitzgerald*'s unique characteristics—the modular construction, the use of welds over rivets, the extraordinary flexibility of the hull, the lowering of the Plimsoll Line, and whatever damage she might have suffered over Six Fathom Shoal—would all be tested by the once-in-a-lifetime conditions on Lake Superior. The fully loaded *Fitzgerald* had only 11.5 feet of freeboard on a good day, and this was not a good day. The question no longer was whether the *Fitzgerald* could withstand such relentless punishment, but how long before she succumbed.

"We Are Holding Our Own"

Monday, November 10. 7 p.m.

CAPTAIN MCSORLEY KNEW THIS WAS NO TIME TO stand on ceremony.

While he tried to coax his listing, wounded ship toward Whitefish Bay, he tried several times to alert people on shore that his ship was in trouble—serious trouble. But he often couldn't get through; and when he did, the receiver often couldn't help—or wouldn't.

At one point McSorley managed to contact the Coast Guard station in Sault Ste. Marie, called Group Soo, only to reach Petty Officer Philip Branch, a rookie watchman who repeatedly failed to grasp the urgency of McSorley's situation. He did not pass on McSorley's concerns, offer any help, or alert anyone else at the station.

By 7 p.m., Captain Cooper informed McSorley that the *Anderson* could once again track the *Fitzgerald* on her radar and that the *Fitzgerald*'s directional line was close to where it needed to be to reach Whitefish Bay. Cooper assumed the *Fitzgerald* would soon reach safe harbor.

Cooper also told McSorley that the *Fitzgerald* was now just ten miles ahead of the *Anderson*. In just two hours, by intentionally slowing down, McSorley had let the *Anderson* close the gap between them by five miles. But in the process, he had also unwittingly allowed the epicenter of the incoming storm system to beat the *Fitzgerald* to their rendezvous point in front of Whitefish Bay, while his ship filled with water.

On shore and at sea, people were now clocking winds gusting up to one hundred miles per hour—powerful enough to knock over vans, trucks, and mobile homes. David Schwab's computer model of the storm shows the area around Whitefish Bay shifting from calm to ferocious in just minutes.

When Schwab plugs the *Fitzgerald*'s locations and times into his model, a haunting pattern emerges: "When the storm was at its worst," Schwab says, "the *Edmund Fitzgerald* got to the worst possible place, at the worst possible time."

IF CREWS ON the Great Lakes could have picked one captain to get them through a once-in-a-lifetime storm, they would have voted for McSorley in a landslide.

"McSorley was a heavy-weather captain," says Tom Walton, who had served as a porter on the *Fitzgerald* in 1963, along with his father Wade. His uncle Grant, an oiler, was on the *Fitzgerald* that night. "He had that reputation as somebody who could take care of his ship in bad weather and get where he had to go. But I don't think he'd ever seen, even in forty years, anything quite the match of what he saw that night. You had these colliding weather systems. As the day wore on it just got worse and worse.

"I mean this is—what do they call it?—the storm of the century. It's a phrase that's misused, and overused, I think. But if ever there was a time when the cliché 'storm of the century' applied, this was it.

"How ironic at the very end of McSorley's career, he gets the worst storm he's ever seen."

Monday, November 10. 7:10 p.m.

At 7:10 p.m., a mate on the *Anderson* radioed McSorley to tell him to watch out for a small boat heading in the opposite direction toward the *Fitzgerald*'s path, then asked how he and the *Fitzgerald* were doing.

> *ANDERSON* MATE: *Fitzgerald*, this is the *Anderson*. Have you checked down?
>
> MCSORLEY: Yes we have.
>
> *ANDERSON* MATE: *Fitzgerald*, we are about ten miles behind you, and gaining about one and a half miles per hour. *Fitzgerald*, there is a target [another ship] nineteen

miles ahead of us. So the target would be nine miles on ahead of you.

McSorley: Well, am I going to clear?

Anderson mate: Yes. He is going to pass to the west of you.

McSorley: Well, fine.

The fact that the *Anderson*'s mate mentioned a small boat passing by the *Fitzgerald*, that was not having any particular difficulty, is another indication the *Anderson* did not perceive the danger the *Fitzgerald* was in.

Anderson mate: By the way, *Fitzgerald*, how are you making out with your problem?

McSorley: We are holding our own.

Anderson mate: Okay, fine. I'll be talking to you later.

"I came to the wheelhouse shortly after this call," Cooper later testified. ". . . After this call we kind of relaxed, looking forward to the shelter of Whitefish Bay. Sometime later, one half hour to forty-five minutes, we were trying to pick up the *Fitzgerald* . . . and thought we could make out a target once in a while about seven miles [away] which coincided with the speed at which we had been closing.

"We then tried to contact the *Fitzgerald* again almost continuously and received no answer."

Just like that, the *Fitzgerald* had turned invisible, and gone silent.

McSorley's simple, stoic statement, "We are holding our own," are the last known words from the *Edmund Fitzgerald*.

XIV

THE SAILOR'S CODE

They Would Do It for Us

JUST MINUTES AFTER THE *ARTHUR M. ANDERSON* LOST track of the *Fitzgerald* the waves settled down to twenty feet, the snowstorm suddenly stopped, and visibility miraculously cleared. Captain Cooper and his crew had little doubt that the *Fitzgerald* would pull through.

After the *Anderson*'s last talk with McSorley at 7:10, the crew estimated the *Fitzgerald* had been running about nine miles ahead of them—close enough to see her on the radar, and possibly to track her running lights by sight. When the *Anderson* crew couldn't spot the *Fitzgerald*'s lights with binoculars, or find her on radar, Captain Cooper still didn't fear the worst. He assumed the *Fitzgerald* had suffered a power outage, common enough in heavy seas, and advised his crew to keep an eye out for a silhouette on the horizon.

When *Anderson* first mate Morgan Clark tried to radio the *Fitzgerald* and got nothing, he then attempted to contact other ships in the area, and again received no response. This raised the possibility that the problem was not that the *Fitzgerald*'s communication equipment had failed, but the *Anderson*'s. To test that theory Captain Cooper radioed the *William Clay Ford*, which immediately confirmed that the *Anderson*'s signal was loud and clear—good news and bad news.

Monday, November 10. 7:39 p.m.

The *Arthur M. Anderson* was still fighting her way to Whitefish Bay, just as persistently as she was trying to contact the *Fitzgerald*. Having confirmed that the *Anderson*'s radio was in fine working order, Captain Cooper called the Coast Guard station in Sault Ste. Marie, Group Soo, on channel 16, a wavelength reserved for ships in distress.

USCG Petty Officer Philip Branch, the same Coast Guard agent who had largely dismissed Captain McSorley's worries when he had radioed earlier, interrupted Cooper's concerns to tell him to call back on Channel 12 so they could keep Channel 16 open for ships in distress. Unless Petty Officer Branch was listening to Captain McSorley himself on Channel 16, it is hard to imagine which ship on the Great Lakes might have had more distress to report than the *Anderson*, whose captain was trying to alert anyone who could help that he couldn't locate one of the largest ships on the Great Lakes. Cooper must have been mystified by Branch's instructions, but he did as directed—only to get no response on Channel 12.

Cooper, still focused on getting his own ship safely into Whitefish Bay, and with a heightened sense of urgency due to *Fitzgerald*'s problems, was growing desperate to reach the *Fitzgerald*, too. While sailing his ship through high seas Cooper repeatedly radioed the USCG's Channel 12, as he'd been told, and finally got through at 7:54, a delay of fifteen minutes—more than it takes for a human body in Lake Superior to succumb to hypothermia, freeze, and drown.

When Petty Officer Branch answered on Channel 12, Cooper told him the *Fitzgerald* had been in trouble and seemed to be out of communication. Branch responded by telling Cooper to keep an eye out for a sixteen-foot boat lost at sea—a clear sign that Branch had utterly failed to grasp the gravity of Cooper's message. (The small craft would make it safely to shore.)

After Cooper and his crew spent another exhausting half hour battling to keep their ship afloat while rolling side to side in the twenty-foot troughs, at 8:25 p.m. Cooper again radioed the USCG station at Sault Ste. Marie to report that he still hadn't heard or seen the *Fitzgerald*, and it had now been more than an hour. After receiving no particular response, Cooper radioed USCG's Group Soo again at 8:45, and again at 9:03, when he got Petty Officer Branch once more. Cooper, now far more concerned about the *Fitzgerald* than his own ship, was direct: He now believed the *Edmund Fitzgerald* was "missing." This was Cooper's most ominous radio transmission thus far.

"I am very concerned with the welfare of the steamer *Fitzgerald*,"

Cooper told Branch. "He was right in front of us experiencing a little difficulty. He was taking on a small amount of water and most of the upbound ships have passed him. I can see no lights as before, and I don't have him on radar. I just hope he didn't take a nosedive."

Captain Cooper's concerns once again went nowhere.

During one of the many investigations that followed the *Fitzgerald*'s sinking, Branch had his chance to explain his responses to McSorley's and Cooper's calls about the *Fitzgerald*'s increasingly dire situation.

"I considered it serious," he testified, "but at the time it was not urgent."

Branch's answer defies explanation. He received no censure for his actions on November 10.

WHILE COOPER HAD been trying to get through, in every sense of the phrase, to Petty Officer Branch, someone at the Coast Guard's Group Soo had the good sense to try to radio the *Fitzgerald*. When that failed, they contacted marine radio station WLC in Rogers City, Michigan, to try to reach the *Fitzgerald*—but again, the *Fitzgerald* did not respond.

By 8:40 p.m., some ninety minutes after the *Anderson*'s last exchange with McSorley, the USCG's Group Soo was beginning to share Captain Cooper's concerns about the *Fitzgerald* and sent a message to the Coast Guard rescue coordination center in Cleveland, Ohio. Just one minute after Group Soo relayed the news to the Cleveland rescue center, the officers there contacted the Coast Guard air station in Traverse City to send out a search plane. Then Group Soo alerted the Canadian rescue center in Trenton, Ontario, located on the east end of Lake Ontario some five hundred miles from the Soo Locks, to inform them of the *Fitzgerald*'s situation.

The Coast Guard's motto is *Semper Paratus*, which means "always prepared." Unfortunately, the Coast Guard's best-positioned unit to conduct search and rescue efforts for the *Fitzgerald*, Group Soo itself, was willing but unprepared. The *Naugatuck*, one of the USCG's ice-breaking tugboats based in Sault Ste. Marie, had been docked before the storm for routine maintenance. The Coast Guard hurried to get the *Naugatuck* ready, but since she was prohibited from going out in winds over sixty knots (sixty-nine miles per hour), the Coast Guard gave her strict instructions to stay within Whitefish Bay, which was relatively safe and already well patrolled by other ships. Wherever the *Fitzgerald* might have been that night, Whitefish Bay was probably one of the few places on Lake Superior they could safely eliminate. But the *Naugatuck* could not complete that duty either because another mechanical failure forced her back into the dock until 9 a.m. the next day.

Group Soo, the *Fitzgerald*'s best hope, would be sitting this one out.

Monday, November 10. 8:59 p.m.

The *Anderson* slogged along, rocking back and forth and smashing down with each colossal wave, but she continued to make steady progress toward Whitefish Bay. After a full day spent fighting the worst storm of their lives, the *Anderson*'s captain and crew never did experience the great relief of seeing the Whitefish Point lighthouse welcoming them to safe harbor. Still, they did manage to coax their ship across the threshold of Whitefish Bay in fifty-five-mile-per-hour winds at 8:59 p.m.

They scanned the horizon for a little island in the middle of Whitefish Bay, barely on the Canadian side, called Ile Parisienne. An uninhabited island that runs five miles north to south and one mile across, its most important feature is a lighthouse at the southern tip. Ile Parisienne also serves as the call-in point for ships heading downbound into the Soo Locks. Once a ship reaches Ile Parisienne it's permitted to call in to the lock master, who gives the ship its place in line. Because ships cannot change their position once the lock master assigns them their number, Ile Parisienne ends the race from Superior to the Soo Locks.

When the *Anderson* reached Ile Parisienne, the tortoise officially got there first, after all.

But they would not celebrate beating the faster *Fitzgerald* to Ile Parisienne, and securing the *Anderson*'s spot in line for the Soo Locks ahead of her rival, as the crew's triumph was quickly extinguished by their worries over the *Fitzgerald*'s fate. Before the *Anderson* had even dropped anchor the USCG told Cooper what he already knew: The *Fitzgerald* was missing.

"I was in the mess room when I heard," Rick Barthuli says. "Doesn't take long. Word spreads through the ship like lightning. And then, everything changes."

If the radio on the *Anderson* had suddenly crackled to life and Captain McSorley's steady voice had come through, assuring everyone the *Fitzgerald* had made it to Whitefish Bay, Cooper's night would have been over, and he and his crew could have finally relaxed, even in the heavy waves still buffeting their boat in the bay. But if no one could find the *Fitzgerald* by sight, radio, or radar, Cooper knew that would immediately raise a deeply uncomfortable question: Should the *Anderson* leave the hard-won safety of Whitefish Bay to go back out and look for the *Fitzgerald*—or lay anchor, and count her blessings?

Four centuries of Great Lakes shipping have witnessed untold numbers of sailors and elite Coast Guard teams risk their lives to pull off dramatic rescues. But the lakes have also seen too many heroes head into troubled waters only to sacrifice their own lives. The odds of finding a missing ship, especially one as big as the *Fitzgerald*, are much lower than the odds of drowning in the effort.

No one said it, but it was understood: At this point, anyone attempting a rescue would probably not be looking for the *Edmund Fitzgerald*, which had almost certainly sunk somewhere along the last miles of her route. Instead, they would be looking for a few freezing survivors hanging on for dear life in a flimsy raft. The men in Whitefish Bay knew the stories of the *Bradley* in 1958 and the *Morrell* in 1966, and how the three sailors from those two wrecks never would have survived if brave sailors and Coasties hadn't risked their own lives to go find them.

These were the tales they shared late at night for the rookies. It's a safe bet every single sailor, young and old alike, had imagined himself clutching one of those rafts, soaked and shivering, bobbing up and down in twenty- and thirty-foot waves, wondering if they would ever see their parents, their wives, or their children again. They knew their last strand of hope would be the knowledge that, yes, somewhere out there, some stranger would gamble his own life to save theirs.

The decision to go back out in a horrible storm to look for a troubled vessel no one could find was not made on paper, and certainly not derived from rational self-interest, except in this regard: If you ever expect someone to come for you in your hour of desperation someday, you have to go look for them—no matter the odds. But when the question—*Will you go?*—is actually put to sailors at the worst possible time, and the decision has to be made on the spot, without any analysis, it's not self-interest that motivates a captain to say yes. It's an impulse some sailors have, and others don't.

Captain Charles "Chuck" Milradt, the commanding officer of Group Soo, asked Captain Cooper the question he'd hoped not to hear.

> SOO CONTROL: Roger, well, again . . . do you think you could come about and go back and take a look in the area?
> COOPER: I'll go back and take a look, but God, I'm afraid I'm going to take a hell of a beating out there on it . . . I'll turn around and give it a whirl, but God, I don't know. I'll give it a try.
> SOO CONTROL: . . . That would be good, if you could turn around and head out that way . . .
> COOPER: Soo Control, do you realize what the conditions are like out there?
> SOO CONTROL: [no answer]
> COOPER [AGAIN]: Soo Control, you *do* realize what the conditions are out there?

Milradt didn't answer Cooper's question, but we can: He had no idea.

But then, how could he? No matter how outlandish the conditions were at Group Soo, land is land, water is water, and waves are waves. Cooper had already been out on the water, fighting the biggest waves he would ever face, while Milradt and company were safely on land. Even with waves crashing *over* their buildings on shore, they hadn't seen what Cooper had seen, or experienced the fear he had felt for his men and himself.

Now they were asking Cooper and his crew, in a 767-foot-long ship still weighed down with twenty thousand tons of taconite, to do what the Coast Guard, which was equipped with boats specifically designed for rescues and crews highly trained to execute them, would not be doing: go back out to look for a ship that couldn't be found.

"I was reluctant to go, really I was," Cooper confessed years later in a video interview. When Commander Milradt had told Cooper, "'There's a ship on the bottom out there,' I felt like saying, 'That could be two if I go back.' But, I finally decided I'd go out."

Before Captain Cooper had even laid anchor he turned the *Anderson* around and plowed back out toward the Shipwreck Coast, the most dangerous stretch of the Great Lakes, during the storm of the century, to look for a ship he knew could not be found.

"WHEN WE GOT into Whitefish Bay the storm's still shitty," says former *Anderson* engineer Rick Barthuli. "From where I was in the engine room, it seemed like it hadn't diminished at all. Then the Coast Guard asks Cooper to go back out. He didn't tell us, but we knew we were going out. Know why? The mess room. Cook knows everything.

"Everybody goes, 'Ohhh shit.' We knew how bad it was. Cooper might have hesitated, but we didn't. We hadn't even anchored yet, but once we heard the *Fitz* was missing, we knew we had to go out.

"We knew Cooper could have lost the *Anderson* that night, with us on it. But not going back out? No. Going back out *was* a really bad idea, but there wasn't anyone debating it on board.

"I knew it was the *Fitzgerald*. I think we all did. But that night I didn't know Tom [Bentsen, John Hayes's best man to be] was onboard the *Fitz*. I didn't know [fellow GLMA student David "Cowboy"] Weiss was on the *Fitz*. I didn't learn who was on the *Fitz* for a week.

"But that wasn't why we went."

When Barthuli learned that Bentsen was on the ship, he says, "We knew the odds weren't great that Tom somehow survived, but I figured if anyone in the world could beat the odds, it would be Tom, because he was an odds beater. But the odds ultimately didn't matter. That wasn't the point. You go back out because that's what you do—and they would have done it for us. Guaranteed.

"Everyone's awake. No one was sleeping—not in that storm. Then you can feel it: We're coming about. We're going out. This is it."

Having cheated death once, it seemed insane to put their lives back on the table just a few minutes later and throw the dice again. It was not only the sailor's code that forced them back out, but the hope that somehow, somewhere, there were freezing sailors clinging to a raft, hoping beyond hope that someone was coming to save them. The odds might have been long, but everyone knew stranger things had happened—with the survivors from the *Bradley* and *Morrell* as proof.

"Cooper went back out," says GLMA Superintendent Tanner. "Didn't surprise me at all. Not one bit. Top-notch guy. And the crew was the same way. 'Let's go.'

"There's an unwritten code. Oh, absolutely there is. When someone is in trouble out there, you do whatever you can. You just have to. They couldn't just stay on the sidelines. Of course at that time no one really knew where the *Fitz* went down, and it was dangerous, and they knew that, too.

"But they went."

"We Have to Go Out, but We Don't Have to Come Back"

THE *ANDERSON* WAS THE FIRST SHIP GROUP SOO COMMANDER Chuck Milradt asked to go back out, but not the last.

His list encompassed virtually every sizeable ship in or near Whitefish Bay that night. Of those, only the *William Clay Ford* and the *Hilda Marjanne* initially accepted the mission, and the *Hilda Marjanne* turned back to Whitefish Bay within thirty minutes.

"The *William Clay Ford* was already at anchor," Barthuli says, "and they *still* pulled up and went out. That's even more noble. They're heroes, in my book."

John Tanner knew the *Ford* skipper, Don Erickson, a native of Ontonagon, in Michigan's Upper Peninsula. As a teenager Erickson lied about his age to enlist in the Navy, and emerged a decorated World War II veteran. He was the kind of guy Tanner fully expected to take his ship back out—and he did.

"First class," Tanner says, with a respectful nod.

Commander Milradt also asked upbound saltwater ships *Benfri*, *Nanfri*, and *Avafors*, which were all near where the *Fitzgerald* had made its last radio contact with the *Anderson*, to "reverse course and assist in the search," the Coast Guard later reported. "All three replied that they did not believe they could reverse course without hazard to their vessels, because of the severe weather conditions."

"There were some salties that refused to go out," Barthuli says. "Yeah, they were cowards, but they weren't stupid. And I can't say that I blame them. I think some were empty and didn't have enough ballast to make them really seaworthy, so they were really going to get the shit kicked out of them. But then I guess we knew on the *Anderson* we were going to get the shit kicked out of us, too, and we went."

If any ocean-going sailors were tempted to condescend to the Great Lakes sailors, they thought better of it that night. The Great Lakes had once again earned the respect of the salties.

THE *ANDERSON* TURNED to leave the security of Whitefish Bay at about 9 p.m., along with the *William Clay Ford*. After Group Soo followed up its initial plea by sending out "urgent broadcasts" at 9:45 and 10 p.m., those two ships were soon joined by the *Armco*, *Reserve*, *Roger Blough*, *William R. Roesch*, and *Wilfred Sykes*, which had caught up to the *Anderson* after stopping in Thunder Bay, Ontario, on the first day, plus three Canadian ships: the *Frontenac*, *Joan O. McKeller*, and *Murray Bay*.

Going headfirst into the wind and waves took these ten ships a few long hours to get back to where the *Fitzgerald* had last been heard. But the worst was still to come.

What the sailors feared most that night was not going out into that historic storm, but turning around to come back. Whether these ships found the *Fitzgerald* or some desperate men in a raft or not, at some point the captains would have to perform the scariest maneuver of the night, and probably their careers: turning their big ships around in the huge waves, and going broadside against them while the waves breached the deck. Every sailor onboard every ship that was going back out already knew that the turn could capsize, break, or simply drown their ship.

"Turning a big ship around in a storm is *very* dangerous," John Tanner says. "Because you're in the trough—rolling between the waves—and all stability is compromised. During that turnaround you're at the mercy of forces you don't control. And it's harder at night, because you can't see the waves well enough to determine which one is the smallest to turn on. So you just have to guess, and go."

"When you make that turn, everything on board that's not secured is going to get trashed," John Hayes adds. "Whatever is in your room is going to get tossed to the other side: TVs, books, everything. In the engine room your tools are going to stand out from the wall at ninety degrees—if they don't go flying themselves. There's a 'dread factor' too, because you know what's coming."

Those who heard the call received one minor break on their way back out.

"It was actually calmer going into the lake than it had been going into the bay," Rick Barthuli says. "Going back out, we were smashing into the waves: bam, bam, bam! Okay, that's bad. But you knew we were going to take a horrible beating—and we did. The hard part is making the turn. The waves are bad, but the trough is worse, and to turn, you have to go down into the trough, but then you have to have enough power to claw back out of it."

Given the towering waves, performing a routine "zigzag" search grid was impossible. The ships could only go out to the last coordinates the *Fitzgerald* was known to be sailing, execute a harrowing turnabout, then return to Whitefish Bay. The entire trip would take about five to ten hours—and that was if all went well.

Did Barthuli remember that turnaround? He gives a grim, dry chuckle.

"You kidding? Everything is sliding off everywhere. Take your books off the bookshelf, make sure your TV is tied down. Yeah, I remember it."

Was he scared? Barthuli takes the question seriously. After pondering it for a few moments, he finally says, "*Concerned*. Nobody had a life jacket on. Wouldn't do you any good anyway. The cold water would have you dead in five minutes."

Barthuli isn't being brave, but honest.

"Sailors, the ones who last, are adrenaline junkies," he explains. "That's what we signed up for. When a crisis gets worse, some folks get calmer. That's what happens on a ship, or on a plane, if they're any good. I dated a few nurses. Same thing."

After an hour of turning—rocking and rolling, praying they would pull out of each trough—the *Anderson* started smashing into waves again, surfing on top of them and diving into them. That's when the *Anderson* crew knew they had made the turn successfully, and were heading back to Whitefish Bay.

They were relieved to have survived the rescue mission, but they also knew they had come up empty-handed. Even with their search lights working across the waves, they hadn't seen any survivors floating up and down in the distance, frantically waving their arms and yelling to be rescued, or even flares. No, nothing except a shattered lifeboat bobbing on the water, which they retrieved. It was the *Fitzgerald*'s.

The ship the *Anderson* had been trying to catch for two days had vanished.

WHILE THE COAST Guard's Group Soo struggled to get a ship ready to go out on Lake Superior to search for the *Fitzgerald*, the Coast Guard's Duluth station 350 miles away heard the call.

On Monday night the sailors on the USCG *Woodrush*, which had just returned to Duluth the day before from its two-week trip collecting buoys on Lake Superior, were enjoying a rare full day off for the entire crew. Some of them had gone to the local bowling alley, but Michael Zronek and three mates who rented an apartment on Duluth's hillside were settling in to watch Monday Night Football. They ordered some pizza and picked up plenty of beer: Old Milwaukee ("The good stuff"), which fit any budget.

Monday Night Football, then in its sixth year, was still a novelty. Before cable TV, ESPN, and Thursday Night Football, this was your only chance to see an NFL game outside of Sunday. For the crew of the *Woodrush* it was one of their few chances to see any game, since they usually couldn't pick up a TV signal once they were out on Lake Superior. Broadcast on Duluth's local ABC station, the game featured the Kansas City Chiefs playing the Dallas Cowboys, with Frank Gifford calling the play-by-play and "Dandy" Don Meredith and Howard Cosell providing color commentary.

At 7 p.m. CST, Zronek and friends had just hunkered down when a chyron ran across the bottom of the screen: "All crew members of the USCG *Woodrush* to report to the ship." Just a few seconds later their phone rang, with someone from their USCG unit on the other end.

"We had no idea why we were being recalled," Zronek says. "Never happened before, so we thought it was a drill. We didn't know if we were even going out."

Zronek's orders: "Get in uniform, find food, supplies, fuel."

After a few weeks on Superior the *Woodrush* was out of almost everything, as expected. Since Zronek was the man in charge of supplying the ship, that was his problem now, and not a small one. On a Monday night in Duluth in 1975 there weren't any all-night big box stores to ransack, so Zronek had to beg, borrow, and steal from the Coast Guard station and then the lighthouses on Wisconsin's Apostle Islands to get everything from canned casseroles to toothpaste and toilet paper, and enough of all of it to last at least a week, and who knew how much longer?

In contrast to the balmy weather the *Woodrush* crew enjoyed when they were coming home the day before, while passing the *Fitzgerald* on her way out, when they reported to the *Woodrush* Monday night at around 10 p.m. CST, Zronek recalls, "Man, it was raining cats and dogs, wind howling, huge waves. That was in *port*—and Duluth is protected, too. The boat was moving, and I mean *really* moving, and it was tied up. It was hard just to get up the gangway to the ship."

They were still missing a half dozen sailors they couldn't reach, but Captain Jim Hobaugh made the command decision to leave without them. Only when the *Woodrush* had cleared Duluth's break wall did Hobaugh reveal their mission: They were headed to Whitefish Bay because, he said, "The *Fitzgerald* is in trouble."

"That's all we knew," Zronek says. "We'd seen the *Fitz* before, many times, and I'd taken pictures of her when we were out icebreaking one time. She was still the biggest name on the Great Lakes."

Captain Hobaugh added one more thing, "the same line that we'd been hearing from day one in boot camp," Zronek says. "Captain said, 'We have to go out, but we don't have to come back.'

"That means we're honor bound to try to save them, but don't screw it up, or we'll go down too.

"So we have to go out. That's an order."

The Word Goes Out

BACK IN TWO HARBORS, MINNESOTA, FORMER *FITZGERALD* deckhand Craig Ellquist was thinking about his friends on the ship that night.

Al Ruberg, who owned Al's Dairy in Two Harbors, had persuaded Ellquist in March of that year to spend his summer delivering milk instead of returning to the *Fitzgerald*. Ellquist agreed, but visited with his *Fitz* friends whenever they were in town, and still thought he might get back on the ship the following season.

When Ellquist, nineteen, and Ruberg finished all their deliveries on November 10, they got in Ruberg's truck, a red International Harvester Scout, and stopped at the parking lot of Betty's Pies overlooking Lake Superior. Ruberg was not a drinker, so they decided to park there "just to listen to the radio and bullshit and look at the lake," Ellquist says. Ruberg turned the Scout's lights on so they could see Lake Superior better, and watch the waves crashing over the rock cliffs.

"We'd never seen waves like these," says Ellquist, a Two Harbors native.

Ruberg said, "Wow, you're probably glad you're not on the *Fitz* tonight!"

"Nah, these boats can handle this kind of weather," Ellquist replied, and he spoke from experience. "This is no big deal for them."

Then the news anchor came on the radio: "Breaking news: the *Arthur M. Anderson* has reported the *Edmund Fitzgerald* has been out of contact."

That was the first Ellquist had heard of any trouble, but he still wasn't concerned.

"Well," Ellquist said to Ruberg, "I think their radar probably isn't working properly, but it'll show up. They'll find it. They'll be all right."

"I wasn't that worried," Ellquist recalls. "Not that night."

Ellquist went back to his parents' home in Two Harbors, and slept soundly.

THAT SAME NIGHT Canadian singer-songwriter Gordon Lightfoot was working on his next song in the third-floor attic room of his Toronto home. A favorite of Bob Dylan, who was not known for praising his peers, Lightfoot, already considered one of Canada's greatest songwriters, would be covered by everyone from Elvis Presley to Sarah McLachlan.

But even as Lightfoot had notched eleven top-hundred U.S. hits—including "If You Could Read My Mind," "Sundown," and "Carefree Highway," all of which hit number one on the American contemporary chart—he had been battling alcohol and drugs. In 1973, after ten years and two children, he divorced his first wife, a Swede named Brita Ingegerd Olaisson, who had been the inspiration for "If You Could Read My Mind."

About the only places Lightfoot felt truly comfortable during this tumultuous time were his third-floor attic room, where he composed his songs, and on stage, where he performed them.

On Monday night, November 10, he recalled, "I already had a melody in my mind. It was from an old Irish dirge that I heard when I was about three and a half years old. I think it was one of the first pieces of music that registered to me as being a piece of music. That's where the melody comes from, from an old Irish folk song."

From its origins, the piece Lightfoot was working on was about as elemental as a song can be. He didn't have any lyrics yet, because he didn't have any idea what the song was about.

He took a break at about 10 p.m. to go down to his second-floor kitchen and get a cup of coffee, when his thoughts started to drift to the Great Lakes. Lightfoot was an experienced Lake Superior recreational sailor who'd raced in the rigorous Port Huron-to-Mackinac Island regatta. That night, he remembered, "The wind was howling even in Toronto, and I went back up to the attic thinking, 'I wonder what it's like up on Lake Superior.' It must've been awful."

Lightfoot climbed the stairs back to his attic and resumed working on his sea shanty, waiting for the words to arrive.

A WEEK OR so earlier Ernest McSorley and Silver Bay Reserve Mining foreman Don Frericks had sat down for lunch aboard the *Edmund Fitzgerald*, as was their habit whenever the *Fitzgerald* loaded in Silver Bay. McSorley had told Frericks that he and his crew planned to end the season with an extra trip the following week from Superior, Wisconsin, to Zug Island, so McSorley could apply his bonus to his wife's health care.

On Monday nights Don's son Doug, fourteen, and his friends attended Junior Rifle Club. Their shooting range ended where a twenty-five-foot cliff overlooking Lake Superior began. On Monday, November 10, "the wind was *howling* that night," Doug Frericks says. "Just incredible. The waves were hitting the cliff so high the spray was going over it and hitting the clubhouse, where we were."

When Doug got home he couldn't wait to give his father his report: "Dad, the lake is just going *crazy*!"

When Don Frericks got home after a hard day's work he liked to sit on the couch with his beefy left arm on the arm rest, watching TV. On Mondays that meant Monday Night Football on Duluth's ABC affiliate, WDIO. Just a beat or two after Doug's words left his mouth, local anchor Dennis Anderson interrupted the game. Described by northern Minnesotans as "our Walter Cronkite; if he said it, that's it," Anderson's voice was the most trusted in the area.

"We have breaking news," Anderson said. "The *Edmund Fitzgerald* is lost."

Big Don Frericks didn't shock easily. His son had seen his father, a "big brick wall of a man," cry only once, after Don's father died. But this news sent Don reeling.

Thinking of Captain McSorley, Don Frericks protested, "I just had lunch with him!" It couldn't be true.

"Dad never showed emotion," Doug says. "He didn't cry. He never cried. And then you see him crying at this. Later he'd say, 'I wasn't crying.' But he had tears flowing down his face. No hiding it."

WITHOUT ANY OFFICIAL word coming from Columbia to the families, word spread via a few brief reports on WDIO in Duluth and radio stations WSOO in Sault Ste. Marie and WLC in Rogers City, Michigan. But no one could confirm anything more than the simple fact that the *Edmund Fitzgerald* had been reported missing.

Families started calling families. Although most crew families knew only a few of their husband's, father's, or son's colleagues, and fewer phone numbers, support groups grew spontaneously among those with a connection to the ship, and they started swapping numbers. Anyone who had a sailor on the Great Lakes who hadn't called home that night knew their loved one could be in grave danger. All the families could do was watch the news, call anyone they knew, wait by the phone, and hope and pray. It wasn't much.

Just up the road from the Frerickses' home in Silver Bay, Nolan Church's wife Thelma was at home with Michael, seventeen, the youngest of their five children.

After the family adventure in Duluth, when Nolan insisted on buying all the Church women something nice at the mall followed by a Chinese dinner, his daughter Bonnie Church Kellerman drove back to Rockford, Minnesota, and started preparing for the fifth birthday of her oldest child, Deanna, which fell on November 11, 1975. Bonnie was busy wrapping presents in their living room while her husband watched Monday Night Football. Then their phone rang.

Her sisters, Marilynn and Debbie, had returned to their families in Two Harbors. When Marilynn walked into her home with her luggage and packages, her husband, Steve, was also watching Monday Night Football. As she took her boots off in their foyer, she thought she caught someone interrupting the game with breaking news: The *Edmund Fitzgerald* was missing. She dropped her bags and walked into the living room.

"What did they just say about the *Fitz*?"

"You're just hearing things," Steve replied. "We just dropped your dad off!"

But a few seconds later their phone rang. It was Marilynn's aunt Dorthea, who told Marilynn that her mom, Thelma, needed Marilynn at the family home in Silver Bay as soon as possible. Then Dorthea explained why: Her husband, Erling Pederson—Thelma's brother—worked at the Reserve Mining plant in Silver Bay and had just heard the *Fitzgerald* was missing.

Marilynn and Steve dropped what they were doing, picked up her sister Debbie in Two Harbors, and headed back to Silver Bay. When they got to the Churches', their modest, tidy home was already packed, with everyone standing around Thelma's tiny transistor radio in the kitchen, listening for news. When no updates came by radio or phone, everyone stayed overnight.

The next morning Dennis Anderson came on Duluth's WDIO to deliver the news that the *Edmund Fitzgerald* was still missing, without a trace, and there were no signs yet of any survivors.

"He was so sad," Marilynn recalls. "I think he was crying."

A few minutes later Thelma's brother Erling called from the Reserve Mining plant, and confirmed it was no rumor. The *Fitzgerald* was gone.

"I couldn't believe it," Marilynn says. "We'd just been up here, seeing Dad off at the dock. It couldn't be!"

The members of the Church family who were not in the area started driving and flying in from around the country to be together in Nolan Church's home in Silver Bay.

IN EARLY 1975 Tom Walton had moved from Toledo to Monterey, California, swapping his job as an editor at the *Toledo Blade* for the *County Herald*, both of which were owned by the Block family. Walton would work fourteen years in Monterey before returning to Toledo in 1989.

On November 10, 1975, Walton was getting ready for bed at his home in Monterey when he heard the TV in the other room. It was 11 p.m. in California, three hours behind Michigan.

Walton turned on the *ABC Evening News* with Harry Reasoner, who had grown up in Minneapolis and had an affinity for the Great Lakes and the shipping industry. While Walton brushed his teeth he heard Reasoner in the background say, "A Great Lake ship is feared lost on Lake Superior."

Before Reasoner mentioned the ship's name, an unwelcome thought popped into Walton's mind: "I think it's the *Fitz*. Not my dad's ship, either, the *Armco*, but the *Fitz*. Now I'm thinking, *Oh, man, I hope I'm wrong. And I hope whatever boat it is, they find it*. But I had this awful feeling. I just *knew*. And then Reasoner said the name, '*Edmund Fitzgerald*.' My dad wasn't on it, but I knew my uncle Grant was.

"Reasoner said, 'The sea search is continuing for possible survivors of the *Edmund Fitzgerald*, a 729-foot ore carrier . . . The ship and its twenty-nine-man crew vanished in a storm with eighty-mile-per-hour winds . . .'

"But I knew there would be no survivors," Walton says. "There couldn't be. You're not going to kid a sailor. So I knew at that moment that I'd lost my uncle."

Because Walton's uncle Grant worked the four-to-eight shift, morning and night, Tom knew his uncle was probably working in the engine room when the ship went down.

While some sailors use accrued vacation time to go home in November and avoid the nasty weather, both Walton's uncle Grant and his father, Wade, always kept going.

"They were lakers," Walton says. "And that's where they wanted to be. They needed to be out there."

Walton's thoughts then turned to his father, the chief engineer on the *Armco*, also operated by Columbia. Wade could have just as easily been assigned to the *Fitzgerald*, instead of his good friend George Holl.

"It was only through good fortune and the grace of God," Tom Walton says, "that my dad was not on the *Fitzgerald* that night."

HEIDI WILHELM, TWELVE, the sixth of Blaine Wilhelm's seven children, was at home that night, a school night, looking forward to her father coming home in a few days to Moquah, Wisconsin, just off Lake Superior. Blaine served as an oiler on the *Fitzgerald*, the man with the coffee can full of change.

That Monday night Heidi's quiet evening at home was interrupted when their neighbors knocked on their door to tell them they had just heard something on the news about a ship missing on Superior. When the

Wilhelms turned on their TV, WDIO's Dennis Anderson announced on the ten o'clock news that the *Edmund Fitzgerald* was missing. The news sent Heidi spinning.

"I don't remember everything," she says. "It was so traumatic. I think I already knew in the back of my mind, in that instant, that he wasn't coming home."

When Heidi couldn't sleep she went down to the kitchen and curled up. Her mother was on the phone in the kitchen "trying to get someone, *anyone*," at Columbia to answer the phone. After many attempts her mother finally got through to the company operator, and explained the situation, but no one gave her any information, or called her back that night—or any other.

Craig Ellquist had listened to the news reports on Monday night with his friend Al Ruberg in Al's International Harvester pickup truck. But because the newscasters hadn't said that the *Fitzgerald* had actually sunk, only that it was missing, Ellquist went to bed that night certain that the big ship would be found, and his friends onboard would be safe.

At 7 a.m. the next morning Ellquist and Ruberg had just started their milk runs when the news started rolling in: The *Fitzgerald* was still missing. Ellquist started thinking about his friends on the ship, especially Eugene "Red" O'Brien, the fifty-year-old wheelsman who took Ellquist to Tony Packo's in Toledo for the famous chicken paprikash, boiled with dumplings. O'Brien always insisted on paying for both of them.

Ellquist's long list of deliveries prevented him from stopping to watch the news, but whenever he ducked into a store or restaurant he would grab snippets of the Channel 10 newscast out of Duluth, and he listened during his runs on the delivery truck's radio.

Stop by stop that morning, the weight of it started to sink in: The *Edmund Fitzgerald* had gone under, with all his friends on it.

Many family and friends of the *Edmund Fitzgerald* crew didn't hear any news at all that night.

The next morning, Tuesday, November 11, 1975, reports started reaching them at their breakfast tables, though many refused to believe them.

Cindy LoCicero, the girlfriend of David "Cowboy" Weiss, was just waking up to start her day as a senior at Benzie Central High School when her father knocked on her bedroom door. He told her a ship was missing, and added sadly, "I think David was on that ship."

"What ship?" she asked. "What are you talking about?"

They went downstairs to watch the 7&4 news, out of Traverse City, which confirmed it.

"It took quite a while for it to hit me, to understand what had really happened," LoCicero says. "I think I was still in shock. I was thinking that David wasn't really out there, on the ship. He was always late for everything, so I was thinking he was late for the ship—the one time I wished he was."

The LoCiceros sat there in silence, eating breakfast while watching the news. Then Cindy went to school, like any other day. Since most of her classmates were from farm families they didn't know much about shipping, the *Edmund Fitzgerald*, or what the news meant.

"They didn't really understand what had happened," LoCicero says, "so it didn't seem real to me, either. That made it harder."

On that same Tuesday morning in North Olmsted, Ohio, Aunt Ruth, Bruce Hudson's mom, got on the road by 6:30, like she did every weekday, to work the early shift at the Bonne Bell Cosmetics factory.

She had heard nothing about the ship the night before, so she was unprepared when she turned on the car radio on the way to work and heard the anchor say the *Edmund Fitzgerald* was gone, with no survivors. She pulled over, shaking her head, too stunned to cry at first.

Later she would say she didn't know how she made it all the way back home. When she did, the first call she made was to her sister, Pam Woodman Wittig's mother.

Pam was fourteen years old in 1975. Her father, a truck driver, had heard the news the night before on his ham radio, but he figured it had to be the wrong ship. The Woodmans had recently bought a new house, so Pam proudly hosted her friend Tina that Monday night. They were still sleeping on the floor of the TV room the next morning when they were woken up by Pam's mom on the phone, shouting, "No! No, it can't be!" then she started to sob.

"It didn't feel real," Pam says. "Not at all."

Like a lot of the family members, Wittig says, "I don't remember a lot about the days after that, to be honest. It's mostly a blur. People came by I didn't know. Aunt Ruth was in a daze."

NINETY-FOUR MILES AWAY in Oregon, Ohio, Bruce Hudson's girlfriend, Cindy Reynolds, went downstairs for breakfast. She was now about three months pregnant, but no one knew except her best friend, Cyndi George, and Bruce Hudson himself, the father. It was a lot to carry for a seventeen-year-old high school senior, but Reynolds was still passing her classes, making good money waiting tables, and keeping her secret to herself.

When she sat down at the breakfast table her mother mentioned that the *Edmund Fitzgerald* had been in the news.

"They say it might have gone down," she said.

Even though her mother had said it, clear as could be, it didn't stick.

Ships don't go down, Cindy thought. She'd been on the *Ashland* many times at the Toledo dock, when Bruce was taking care of it the previous winter. She knew how big freighters were, and the *Fitzgerald* was bigger than the *Ashland*. *"No way* that *ship went down. It's huge! If it's foggy, they'll find it. Gotta be somewhere up there, so I'm not going to worry about it."*

Just two months earlier she had told Bruce over the phone that he was going to be a father. She still hadn't seen him in person since she learned she was pregnant—and now he was simply gone, leaving her alone to raise their child?

She forced both thoughts out of her mind.

"I'm already living in fear of my parents' reaction to my getting pregnant," she recalls, "so now I'm just in denial. *No way I'm pregnant! No way Bruce's ship went down!* No time for tears. I'm getting ready for school."

She collected her books, and headed off. Her classes and friends kept her mind off the inconceivable news, but when she came home there was no escaping from it. The *Edmund Fitzgerald* was all over the TV, and the news was only getting worse, hour by hour: still no signs of any survivors.

"And that's when it hit me: *This is for real.*"

Reynolds's first wave of grief was quickly followed by a second: *"Oh no, now I'm pregnant, and all they're finding is lifeboats. I'm having a baby, and the father is gone."*

The full weight of the tragedy landed hard on twenty-nine families that morning, but perhaps no one carried a heavier burden than the deck-hand's girlfriend in Oregon, Ohio.

Cindy Reynolds had no idea what to do, or where to turn.

XV

SEARCHING

The First Draft of History

On Monday evening, November 10, Harry Atkins, an Associated Press reporter based in the Detroit bureau, was working at their downtown office.

Up in Whitefish Bay, an "old hermit" Atkins knew about was listening to his radio.

"His one joy in life was listening to the ship-to-shore stations," Atkins says, "eavesdropping on the captains talking to one another."

When the hermit heard McSorley and Cooper radioing back and forth during the horrible storm, he tipped off Sault Ste. Marie's WSOO radio station, which contacted the Sault Ste. Marie *Evening News*, one of Michigan's fifty-three daily papers. Since they were all members of the Associated Press, it made sense for an *Evening News* reporter to call the AP's Detroit bureau, which employed twenty-six staffers at the time.

There, on the spot, the Detroit bureau chief made the decision to send a reporter and photographer on a rare overnight trip, all the way to Sault Ste. Marie, Michigan. He picked Atkins because he'd already written some good stories about the Upper Peninsula, a region he loved, and then told Atkins to pick a photographer.

"When it comes to photographers, you must know they're all nuts," Atkins says. "John Hillery was no exception, but that's what you need. I knew I could count on him to come through with the goods."

When the duo reached the Mackinac Bridge just before dawn on November 11, Hillery saw something that made him grab his camera, jump out of the car, and start shooting: Truck driver Ivan Wilder and his eleven-year-old son had made it across three-quarters of the bridge when the wind picked up their trailer and smashed it down onto the trunk of a car driving alongside them. The bridge authorities would soon close the bridge, but not before Atkins and Hillery slipped across it.

Hillery's instincts were right, his photo was good, and it was soon rocketing throughout AP bureaus worldwide.

At 8 a.m. on Tuesday, November 11, Atkins and Hillery arrived at the Sault Ste. Marie *Evening News*, where the editor in chief was nice enough to set up workspaces for the two. Atkins figured he should observe the search effort from above, and Hillery needed shots of it, so Atkins started calling around to rent a plane. But when he kept striking out, he feared the whole trip would be a wash.

Help came from across the desk, where one of the local reporters had been overhearing his calls. He told Atkins he had a friend with a plane, and would Atkins want him to ask?

That's how Atkins and Hillery found themselves in a four-seat Cessna at the mercy of a retired Navy pilot with steel gray hair, combed straight back, and his forty-something girlfriend with a beehive hairdo. When they flew over the search ships, Atkins says, "Hillery—who, like I said, was nuts—keeps telling the pilot, 'If you could just get over there,' 'If you could just go back that way,' and then, 'If you could just tilt the plane a bit this way'—so he could take his shot beyond the wings."

"Every time it was 'No problem!' *Rrrrawr.* He'd do it just like Hillery asked."

They weren't up too long when the Coast Guard ordered, "All aircraft out of the area!" The pilot turned his radio off, kept flying, and added a tour of the Soo Locks for color. Atkins and Hillery got everything they needed to file their story, a Xerox copy of which Atkins saved.

16:12 11/11/75
BY HARRY ATKINS
Associated Press
November 11, 1975
SAULT STE. MARIE, Mich. (AP)—

Atkins opened his story with a quote from Captain Charles Milradt, commander of Group Soo: "Lake Superior seldom coughs up her victims unless they're wearing life jackets. As of this time, we have no reason to believe the men of the *Fitzgerald* had time to get into life jackets."

Atkins covered all the essential points:

- The twenty-nine-member crew of the 729-foot *Edmund Fitzgerald*, "once the largest ore-carrier on Lake Superior, went down in 520 feet of water about 7:30 p.m. Monday. . . . The 729-foot vessel vanished from radar screens as winds of hurricane force—of 75 miles per hour—raised waves to 25 feet in 42-degree weather."
- "The Coast Guard said the *Fitzgerald* may have broken up and sunk before a distress call could be made. . . . The *Fitzgerald* was taking on water but its pumps were working and the vessel was not in immediate danger.
- "One Coast Guard spokesman said the *Fitzgerald* 'probably broke in two.' But Ens. Kenneth Baker added that a hatch cover could have blown off, causing the vessel to take on water."
- "The vessel, owned by the Northwestern Mutual Life Insurance Co. of Milwaukee, was loaded with about 26,000 tons of taconite pellets on Sunday at Superior, Wis., and was bound for Detroit, officials said."

IT'S STRIKING HOW many difficult facts Atkins reported accurately in a few hours using only a notebook and an office phone. From his research and his writing, it's clear Atkins cared about this story more than the job required.

But perhaps the most interesting thing about the piece Atkins sent to Detroit is what it *didn't* include: any mention of the Mariners' Church or its pastor ringing the bell twenty-nine times, especially since those scenes appeared in the final draft of Atkins's story that went out on the AP wires worldwide, facts that would leave a lasting impression.

"I never wrote about the bell ringing twenty-nine times," Atkins says, with disarming honesty. "It wasn't me! I was in the Sault at the time, and had no idea what was happening at Mariners' in Detroit."

Atkins suspects that someone in the Detroit AP office read his story as it came in. When they heard the bell chiming at Mariners' Church, just a few blocks away, they must have walked down to witness Father Richard Ingalls Sr.—who had taken his son on a private tour of the *Fitzgerald* when it was being built eighteen years earlier—ringing the bell.

Atkins later wrote to Michael Graczyk, who was Michigan's AP news editor in 1975, to ask if he knew who added the passage about Mariners' Church.

"I didn't send anyone over to the church to talk to the priest," Graczyk wrote back. "And if anyone had sent someone it would have been me."

But, Atkins says, "the bell is so essential to the story that I've wondered for years."

The final version of Atkins's story, including the Mariners' Church pastor tolling the bell twenty-nine times, went out on the wire to the AP's 6,500 member papers around the world, including the *Los Angeles Times*.

DUE TO THE reports from Dennis Anderson at Duluth's Channel 10, Harry Reasoner on the *ABC Evening News*, and Harry Atkins at the Associated Press, the *Edmund Fitzgerald*'s disappearance was soon picked up by all the media available in 1975. The interest in the wreck prompted *Newsweek* to assign a half-page story for its November 24, 1975, issue, exactly two weeks after the ship sank, that was replete with phrases that still resonate today.

Almost buried among that issue's forty-four stories, eight department dispatches, and various columns—including the debut of a thirty-four-year-old columnist named George Will—was a story on page 48 titled "Great Lakes: The Cruelest Month." At the end of the piece it credits "James R. Gaines with Jon Lowell in Detroit."

Looking back, Gaines is surprised he got a byline on the piece, because *Newsweek* reporters typically didn't get one if an article wasn't longer than a page. But this story was exceptional in several ways, which his editors probably recognized in giving it the space they did.

Gaines had attended the University of Michigan, where he spent more time working for the acclaimed student paper, *The Michigan Daily*, than he did on his English major. Still, soon after he arrived at *Newsweek* in late 1972, he realized he had a lot to learn.

"Look, I just wasn't very good," he says. "I'm close to saying I learned everything I know at *Newsweek*, especially about writing short, cogent pieces with a little style. I probably couldn't have written that story even one year beforehand. I credit the guys who were there much, much longer than I had been, who were extremely friendly and helpful. There was no competition, just a spirit of 'let's band together and get it done.'"

Gaines quickly got up to speed by "being edited and torn up by two great editors, Peter Goldman and David Alpern—and being humbled, twice a week. Go through enough of that, you learn how to crunch it all down, right to the story's essential nuggets."

The *Fitzgerald* assignment started with Detroit bureau chief Jon Lowell conducting most of the reporting, then sending his file to New York, where Gaines began sorting through the pieces.

"Between Jon and me, who wrote it?" Gaines asks. "I don't know, but generally the lines from the reporters' file didn't get into the story. Jon was really good, though, and I may have used a line or two of his. When I read it now, I'm glad I was able to write it as I did.

"The *Edmund Fitzgerald* was national news—but only sort of. It was more poetry than news, like an obituary. It's a really sad story. It was not hard to make it sing."

AND SING IT does, from the very first words: "According to a legend of the Chippewa tribe, the lake they once called Gitche Gumee 'never gives up her dead.'"

The story continued, "Modern-day mariners of Lake Superior know the legend has some basis in fact: the largest and most treacherous of all the Great Lakes, Superior is also the coldest—deadly not only to man but also to the organisms that infest drowned bodies and bring them to the surface."

"During the gales of November," the *Newsweek* authors added, "the lakes can become especially forbidding."

They then listed other Great Lakes tragedies that occurred on the same deadly day, November 10: the storm of 1913, which killed 254 people; another in 1930, when 67 drowned; and finally the *Edmund Fitzgerald*, whose twenty-nine-man crew "vanished without a trace in a nighttime torrent of slashing winds and waves on Lake Superior," Gaines writes. "When the *Edmund Fitzgerald* steamed from port at Superior, Wisconsin, on a sunny Sunday afternoon, [it was] one of the largest ships on the Great Lakes, and its skipper, Ernest McSorley, was a veteran of 44 years on the lakes.

"But the next day," the story continued, "the storm hit Lake Superior and the *Fitzgerald*; by evening the ship was rocking through thirty-foot waves, and fighting hurricane force winds. Only fifteen miles from the relative calm of Whitefish Bay, McSorley radioed the ore ship *Arthur M. Anderson*, which was a few miles behind, that he was taking on some water . . ."

Gaines closed the piece by writing, "And in the stone, 126-year-old Mariners' Church in downtown Detroit, a minister offered prayers for the lost seamen and tolled the church bell twenty-nine times in grim tribute to the unslaked furies of Lake Superior."

Gaines and Lowell got a lot done in just 534 words. They didn't merely deliver the news but the lore behind it, capturing the heart of the story so well that their lines took root in the mind of at least one reader.

"We Didn't Feel Any Better About It"

Tuesday, November 11, 1975, dawned almost as pleasantly in Whitefish Bay as Sunday, November 9.

The storm still raged on the Great Lakes below, but not on Superior, where the waters spread out smooth as glass, as if nothing had happened the day before. But if Lake Superior had a short memory, the people on it did not.

Ships, helicopters, planes, and even a local seventy-five-foot tugboat, James MacDonald's *James D.*, searched the waters. Twelve hours earlier, on Monday night, MacDonald had been tempted to take his tugboat out of tiny Mamainse Harbor, near Batchawana Bay, Ontario, sixty miles north of the Soo Locks on the Canadian coast, to go look for the *Fitzgerald* or any possible survivors. But when the waves threatened to knock down a government dock and shed near MacDonald's boat, all spared by a brick wall the village had built just the year before, MacDonald thought better of it. He and a friend spent the night in his boat to make sure it didn't go out on its own, which it attempted to do several times by ripping away from the dock.

The two sat in MacDonald's boat while it rocked violently back and forth and they listened to the captains talking on the marine band radio. When Captain Cooper asked about lights on the lake, MacDonald got on the radio to tell Cooper all the lights on shore had been knocked out, and "the only lights he'd be seeing were car lights" on the Trans-Canada Highway, which runs along Lake Superior's eastern shore, on its way to both national coasts.

Later that night MacDonald heard Captain Cooper talking with the Coast Guard's Group Soo Commander Chuck Milradt.

"I was kinda surprised when the Coast Guard asked the *Anderson* to turn back," MacDonald says. "You can't imagine a boat of that length trying to turn around in that sea—pert near impossible. But he did it."

The next morning, Tuesday, November 11, MacDonald joined the armada of ships looking for survivors and collecting what the *Fitzgerald* had left behind, most of which washed up on Canadian shores. MacDonald himself pulled in lanterns, flare guns, almost three dozen life jackets, a rubber life raft, and one of the two steel lifeboats, still attached to its slings, indicating that no one had had enough time to release it. MacDonald gave everything he found to the Ontario Provincial Police, although a lot of it would end up in museums, on the walls of Lake Superior bars, and in collectors' homes.

The *Fitzgerald*'s second lifeboat was retrieved by another Columbia ship, the *William R. Roesch*, and in far worse shape. The *Fitzgerald*'s lifeboats were attached to davits, which look like mini-cranes. This allows for quick release, but since the boats were not used, they remained attached to the davits on the ship's way down. Because the lifeboat had an air tank attached, and air from the atmosphere was also trapped underneath, it eventually broke loose from the davits to return to the surface, completely mangled.

"Those two sources of air would have ripped the lifeboat off the davits, which is not easily done," John Tanner says. "That had to be a very violent act."

Michael Zronek and his mates on the Coast Guard's *Woodrush* made the twenty-hour trip from Duluth to Whitefish Bay by Tuesday night, and immediately started running a search grid. Over the course of several days they spotted oil here and there and picked up some debris, but found no sign of survivors.

"I'd been in Lake Superior that spring," Zronek says, recalling when he had volunteered to be the man overboard for a Coast Guard drill. "I knew the answer. I lasted just ten minutes before my limbs became numb, and I was wearing a full-body wet suit. But you always hold out hope that someone could survive, so you keep looking."

At noon on Monday, November 10, John Hayes's ship, the ST *Crapo*, had docked at its home port of Alpena, Michigan, in a bay on Lake

Huron about one hundred miles southeast of Whitefish Bay. After Hayes got off his shift at midnight he walked up the street to Joe's Bar, the sailors' Alpena spot. The TVs overhead were usually ignored, outside of a big game, but when the local news came on that night the bar became silent. The local anchor said the *Edmund Fitzgerald* was still missing but the search continued.

Hayes finished his beer, then wandered back to the docks with a lot to think about. He knew his best friend, Tom Bentsen, whom Hayes had asked to be his best man the next summer, was on the *Fitz*. Hayes also knew what the newscast probably meant.

For the sailors on the seas, however, there was no stopping to mourn or attend a service—not even for your best man. These were Great Lakes sailors, paid to deliver their cargo. With the storm still sending up waves on Lake Huron and Lake Michigan big enough to hide half the *Crapo*'s smokestack under green waves, the *Crapo* made her way from Alpena to Muskegon to deliver another load of cement.

Arriving on Thursday, November 13, Hayes and his mates decided to go out for a steak-and-lobster dinner to mourn their friends and show gratitude for their own good fortune. A fellow sailor named Rodney Ruell picked up the tab, Hayes says, "and he didn't have any more money than we did. We put down a two-hundred-dollar tip.

"It was unspeakably sad to lose Tom—and at the same time, good to be alive."

No one working on a Great Lakes freighter that week was taking that for granted.

The next day, Friday, November 14, in Dover, Delaware, doctors tended to Heidi Wilhelm's sister, Candace, who was pregnant with her first child, and oiler Blaine Wilhelm's first grandchild. Fearing the news of her father's ship would affect Candace's blood pressure and endanger the baby, they decided to keep the tragedy from her until after she delivered.

That Friday Candace gave birth to Michelle Haithcok Flores, a healthy, hardy baby girl. One day later the doctors finally gave Candace the horrible news: four days before, their father had gone down with his ship.

The bargain all the crewmen on the *Fitzgerald* had signed up for was a hard one, but straightforward: The work will be taxing, and you will miss most of your family's best moments, but you will retire relatively young, with a good pension and nothing to do but hunt, fish, and play cards, pool, and golf. Best of all, you'll have plenty of time and energy to spend with your grandchildren.

The *Fitzgerald*'s twenty-nine crewmen and their families had all paid their deposits up front, but never got to enjoy the sweet side of the deal.

THAT SAME DAY a U.S. Navy crew flying a Lockheed P-3 Orion over Lake Superior detected magnetic anomalies about eight miles northwest of Canada's Pancake Bay Provincial Park, fifteen miles west of Deadman's Cove, and just seventeen miles from the entrance to Whitefish Bay.

A week later the *Woodrush* went back with a sonar and confirmed the Navy's preliminary findings: The SS *Edmund Fitzgerald* lay 530 feet below the surface of Lake Superior, in two parts. The first mystery had been solved.

Despite the success of their mission, *Woodrush* crewman Michael Zronek says, "We didn't feel any better about it."

The *Woodrush* crew made the twenty-hour trip back to Duluth in somber silence.

The Clues They Left

IN MAY OF 1976, SIX MONTHS AFTER THE *FITZGERALD* went down, the U.S. Navy sent a new expedition to the *Fitzgerald*'s final resting place. It was led by the fifteen-foot-long Cable-Controlled Underwater Recovery Vehicle known as CURV III, which achieved international fame in 1968 for bringing up a nuclear warhead off the coast of Spain in 2,800 feet of water.

Equipped with lights, cameras, and a robotic arm for the mission in Lake Superior, CURV III took twelve dives down to the *Fitzgerald* and recorded 43,255 feet of video tape. On May 20, she captured the name *Edmund Fitzgerald* on the stern, marking the first official identification of the vessel.

CURV III found the ship in two sections: 235 feet of the stern lying upside down, and 276 feet of the bow right side up. They sit in cold mud, which also covers much of the deck. The 170-foot gap between the two sections is strewn with the shredded metal, much of which used to comprise the middle of the ship.

The twenty-nine men remain entombed inside the *Edmund Fitzgerald*.

EVERYONE ON THE *Titanic* knew the night she went down that the iceberg was the culprit, yet no one could find the ship for seventy-three years, whereas finding the *Edmund Fitzgerald* has proven far easier than determining why it sank.

What happened?

That basic question has produced thousands of pages of complicated answers, including a handful of thick government reports, a couple dozen books, and just as many documentaries—but no final answers.

Some of the possible causes include: the design of the ship itself; the hatches; record waves; fatigue and navigational error; and Six Fathom Shoal.

The Design

Hull 301, which would become the *Edmund Fitzgerald*, was the first vessel built at the Great Lakes Engineering Works using a new method of modular construction, and with welding often used in place of riveting. Both innovations gave the ship more flexibility, allowing it to bend but not break in heavy seas, but perhaps too much. Richard Orgel, who served as McSorley's second mate on the *Fitzgerald* in 1972 and 1973, testified that the ship had a tendency to bend and spring during storms "like a diving board after somebody has jumped off." If the *Fitzgerald*'s hull had twisted too much it would have made it that much harder to steer, and if it had flexed too much too often, it could have eventually cracked, the odds of which go up with overloading and heavy seas, and the possibility of a final rogue wave. George H. "Red" Burgner, the *Edmund Fitzgerald*'s celebrated cook, spent ten shipping seasons cooking on the *Fitzgerald* in the sixties and seventies, and seven winters as the *Fitzgerald*'s ship-keeper in Toledo. He knew the ship as well as anyone, and testified in a deposition that the keel was only "tack welded," and that he had seen for himself that many of the welds had broken. After this deposition, the Marine Board of Inquiry did not ask Burgner to testify.

The Hatches

The *Fitzgerald*'s cargo hatches have the dubious distinction of being the first and best-known suspect, in part because they would be the easiest answer: If the deckhands failed to completely clamp down the hatches, or if the waves caused the clamps or hatches to fail, tons of water would have invaded the immense cargo holds and quickly sunk the ship. Support for this theory comes from the CURV III videos, which show some of the clamps undone and some hatches collapsed.

But others point out that such damage could have occurred after the ship collided with the bottom of the lake, especially with the extraordinary pressure 530 feet below the surface, made worse by trapped air bubbles. If the clamps or hatches had failed, so many tons of water would have come in with the next green wave that the ship would have sunk almost immediately, and not limped on for hours, as it did. Further, photos of the right-side-up bow section show the clamps had been properly secured after all.

Those who previously worked as *Fitzgerald* deckhands, including Craig Ellquist and Patrick Devine, steadfastly insist First Mate John McCarthy never would have permitted the *Fitz* to leave Burlington Dock No. 1 in November without the deckhands securing the clamps first.

"There is *no* way they went out that day without clamping down *all* the clamps," says Devine, who worked on the ship just two months before the tragedy. "It was November, and they knew they were in for a rough one. That was just protocol."

Record Waves

Whatever happened to the *Fitzgerald* before 7 p.m. on November 10, we know she was in a weakened state due to the list McSorley mentioned in two calls, which made her as vulnerable as a three-legged animal at the back of the pack. Almost anything could have provided the final straw, including a rogue wave or simply the inevitable result of the ship taking on too much water, minute by minute, until her bow finally dived too deeply into a wave, and couldn't come back up.

Fatigue and Navigational Error

McSorley's status as the best captain on the Great Lakes was well earned, but even his many admirers concede he was going too fast in heavy seas that night, and that he sailed too close to Six Fathom Shoal. Lack of sleep combined with motion fatigue would have tested any captain in that situation, but without witnesses it's impossible to say how much those demons affected McSorley, if at all.

"With McSorley, it's hard to know what he knew, what he said, even where he thought his ship was on the lake," Barthuli says. "But we know they were going too fast, especially sailing blind [without radars, lighthouses, or beacons]. I think he probably didn't know he was heading right for the shoal. Even a half mile current can make a big difference in your line."

Six Fathom Shoal

It's entirely plausible that McSorley, with a dangerous combination of sleep deprivation, motion fatigue, a lack of familiarity with the northern route, outdated charts and possibly the wrong charts, no working radars, lighthouses, or beacons, record waves, and too much speed, sent his ship right over the perilous Six Fathom Shoal, bounced the boat off the bedrock, and inflicted structural damage that ultimately led to the *Fitzgerald*'s sinking.

"Hitting bottom could tear into the hull plating," University of Michigan naval architecture professor Matthew Collette says, "and those cracks start growing, wave by wave, until it finally snaps. If that is true, then the rest of the damage is inconsequential, because at some point a wave is going to be big enough to send it down.

"Some say a rogue wave could have knocked out the radars, busted the hatches, and started flooding. Perhaps. But if the ship had just gotten whacked with a rogue wave, the radars would be low on the captain's list of concerns. He wouldn't have mentioned them to the *Anderson*. If you know you're flooding, that's the first thing you'd tell Captain Cooper. That is orders of magnitude more important than the radars."

Within a year of the accident Oglebay Norton, Columbia Transportation's parent company, quietly commissioned the Great Lakes' top nautical investigator, Dick Race, to explore Six Fathom Shoal.

A wiry man with leathery skin and a white-haired brush cut, Race had a handshake that would crush an unsuspecting greeter's hand, and a colloquial way of talking that put his listeners at ease.

"How ya doin' there, young fella? Good handshake ya got there!"

"He'd talk to anyone," recalls one of his proteges, Ed Wiltse, now captain of the popular SS *Badger*, which ferries cars and passengers across

Lake Michigan. "He could be a bit of an absent-minded professor, but he was *brilliant*."

After World War II Race worked on the Motorola team that designed the radar and sonar systems that much of the world used for decades. He preferred working for himself, however, and eventually designed his own research boat, the *Neptune*, a sixty-five-footer built with the latest equipment, much of which he had created himself.

A skilled diver, Race gained notice on the Great Lakes for finding Flight 389, a Boeing 727 that went down in Lake Michigan on August 16, 1965, near Chicago. He was universally considered the best in the field, and often worked with the federal government and the Chicago Police Department Marine Unit, where Race stored the *Neptune*.

"He was a mentor, in many ways," says retired Chicago Police Department lieutenant Earl Zuelke, whose views echo those of other Great Lakes leaders Race worked with. "An older guy who had a very deep background, a lot of stories, and was always available. He was a global expert, and I thought the world of him."

When Oglebay Norton hired Race to investigate the *Edmund Fitzgerald*'s sinking, he anchored the *Neptune* at Six Fathom Shoal and started diving. He would put all his findings in his report for Oglebay Norton, but it was strictly confidential and protected by a nondisclosure agreement. Considerable efforts to find the report have come up short.

But Race did talk with three people—Ed Wiltse, Earl Zuelke, and John Tanner, all close friends of Race's—about his exploration of Six Fathom Shoal. His comments to all three colleagues were consistent: On the hard bedrock of Six Fathom Shoal he found the *Fitzgerald*'s distinctive maroon paint, still clearly visible and embedded in the stone about six months after it sank. Race told them he also discovered clear scraping scars on a large rock nearby.

Based on Race's findings and the damage that can be seen toward the middle of the *Fitzgerald*'s hull—not on the stern, as many assumed—he told those three friends that he believed the *Fitzgerald* had bottomed out on the shoals and damaged its hull, which allowed water to rush in, creating the starboard list McSorley complained about.

In fact, in 1983—eight years after the *Fitzgerald* sank, and seven after Race investigated Six Fathom Shoal—he talked with reporter Mark

Fellows from *Harbor Light/Summer Life* magazine, in Harbor Springs, Michigan, for a profile. Almost as an aside, Fellows wrote, "Dick has since been involved in surveying the area in which the *Edmund Fitzgerald* sank in Lake Superior, but was pulled off that job by what he described as 'politics.' It is his belief the giant ore carrier ran aground on an uncharted shoal before sinking."

Since we know Race investigated the shoal himself a few months after the *Fitzgerald* sank, it seems fair to assume his "belief" that the *Fitz* bottomed out on the shoal was based on his own findings—findings he could not share publicly as fact since he had been commissioned to produce a confidential report for Oglebay Norton. (Because Race died in 2001, we're left to guess what "politics" might have taken him off the investigation.)

If the *Fitzgerald* did start taking on water after bottoming out at Six Fathom Shoal, then McSorley's uncharacteristic decision to slow down to allow the *Anderson* to catch up could have cost him and his crew a vital hour or more of buoyancy, which would have been almost exactly what they needed to cover the last seventeen miles to Whitefish Bay. But then McSorley was probably not aware of any damage to the hull, or he would have mentioned that in his radio dispatches, and not have wasted precious minutes waiting for the *Anderson*.

We cannot be entirely sure, however, because Oglebay Norton kept Race's study private—a big mistake, Tanner believes.

"The downsides of a lot of American corporations: They're too tight with information when things go wrong," he says. "You're not likely to find malice or incompetence. I think they should be more transparent, and see where it leads. That way you gain trust."

We will never have the whole story of the *Edmund Fitzgerald*'s final day, due to the simple fact that no one survived and almost every piece of evidence we have is incomplete. Some of that is due to bad luck, but not all.

Peter Groh served as Oglebay Norton's purchasing agent from 2001 to 2006, during which the company went bankrupt in 2004. Four years later, in 2008, it was purchased by a Belgian company, the Carmeuse Group.

"I was involved with getting rid of their records that were in long-term storage," Groh says. "This would have been around 2006. And I can tell you this for a fact: there were only two or three boxes that we could not locate, and those were the boxes on the *Edmund Fitzgerald*. Supposed to be some videos in there, too," possibly including footage from Dick Race's exploratory dives on Six Fathom Shoal.

"They were taken out and never returned," Groh adds, "and I don't know what ever happened to them. I don't think there was any record of who signed them out, either. All the other company records on the inventories were there. Only those boxes were missing.

"Go figure."

The Captain's Blind Spot

Another factor is a blind spot common to all captains and crews: because your ship has never sunk before, you don't believe that it ever could.

"You get a 'confirmation bias,'" University of Michigan professor Matthew Collette says. "A captain thinks, 'In my 30-year career, I've faced all kinds of weather and problems, and we've always gotten there. So that's going to happen this time, too, because nothing else ever has.'

"But a storm is an entirely binary event. Either you make it to shore, or you sink. There's no shade of gray. So when sailors survive they never know how *close* to sinking they might have been. The only people who know what it's like to experience a sinking are already on the bottom, and they can't warn you."

In that sense all sailors are sailing blind. Like walking near the edge of the Grand Canyon with a blinder on, if you walk away safely, you'll never know how close to disaster you really were.

"I feel for the captain," Collette adds. "The last hour or two McSorley has very few options, none of them are very good, and he really has no good way to weigh them. The margin to failure is not visible to him and his crew. They don't know how close they're getting to the edge.

"But there is no way to call time-out. This is not football. Your options are pretty limited, so you stick to your plan, and hope for the best. That's about all that's available to you."

Another flaw common to many studies of the *Edmund Fitzgerald* is the temptation to identify a single cause for the catastrophe.

"I've looked at the reports," says Collette. "I've studied this throughout my career. But I don't think it's possible to pin it down to one factor, with certainty. What you can see, very quickly, is there were multiple possible causes, and those added up to circumstances that the ship could no longer handle. But who can say for sure?

"Too much water in the ship, and it's going to sink. That's pretty basic."

THE MYSTERY LIVES on for millions of people still interested in the *Edmund Fitzgerald*, which adds to the ship's enduring attraction. But for the families of the sailors, the unanswered questions hold no power.

"Someone asked me, 'Don't you want to know the reasons why it went down?'" says Deb Champeau, Buck's daughter. "None of us do. Not anymore."

"At this point?" asks Heidi Brabon, daughter of Blaine Wilhelm. "*How* dad's ship went down matters absolutely not at all. It won't change anything for us."

Marilynn Church Peterson, daughter of porter Nolan Church, agrees. "Everyone can have their own theory, and I've probably heard them all. It's something where no one's going to really know. And I'm okay with that."

Tom Walton, his father, and his uncle all served on the *Fitzgerald*, and his uncle Grant remains with the ship. Tom has given the *Fitzgerald* as much careful deliberation as anyone, which he ultimately boils down to one elementary thought: "Surely the mighty *Fitz* would have been considered the least likely ship to succumb to the sea. But this time the sea won."

FOR ALL THE competing theories, reports, books, and films on the *Fitzgerald*'s fate, almost everyone agrees that the ship's ultimate demise occurred with alarming speed. Perhaps the strongest argument for that conclusion is the simplest: For a seasoned captain like Ernest McSorley to fail to send out a distress signal, or order his crew to launch their lifeboats or don lifejackets, he must not have had even a minute's warning, or else he surely would have taken those fundamental precautions.

"If there's any consolation here," Matthew Collette offers, "it's that the end probably happened very quickly."

"I have no doubt she ultimately drove that bow into a wave," Rick Barthuli says, "and then she went down—fast. I don't think the crew knew they were going down, until maybe the last thirty seconds. The final throes must've been so bad and so fast, they wouldn't have realized she was going down until it happened."

Reports suggest that the same ship that had a top speed of sixteen miles per hour on the water went down to the lake floor at thirty-five miles per hour, which might also explain some of the damage we see today.

The crew's family members have spent decades imagining—and sometimes trying to block out—their loved ones' final minutes.

Perhaps Bruce Hudson and Mark Thomas were alleviating their fears with gallows humor, and joking about how happy they would be once they got to Toledo and hopped into Hudson's burgundy Dodge Challenger to take off for California, leaving it all behind for a month before Hudson's life got serious. Maybe Paul Riippa looked at Eddie Bindon with the urgent question "What was *that*?!"

And there could have been a moment, somewhere near the very end, when Captain Ernest McSorley made eye contact with his wheelsman and best friend, John Simmons—with whom he had just been discussing a day or two earlier their last trip together before both retired—with the horrifying realization: *This is really it.*

Like with so many questions the *Edmund Fitzgerald* raises, we will never know the answers to those, either.

Aunt Ruth herself said it best when she observed, "Only thirty know what happened: twenty-nine men, and God."

But they're not talking, so the rest of us are just guessing.

XVI

ALL THAT REMAINS

"It Doesn't Seem Real"

SHOCK AND GRIEF OVERWHELMED THE FAMILIES—YET they still had to act.

Six days after the *Edmund Fitzgerald* went down, the Hudsons held a service for Bruce at the Methodist church in North Olmsted, Ohio. Aunt Ruth picked "Michael Row Your Boat Ashore."

Michael row your boat ashore, hallelujah
The River Jordan is chilly and cold, hallelujah
Chills the body but not the soul, hallelujah

Bruce's shiny burgundy Dodge Challenger waited at the docks in Toledo for its owner to return, as patiently as a loyal dog. After the *Fitzgerald* sank Aunt Ruth had to arrange to retrieve her son's prized possession, with the Columbia sticker on the window.

Far easier was Ruth's decision to keep Kelly, Bruce's German shepherd. Aunt Ruth was already in the habit of treating Kelly, someone both she and Bruce loved, as an extension of her son when he was sailing for the season. With Bruce gone, taking care of Kelly was a blessing, a small but vital consolation for the immeasurable loss she suffered.

"As you get older, the simple things in life really make a difference," Ruth's niece Pam Wittig says. "Aunt Ruth *loved* that dog. You didn't get too close to Aunt Ruth without Kelly checking you out first! If Kelly liked you, Aunt Ruth figured you must be okay."

For months after losing her only child, Aunt Ruth had no reason to believe Bruce had left her anything but a few mementos, a shiny new car, a beautiful dog, and an irreparable hole in her heart. But her deep and abiding love for her son, and even the grief that came with it, got her through each day.

Helen Bindon, Eddie's wife of twenty-five years, was caught in the same vortex of disbelief and anguish. A few days after she received the shattering news, the two-carat diamond ring Eddie had bought for her in Duluth during his last day on shore, then entrusted to his friend, arrived in the mail—a surprise gift to celebrate their twenty-fifth anniversary. Helen's tears flowed anew.

Helen never remarried, and wore Eddie's anniversary ring the rest of her life.

"The day the ship was launched was probably the happiest day of my father's life," Edmund Fitzgerald's son, Edmund Bacon Fitzgerald, had recalled years later, then added: "The day it was lost was probably the worst day of his life."

Edmund Fitzgerald did not know any of the men on the ship, and his company had hired Oglebay Norton's subsidiary Columbia Transportation to operate it from her first day on the lakes, but the vessel still bore his name, his wife christened it, and it represented a dream fulfilled for generations of Fitzgeralds. The ship meant his family of Irish immigrants had arrived, in the most spectacular fashion. Fitzgerald beamed when his VIP friends came back from their trips gushing about the *Fitz*'s records, her crew, and the unsurpassed quality of the ship itself, right down to the lavish meals. Now he knew his legacy would be eclipsed by the name of the ship on the bottom of Lake Superior, and the men forever trapped inside.

Michael Cudahy, a spry ninety-four-year-old Milwaukee business leader and philanthropist, knew Edmund Fitzgerald well.

"There was a weight he carried around after that," Cudahy said. "He didn't like to talk about it."

Tom Bentsen, who had dropped out of the Great Lakes Maritime Academy to become an oiler on the *Fitzgerald*, was one of those sailors attracted to sailing to get farther from his father, Harold, a successful businessman. As soon as Harold found out about the *Fitzgerald*'s fate, he drove from his home in St. Joseph, Michigan, to his son's apartment in Traverse City.

"Tom Bentsen's dad, Harold, came up right afterward," Rick Barthuli says. "I liked him. I liked Tom's mom, too, but I know their divorce was rough. Just goes to show, you never know.

"Tom's dad went right up to Lake Superior. He was looking in the right places, too, on the Canadian side of Superior, where all the debris washed up. But that's all anyone found."

Harold Bentsen had hoped to repair the rift with his son, but their chance to reconcile one day had gone down with the ship.

AARON WEISS, THE father of David "Cowboy" Weiss, the cadet whom John Tanner had convinced to stay on the *Fitzgerald* to clear his name, flew from California for his son's memorial service at the Great Lakes Maritime Academy.

After the service he sought out John Tanner. Although they had never met before, Aaron asked Tanner a point-blank question: "I know David wanted to transfer ships. Why didn't he?"

Tanner was the only person still alive who knew the answer. He could have told Mr. Weiss just about anything, hemmed and hawed, or just feigned ignorance. But Tanner answered David's father as directly as he had been questioned.

"I had to explain to his father what had happened," Tanner says, his voice turning soft. "He was a mild man, probably middle management. I told him the truth: David, he wanted to get off the *Fitz*. But I told David he needed to stay on the ship, make the situation right, and he'd be better off in the long run.

"What else could I do? It wasn't pleasant. It was very hard. But his dad understood, and he was gracious. I've always been grateful for that.

"But to talk to a father about the death of his son—that's . . . tough. You can't talk about this and not wonder how it could have been different."

A half century after that difficult conversation, recounting it forced Tanner to look away for a moment, then out the window. Then he looked back, his eyes red.

"That was tough."

Ten years later Weiss's younger brother came to Traverse City to tour the academy and retrace his brother's steps. He wanted to walk where David had walked, and feel what David must have felt, just to be a little closer to a brother he would never see again.

IN THE MONTHS after the sinking, seventeen-year-old Debbie Champeau developed the habit of magical thinking about her father, Buck, the third engineer on the ship.

She would tell herself, "He found a cave somewhere—and he's alive! He'll never miss my high school graduation, because he's all about education."

Eight months later, when she walked up to receive her diploma at St. Pius XI, she stopped on the stage and looked around to see if her father was near the door, walking in, as she somehow expected him to be. When he didn't appear, she says, "That's when I finally thought, *Education meant everything to him, and if he could swim across Lake Superior to be here, he'd be here.* Because I knew he would never, ever miss my graduation. Only then did I know, *really* know, with tears in my eyes, that this is final. He's gone.

"The loss gets harder when you don't have a funeral. You miss that. It doesn't seem real. You don't have a sense of closure. It was my goal to bring Dad's body home."

They had already bought a grave for Buck at his family's plot in Sturgeon Bay, but they weren't sure what to do with it. Should they try to retrieve his body from the ship? That was when Debbie learned how many other people were affected by the sinking, and the impossibility of trying to find her father without disturbing the others, or endangering the divers.

"Dad would never want anyone to risk their lives for him," she decided. "And he was a Marine: You stay with your men."

That was hard for Buck's youngest brother, Jack, to accept. When Jack served in Vietnam, Buck had often told him that if anything happened to him overseas, Buck would be sure to bring Jack home for a proper funeral. When Jack couldn't do the same for Buck, he was devastated.

"He couldn't," Debbie says. "No one could. But he just couldn't accept that."

The family still has an empty grave in Sturgeon Bay, with Buck Champeau's marker above it.

COLUMBIA OFFERED SOME of the families the victims' last paycheck ($568.25 for a deckhand) and $750 for the victim's lost personal effects, an amount determined by their labor contract, but other families didn't receive even those checks.

When Columbia offered nothing else, the families had little recourse but to file wrongful death lawsuits, for which Columbia paid whatever the families' individual attorneys could negotiate. Some families received about $35,000, or a little more than a year's wages for a deckhand making overtime, and others marginally more. Columbia seemed eager to get the settlements signed before the investigative reports were published and studied, fearing those might point the blame at the company or captain, which could greatly increase Columbia's liability.

Beyond the checks, Columbia had little to say.

"Nobody from Columbia has ever talked with anyone from the families," says Heidi Brabon, Blaine Wilhelm's daughter. "No apologies. Nothing."

"We never heard from the company for weeks," Marilynn Church Peterson confirms. "They finally sent mom a fruit basket—not quite the right thing."

Aunt Ruth never heard anything from Columbia.

"Nothing," her niece Pam Wittig says. "I do not believe Aunt Ruth ever got a response from the company.

"Nothing."

The Ballad

After the *Edmund Fitzgerald* sank, Gordon Lightfoot read Harry Atkins's Associated Press story in the *Los Angeles Times*, then Jim Gaines's piece in *Newsweek* two weeks after the wreck. Lightfoot biographer Nicholas Jennings tells us Lightfoot read the opening line of the *Newsweek* story "and was instantly captivated."

"When the *Edmund Fitzgerald* went down I imagined what that wave might have been like," Lightfoot said. He added that the *Newsweek* piece "really moved" him, but it struck him that the twenty-nine men deserved more than a half page in a national news magazine.

Lightfoot felt that he was getting close on his sea shanty melody, which seemed to fit his subject's somber and mysterious mood, so he started working on the words.

"It was quite an undertaking to do that," he said. "I went and bought all of the old newspapers, got everything in chronological order."

With the AP, *Newsweek*, and other stories laid out in front of him, Lightfoot began by writing about "the big lake they call Gitche Gumee," the "load of iron ore" that weighed twenty-six thousand tons, "the gales of November," and "the maritime sailors' cathedral," where "the church bell chimed 'til it rang twenty-nine times / For each man on the *Edmund Fitzgerald*."

The troubadour had done his homework.

The song's 478 words, just 56 shy of the *Newsweek* article itself, told the story with both economy and feeling, two masters that are hard to please in one song.

Still, Lightfoot remained deeply unsure of this piece, particularly his lyrics, due to the sensitivity of the subject. He feared being inaccurate, corny, or worse, appearing to exploit a tragedy for profit. But more than that, as a fellow sailor and a child of the Great Lakes, and as a musician whose first song he ever recalled was now playing in his head, decades later, this song—whatever it was—was deeply personal. It was something he *felt*.

Lightfoot couldn't put the song out of his mind, tinkering with it for months—but always keeping it to himself.

BY DECEMBER OF 1975 Lightfoot felt he had enough songs ready for his next album, *Summertime Dream*. It was time to gather his longtime bassist Rick Haynes, guitarists Terry Clements and Pee Wee Charles, and a new drummer, Barry Keane, to rehearse the tunes in the solarium of Lightfoot's home.

Lightfoot took a working man's approach to his music, and he expected his band to do so, too. After practicing long hours Monday through Friday, Keane recalls, they had about a dozen songs "in pretty good shape. But at the end of each rehearsal Gord started strumming this new song, in six-eight time, which you don't hear very often. Terry and Pee Wee would work out parts of it. Rick might have played a note or two, that's all, and I never played a single beat on it.

"But before they ever got going on it Gord would always stop and say, 'No no. It's not ready yet. Don't worry about it. Look, this is a song about a shipwreck—a real one.'"

Then Lightfoot would drop the subject, every time.

In the spring of 1976 Lightfoot summoned his band to Eastern Sound Studios on Yorkville Avenue in Toronto for a five-day session, noon to six each day, to put *Summertime Dream* on vinyl. In the meantime Lightfoot had figured out how the guitar parts for his new sea shanty would go, but he still wouldn't dare sing the lyrics to anyone, nor did he plan on recording the song for this album, if ever.

But the pattern held. On Monday, after getting a handful of songs polished enough to put "in the can," Lightfoot started fiddling with the sea shanty again, but shortly after the others joined him he abruptly stopped.

"No, no, we're not doing it."

The same thing happened Tuesday, and again Wednesday: After getting a few more songs on tape, he'd start playing the new song, and then shut it down.

"It isn't ready," he insisted. "And it's not going to be on the album."

The band still hadn't heard the whole song, just some chords and bars, and no lyrics.

By 3 p.m. on Thursday they had finished recording ten songs for the new album, a full day and a half before their studio rental ran out.

"Gord said, 'Okay, we're done. Thank you guys.'" Keane says. "This was back in the seventies, when no one finished early. But we were a tight group, and knew what we were doing."

The bandmembers had already started packing up when studio engineer Kenny Friesen hit the talk-back button in the booth to speak to the band. "What about that shipwreck song?"

Lightfoot once again protested that it wasn't ready.

Friesen countered, "Look, you've got the guys here and you've got the studio booked for five days. You're paying for it either way. Might as well try it."

"There was a long pause," Keane recalls. "Then Gord said, 'All right.'"

Lightfoot turned to his guitarists and said, "Terry and Pee Wee, do your thing."

Keane, lost, had to speak up.

"When do you want me to come in?" Lightfoot's drummer had never played a single note on the mystery song to that point, and had no idea what Lightfoot wanted.

"I'll give you a nod," Lightfoot said. Since Lightfoot would be sitting across from Keane, right outside the drum booth, that seemed simple enough.

Lightfoot asked Friesen to turn the lights down, which set the mood, then paused, closed his eyes, and started strumming the song's first notes. When he was already ninety seconds in—approaching the entire length of most popular songs—he still hadn't given Keane the nod to start, so Keane figured he had forgotten him, and the song was about to end.

"But no," Keane says, "right before the third verse Gord gave me a nod, just like he said he would, and I jump in."

At exactly 1:34, right after Lightfoot sang,

and later that night when the ship's bell rang
could it be the north wind they'd been feelin'?

He nodded to Keane, who came in with a strong tom fill, to mimic a storm crashing down. It was a bold move, especially for someone who hadn't yet secured a full-time spot in Lightfoot's band—and exactly the right one.

"None of us had heard the whole song," Keane explains. "So we all just played what we felt."

Right after Keane's thunder, Lightfoot sang,

The wind in the wires made a tattle-tale sound
and a wave broke over the railing

Keane had provided the perfect transition to the storm itself. It's impossible to imagine the song without it.

After twenty-eight two-line stanzas, lasting five minutes and fifty-eight seconds, they reached the end of the song, improvising the entire way—then looked at each other, pleasantly surprised.

What was that?

Whatever it was, Keane says, "it was actually pretty darn good. But Gord's a perfectionist, so he says, 'Well, we should try it again.' So we tried it again. Then maybe a third time. Then Gord says, 'We've got another day of studio time, so let's try it for real tomorrow, and do this thing right.'"

On Friday they played it again three or four times, Keane says, "but we never got it as good. The first time we played it the day before, there was that creative tension. Gord was putting his heart and soul into it. You can *hear* it. The other guys felt the same tension, because we'd never heard the song, and nobody wanted to screw it up. And that tension led to some good stuff. We weren't *thinking*. We all just played what we felt.

"You're always trying to make it better—but each time you play it, it takes some of the soul out if it, because it becomes more clinical, more technical. You want to perfect it, but that song didn't need to be *perfected*. It needed to be raw, organic."

When they played back the various takes, they reached a surprising consensus: The first take on Thursday *was* their best. "That's it," they said. "That's the one."

But Lightfoot's band was not a democracy. He had the only vote that mattered, yet to their surprise he agreed with them: The first take was their best. The version people have been hearing on the radio for decades is actually the first time the band ever played the song.

"Look, if you're not in the music business, you probably don't know that first takes get on albums *sometimes*," Keane explains. "But the first time you ever *played* the song? *Never.* Never, never, never. That *never* happens. And it almost didn't happen that time. It was *that* close. The album was done!"

When they left the studio, they all felt that they had created something special.

"But did I know it was going to be a hit?" Keane asks. "Not a chance in hell. It was long. *Six minutes*. It didn't have a chorus. It didn't have a hook, no 'Yummy yummy yummy, I got love in my tummy.' It didn't check any of the boxes you need for a hit. I didn't think it had a *chance* to be a hit—and I was in the record business.

"No. No chance."

An Unexpected Hit

Shortly after the album came out the band appeared on *The Midnight Special*, a popular show featuring live music, to promote Lightfoot's new album, *Summertime Dream*. The album had eleven songs, and they played six that night—but not "The Wreck of the Edmund Fitzgerald," which they felt was too long, with little commercial appeal.

A few months later Lightfoot and his band traveled to Los Angeles for a series of shows at the Universal Amphitheatre. While in town Warner Brothers asked Lightfoot to meet with Mo Ostin, their president, to discuss which song to push as a single from the *Summertime Dream* album. Lightfoot asked Keane to come along.

"We sit down," Keane says, "and Mo says, 'You know what, Gordon, we're getting some reaction to the shipwreck song on FM.'"

When Ostin asked Lightfoot what he thought of turning it into a single, Lightfoot and Keane looked at each other "in complete disbelief," Keane says. "We know Mo's a smart man, but really? We couldn't believe what we were hearing."

Almost everyone personally attached to the *Fitzgerald* remembers the first time they heard, "The Wreck of the Edmund Fitzgerald."

John Hayes was working on the ST *Crapo*. He and Helen planned to get married on August 21, 1976, though the death of his best man, Tom Bentsen, naturally hung over them.

"It was a windy, nasty night on Lake Michigan," Hayes says. "I'd just helped load the coal for the boilers with a flashlight. When we finished

I hopped on my bunk with my AM radio and I just happened to hear Lightfoot's song that night. First time.

"It was eerie. Man, he got it right.

"The biggest thing for me is the opening guitar riff. Everyone knows that now. No matter what I'm doing when the song starts, I hear that, and I stop. Gets to me. Every time."

The unlikely single topped the Canadian chart, the U.S. country chart, and finished 1976 on the Billboard 100 chart second only to Rod Stewart's "Tonight's the Night," a song that checked all the usual boxes for a hit: short—at three minutes and thirty-four seconds, almost three minutes shorter than "The Wreck"—peppy, with a memorable chorus and hook, plus the bonus of Stewart's girlfriend, Britt Ekland, cooing in the background, the "Me Generation" personified. It embodied everything "The Wreck of the Edmund Fitzgerald" did not.

"I just listened to 'The Wreck of the Edmund Fitzgerald' for the first time in a while," *Rolling Stone* editor Christian Hoard says, "and I have to say it's remarkable that it was such a big pop hit: no chorus, no bridge, no hook, just the same melody repeated over seven eight-line stanzas for nearly seven minutes. I mean, 'Hotel California,' another dark and lengthy story song from the same era, still had a chorus *and* an amazing guitar coda.

"I'd venture 'Wreck' is one of the *wordiest* top five hits until rap came along. Compelling melody for sure, but I have to assume that what people loved so much was hearing the *story* in such detail. That's some old-school troubadour stuff, a ballad in the classic sense."

Perhaps Hoard's insights explain why Lightfoot was so reluctant to share it in its embryonic stage. Lightfoot's song broke all the rules, and he knew it. But Hoard is right: The story was too compelling to ignore. Like Lightfoot's sources, the AP's Harry Atkins and *Newsweek*'s Jim Gaines, Lightfoot cared about the *Edmund Fitzgerald* more than he had to, and people could feel it.

A FEW MONTHS after the meeting with Warner Brothers' president in Los Angeles Lightfoot's band played a tour stop at Kalamazoo, Michigan's K-Wings Stadium. It holds about five thousand people, but packed six thousand that night.

"I can still see their faces pressed up against wire screens around the stage," Keane says. "It was like that for the whole concert—but you can imagine how it got amped up when we played 'The Wreck of the Edmund Fitzgerald.'"

In addition to the song's unusual structure and forbidding length, the tune was limited by Lightfoot himself, who refused to market the piece in the usual manner.

"Gord wasn't big on playing hits," Keane says with a chuckle. "He would always say, 'To thine own self be true.' At our concerts he liked to play *his* favorites. We'd say, 'Hey Gord, why don't we play "Carefree Highway"? Big hit, everyone likes it.' And he'd say, 'Ah they all know that one.' Right! Isn't that the point?

"He drove Warner Bros. absolutely *nuts*! We'd produce a new album, and *not* tour, because Gord was afraid people would think we're just trying to sell records. Well, wasn't that the idea? A very Canadian response. A very Lightfoot response."

And yet, Lightfoot's stubborn purity is surely why listeners recognize his sincerity in memorializing such a tragic event. The next year he accepted an invitation from the Reverend Ingalls, the pastor who rang the bell twenty-nine times, to play at the Mariners' Church in Detroit. Lightfoot brought only Terry Clements and Rick Haynes, a barebones band.

"Just us, and a small amplifier playing at the front," Haynes says. "As simple and pure as it gets."

After they finished the song Reverend Ingalls approached Lightfoot, appreciatively and respectfully, to point out that Mariners' wasn't a "musty old hall," as Lightfoot's lyrics said, but clean and bright.

Lightfoot agreed. Whenever they played the song after that, he changed the lyric from "musty old hall" to "rustic old hall."

One of the theories investigators had posited to explain the *Fitzgerald*'s sinking was improperly clamped hatches, which prompted Lightfoot to write one of his most famous stanzas:

When suppertime came, the old cook came on deck
sayin', "Fellas, it's too rough to feed ya."
At seven p.m., a main hatchway caved in
he said "Fellas, it's been good to know ya"

After investigators were able to send a submarine to examine the ship 530 feet below the surface, they discovered that Mark Thomas, Paul Riippa, and muscle car aficionado Bruce Hudson had, in fact, done their jobs correctly, to the great relief of Hudson's mother, Ruth. Lightfoot changed that lyric, too.

At seven p.m., it grew dark, it was then
he said "Fellas, it's been good to know ya"

"That's how much Gord really cared about 'the wives and the sons and the daughters,'" Keane says.

Bassist Rick Haynes agrees. "Gord wanted the families to have peace."

Lightfoot even double-checked lines in the song that were verifiably accurate.

"One time Gord and I had a heated argument," Haynes says. "He said, 'It *can't* be twenty-six thousand tons. That's impossible! It has to be twenty-six hundred tons!'

"Gord, you got it right the first time," Haynes said. "That's what those ships carry!"

Lightfoot and his bandmates have been careful about how and where they play it, too. When Jimmy Fallon wanted to do a comedy bit based on the song, Lightfoot rejected the idea out of hand, before it could go anywhere.

THE FEAR LIGHTFOOT had of being perceived as an opportunist, especially by the families, was dispelled.

"I had quit following the *Fitzgerald* story," former *Fitzgerald* deckhand Patrick Devine says. "I just couldn't deal with it emotionally. But when the song first came out the next year, I was furious! I felt like a lot of people were taking advantage of other people's suffering. I was really irritated.

"But the following year I was at one of the memorials when Helen Bindon, widow of Eddie Bindon, who had been so good to me, came up to me and said, 'Have you heard that new song?' She appreciated it—even if I didn't. It stunned me. Well, she lost her husband, and she loves the song, so what's my problem?"

Like Devine, when Marilynn Church Peterson, one of Nolan Church's five children, heard the song for the first time, "I hated it. My first thought was he just wants to make money off it."

Marilynn's view changed twenty-six years later, on May 5, 2002, when she and five family members went to see Lightfoot and his band play in Duluth. After a moving concert, Lightfoot invited them all backstage.

"When I heard him play it live I knew he really cared about the song," Marilynn says. "And backstage he asked what I thought of it. I assured him it was a great tribute. He truly cared about all the families involved—and I felt that he truly cared about my feelings."

Like many of the survivors, since the sinking Marilynn Church Peterson has never gone back out on Lake Superior, the lake she grew up on. As a rule, the younger the survivor, the more likely they were to succumb to self-medication through drinking and drugs. Most ultimately came out of it, but not all.

"It was very hard on Mike," Bonnie Church Kellerman says, referring to their youngest sibling, who was just seventeen when their father died.

"He had a really hard life after that, and chose the wrong direction," Marilynn says. "At that age, I don't think he ever got over it."

The families have little choice but to savor the silver linings, including the song itself.

"Our dad has so many grandchildren, great-grandchildren, and now even great-great-grandchildren," Marilynn says. "They never got to meet him, but they love the song, and at family functions we always play it."

Cindy Reynolds, Bruce Hudson's girlfriend, remembers the immediate effect the song had on her and Ruth Hudson.

"We listened to it and listened to it," Reynolds says. "And Ruth thought it was unbelievable that he could put together those words that fast. She wondered how he could know how it felt, because it felt like he did.

"Even now, when I hear the song, it gets me reminiscing about Bruce. And sometimes I have to pull over, and listen in peace."

That might be Lightfoot's best review.

Lightfoot, after the unexpected success of "The Wreck of the Edmund Fitzgerald," pulled out of his tailspin, got clean and sober, and embarked on thousands of concerts over the next four decades.

If Lightfoot was initially uncertain about his new song, by 2002 he knew exactly where it stood in his body of work. He told Roger LeLievre, then at *The Ann Arbor News*, that "The Wreck of the Edmund Fitzgerald" "is my greatest achievement. It's a song you can't turn your back on. You can't walk away from the people either. The song has a sound and total feel all its own. We've sung it at every show since the day we wrote it. It's a true song and a great song. It's stood the test of time."

Former GLMA superintendent John Tanner met Lightfoot a few times backstage with the GLMA scholarship recipients. "If I had to pick one word to describe him and his music," Tanner says, "it's 'pure.' Gordon Lightfoot is pure."

That explains why fans, from overseas to the *Fitzgerald* families themselves, are so attracted to "The Wreck of the Edmund Fitzgerald": It's a true song.

For the fortieth anniversary of the sinking in 2015, bassist Rick Haynes and Lightfoot flew from a concert in Utica, New York, on their only day off from their tour, to the Upper Peninsula, then drove to Whitefish Point for an event—and not to play, just to be there with the families.

"I remember walking out to the water off Whitefish Point," Haynes says, "and sitting in the sand, and just looking out there. This is a song that I've sung thousands of times, and the men we sing about are just fifteen miles out there.

"So close to safety. It gets you."

The Deckhand's Baby

BACK IN OREGON, OHIO, SEVENTEEN-YEAR-OLD CINDY Reynolds had completed all the credits she needed to earn her high school diploma by January 1976, and continued to wait tables at the supper club. Because she still wasn't showing at almost eight months of pregnancy, her classmates, coworkers, and even her parents didn't know she was expecting. Only her best friend, Cyndi George, knew the truth.

"I just went totally quiet about it for months," Cindy Reynolds says. "Now that I look back, I don't know how I did it."

With only a month left in her pregnancy, Cindy's mother finally confronted her.

"I don't know how she found out," Cindy says. "But one day she said, 'I hear you're expecting,' in a tone of voice you don't forget. Then she asked, 'What are you going to do about it?'

"'It's too late to do anything,'" Cindy said. "'It's due in three weeks.'"

Cindy finally made a doctor's appointment, which she had been avoiding out of fear her parents would find out. The doctor assured her that everything seemed fine, but because Cindy had received no prenatal care and taken no vitamins, he added, "I am not responsible for what happens to this child"—not exactly what a pregnant seventeen-year-old whose boyfriend had died tragically needed to hear.

On Saturday, May 22, 1976, Cindy worked her usual shift at the supper club. Then, two days later, on Monday morning, May 24, as soon as she woke up she told her mother, "It's time. Can you take me to the hospital?'"

Her mom said, "Sure. I'm going to call Grandma and see if she wants to come."

"I don't know if we have time for that!"

They got to the hospital at 8:30 a.m., and at 11:30 Cindy delivered a healthy baby girl: Heather Lee Reynolds.

"Lee" was Bruce's middle name.

Cindy still hadn't told Ruth Hudson, who did not even know Cindy was pregnant.

"Ruth was fifty when the ship went down," Cindy says, "and already menopausal, and emotional. Bruce was her only son, and she poured herself into him."

Although Bruce had been boldly independent in some ways, in others he was still a mama's boy who loved going home to be fussed over. For her part, Ruth had started to let go of her son only when he began working on the *Fitzgerald*.

"She wasn't really ready for Bruce to start sailing," Cindy says. "Then the ship goes down. That's all at once. No preparing for that. I can't imagine what that was like for her."

A couple weeks after Cindy gave birth to Heather Lee, she screwed up her courage yet again and called Bruce's mom. After Ruth heard the stunning news—her second shock of a lifetime in just six months—she went silent for a moment. Then she said, "I need to digest this for a while. I'm not saying I don't believe you. I've just got to pray on this."

Ruth called back the next day, and asked Cindy a few questions. Cindy made it clear that Bruce was definitely the father, but added, "Look, I'm not asking for nothing. I just want you to know," and left it at that. What Ruth did next would be up to her.

On June 2, 1976, eight days after Cindy had given birth to Heather, her high school class would conduct its graduation ceremony. Although Cindy had completed her coursework in January, six months later she had no interest in walking across the stage—but her best friend was having none of it.

"You are going to walk," Cyndi George told Cindy Reynolds. It was not phrased as a question.

"No, I'm not."

"Yes. You are."

And that was that.

As Reynolds watched her classmates receive their diplomas, she soon discovered she was far from alone. In a class of 380 graduates, about 190 of them women, 13 were visibly pregnant.

"Thirteen!" Reynolds says. "We counted them as they walked across the stage. But no one knew I was pregnant, so maybe there were more."

If her class had just five more students who were secretly pregnant, that would mark 10 percent of the graduating women. It was a different era.

Thanks to Cindy's friends at the supper club, who threw her a baby shower, Cindy and her daughter had just about everything they needed to get started. The two lived in Cindy's room at her parents' home, with Heather sleeping in the drawer next to Cindy's bed.

"When I look back at everything that happened," Cindy says, "I can't believe we all survived."

A FEW WEEKS after Cindy's first call to Bruce's mother, Ruth invited Cindy and Heather to visit later that summer, when Heather would be just a few months old. It went so well that, every month or so, Ruth would take Heather back to North Olmsted for a whole weekend, giving Cindy a much-needed break, and Ruth time with her new granddaughter. When Heather was old enough Ruth started taking her on shopping trips, which soon became their favorite shared pastime.

"I'm not a shopper," Cindy says, "so this was not for me! I'd ask them, 'Do you guys really gotta touch every piece of clothing? Find something, and let's go!' But that's not how they did it. Heather said, 'This is shopping, Mama!'"

Ruth Hudson had lost her only child, then six months later gained her only grandchild. Pouring herself into Bruce had caused her unimaginable heartbreak when he drowned, but she couldn't resist doing the same for her grandchild, no matter the risks.

The poet Louise Gluck asks, "Why love what you will lose?"

Then she answers her own question: "There is nothing else to love."

Protecting the Living

After the *Bradley* broke apart in 1958, very little changed.

When the *Morrell* went down in 1966, industry leaders paid lip service to reforms, but their half-hearted efforts soon faded.

But when the *Edmund Fitzgerald* sank, the shockwaves it sent throughout the shipping industry and beyond provided the wake-up call that was sorely needed to prompt changes that have stuck, and saved lives.

"The *Fitzgerald* was a very tragic thing," former GLMA superintendent John Tanner says. "But the safety reforms that were triggered by that accident were incredible."

Fifty years ago captains would receive two short "reports of weather" each day about what was happening at that time, plus two short forecasts from Marine Forecast (MAFOR), and occasional calls from other ships reporting what they were experiencing on the seas.

"But it was random," Tanner says. "No system to it at all. That's all we had. Well, you look at the *Fitzgerald*, and it clearly wasn't enough—not even close. If Captain McSorley had more information, he probably wouldn't have been out there, or at least he'd have gone a different way."

If McSorley had the data then that captains receive today, before and during their trips, he would have been far more likely to have kept the *Fitzgerald* at Superior's Burlington Dock No. 1 a day longer, or found safe harbor along the way. If he did decide to press on, he would have at least taken the faster route straight across Lake Superior. That would have spared McSorley the less familiar northern route, with outdated charts and the perilous Six Fathom Shoal looming, and saved the *Fitzgerald* fourteen or more hours, keeping it well ahead of the storm's epicenter in the race to Whitefish Bay.

Regardless of which route he took, McSorley also would not have slowed down to wait for the *Anderson* if he knew the center of the storm was headed to meet his ship at Whitefish Point. Those two decisions alone would have likely delivered the *Fitzgerald* to safety. In fact, if he had taken the northern route but been aware of fifty-footers heading to Whitefish Bay, a seasoned captain like McSorley would have sought shelter and waited out the worst of it, *before* crossing Caribou Island and Six Fathom Shoal.

Thanks to the unprecedented global attention the *Fitzgerald*'s demise received, the Coast Guard, the shipping companies, and the Lake Carriers' Association all worked together to improve radars, satellites, computers, and communication systems between ships and shore, and to make sure better electronic components were installed in all freighters. Every ship now has enough information to ensure such a tragedy never happens again.

"It is *completely* different today," Tanner says. "With all that technology, you're going to know what's actually happening out there much earlier, and much more thoroughly. The weather reports get to the captains much quicker now, almost in real time. Really, it's just unbelievable what they have today compared to what we had back then."

Perhaps the most fundamental change in Great Lakes shipping since the *Fitzgerald* is not technology but a renewed emphasis on plain old common sense. Corporate avarice and the captains' macho mentality have finally taken a backseat to cool-headed assessments of the relative risks and rewards of charging ahead versus waiting for better weather. Even without considering the incalculable cost of human life, trying to save a few hours by pushing through a storm is not worth the risk of losing a 729-foot ship carrying twenty-six thousand tons of taconite, a loss of $24 million in 1975, or $140 million today. Just one day later, Superior was glass.

"Those types of storms were typically occurring every thirty years or so," Michigan Tech's Guy Meadows says. "They appear more frequently now, and will likely continue to into the future. But now the forecasts are much better, and I am amazed how much more careful the captains are than they used to be. When those big blows come now, they hide without hesitation behind the Keweenaw. Doesn't take much for them to seek shelter. They are more cautious now than they were in *Fitzgerald*'s day."

On November 11, 2024, the day after the forty-ninth anniversary ceremony at the Great Lakes Shipwreck Museum at Whitefish Point, faithfully attended each year by the family members, the winds approached thirty miles per hour on Lake Superior and the waves kicked up to ten feet. Not much by *Fitzgerald* standards, but nearly fifty years later it was enough for *every ship* in Whitefish Bay to lay anchor, perhaps the most sincere homage the sailors could pay to the *Fitzgerald*'s crew. That's how much things have changed.

The most eye-opening outcome of all these reforms is this: In the half century since the *Edmund Fitzgerald* went under, *not one commercial ship* has sunk on the Great Lakes, by far the longest run of safe trips since the French fur traders started traversing the same waters four hundred years ago.

"As hard it was to lose twenty-nine men, think how many lives have been saved since," John Tanner says. "Would that have happened without the *Fitzgerald*? I sincerely doubt it. When do you fix anything? When it's broken."

When talking with the families of the victims, you notice how often they make that very point: As devastating as it was to lose their fathers, their uncles, their brothers, their cousins, and their boyfriends, they are acutely aware that no commercial ships have suffered a similar fate since, and they justly take pride in that fact. The immeasurable sacrfices of that day were not made in vain.

But that does not bring back the twenty-nine men whose loved ones still grieve.

Raising the Bell

After her initial shock wore off, Ruth Hudson fell hopelessly in love with her new granddaughter, Heather Lee Reynolds, but the heartache she felt over her lost son never relented.

Aunt Ruth channeled her grief into action, working ceaselessly to preserve the memory of her son and his shipmates. But how best to honor the dead? Some fifteen years after the shipwreck the answer came to Tom Farnquist, then the director of the Great Lakes Shipwreck Museum: retrieve the *Fitzgerald*'s bell. But what now seems like an obvious idea was initially quite controversial.

"Some families didn't think the bell should be brought up, but left there, forever," Cindy Reynolds says. "And then some thought, if you do bring it up, you should not put it in a museum, but in the Mariners' Church."

After many long, hard conversations, Aunt Ruth and the other families decided Farnquist was right: They should recover the two-hundred-pound bell from the bow of the *Fitzgerald*, if they could, and display it at the Great Lakes Shipwreck Museum, home of the Whitefish Point lighthouse. Opened in 1849, it is the oldest operating beacon on Lake Superior, and the closest to the *Edmund Fitzgerald*'s final resting place seventeen miles to the northwest.

With the support of most of the families, if not all, Ruth Hudson did what she always did, and got to work.

"Ruth and I drove all over, working on that," Cindy Reynolds says. "Quebec, Ottawa, Michigan, talking to all the governments involved."

In the days before cell phones and email, Aunt Ruth spent hundreds of hours writing letters, making phone calls, and arranging meetings with Canadian and American government officials. The cost of stamps and long-distance calls ran into the thousands, an expense she could barely afford on her Bonne Bell Cosmetics factory wages or, later, her pension. But she pressed on, determined that her son would not be forgotten.

What price can a mother put on her love for her only child?

Over time Aunt Ruth and Cheryl Rozman, Ransom Cundy's hardworking and devoted daughter, gained unanimous support from the family members. Then they secured the permission of the Canadian and United States governments to send another expedition down to the ship to retrieve the bell, and tastefully display it as the centerpiece of the Great Lakes Shipwreck Museum.

On Tuesday, July 4, 1995, the Coast Guard's premier Great Lakes ice breaker, the *Mackinaw*, sailed to where the *Fitzgerald* now lies, just on the Canadian side of the border:

46 degrees, 59 minutes north latitude
85 degrees, 6 minutes west longitude

Two submersibles and a diver wearing a specially designed "Newtsuit" to survive the immense water pressure descended 530 feet to remove the *Fitzgerald*'s original bronze bell, which weighs two hundred pounds, with underwater cutting torches. After freeing the bell from the roof of the pilothouse, where it had sat in darkness for two decades, they replaced it with a replica engraved with the twenty-nine names on it as a permanent grave marker.

Floating near the *Mackinaw*, the *Northlander* carried the *Fitzgerald* families. While a single trumpet played, they watched the original bell break the surface of Lake Superior at 1:25 p.m.

Buck Champeau had often pledged to his younger brother Jack, who served in Vietnam, that if anything happened to him overseas, Buck would bring him back. Jack always felt guilty that he could not do the same for Buck. On this day, after government officials set the recovered bell up on a podium, they asked Jack Champeau to be the first to ring it—the best he could do for his brother.

Three days later, in a ceremony the family members named "Call to the Last Watch," they rang the bell thirty times—twenty-nine for each man lost on the *Fitzgerald* and once for the thirty thousand sailors who have lost their lives on the Great Lakes.

"It was kind of like being in church, if that makes any sense," says John Tanner, who had been invited to join the families on the *Northlander* that day. "It wasn't sad, as much as it was respectful. This was a cemetery below us, and we knew they're still there. It was solemn.

"It's one thing to feel bad for your friend, or your students, in my case. But when you're looking into the eyes of the mother of one of those men, that's different. That's hard."

Today the *Edmund Fitzgerald*'s original bronze bell, freshly polished, shines at the Great Lakes Shipwreck Museum. Every November 10 current director Bruce Lynn invites the family and friends of the victims back for a private ceremony. When a Coast Guard officer announces each name, the closest family member or friend present rises, walks up to the bell, and rings it in their honor.

"When I see the bell," says John Hayes, who once rang it for his best friend, Tom Bentsen, "it triggers something in me. There's always survivor's guilt. Tom and I were very reckless back then, although he 'did reckless' with more panache than I did. We were living for the moment, as you do at that age. Why did I get a chance to get my life squared away and stop doing the stupid things you do as a young man, and Tom never got that chance? I've got grandkids now."

Hayes thinks of Cindy Gagnier, Bentsen's girlfriend the last year of his life. They had just gotten engaged that season.

"She was a great girl and could have helped Tom clean up his act, like my wife helped me clean up mine, but she never got the chance. The realization of all that makes it worse.

"Sometimes it's the silence that gets me. No survivors. Not even a peep."

For Third Mate Michael Armagost's wife, Janice, the recovery of the bell marked the end of a journey that she, Aunt Ruth, and the others had traveled for two decades. Once the bell came up, Janice told the other families: "That's my closure. I'm done."

Understandable, but Aunt Ruth soon decided she had more to do.

In July of 1994 a wealthy businessman named Fred Shannon organized an expedition he named "DeepQuest" that conducted seven dives over three days, which obtained some of the clearest footage of the site. Most controversially, the video captured one of the twenty-nine bodies, which could be seen wearing a lifejacket. That's unusual for a Great Lakes sailor, and suggests that at least one crewman believed they were in danger of sinking, or perhaps he had been one of the sailors on the deck trying to tie the ship together with the cable from the winch.

Aunt Ruth felt deeply offended by Shannon's unauthorized filming, especially the footage of the sailor in the lifejacket. She and the other families insisted that he cease his filming immediately and not sell his film to the public, but they had no power to enforce their wishes.

After Shannon refused, Cindy Reynolds wrote him a letter asking for a copy of the footage so she would have a better sense of what had happened to the father of her child. Not only did Shannon decline her request, "he sent me a nasty letter," Reynolds says. "And he harassed Aunt Ruth for years. Who does that? I gave him an earful."

So did Pam Wittig, Aunt Ruth's niece, after Shannon kept calling Aunt Ruth, trying to persuade her to give her blessings for diving on the site.

"He wanted to sensationalize it, and she wanted to keep it a gravesite," Pam says. "I had to call him one time and say, 'Leave her alone.' She never had a good thing to say about him."

While most people found Ruth Hudson unusually friendly and kind, "If she didn't like you, she didn't like you," Cindy Reynolds says. "And she did not like him."

Fred Shannon had made a small but surprisingly powerful enemy.

The experience convinced Aunt Ruth and the other families they needed to prohibit anyone from exploring the remains again. This would not be simple, because the *Fitzgerald* lies 530 feet below the surface in dark, cold waters, and just on the Canadian side.

Once again Aunt Ruth rolled up her sleeves, this time to persuade the Canadian government to declare the shipwreck a national gravesite, which would protect her son and the other crewmen from profiteers and grifters eager to exploit their loss for fame or fortune.

"Aunt Ruth kept everything in envelopes," Pam Wittig says. "She was tight with a penny, a child of the Depression, after all. But she spent a lot of her money tracking down everybody connected to the ship to get that passed."

"The bell and the gravesite, they were both hard to get done," Cindy Reynolds says. "Lots of letters. Lots of calls. Lots of trips. And lots of talking to one person, just to get a hold of the next person, and then you've got to talk to the secretary—and if you're not careful they'll send you back to the first person. And in Canada, it seemed like they're 'on holiday' all the time! And here comes this little woman to talk to all these big government officials in suits sitting around a table. We had two good lawyers, but Ruth was always the driving force."

In the process Cindy and Ruth became partners who learned to rely on each other.

"She'd be writing a letter and ask me, 'How does this sound? This is what I want to do. What do you think?'" Cindy says. "We were a team."

On July 17, 1999, their work came to fruition at a ceremony aboard the Coast Guard cutter *Mackinaw*, positioned directly above the *Fitzgerald* on Lake Superior. With the Mariners' Church pastor, the Reverend Richard Ingalls, Sr., presiding, the wreck of the *Edmund Fitzgerald* was legally consecrated as a gravesite, one which cannot be visited without the approval of the Canadian government.

The twenty-nine men have been left in peace.

EPILOGUE

WHEN CRAIG ELLQUIST SAYS, "THERE BUT FOR THE grace of God go I," it's not just a phrase.

He had planned to return to the *Edmund Fitzgerald* for the '75 season, which would have been his second as a deckhand. It was work he enjoyed with people he liked. But when Al Ruberg convinced him to spend the summer delivering milk in Two Harbors, Ellquist decided to put off the *Fitzgerald* for at least a few months.

In the half century since, Ellquist has not been able to shake that day, nor the memories of his friends on board—friends he would have been sailing with on November 10 if not for Al Ruberg, who passed away a few years ago.

"I'm still in contact with Al's family," he says. "He saved my life. But it still haunts me to this day. It does."

In an unexpected turn of events, Ellquist's daughter, Julie, married Bryan Peterson, the son of Marilynn Church Peterson and grandson of Nolan Church, the *Fitzgerald*'s fifty-five-year-old porter. The young couple now has three children of their own they're raising in Two Harbors.

The Churches know the same fates that claimed their father also spared Craig Ellquist, which ultimately made possible three of Nolan's thirty-one great-grandchildren.

"For that," Marilynn Church Peterson says, "we are grateful."

WHEN BRUCE HUDSON returned to the *Fitzgerald* in September of 1975, Patrick Devine got bumped off. He wasn't happy about it, but he soon went out on another Columbia ship for one last run to finish the season. He enrolled for the fall quarter at the University of Toledo, and then boarded another Columbia ship that spring.

But Devine couldn't get the *Fitzgerald* and his friends off his mind. It didn't help that on three occasions, when his ship pulled into port he saw the wreck investigators from the Coast Guard, the National

Transportation Safety Board, and others waiting for him on the dock to ask more questions.

Late in the 1976 shipping season Devine dislocated his right shoulder working onboard. He tried to come back the following season, but inevitably he reinjured it.

"I thought, *'You know what, I'm done with this,'*" he says. "But really, I was done with shipping when the *Fitzgerald* sank. I went back out because I didn't know what else to do. But I was just going through the motions, trying to digest everything. It was too much.

"I already had my problems with alcohol before she sank. But after she went down, I just crawled down into a bottle and hid."

It is rare to find a victim's family that has not had someone struggle with drugs or alcohol after the *Fitzgerald* went down, and some have been lost. Devine was almost one of them.

"Took me a long time to pull out of it," he says. Thanks to Alcoholics Anonymous and his family, Devine has been sober for forty years, and enjoyed a successful career in the restaurant business, a life very far from the docks.

"I learned that the way for me to stay sober was to reduce my stress," he says. "Now, maybe running a fine-dining restaurant sounds stressful to most people, but it worked for me."

It also allowed him to meet Cheryl Armor.

"I fell in love immediately," Devine says.

They married, and years later retired happily out West. But Devine still thinks of the *Edmund Fitzgerald* and his friends, particularly Eddie Bindon, his forty-seven-year-old protector, and Paul Riippa, his fellow deckhand. The night Bruce Hudson replaced Devine on the *Fitzgerald* the ship happened to be in Ashtabula, Riippa's hometown, so Riippa invited Devine to spend the night at his folks' house, a kindness Devine never forgot. Devine also remembers giving Riippa the Moody Blues cassette he liked so much when they said goodbye.

"And that went down with the boat," Devine says. "I assure you it did."

Devine eventually made peace with his demanding father, the judge. When his dad was hospitalized for a back injury, he and Patrick talked for two weeks.

"At one point Dad got real quiet, and he said, 'You know Patrick, I'm beginning to understand why you've lived the way you do.' And that's it: the closest he ever came to giving me a compliment."

Devine smiles at the memory. It took a lot of years, willpower, and help, but Patrick Devine stands squarely on solid ground, for good.

Tom Walton has followed the *Fitzgerald* since he served as a porter on the great ship in 1963, a position that gave him the run of the boat.

"I explored every inch of that ship because I was a kid, too," he says, "and I was fascinated by it all. And at that age, it stays with you. I remember it all so vividly. I know all the stairways and officers' quarters and the crews' cabins, the laundry, the passengers' rooms."

His father Wade, an engineer, joined him onboard during that magical summer of 1963, and twelve years later his uncle Grant, an oiler, went down with the ship. Walton, who became a respected editor and later a columnist with the *Toledo Blade*, under the name Thomas Walton, has been writing and speaking about the *Fitzgerald* for fifty years.

"I'm always aware of it," he says. "It's only in November, when the anniversary comes around, that others are."

One of Walton's themes: how much his father and uncle loved their work.

"My dad was a laker, and on the Great Lakes was where he wanted to be. Even so, my father retired not long after the *Fitz* went down. He had lost his brother and he had lost his love for what he was doing. He had also lost many good friends, including several I knew because they had been to our house so often in the offseason. Ed Bindon. Bob Rafferty. Russ Haskell. And of course, Captain McSorley.

"I can still see their faces."

McSorley's widow Nellie was in ill health in 1975, but thanks to Ernest's plans she received the care she needed and lived eighteen more years before passing away in 1993, at the ripe age of 82.

One scene Walton did not see but still envisions: the ship's demise.

"I constantly flash back in my mind's eye to what it must have been like for them, at the end. For a long time I would have dreams about it, imagining those final few moments for Uncle Grant."

Grant Walton was probably on the four-to-eight shift. At 7 p.m., therefore, he would have been on duty in the engine room.

"I can just picture that engine room so clearly, and the terror of that moment. It's frightening to contemplate. Nothing was watertight, including the sleeping quarters. The water's coming in, by the tons, and it's freezing.

"To be trapped in that stern, as it's filling rapidly with water . . . You're not going anywhere. You're in total darkness, no hope—and you know it. They might have lived for a few minutes, about as long as you could hold your breath. But that would have been it.

"That haunted me for the longest time.

"I don't dream about it anymore, but I think about it every day.

"Every single day."

MANY OF THE family members, close friends, and girlfriends have recurring dreams of their loved ones on the water.

Cindy LoCicero, the high school senior who dated David "Cowboy" Weiss, started having dreams of Weiss soon after the ship sank.

"I would dream he was in a raft and got rescued—again and again," she says. "And then you wake up, and you know he's still gone. It took me a long time to come to terms with it."

LoCicero attended the first memorial service at the Great Lakes Maritime Academy in Traverse City, which they've held every year since. Cindy's father walked her over to meet Weiss's parents, who knew of her and received her warmly. She continued to go to the memorial services for thirty years—but always standing in the back, out of deference to the wives and the daughters, where she could be seen quietly crying, and rubbing the necklace Weiss had given her.

For the tenth anniversary at the GLMA the Weisses took LoCicero with them. When they showed a video of all twenty-nine sailors, LoCicero started crying, and Weiss's mother, Selma, said, "You really did love him, didn't you?"

"Yes, I really did."

Selma Weiss gave LoCicero a picture of David that she's kept in her purse ever since. It's now very worn.

"It was probably one of the few that she had of him," LoCicero says, "so that was generous."

Years later when LoCicero was in California she drove past the Weisses' house, and stopped to look, and think. She just wanted to see it, and imagine a life that almost was.

As a high school junior during the spring of 1975, Debbie Champeau had sent a letter to her father, Buck, when he was on the *Fitzgerald*, asking for money for a new dress, new shoes, and a fancy new hair style for her junior prom. He generously agreed to pay for all of it, provided she came home from the dance at 11 p.m., and she did—that time.

After the *Fitzgerald* went down the Champeaus had to get her father's car, the Oldsmobile, parked at the dock in Toledo.

"Dad's car was blueish, a four door, nothing huge, and it was a stick shift," Debbie says. "I didn't know how to drive a stick shift, so I couldn't drive it home, and my mom didn't drive at all. So his brother Tom and I picked it up."

When they pulled up to Buck's car, Debbie went right to the glove box, the old metal kind with a keyhole. When she opened it, sure enough, the letter she had sent him about her junior prom was right on top, and another envelope containing a few pictures of her: one of her in the fourth grade, and another of her in the prom dress he'd paid for.

"He'd saved them, and put them in the glove box," she says. "So they would be waiting for him in Toledo when he finished the season."

Debbie still has the list of rules her dad wrote out for her when he gave Debbie her first car, the Rambler, but she would wait forty years before she read it again. Yes, it was about car maintenance, but Debbie says, "Every one of these rules you could live your life by."

Buck Champeau liked to help the men at the Milwaukee Rescue Mission, including one man named Caput. Eventually Caput went clean and sober, and got a good job on his own. Years later, Caput told Debbie, "If it wasn't for your dad, I wouldn't be alive."

Debbie still gets a Christmas card in the mail from the mission, and always replies with a donation in her father's name: *Buck Champeau.*

Buck had been a proud Marine, but when Debbie's youngest daughter, Rachel, wanted to sign up right out of high school, Debbie was having none of it. Rachel eventually wore Debbie down, joined the Marines, and served in Fallujah, Iraq, as an aviation mechanic, working on helicopters.

"I was terrified when she was over there," Debbie admits. "She's so petite she couldn't put a bomb into the Hueys, so she had to get on her back and push the bombs in place with her legs! But she found a way, and got it done. Her grandpa would be very proud.

"*I'm* very proud of her. She says, 'Once a Marine, always a Marine.' Just like her grandfather."

As a teenager Debbie had recurring nightmares "seeing my dad that horrible night reaching out with one hand out of the water. His hand was reaching out to me. I tried to grab it to pull him out, but I never could save him. I was so close, but I could never get him out of that horrific storm. This dream haunted me for a very long time.

"I have been able to come to peace with Lake Superior because the families fought to make the wreckage a burial site to be protected, and not tampered with. I know when I am long gone, my children and grandchildren will continue to protect my dad."

WHEN THE *FITZGERALD* foundered Bruce Hudson was just twenty-two years old—and always will be.

After he was gone, Pam Wittig recalls, "Aunt Ruth would often say things like, 'Can you imagine him as a dad? He'd be forty now.' Then, 'He'd be fifty now. I can picture him.' "

Ruth Hudson would have had to content herself with her memories, her imagination, and Bruce's dog Kelly, if it were not for the arrival of Cindy and Bruce's daughter, Heather, followed by Heather's four children—Ruth's great-grandchildren. They gave Ruth Hudson a name she never thought she would have after she lost her only child: Grandma Ruth.

Ruth doted on them all, but she had an especially soft spot for Heather's oldest boy, Austin, now twenty-six. If fortune had cost Ruth Hudson her only child, it also gave her, just as unexpectedly, a great-grandson who is the spitting image of her son, and even shares his grandfather's mannerisms.

"Oh my gosh!" Pam Wittig says. "Austin looks *just like* Bruce! And Aunt Ruth loved that kid—oh my god, how she loved that kid."

As Aunt Ruth approached ninety she invited Cindy over so they could go through Ruth's possessions, sorting through Bruce's things.

"Ruth gave me everything," Cindy says, including a handful of taconite pellets that had come up from the *Edmund Fitzgerald* with the bell. Cindy has saved them in a jar of Lake Superior's pure water, and gave some to her daughter, Heather, who keeps hers in her purse—a piece of the father she never met.

The day Ruth gave Bruce's remaining effects to Cindy had some light moments, too. Cindy had always thought the purple skull bong she bought Bruce for his birthday had gone down with the ship.

"But then Ruth pulls this thing out of the closet one day," she says, "long after he was gone, and says, 'I have no idea what this is!'"

Thinking fast, Cindy replied, "I think you burn incense in it."

Ruth seem satisfied with that answer, so Cindy asked, "Can I have it?"

To this day, Cindy keeps Bruce's purple skull bong in a special place.

In early November of 2015, when Aunt Ruth was ninety, she and her niece, Pam Wittig, decided Ruth should move in with Pam and her husband in South Carolina.

With the fortieth anniversary of the tragedy just a few days away, Aunt Ruth made Pam promise that she would go to Whitefish Point in Ruth's place, and ring the bell in honor of Bruce. Pam agreed.

Aunt Ruth then told Pam that she planned to go—pass away—right before November 10, so she could be with Bruce to watch the fortieth anniversary ceremony together.

When Wittig left Columbia, South Carolina, for Whitefish Point on November 7, Aunt Ruth could barely speak. Wittig's husband stayed behind to take care of Ruth, and they were soon joined by Cindy Reynolds and Heather, who drove down from Ohio.

"I'm so glad it worked out that way," Cindy says. "It was so good to be with Ruth."

After Pam arrived at the Great Lakes Shipwreck Museum on November 9, Cindy called her to let her know Aunt Ruth was near the end.

It so happened that Gordon Lightfoot and Rick Haynes, his loyal bassist, had come to Whitefish Point that day just to visit with the families at the museum campus's crews quarters, where the families stay. When Lightfoot saw Pam Wittig in the kitchen, where everyone tends to gather, he immediately asked her where the irrepressible Aunt Ruth was. Pam told him that Aunt Ruth was back in South Carolina, and likely on her death bed.

Lightfoot said, "I need to call her."

After Pam warned him that Aunt Ruth could barely speak, she dialed Aunt Ruth's number, and handed the phone to Lightfoot.

"He talked to her very casually," Pam says, "just like an old friend. Which they were."

Back in Columbia, South Carolina, Cindy Reynolds helped Aunt Ruth on the other end.

"Ruth told him that she would be going that day," Reynolds recalls, "dying, so she could spend the fortieth anniversary in heaven with Bruce the next day. She said, 'Bruce has been alone too long.' "

When the two finished their call, Aunt Ruth turned to Cindy and whispered, "I just got off the phone with Gordon."

"She was very weak," Cindy says. "But she got those words out. When I see the photo of Gordon in that kitchen, on the phone with Ruth, it still gives me chills."

True to her word, a few hours later, around 4 p.m. on Sunday, November 9, Ruth Hudson gently passed away.

THE TRAGEDY ALSO performed some unexpected work.

While the men on the *Edmund Fitzgerald* got along unusually well, forging close friendships with their fellow crewmen, the families themselves barely knew each other before the accident. They were aware of their loved ones' friends on the ship, but few met them, and they knew almost nothing about the other families.

But after the shipwreck the families started meeting at memorials, working together to retrieve the bell, and getting the governments to declare the broken ship a gravesite. In the process they too forged friendships with people they would otherwise never have known.

"We've become a family," says Heidi Brabon, daughter of Blaine Wilhelm. "A *family*—truly."

She says this at the kitchen table in the crews quarters at Whitefish Point—where Gordon Lightfoot had called Aunt Ruth years before—surrounded by Pam Wittig, Debbie Champeau, and some of their children and grandchildren, who nod vigorously.

"And these are the people who've got your back," Pam Wittig says.

They meet at least once a year. They catch up on their families, swap pictures and stories, and enjoy a few drinks and laughs, too—the kind you can share with trusted friends. They keep in touch, and they help each other keep going.

"When Dad died," Heidi Brabon says of Blaine Wilhelm, "two of my older sisters were already out of the house, so Mom raised the five kids still left at home by herself. She got Social Security for all five of us, and his pension of a whopping seventy-five dollars a month. But she did it."

The following generations of *Fitzgerald* families have made their way, too, and stayed close.

Brabon gestures to her daughter, Sarah, sitting next to her at the crews quarters' big, solid kitchen table, the centerpiece for their gatherings.

"Sarah was born on November 10, 1998—exactly twenty-three years after Dad's ship went down. On her twenty-first birthday, in 2019, she got a tattoo."

Sarah pulls up the sleeve of her sweatshirt to reveal five words artfully inscribed on the inside of her left forearm, in distinct black letters:

"*We are holding our own.*"

And so they are.

ACKNOWLEDGMENTS

When I decided to write a book about Great Lakes shipping in general and the *Edmund Fitzgerald* in particular, I had a lot to learn, from the Great Lakes themselves to mining, manufacturing, meteorology, and shipping itself, for starters. That meant I had to do a lot of reading, so my first thanks goes to the authors of the many books on all these subjects and more, whose work made it possible for me to tell this story. (These are listed in the source notes and the bibliography.)

I started three years ago by reaching out to the Great Lakes shipping experts I knew at Northwestern Michigan College's Great Lakes Maritime Academy (GLMA) in Traverse City: board member Ross Childs, who connected me to President Nick Nissley, and former GLMA superintendent John Tanner, whom I relied on for his expertise on more matters big and small, general and specific, than anyone else. I cannot count the number of calls and emails I've made to him, but he might be able to. He was consistently kind, knowledgeable, and patient.

He in turn connected me to three vital sources, all former students of his: Rick Barthuli, John Hayes, and Craig "Red Dog" Silliven. I called and emailed Hayes almost as often as I did Tanner, and he was just as helpful. He took me to Green Bay to see his old ship, the ST *Crapo*, before it was scrapped, and joined me on another trip to Silver Bay, Minnesota, then down the Head of the Lakes to Superior, Wisconsin. Silliven is one of the few surviving former crewmen of the *Edmund Fitzgerald*, and offered rare firsthand accounts of the *Fitz*, Captain Ernest McSorley, and more. Rick Barthuli might be the last surviving crewman from the *Arthur M. Anderson* who sailed on that fateful night in November 1975. His memories of the ship, Captain Bernie Cooper, and that treacherous journey were invaluable. Talking with these four insiders during long lunches at Traverse City's Elks Lodge 323 was as valuable as it was memorable.

Terry Sullivan spent a summer in college as a deckhand on the *Armco* in 1971, with Captain McSorley and most of his team before they were promoted to the *Edmund Fitzgerald*. Patrick Devine and Craig Ellquist served as deckhands on the *Edmund Fitzgerald* herself, surely among the few still living who can say that; their descriptions of the ship, the crewmen, and life on the *Fitz* added greatly to this story. Frank Kobasic told me about working with Blaine Wilhelm on the SS *Reserve*. James Weakley, President of the Lake Carriers Association (LCA) provided valuable data. SS *Badger* Captain Ed Wiltse and retired Chicago Police Department lieutenant Earl Zuelke shared their knowledge of Dick Race and his investigation of Six Fathom Shoal. Retired Michigan State University journalism professor Mark Fellows patiently answered my questions about his story on Dick Race in *Harbor Lights*. Peter Groh, a former purchasing agent with Oglebay Norton, provided firsthand testimony about how, after the company went bankrupt, the boxes of papers on the *Edmund Fitzgerald* could not be found.

One of the great pleasures of this project was traveling the beautiful, largely unspoiled country of the Great Lakes, and meeting hard-working, straightforward people with little ego or pretense. Without any self-interest to speak of, they bent over backwards to help.

My two trips up to the Head of the Lakes produced a treasure trove of information thanks to the innate friendliness of the people who live and work there, and sometimes pure dumb luck. When Hayes and I first walked into the Silver Bay Municipal Liquor and Lounge, we started talking with Tom Byrnes, who just happened to be the bartender who served the *Fitzgerald* crew fifty years ago. A few hours later, while walking into the American Legion Post 109 in Two Harbors, Minnesota, we literally ran into big Doug Frericks—not hard to do, given his size—who started telling us the remarkable story of his father, Don Frericks, and his lunches with Captain Ernest McSorley. He indulged my many follow-up calls to get those scenes just right.

In Duluth I talked with former University of Minnesota Duluth hockey star Scott "Skeeter" Moore; retired Coast Guard first class petty officer Michael Zronek, who served on the USCG *Woodrush*; and Patrick Labadie, the former director of the Canal Park Marine Museum, all of whom told me stories about the town, the cold weather, the cold water, and the *Fitzgerald* itself. In Superior I made several visits to the President Bar and Liquor Store, where James Bolin, a bartender in 1975 and the owner now, told me of the crew's last stop; Lloyd

Woodhull and Jeff Zackovec patiently explained to me how the Allouez Taconite Facility delivers tons of taconite by conveyor belts to the same docks that loaded the *Fitzgerald*; and Jeff Johnson and Kelly Murphy, who were the pilot fish on this mission, put me in touch with Jeff Ahlborg and Milton Aho, who loaded the *Fitzgerald* before her last run.

In Marquette, former Northern Michigan University journalism student Pat Schutte shared his interview with a witness to the great storm. His friend Kevin "Spyder" Nylund and Kevin's daughter Maddie went out in freezing Lake Superior to determine that Picnic Rock is, indeed, sixteen feet high.

In Whitefish Point, Great Lakes Shipwreck Museum Director Bruce Lynn quickly established himself as one of my most important teammates. He not only provided his great museum and staff, he lent his own credibility to encourage the *Fitzgerald* family members to talk with me, which is the heart of this book. He and his coauthor, Chris Winters, also allowed me to use wonderful photos from *The Legend Lives On*, one of the best books on the *Edmund Fitzgerald,* and the most visually appealing.

Michelle Briggs, the U.S. Army Corps of Engineers' chief park ranger at the Soo Locks, gave me a private four-hour tour of the locks themselves when they were empty in January 2024, and answered questions for months. Andrea Guerriero, the unofficial queen of Great Lakes shipping and the webmaster of DRE Designs, a popular site covering Great Lakes shipping, is connected to virtually every ship that goes through the Soo Locks, and she frequently put me in touch with people who were eager to assist.

Her long list included Mike Peterson, the General Manager of the Great Lakes Fleet/Key Lakes Shipping, who not only invited me to take a trip on the *Arthur M. Anderson*, the second most important ship in this story, but picked me up at the Duluth airport at midnight and delivered me to the dock. Captain Ken Senff and crewmen Keith Baker, Jim Boyle, Christian Leathers, Andy McGinn, Gary Senff, Bob Slight, and Leo Wintreich offered hospitality, expertise, and an experience that informs this book. Tom Wiater, another GLMA graduate, rose to captain, created his own company, and now owns the *Edward L. Ryerson* ("Fast *Eddie*"). He spent several hours giving me a detailed tour of the ship, which is very similar to the *Fitzgerald*, and provided several key insights that you see in the final product. He also arranged a berth for me on the *Wilfred Sykes*, which was on Lake Superior on November 10, 1975, captained by Michael Grzesiek. He and his crew—Andrew Centala, Jason "Opie" Craycraft, Chris Green, Ron Hebner, John Lyon, and Nick Zarafonitis—gave me my first experience on a Great Lakes freighter. Those two trips improved this story in too many ways to quantify. On both ships I gained five pounds in three days. The rumors are true: The quality and quantity of the food is unmatched anywhere on land.

Paul Nesbitt's warm retelling of his father working on Zug Island, then proudly welding the *Edmund Fitzgerald*, is a favorite piece of mine.

In Toledo I relied on the great Christine Brennan, *USA Today* sports columnist, best-selling author, and native of Ottawa Hills, Ohio, a Toledo suburb; John and Gus Mancy, who have both run Mancy's, their family's famous steakhouse, and Captain McSorley's favorite; Denise K. Lockie, who waited on McSorley and his crew there in the 1970s; and George Braatz, who wrote a detailed piece about his trip on the *Edmund Fitzgerald* in 1970 for the *Toledo Blade*.

Tom Walton warrants a category of his own. He's the son and nephew of *Edmund Fitzgerald* crewmen, and served as a porter on the *Fitzgerald* himself in 1963. Tom went on to become an editor for the *Toledo Blade* and the *Monterey* (California) *County Herald*, before retiring as a part-time columnist back on the *Blade*, writing under the name Thomas Walton. I believe he knows as much as anyone about the *Edmund Fitzgerald*, inside and out, and has spoken and written on the subject longer and better than all of us. He was extraordinarily generous with his knowledge, clips, and contacts, and always cheerful.

Because the *Edmund Fitzgerald* is such a public story I tapped the talents of several first-rate journalists connected to the saga. Daniel Okrent, author of several best-selling books, among other successes, provided a rich portrait of Detroit in its salad days. Harry Atkins wrote the first feature on the ship's sinking for the Associated Press, and Jim Gaines followed that with the *Newsweek* article that sparked Gorden Lightfoot's song. Both are still very much alive, and explained how those stories came to be. *Rolling Stone* editor Christian Hoard offered his professional review of Lightfoot's song and its unlikely success; the late Detroit DJ Ken Calvert put that song in the context of an unprecedented era of rock; while Daniel Charles Ross, former columnist with *Motor Trend*, compiled a detailed file on the apex of the American automotive industry, and the land yachts and muscle cars that are still admired today. All were overqualified for my requests, but took them seriously, and responded enthusiastically.

As Bruce Lynn himself said at the podium on the forty-eighth anniversary of the sinking, "Were it not for the song, we probably wouldn't be here." The talented painter Mary Steele Gair connected me to the Gordon Lightfoot band, which resulted in many interviews with bassist Rick Haynes and drummer Barry Keane, who spelled out how "The Wreck of the Edmund Fitzgerald" became an unexpected hit. My conversations with Elliot Lurie, songwriter and singer of "Brandy (You're a Fine Girl)," let me in on the creation of the Great Lakes sailors' unofficial anthem. Michelle Ritter of Alfred Music helped me secure the rights to both for this book.

I also benefitted greatly from several academics at the top of their field: Tim Havens and Guy Meadows at Michigan Tech's Great Lakes Research Center; Matthew Collette and Brendan Falkowski of the University of Michigan's Department of Naval Architecture and Marine Engineering; and David Schwab, who worked at both those universities before taking his talents to the National Oceanic and Atmospheric Administration. Northwestern Mutual Insurance board member James Hackett, CEO John E. Schlifske, and archivist Aileen Caldwell gave me access to boxes and boxes of documents at their headquarters in Milwaukee.

A band of smart, eager college students found facts and figures faster than I could, and helped me sort through a small mountain of sources for the information we needed. They were a joy to work with, and if you can hire one of them, you're lucky. Thank you Carter Bankowski, Aubrey Fitts, Jake Ruffer, Jack Schmelzinger, and Sam Woiteshek.

I first pitched this idea two decades ago, but it took Jay Mandel, superagent at William Morris Endeavor, and his assistant, Liv Guion, to make it a reality. Great thanks for your skill and support.

At W. W. Norton/Liveright, Pete Simon took an immediate interest in the subject, a passion that never faded over this arduous three-year process. He invested far more of his time, brain, and red pen than editors commonly do these days, reflecting his deep commitment to this book, and his desire to get it right. Kadiatou Keita has been sharp, responsive, and fun to work with throughout.

The team at Norton/Liveright is top-shelf, including Steve Attardo, Julia Druskin, Anna Oler, Rebecca Homiski, Rebecca Springer, Susan Sanfrey, Renata Mitchell, Peter Miller, Clio Hamilton, Nick Curley, Steven Pace, Karen Rice, Sharon Gamboa, and Meg Sherman. Thanks to you all, and to copyeditor Emily Andrukaitis.

This is a visual story, which is why the sharp, artistic maps of David Atkinson are so important. Great Lakes photographer Roger LeLievre contributed several photos to the inserts, and helped collate, select, and organize the rest as the book's photo editor. His assistant, William Soleau, clarified a few photos to great effect.

I always recruit a band of savvy readers to review my various drafts and give me feedback, but this time I needed a small army. In addition to many of the people above, who read parts or all of the manuscript for factual accuracy and more, my volunteers included Jim Austin, Jim Carty, Stephanie "Snickerdoodles" Cedergren, who also contributed research, Jonathan Cohn, Tom Ivacko, John Kryk, Scott Lasser, Thomas LeBien, Alan "Doc" Loehr, Bruce Lynn, Marc Savard, Rod Sorge, Nick Standiford, Ted Standiford, and James Tobin. If you enjoyed this book you can thank these readers, who identified a lot of burrs, made sure I kept the best stuff, and helped me cut the book in half (yes, you read that right), including paring back lengthy sections on the investigations and reports, which are the centerpiece of most books on the *Fitzgerald*.

Their work helped me focus on the soul of the story, the twenty-nine crewmen, whom I got to know through their families and friends (many of the latter thanked above). Half a century later the sinking of the *Edmund Fitzgerald* naturally remains a deeply sensitive subject, one that has often been mishandled. For the families to trust me with their stories represented both an honor and an obligation. A deep thank-you to Cindy Reynolds Berlincourt, Heidi Wilhelm Brabon, Debbie Champeau Gomez, Bonnie Church Kellerman, Marilynn Church Peterson, Cindy LoCicero Sauer, and Pam Woodman Wittig.

This is the first book I've finished without my parents along for the ride, but I still feel their love and support—a blessing, truly.

As usual, my wife Christie and son Teddy sacrificed more than anyone, especially when I was researching or writing far away, or simply working too late, too long. Christie also assisted with the research, compiled the bibliography, and helped me make countless editorial decisions, right down to word choices. They both were unfailingly supportive, and my love for them knows no depths.

It was eight-year-old Teddy who showed me a bit of what life was like for sailing families, in a way no one else could. After I got off the *Arthur M. Anderson* in Toledo, my wife and son pulled into the parking lot. I hadn't seen them in a week.

Teddy came bursting from the car and ran full speed for a hundred feet or so, with no let up. When I got on my knees to catch him he launched himself into me full force, then hugged me harder than anyone ever had before. I had never felt so missed.

That represented a tiny fraction of what these sailing families have been enduring every year, for decades—but that's when I understood what this story was all about: fathers and families, the sacrifices they make, and the love that binds them forever, even after one of them is gone.

THE CREW OF THE *EDMUND FITZGERALD*

Michael E. Armagost, 37, third mate, Iron River, Wisconsin
Frederick J. Beetcher, 56, porter, Superior, Wisconsin
Thomas H. Bentsen, 23, oiler, St. Joseph, Michigan
Edward F. Bindon, 47, first assistant engineer, Fairport Harbor, Ohio
Thomas D. Borgeson, 41, maintenance man, Duluth, Minnesota
Oliver J. Champeau, 41, third assistant engineer, Sturgeon Bay, Wisconsin
Nolan S. Church, 55, porter, Silver Bay, Minnesota
Ransom E. Cundy, 53, watchman, Superior, Wisconsin
Thomas E. Edwards, 50, second assistant engineer, Oregon, Ohio
Russell G. Haskell, 40, second assistant engineer, Millbury, Ohio
George J. Holl, 60, chief engineer, Cabot, Pennsylvania
Bruce L. Hudson, 22, deckhand, North Olmsted, Ohio
Allen G. Kalmon, 43, second cook, Washburn, Wisconsin
Gordon F. MacLellan, 30, wiper, Clearwater, Florida, and Presque Isle, Michigan
Joseph W. Mazes, 59, special maintenance man, Ashland, Wisconsin
John H. McCarthy, 62, first mate, Bay Village, Ohio
Ernest M. McSorley, 63, captain, Toledo, Ohio
Eugene W. O'Brien, 50, wheelsman, Toledo, Ohio
Karl A. Peckol, 20, watchman, Ashtabula, Ohio
John J. Poviach, 59, wheelsman, Bradenton, Florida
James A. Pratt, 44, second mate, Lakewood, Ohio
Robert C. Rafferty, 62, steward, Toledo, Ohio
Paul M. Riippa, 22, deckhand, Ashtabula, Ohio
John D. Simmons, 63, wheelsman, Ashland, Wisconsin
William J. Spengler, 59, watchman, Toledo, Ohio
Mark A. Thomas, 21, deckhand, Richmond Heights, Ohio
Ralph G. Walton, 58, oiler, Fremont, Ohio
David E. Weiss, 22, cadet, Agoura, California
Blaine H. Wilhelm, 52, oiler, Moquah, Wisconsin

LIST OF SIGNIFICANT PEOPLE

To help readers keep the cast of characters straight, here is a partial list of significant people who appear in the book.

Harry Atkins: Associated Press reporter from its Detroit bureau whose feature on the *Edmund Fitzgerald*'s sinking went global and inspired stories from *Newsweek* and others.

Rick Barthuli: Great Lakes Maritime Academy graduate who rose to chief engineer during his forty-three-year career. Second assistant on the *Arthur M. Anderson* on November 9 and 10, 1975, when it sailed alongside the *Edmund Fitzgerald.*

Cindy Reynolds Berlincourt: the girlfriend of *Fitzgerald* deckhand Bruce Hudson and mother of their child, Heather.

Heidi Wilhelm Brabon: sixth of Blaine Wilhelm's seven children. Blaine was an oiler on the *Edmund Fitzgerald* from Moquah, Wisconsin.

Christine Brennan: *USA Today* sports columnist, best-selling author, and native of Ottawa Hills, Ohio, a Toledo suburb.

Michelle Briggs: current chief park ranger of the Soo Locks.

Tom Byrnes: veteran bartender at the Silver Bay Municipal Liquor and Lounge since 1975, who knew the crew of the *Edmund Fitzgerald.*

Patrick Devine: oiler and deckhand who served on ten Great Lakes freighters in the 1970s, including the *Edmund Fitzgerald* in the summer of 1975, when he substituted for Bruce Hudson.

Craig Ellquist: deckhand on the *Edmund Fitzgerald* in the winter of 1974–75, who decided not to return to the ship in the spring of 1975 to take a job delivering milk in Two Harbors, Minnesota.

Brendan Falkowski: graduate student in the University of Michigan's department of naval architecture.

Doug Frericks: son of Don Frericks, a former foreman at Reserve Mining in Silver Bay, Minnesota. Don was a close friend of *Fitzgerald* captain Ernest McSorley.

Jim Gaines: a former *Newsweek* reporter who composed one of the articles Gordon Lightfoot read on the *Edmund Fitzgerald*'s sinking, including some of the lines Lightfoot would use in his famous song.

Debbie Champeau Gomez: only child of Oliver "Buck" Champeau, third assistant engineer on the *Edmund Fitzgerald*, from Milwaukee, Wisconsin.

Peter Groh: former purchasing agent for Oglebay Norton, which leased the *Fitzgerald*.

John Hayes: graduate of GLMA and friend of Tom Bentsen, who became an oiler on the *Edmund Fitzgerald*. Hayes asked Bentsen to be his best man, and would later become a chief engineer on the Great Lakes.

Rick Haynes: longtime bassist in Gordon Lightfoot's band, dating back to 1968.

"Aunt Ruth" Hudson: Mother of *Fitzgerald* deckhand Bruce Hudson.

Barry Keane: drummer for Gordon Lightfoot's band, since 1975.

Bonnie Church Kellerman: second child of Nolan Church, porter on the *Edmund Fitzgerald*.

Frank Kobasic: former oiler on the *Reserve*, and friend of fellow oiler Blaine Wilhelm, who would later serve on the *Edmund Fitzgerald*.

Patrick Labadie: former director of the Canal Park Marine Museum in Duluth, and possibly the last person on land to see the *Edmund Fitzgerald*.

Roger LeLievre: Sault Ste. Marie native who worked as a reporter and editor for *The Ann Arbor News*, and is the publisher and editor of *Know Your Ships*.

Cindy LoCicero Sauer: girlfriend of David "Cowboy" Weiss, a GLMA cadet who served on the *Edmund Fitzgerald*.

Denise K. Lockie: a former waitress at Mancy's Steakhouse in Toledo.

Elliot Lurie: lead singer of Looking Glass and author of "Brandy (You're a Fine Girl)," a number one hit in the U.S. in 1972.

Bruce Lynn: current director of the Great Lakes Shipwreck Museum, and coauthor with Chris Winters of *The Legend Lives On*.

Gus Mancy: grandson of the founder of Mancy's Steakhouse in Toledo, who ran the restaurant with his twin brother for many years and knew Captain McSorley, his daughter, and the crew.

John Mancy: great-grandson of the founder of Mancy's Steakhouse, and son of Gus.

Guy Meadows: founder of Michigan Technological University's Great Lakes Research Center on Lake Superior.

Paul Nesbitt: son of Grover Nesbitt, one of the welders who helped construct the *Edmund Fitzgerald.*

Daniel Okrent: Detroit native and best-selling author who wrote a seminal cover story for *Time* magazine in 2009, "The Tragedy of Detroit: The Death—and Possible Life—of a Great City."

Marilynn Church Peterson: daughter of Nolan Church, porter on the *Edmund Fitzgerald.*

Dick Race: a nautical investigator on the Great Lakes who was commissioned in 1976 by Oglebay Norton, which leased the *Edmund Fitzgerald,* to investigate its sinking.

Pat Schutte: former *Ann Arbor News* reporter and Northern Michigan University student who interviewed one of the witnesses of the November 1975 storm in Marquette.

David Schwab: retired University of Michigan professor of naval architecture, and National Oceanic and Atmospheric Administration oceanographer.

Craig "Red Dog" Silliven: GLMA graduate and cadet on the *Edmund Fitzgerald* who earned his masters license (captain) on the Great Lakes and on the Atlantic.

Terry Sullivan: a deckhand on the *Armco* during the summer of 1971, where he worked with Captain Ernest McSorley and other crew members who would be promoted to the *Edmund Fitzgerald* in 1972.

John Tanner: former Great Lakes sailor, GLMA professor, and superintendent who taught David "Cowboy" Weiss, cadet on the *Edmund Fitzgerald*, and visited the ship.

Tom Walton: son of Wade Walton, a former chief engineer on the *Edmund Fitzgerald*, and nephew of Grant Walton, an oiler on the *Fitzgerald* in 1975. Tom himself worked as a porter on the *Fitzgerald* in 1963.

Tom Wiater: GLMA alumnus who rose to captain on the Great Lakes and is now president of Central Marine Logistics, which owns the *Edward L. Ryerson* ("Fast *Eddie*").

Ed Wiltse: GLMA alumnus who is now the captain of the SS *Badger*, and a trusted friend of Dick Race, who investigated the sinking of the *Edmund Fitzgerald.*

Pam Woodman Wittig: niece of Ruth Hudson ("Aunt Ruth"), the mother of Bruce Hudson, Pam's cousin.

Michael Zronek: served on the U.S. Coast Guard's *Woodrush*, which ran a rescue and recovery mission after the *Fitzgerald* sank.

Earl Zuelke: now-retired Chicago Police Department lieutenant who directed the department's boats and divers, and a friend of Dick Race, the Great Lakes wreck investigator.

THE WRECK OF THE EDMUND FITZGERALD

By Gordon Lightfoot

The legend lives on from the Chippewa on down
of the big lake they call Gitche Gumee
The lake, it is said, never gives up her dead
when the skies of November turn gloomy
With a load of iron ore twenty-six thousand tons more
than the *Edmund Fitzgerald* weighed empty
that good ship and true was a bone to be chewed
when the gales of November came early

The ship was the pride of the American side
comin' back from some mill in Wisconsin
As the big freighters go, it was bigger than most
with a crew and good captain well-seasoned
concluding some terms with a couple of steel firms
when they left fully loaded for Cleveland
and later that night when the ship's bell rang
could it be the north wind they'd been feelin'?

The wind in the wires made a tattletale sound
and a wave broke over the railing
and every man knew, as the captain did too
'twas the witch of November come stealin'
The dawn came late and the breakfast had to wait
when the gales of November came slashin'
When afternoon came it was freezin' rain
in the face of a hurricane west wind

When suppertime came, the old cook came on deck
sayin' "Fellas, it's too rough to feed ya"
At seven p.m., a main hatchway caved in
he said "Fellas, it's been good to know ya"

The captain wired in he had water comin' in
and the good ship and crew was in peril
and later that night when his lights went out of sight
came the wreck of the Edmund Fitzgerald

Does anyone know where the love of God goes
when the waves turn the minutes to hours?
The searchers all say they'd have made Whitefish Bay
if they'd put fifteen more miles behind 'er
They might have split up or they might have capsized
they may have broke deep and took water
and all that remains is the faces and the names
of the wives and the sons and the daughters

Lake Huron rolls, Superior sings
in the rooms of her ice-water mansion
Old Michigan steams like a young man's dreams
the islands and bays are for sportsmen
and farther below Lake Ontario
takes in what Lake Erie can send her
and the Iron boats go as the mariners all know
with the gales of November remembered

In a musty old hall in Detroit they prayed
in the maritime sailors' cathedral
the church bell chimed 'til it rang twenty-nine times
for each man on the Edmund Fitzgerald
The legend lives on from the Chippewa on down
of the big lake they call Gitche Gumee
Superior, they said, never gives up her dead
when the gales of November come early

Songwriter: Gordon Lightfoot

BRANDY (YOU'RE A FINE GIRL)

By Elliot Lurie

There's a port on a western bay
And it serves a hundred ships a day
Lonely sailors pass the time away
And talk about their homes

And there's a girl in this harbor town
And she works layin' whiskey down
They say "Brandy fetch another round"
She serves them whisky and wine

The sailors say, "Brandy, you're a fine girl
(you're a fine girl)
What a good wife you would be
(such a fine girl)
Yeah your eyes could steal a sailor from the sea"

Brandy wears a braided chain
Made of finest silver from the north of Spain
A locket that bears the name
Of a man that Brandy loved

He came on a summer's day
Bringing gifts from far away
But he made it clear he couldn't stay
No harbor was his home

The sailor said, "Brandy, you're a fine girl
(you're a fine girl)
What a good wife you would be
(such a fine girl)
But my life, my love, and my lady is the sea"

(doo-doo-doo-doo)
(doo-doo-doo-doo)

Yeah, Brandy used to watch his eyes
When he told his sailor's story
She could feel the ocean fall and rise
She saw its ragin' glory
But he had always told the truth
Lord, he was an honest man
And Brandy does her best to understand

(doo-doo-doo-doo)
(doo-doo-doo-doo)

At night when the bars close down
Brandy walks through a silent town
And loves a man who's not around
She still can hear him say

She hears him say, "Brandy, you're a fine girl
(you're a fine girl)
What a good wife you would be
(such a fine girl)
But my life, my love, and my lady is the sea"

(doo-doo-doo-doo)
(doo-doo-doo-doo)
"Brandy, you're a fine girl
(you're a fine girl)
What a good wife you would be
(such a fine girl)
But my life, my love, and my lady is the sea"
(doo-doo-doo-doo)
(doo-doo-doo-doo)

Source: Musixmatch
Songwriter: Elliot Lurie

GLOSSARY

above deck: shorthand for those who work on the deck crew, including the captain, mates, wheelsmen, and deckhands, among others. Its counterpart is below deck, code for those who work on the engine crew, including the chief engineer, assistant engineers, oilers, wipers, and others.

aft: nautical term for "behind," relative to a position on the ship; *fore* is its counterpart, meaning forward, relative to a position.

***Arthur M. Anderson*:** Named for Arthur Marvin Anderson, a former director of U.S. Steel, the SS *Arthur M. Anderson* launched in Lorain, Ohio, in 1952, six years before the *Fitzgerald*. The *Anderson* stretched 647 feet until the winter of 1975, when U.S. Steel extended the *Anderson* to 767 feet, 38 feet longer than the *Fitzgerald*. She sailed alongside the *Edmund Fitzgerald* on the *Fitz*'s last trip.

ballast pumps: massive devices that suck out water from the ballast tanks. The *Fitzgerald*'s four main electric ballast pumps were designed to pull out an impressive seven thousand gallons of water in a minute, with two auxiliary pumps ready to mop up the rest at two thousand gallons per minute.

ballast tanks: the sealed compartments outlining the hull that can be filled with water when the cargo holds are empty, which gives the ship balance and stability, and to lower the ship in the water so the propellers can work properly.

below deck: shorthand for those who work on the engine crew, including the chief engineer, assistant engineers, oilers, wipers, and others; its counterpart is above deck, code for those who work in the deck crew, including the captain, mates, wheelsmen, and deckhands, among others.

berth: a bed or bunk on a ship, always securely bolted into the floor and walls. The term can also be used for a sailor's room or a ship's slot at a dock for loading or unloading.

bilge pump: a pump at the bottom of a ship, called the bilge, to expel water to avoid listing (leaning one way or the other) or sinking.

boiler: On steam ships the boiler heats water to produce the steam that propels the engines and powers other machines onboard. On older ships boilers occasionally exploded.

bow: the front of a ship; stern is its counterpart, meaning the back of a ship. Great Lakes sailors never say "in the back," because it's considered demeaning to the engine crew that works there. Instead they use *fore* ("forward") and *aft* ("back").

bridge: the area where the captain, mates, wheelsmen, and others navigate the ship, including the pilothouse, chart room, and more.

broadside: the long side of a ship. Waves washing against it can cause the ship to roll side to side in the troughs, which is as unpleasant as it is dangerous.

bulkhead: a wall that divides a ship's cargo hold into separate watertight sections and provides rigidity.

bum boat: Started in Duluth by the Kaner family, "bum boats" were tugboat-sized craft that pulled up alongside the freighters as soon as they docked, offering all manner of snacks, alcohol, cigarettes, books, magazines, and even TVs that ran on DC power, and more. The service spread to Chicago, Detroit, and Toledo, where they catered to the sailors for decades.

cargo hold: Cargo holds are the reason Great Lakes freighters exist, and compose most of the ship itself. The *Fitzgerald* was equipped with three huge cargo holds, which could hold twenty-six thousand long tons of taconite.

chart: term sailors use for navigational maps (i.e., navigational charts). What landlubbers would call a "map room" is always called the chart room by Great Lakes sailors.

chart room: a space on a ship—generally attached to the pilothouse—where navigational charts are kept in long, thin drawers and studied on a desktop.

crest: the top of a wave. On the ocean, salt tends to weigh down crests, making waves smoother and easier to navigate. On the Great Lakes, fresh water creates sharper crests, which are more likely to come crashing down on ships below.

deadhead: To secure a ship to the dock, deckhands tie cables around these devices, about the size and shape of a fire hydrant and installed on both docks and ship decks.

deck: can refer to the top of a ship or to the sides of a lock or other construction (as in a "pool deck"), but are not to be confused with a dock.

deck crane: A deck crane is attached to the ship's deck and runs on rails lining both sides of the ship. The crane rolls back and forth over a ship's hatch covers, which weighed fifty tons on the *Fitzgerald*, picks them up, and sets each down between two hatches, leaving the hatches open so they can be loaded or unloaded. When loading or unloading is complete, the deck crane replaces the hatch covers, one by one, and the ship sails.

deckhand: The lowest ranking of the deck crew, and usually the youngest. As soon as the ship shoves off, the deckhands start clamping the hatches, then sweep the thousands of stray taconite pellets off the deck; when out at sea they paint the ship, among other duties, then unclamp the hatches when the ship approaches the next port.

dock: a structure to which a ship ties up to load and unload, also known as a pier. The word can also be used as a verb, "to dock," as in to tie up at the next dock—or worse, to have your paycheck reduced (or "docked") for an infraction.

downbound: going south, as opposed to upbound (north). On the Great Lakes, however, it means something more specific: the southerly half of a ship's round trip from, say, the Head of the Lakes to Detroit or Toledo, on which even the easterly leg from Duluth to the Soo Locks is considered "downbound."

***Edmund Fitzgerald*:** The SS *Edmund Fitzgerald* (*SS* stands for "steam ship") was commissioned, built, and owned by Northwestern Mutual Insurance in Milwaukee, but leased by Oglebay Norton in Cleveland and operated by its Columbia Transportation division, whose trademark *C* was attached to the *Fitzgerald*'s stack. The *Fitzgerald* was Columbia's flagship throughout its life.

engineer: In this book the term refers not to engineers who work on land, but to those who work below deck and in the stern of a Great Lakes freighter. The chief engineer ranks the highest, followed by the first assistant engineer, two second assistant engineers, and a third assistant engineer. All must pass increasingly difficult tests covering physics, chemical engineering, electrical engineering, and more to climb the ranks. They are responsible for keeping the ship's many mechanical systems running smoothly, especially the engine.

engine room: The term "room" is rather broad here, as the engine room consumes a significant portion of the stern of the ship, and houses the engine, thrusters, and other elements that power the propeller just behind it.

fetch: the distance wind can blow in one direction without interference. The longer the fetch, the greater the likelihood of waves building across a stretch of water. Lake Superior's fetch of 350 miles often makes sailing into Whitefish Bay very perilous, especially in the fall.

first mate: Ranking just below the captains, first mates generally man the pilothouse during all but the trickiest sailing. They supervise everyone working above deck, including the watchmen and the deckhands, and assign them jobs like painting and cleaning, among other tasks. They are also responsible for loading and unloading the ship, and distributing payroll.

fit out: This is a sailor's term for getting on board, ready to work. A ship's entire crew fits out each spring, but crew substitutes might fit out at other points in the shipping season.

following sea: waves that are coming up from behind a ship, against its stern, and pushing it forward.

fore: nautical term for "forward," relative to a position on a ship; *aft* is its counterpart, meaning "behind," relative to a position. "He was standing fore of the deck crane."

freeboard: the space between the water line and the top of the deck. The amount of freeboard a Great Lakes freighter must have is regulated by the U.S. Coast Guard and the American Bureau of Shipping (ABS), and defined by the Plimsoll line.

gale warning: a report from the National Weather Service of storms with 39-to-54-mph winds. Compare storm warning and hurricane force winds.

galley: On a Great Lakes freighter, the galley covers the kitchen and the dining area. On most ships the food is quite good and plentiful; the tables are usually designated for the deck crew, the engine crew, and the officers. The galley is where information circulates most rapidly among the crew.

harbor master: A harbor master is literally the master of a harbor, whom captains must defer to when coming into port. On oceanic ports, the harbor master will assign a local pilot to guide each ship coming into port. On the Great Lakes, ship captains take their ships all the way to the dock by themselves.

hatch: The openings on a ship's deck that allow cargo to be loaded and unloaded, usually with cranes in *Fitzgerald*'s day. At sea they are generally protected by steel hatch covers securely clamped by deckhands. The *Fitzgerald* had twenty-one hatches, each with 68 clamps, for a total of 1,428 clamps.

hatch covers: Made of 5/16-inch-thick steel, these cover the hatches, naturally enough. On the *Fitzgerald*, they measured eleven feet by forty-eight feet, and weighed about seven thousand pounds each.

Head of the Lakes: Taken together, the towns of Silver Bay, Two Harbors, and Duluth, Minnesota, plus Superior, Wisconsin, make up what sailors call "the Head of the Lakes," the western tip of all the Great Lakes. If your ship is hauling taconite, your trip will probably start at one of these ports.

hogging: a phenomenon in which a ship drapes over a wave's crest, with its bow and stern both drooping downward, placing immense pressure on the center of the ship's hull. The opposite of sagging.

Hulett crane: Patented in 1898 by George Hulett, the Huletts were enormous iron giraffes built into the ground that reached over and into a ship's cargo holds, scooped out its cargo, then dropped it into a pile on the dock or directly into a hopper that filled train cars. Huletts could do the job in a fraction of the time of other methods at the time, and for one-third the cost. By the mid-twentieth century seventy-four Hulett cranes had been installed among the Great Lakes' major ports. They were as essential to the Great Lakes shipping boom as the creation of taconite pellets or the Soo Locks themselves, but replaced by self-unloading ships in the 1970s.

hull: the outer shell of the ship, usually made of one-inch-thick steel

hurricane force winds warning: a report from the National Weather Service of storms with winds of 74 mph and beyond. More intense than a gale warning and storm warning.

keel: the rib of steel running along the center of the bottom of a ship, from bow to stern. On small vessels it is external to help stabilize and guide the ship and prevent capsizing. But on Great Lakes freighters the keel is inside the hull, and the bottom of the boat is flat. This allows the ship to clear the shallow waters of the Soo Locks and St. Marys River and its owners to maximize cargo, but will not help stabilize the ship in a storm or prevent capsizing.

Kestner clamps: Used to secure the cargo hatches on most Great Lakes freighters in the *Fitzgerald*'s time, these functioned like large C-clamps. They had to be tightened by hand, or with an iron bar slid into a hole at the top of each clamp, then spun to provide leverage to loosen or tighten the clamp.

knot: a measure of sailing speed, a knot equals one nautical mile per hour, or about 1.15 mph. The typical top speed for a Great Lakes freighter of 15 mph equals about 13 knots. Because Great Lakes navigators use both units, but often favor miles per hour, I've used miles per hour exclusively in this book.

lakers: a slang term for Great Lakes freshwater freighters. They are usually longer and thinner than their oceanic counterparts to get as much cargo through the Soo Locks as possible. Their dimensions also make them less stable and secure in heavy seas.

lee: refers to the side of a land mass like a peninsula or island that is more protected from the wind and waves than the other side. In a storm captains often seek out the "leeward side" of available land to wait out a storm.

list: When a ship leans to its starboard or port side, it is called a "list," and indicates something is out of balance: causes can include improper loading, a shift in cargo, water coming onboard, or damage to the ship itself.

lock: a massive holding tank that, by raising or lowering its water level, allows a ship to go from a higher body of water to a lower one or vice versa, instead of through dangerous rapids or waterfalls.

maintenance men: the lowest ranking of those who work below deck, these two help engineers and others, and assist the wipers in painting, cleaning, and handling the trash, among other duties.

mate: a formal designation for crew working under the captain that includes first, second, and third mates.

nautical mile: A nautical mile measures distance, not speed, and is equal to one minute of latitude, or 1.15 land-measured miles. Nautical miles are most useful for transoceanic navigation, because they take into account the curvature of the earth—less of a consideration on the Great Lakes. A knot equals one nautical mile per hour.

oiler: the engineers' assistant who oils everything that needs to be oiled, takes down all the readings of the engine's many instruments every hour to make sure everything is running smoothly, and does just about anything else the engineers ask.

pilothouse: Part of the bridge, the pilothouse is an enclosed room that houses a ship's steering wheel and navigational instruments. Like most of her peers, the *Fitzgerald*'s pilothouse was located in the bow, though more modern freighters put the pilothouse in the stern.

Plimsoll line: Named for Samuel Plimsoll, this is the line painted and welded on the sides of ships that shows how far down into the water a ship can sink and still be in compliance with regulations. Going below this line is not only illegal but will render insurance companies free from liability if the ship sinks.

port: the left side of a ship (from the stern's perspective); starboard is the right side. For a mnemonic device, *port* has four letters, like "left," while *starboard* is a longer word with two *R*s.

porter: On the *Fitzgerald*, two porters served the crew and VIPs by helping in the kitchen, serving meals, doing laundry, and distributing clean towels and sheets. One porter, called the "bedbug," provided hotel-level service for the officers' rooms, with new towels and bedding daily. (The rest of the crew made their own beds.) The other porter waited on the officers, VIP guests, and crewmen, and washed dishes.

On most ships the porters tended to be young, including college kids working for a summer. But given its coveted status, the *Fitzgerald* could attract older, more experienced porters.

racking roll: this describes a ship's quick back-and-forth movement that occurs when it is fully loaded and rolling in heavy seas. Unpleasant and potentially dangerous.

recreational sailors: To distinguish them from the sailors sailing on Great Lakes freighters, those manning vessels with actual sails are called "recreational sailors" in this book.

rogue wave: a wave that is substantially bigger than those around it. According to the Rayleigh distribution, one in one thousand waves will likely be 1.9 times higher than the highest ones around it, one in five thousand will likely be 2.15 times bigger, and one in ten thousand will likely be 2.23 times taller.

rolling: describes how a ship responds when waves are hitting it broadside, causing it to roll side to side from starboard to port, and back again. While it may sound innocuous compared to crashing into and over waves, rolling is not only unpleasant but much more dangerous, and can lead to foundering or capsizing.

sagging: a phenomenon in which the unsupported middle of a ship sags toward the water below it, exerting a tremendous strain on the hull. This can happen when the ship's bow is raised by one wave and its stern is lifted by another wave behind it—entirely possible for seven-hundred-foot freighters. The opposite of hogging.

sailors and sailing: Although Great Lakes cargo ships have not been equipped with sails for more than a century, their captains and crews are still called "sailors" and their trips "sailing."

salties: a slang term for ocean-bound saltwater freighters, which are generally wider and shorter than their Great Lakes cousins, which are called lakers.

ship vs. boat: These words are used almost interchangeably by Great Lakes sailors when referring to freighters, while ocean sailors call freighters "ships" only. Great Lakes sailors will call small vessels, such as a tugboat or a recreational sailboat, a "boat" rather than a "ship."

shipping season: On the Great Lakes the shipping season runs from late March, after enough ice has broken up to allow ships to sail freely, to mid-January, when the ice clogs the Soo Locks.

shoals: submerged ridges, sandbars, or other shallow plateaus that present a navigational hazard, especially for ships sailing fully loaded. On Lake Superior, Six Fathom Shoal is the most notorious.

SS: "steam ship," as in SS *Edmund Fitzgerald* or SS *Arthur M. Anderson*. Compare with USS ("United States ship"), RMS ("Royal Mail ship"), and HMS ("His [or Her] Majesty's ship").

starboard: the right side of a ship (from the stern's perspective); port is the left side. For a mnemonic device, *starboard* is a longer word with two *R*s, while *port* has four letters, as does "left."

stern: the back of a ship; bow is its counterpart, describing the front of a ship. Great Lakes sailors never say "in the back," which is considered demeaning to the engine crew that works there. Instead they use fore ("forward") and aft ("back").

storm warning: a warning from the National Weather Service of 55-to-73-mph winds. It falls between a gale warning and hurricane force winds warning.

taconite: refers both to a sedimentary rock composed of roughly one-third iron that runs throughout the Iron Range, and to the taconite pellets developed by Edward W.

Davis that are also one-third iron and combined with clay. The *Fitzgerald* was loaded with 26,112 long tons of taconite pellets during its last voyage.

Three Sisters: three rogue waves in succession.

tons vs. long tons: A ton is 2,000 pounds. The Great Lakes shipping industry uses a British unit called "long tons," which are actually 2,240 pounds each, not 2,000. Here tons are used unless specifically described as long tons.

trough: the space between two wave crests; a valley of water between two mountains of waves.

tunnels: On a typical Great Lakes freighter these refer to enclosed walkways that run the length of the ship on both sides, allowing crew to walk back and forth safely during storms and when there are slippery conditions on deck.

upbound: going north, as opposed to downbound (south). On the Great Lakes, however, it means something more specific: the second leg of a ship's round trip from, say, Chicago, Detroit, or Cleveland to the Soo Locks, then west to the Head of the Lakes.

watchman: Ranking below the captain, mates, and wheelsmen, watchmen earn their able-bodied seaman (ABS) endorsement to work on a ship. Their duties include deck maintenance (cleaning, painting, and repairs), standing lookout when the ship is in confined waters or reduced visibility (nighttime, fog, or snow), preparing the ship to enter port by running the hatch crane to remove the hatch covers, and helping to guide the boat into port by telling the captain by walkie-talkie how much space he or she has to work with from each post on the ship.

wheelsman: When the captain or one of the mates is in the pilothouse plotting the ship's course, working with charts and binoculars, they never actually touch the wheel itself. Instead they give their directions to one of three wheelsmen, who perform the actual steering.

winch: Like most ships in its class, the *Fitzgerald* had three winches fore and three aft. These were basically large spools, about four feet high and four feet wide, with three hundred to five hundred feet of one-inch cable coiled around the drum. When the *Fitzgerald* was in port, a deck officer or watchman would push a lever to let the cable out so a deckhand could use it to tie the ship up to the dock. When it came time to push off, he'd pull the lever to pull the cable back in.

wiper: Because all the machines on the *Fitzgerald* had to be hand lubricated, after the oilers oiled everything, the wipers wiped off the excess lubrication on the machines and the floor. The wipers also worked with two maintenance men painting, cleaning, and handling the trash, among other duties.

NOTES

In addition to books, articles, videos, documents, and other sources, I conducted hundreds of interviews with more than a hundred subjects. Unless otherwise noted, the interviews quoted herein were conducted specifically for this book, and were conducted between 2022 and 2025.

My most frequently quoted interview subjects included these sources below. Whenever they're speaking, their quotes were derived from our interviews.

Harry Atkins
Rick Barthuli
Heidi Wilhelm Brabon
Christine Brennan
Michelle Briggs
Tom Byrnes
Debbie Champeau
Bonnie Church Kellerman
Patrick Devine
Craig Ellquist
Brendan Falkowski
Doug Frericks
Jim Gaines
Peter Groh
John Hayes
Rick Haynes
Barry Keane
Frank Kobasic
Patrick Labadie
Roger LeLievre
Cindy LoCicero, now Sauer
Denise K. Lockie
Elliot Lurie
Bruce Lynn
Gus Mancy
John Mancy
Gary Meadows
Paul Nesbitt
Daniel Okrent
Marilynn Church Peterson
Dick Race
Cindy Reynolds, now Berlincourt
David Schwab
Pat Schutte
Craig "Red Dog" Silliven
Terry Sullivan
John Tanner
Tom Walton
Tom Wiater
Ed Wiltse
Pam Woodman Wittig
Michael Zronek
Earl Zuelke

PROLOGUE

1 *On Tuesday, July 4, 1995*: Bruce Lynn and Chris Winters, *The Legend Lives On: SS* Edmund Fitzgerald (Running Light Press in partnership with the Great Lakes Shipwreck Historical Society, 2015), 30.

1 *46 degrees, 59 minutes north latitude*: Thomas Walton, "33 Years On, the *Fitzgerald* Story Still Haunts," *Toledo Blade*, November 10, 2008.

1 *"Aunt Ruth was all of four foot nine"*: interviews with Pam Woodman Wittig.

3 *A good-sized man at six feet*: interviews with Patrick Devine.

I: THE RISKS

7 *in a foot of standing water*: Global Great Lakes, "Lake Superior Overview," accessed February 2, 2025, www.globalgreatlakes.org.

8 *"the most extraordinary spectacle that I have seen in my life"*: Jerry Dennis, *The Living Great Lakes: Searching for the Heart of the Inland Seas* (Thomas Dunne Books, 2003), 5.

8 *"The word 'lake' doesn't do them justice"*: interviews with John Tanner.

9 *"The Great Lakes' waves are what we call"*: interview with Guy Meadows.

9 *two waves at once*: interview with Tim Havens, director, Great Lakes Research Center, Michigan Technological University.

12 *just saw the ship apart*: interview with Mike Grzesiek, captain, *Wilfred Sykes*.

17 *"WHAT HATH GOD WROUGHT?"*: see "Samuel Morse Demonstrates the Telegraph with the Message, 'What hath God wrought?'" *History*, July 20, 2010, www.history.com/this-day-in-history/what-hath-god-wrought.

17 *killing 2,208 people*: David McCullough, *The Johnstown Flood* (Simon & Schuster, 1968), 193–96; National Park Service, Johnstown Flood National Memorial, accessed February 15, 2025, www.nps.gov/jofl/index.htm.

18 *through every storm they'd faced so far*: See Bruce Catton, "The Ultimate Storm," *American Heritage* 35, no. 6 (October/November 1984).

18 *the fall had been glorious*: David G. Brown, *White Hurricane: A Great Lakes November Gale and America's Deadliest Maritime Disaster* (International Marine/McGraw-Hill, 2004), 58.

20 *its deck began to crack*: Brown, *White Hurricane*, 59.

21 *they would have gone down with it*: Hemming, *Ships Gone Missing: The Great Lakes Storm of 1913* (Contemporary Books, 1992), 29–32.

21 *through the blinding blizzard*: Brown, *White Hurricane*, 70–72.

22 *"That little boat will never survive in this storm"*: Classen, "The Wreck and Rescue of the L.C. Waldo—Keweenaw Peninsula—Lake Superior," Mikel B. Classen on the Road, n.d., accessed February 10, 2025, https://mikelbclassen.com/the-wreck-and-rescue-of-the-l-c-waldo-keweenaw-peninsula-lake-superior.

22 *"into their chilled veins"*: Classen, "Wreck and Rescue."

23 *"the blessing of heaven upon our captain and his crew"*: Classen, "Wreck and Rescue."

24 *"Goodbye Forever"*: Brown, *White Hurricane*, 171.

25 *followed by his farewell letter in a bottle*: see "Special Deputy Marshal Christopher Keenan," Officer Down Memorial Page website, accessed February 10, 2025, www.odmp.org/officer/reflections/22863-special-deputy-marshal-christopher-keenan.

25 *their victims forever sworn to silence*: Catton, "The Ultimate Storm," 5.

25 *the advent of gaslights decades before*: Brown, *White Hurricane*, 143.

26 *her teacher and companion, Anne Sullivan*: Brown, *White Hurricane*, 148.

26 *"Goodbye Nellie, ship is breaking up fast"*: Brown, *White Hurricane*, 181–82.

26 *loaded just a few days earlier*: Catton, "The Ultimate Storm," 7.

26 *"gallant fight before giving up"*: Brown, *White Hurricane*, 175.

27 *dreadful duty for his former shipmates*: Catton, "The Ultimate Storm," 6.

27 *"the coin of human life and suffering"*: Brown, *White Hurricane*, 211.

28 *with 254 people aboard*: Catton, "The Ultimate Storm," 1.

28 *"No lake master can recall"*: Catton, "The Ultimate Storm," 3.

28 *less than a month's wage*: Brown, *White Hurricane*, 225–26.

II: THE REWARDS

31 *traders sold millions of beaver pelts*: Robert J. Naiman, Carol A. Johnston, James C. Kelley, "Alteration of North American Streams by Beaver" (PDF). *BioScience* 38, no. 11 (December 1988): 753–62.

32 *pitting the farmers against the new nation's tax collectors*: see Clay Risen, "How America Learned to Love Whiskey," *Atlantic*, December 6, 2013, www.theatlantic.com/national/archive/2013/12/how-america-learned-to-love-whiskey/282110.

32 *and the NCAA for their finals*: John U. Bacon, "The Floor Beneath Their Feet," *Michigan History* (May–June 2001).

32 *"the California Gold Rush"*: Dennis, *The Living Great Lakes*, 125–27.

33 *ratios that suited the locals' lifestyle*: John U. Bacon, "The True Story of 'The Gipper,'" in *The Best of Bacon: Select Cuts* (University of Michigan Press, 2018), 151–63.

33 *"The union blamed the [mining] company"*: interview with William John Foster.

34 *those ranges could support as many as seven mines each*: Ira S. Allison, "The Giants Range Batholith of Minnesota," *Journal of Geology* 33, no. 5 (July 1925): 488–508.

34 *thereby establishing a vertical monopoly*: David Freeman Hawke, *John D.: The Founding Father of the Rockefellers* (Harper & Row, 1980), 203–11.

35 *rubber hockey pucks shatter like porcelain*: Arthur C. Kaminsky and John Powers, *One Goal: A Chronicle of the 1980 U.S. Olympic Hockey Team* (Harper & Row, 1984), 41–49.

35 *a bold move at the time*: John U. Bacon, "How Immigration Shaped Detroit," *Detroit News*, December 3, 1996.

36 *math professor named Edward W. Davis*: Edward W. Davis, *Pioneering with Taconite* (Minnesota Historical Society Press, 1964).

37 *Davis's taconite patents*: Jeffrey T. Manuel, *Taconite Dreams: The Struggle to Sustain Mining on Minnesota's Iron Range, 1915–2000* (University of Minnesota Press, 2015), 1–32.

37 *four times that*: NTSB, *Marine Accident Report*, 10.

39 *every hour, twenty-four hours a day, for years*: "War Production," *The War*, PBS, www.pbs.org/kenburns/the-war/war-production.

39 *dropped 5.4 billion pounds of bombs*: "War Production."

40 *revolved around Detroit*: CNN, "Fortune 500 1957," accessed March 21, 2025, https://money.cnn.com/magazines/fortune/fortune500_archive/full/1957.

42 *the Soviets used to turn back the Nazi invasion*: John U. Bacon, *Blue Ice: The Story of Michigan Hockey* (University of Michigan Press, 2001), 48–50.

43 *as UPS and Amazon do today*: see Dan Austin, "Hudson's Department Store," Historic Detroit, accessed February 10, 2025, https://historicdetroit.org/buildings/hudsons-department-store.

III: TO BUILD A BETTER BOAT

47 *Shipping entails far less friction*: interviews with Roger LeLievre.

47 *moved it two years later to Milwaukee*: see Carl Baehr, "City Streets: The Dreadful Legacy of Charles Nash," Urban Milwaukee, February 16, 2017, accessed February 3, 2025, https://urbanmilwaukee.com/2017/02/16/city-streets-the-dreadful-legacy-of-charles-nash.

48 *Milwaukee's largest shipyard*: Lynn and Winters, *The Legend Lives On*, 21.

48 *decided to name the ship*: Elizabeth Fitzgerald Cutler and Walter M. Hirthe, *Six Fitzgerald Brothers: Lake Captains All* (Wisconsin Marine Historical Society), 189–93.

50 *with greater longitudinal strength, too*: Frederick Stonehouse, *The Wreck of the* Edmund Fitzgerald (Avery Color Studios, Inc., 1977), 24.

53 *two thousand gallons per minute*: Stonehouse, *Wreck*, 18.

53 *the individual pebbles*: NTSB, *Marine Accident Report*, 10.

53 *best-in-class pumps would be rendered largely useless*: Stonehouse, *Wreck*, 18.

54 *water lights to help with night rescue*: Stonehouse, *Wreck*, 22–24.

55 *not the most scientific method*: Stonehouse, *Wreck*, 19–20.

56 *"Hull 301," as the* Fitzgerald *was known until she launched*: Lynn and Winters, *The Legend Lives On*, 21.

56 *"a better future for their three sons"*: Paul Nesbitt, emails to John U. Bacon, May 16, 17, and 18, 2023.

57 *welding and riveting the sections*: Lynn and Winters, *The Legend Lives On*, 21.

58 *the church's importance had grown*: Lynn and Winters, *The Legend Lives On*, 34.

58 *"ride out a storm on a ship like this"*: Lynn and Winters, *The Legend Lives On*, 34.

62 *"When the whistle blew, we drove the wedges!"*: Lynn and Winters, *The Legend Lives On*, 22.

62 *"one of those moments in life that you do not forget"*: Lynn and Winters, *The Legend Lives On*, 21–22.

62 *he had a heart attack, and died on the spot*: Lynn and Winters, *The Legend Lives On*, 21.

63 *"the happiest day of my father's life"*: Lynn and Winters, *The Legend Lives On*, 21.

IV: "IF WE MAKE IT 'TIL DAYLIGHT . . ."

67 *"the last word in freighter construction"*: Mark L. Thompson, *Queen of the Lakes* (Wayne State University Press, 2017), 136–37.

68 *sounds no sailor wants to hear*: Frank Mays with Pat Stayer, Jim Stayer, and Tim Juhl, *If We Make It 'til Daylight: The Story of Frank Mays* (Out of the Blue Productions, 2003). Note: All the information in Part IV comes from Frank Mays's book, unless otherwise indicated.

68 *the ship's power lines snapped*: Department of Transportation, U.S. Coast Guard, *Marine Casualty Report, SS* Edmund Fitzgerald*; Sinking in Lake Superior on November 10, 1975, with Loss of Life*, Report No. USCG 16732/64216, July 26, 1977, 1 and 9–11, www.dco.uscg.mil/Portals/9/DCO%20Documents/5p/CG-5PC/INV/docs/boards/edmundfitz.pdf.

68 *made it impossible to launch or board*: Michael Schumacher, *The Wreck of the* Carl D.*: A True Story of Loss, Survival, and Rescue at Sea* (Indiana University Press, 2008), 53.

69 *it had already become too wet*: Schumacher, *Wreck of the* Carl D., 71–72.

V: PRIDE OF THE AMERICAN SIDE

75 *with televisions, libraries, and writing desks*: Lynn and Winters, *The Legend Lives On*, 22–24.

76 *"anything then available on commercial ocean liners"*: Lynn and Winters, *The Legend Lives On*, 22–24.

76 *pictures for their guests for that very purpose*: George Braatz, "Luxury Cruise on the Great Lakes," *Toledo Blade*, September 1970.

77 *"that's where the similarities end"*: Lynn and Winters, *The Legend Lives On*, 22–24.

80 *tourists ate it all up and nicknamed him "the DJ captain"*: Lynn and Winters, *The Legend Lives On*, 24.

80 "*Wake up, campers! Rise and shine!*": interview with Roger LeLievre.

81 *about 130 Statues of Liberty*: Lynn and Winters, *The Legend Lives On*, 24.

81 *7,000 cars* per shipload: Kevin T. McGee, "Mystery of *Fitz* Lost in the Deep," *Detroit Free Press*, November 10, 1985, 1A, 12A.

82 *kept the crown in 1965 and 1966*: Lynn and Winters, *The Legend Lives On*, 24; Stonehouse, *Wreck*, 13.

82 *1.2 million gross tons through the Soo Locks*: Stonehouse, *Wreck*, 13.

82 *no decline as she aged*: Stonehouse, *Wreck*, 13, 23; Lynn and Winters, *The Legend Lives On*, 24.

82 *the* Fitz *carried 30,260 long tons*: United States Army Corps of Engineers, Detroit District, "Statistical Report of Lake Commerce Passing Through Canals at Sault Ste. Marie, Michigan and Ontario, During Season of 1968."

83 *after he got back on his feet*: Gard, "The Sailor's Champion: Samuel Plimsoll," June 1, 2023, accessed February 10, 2025, www.gard.no/insights/sailor-s-champion-samuel-plimsoll.

86 *39.25 inches, or more than a yard*: Stonehouse, *Wreck*, 26.

87 "*how much money will it bring in?*": Alexis de Tocqueville, "To Ernest de Chabrol, 9 June 1831," in *Selected Letters*, ed. Roger Boesche (University of California Press, 1985).

89 *served at different times on the* Fitz: interviews with Tom Walton. Note: All the information in "The Summer of '63" chapter comes from these Walton interviews, unless otherwise indicated.

92 *"the ship is kept nearly spotless by the crew"*: Braatz, "Luxury Cruise on the Great Lakes."

VI: THIRTY-EIGHT HOURS IN A RAFT

99 *standing on a ship that cracked in half can do that to a man*: Ric Mixter, *Tattletale Sounds: The* Edmund Fitzgerald *Investigations* (Airworthy Productions, 2022), 131.

99 *another had crashed into a lighthouse*: Frederick Stonehouse, *Steel on the Bottom: Great Lakes Shipwrecks* (Avery Color Studios, Inc., 2006), 197–98.

99 *humming along at a brisk 12.3 miles per hour*: Stonehouse, *Steel on the Bottom*, 191.

100 *"There she is!"*: Schumacher, *Wreck of the* Carl D., 176.

100 *told his crew to man their lifeboats*: Mixter, *Tattletale Sounds*, 142–43.

100 *earn a high school diploma, then joined the military*: Dennis Hale, Time Jule, Jim Stayer, and Pat Stayer, *Sole Survivor: A Tale of Shipwreck on the Great Lakes and One Man's Survival Against Overwhelming Odds: Dennis Hale's Own Story* (Lakeshore Charters & Marine Explorations, Inc., 1996), 13.

101 *"For the first time in my life, I felt I really belonged"*: Hale, Jule, Stayer, and Stayer, *Sole Survivor*, 13–17.

101 *before ending her season for good*: Hale, Jule, Stayer, and Stayer, *Sole Survivor*, 26.

101 "*for the rest of my life*": Hale, Jule, Stayer, and Stayer, *Sole Survivor*, 30–33.

102 *went down with the ship*: Jim Bloch, "Marking the 55th Anniversary of Sinking of

Freighter Daniel J. Morrell: Sailor from St. Clair Among 28 Victims," *The Voice*, November 29, 2021, www.voicenews.com/2021/11/29/marking-the-55th-anniversary-of-sinking-of-freighter-daniel-j-morrell.

102 *Charles "Fuzzy" Fosbender, one of the* Morrell*'s wheelsmen*: Hale, Jule, Stayer, and Stayer, *Sole Survivor*, 34.

102 *the* Morrell *hadn't arrived*: Hale, Jule, Stayer, and Stayer, *Sole Survivor*, 36–39.

103 *the families of his fellow crewmen*: Hale, Jule, Stayer, and Stayer, *Sole Survivor*, 46–56.

VII: THE CAPTAIN

107 *62 percent more than the* Fitzgerald*'s highest mark*: Lynn and Winters, *The Legend Lives On*, 24.

109 "*The corporate bean counters watched everything*": interviews with Craig Silliven.

VIII: THE TOLEDO EXPRESS

117 *your life was laid out*: interviews with Tom Byrnes.

119 *they finish each other's sentences*: interview with Bonnie Church Kellerman and Marilynn Church Peterson.

123 *a U-turn to come back to pick him up*: interview with Michael Zronek.

124 *"Well, welcome to Duluth"*: interview with Patrick Labadie.

126 *including the* Fitzgerald *crew*: interview with James Bolin.

128 *the entrance to Whitefish Bay*: Lynn and Winters, *The Legend Lives On*, 9.

130 *the gates open easily*: interview with Michelle Briggs.

130 *"would be like placing one on the moon"*: see Michigan History Center Staff, "The Soo Locks," Michiganology, accessed February 3, 2025, https://michiganology.org/stories/the-soo-locks.

130 *Da Vinci's miter locks*: see "History of the Soo Locks," North Michigan History, n.d., accessed February 3, 2025, https://northernmichiganhistory.com/history-of-the-soo-locks.

131 *even a cholera epidemic*: "The Mitten," *Michigan History*, October 2004.

131 *therefore the South could not lose*: Erik Larson, *The Demon of Unrest: A Saga of Hubris, Heartbreak, and Heroism at the Dawn of the Civil War* (Crown, 2024), 56.

131 *its twin, the Sabin Lock, in 1919*: see "History of the Soo Locks."

132 *to raise or lower a ship twenty-one feet*: U.S. Army Corps of Engineers—Detroit District, *Soo Locks: Sault Ste. Marie, Michigan* (informational pamphlet), February 2023.

132 *from the Head of the Lakes to Toledo and back*: interview with Michelle Briggs; U.S. Army Corps of Engineers—Detroit District, *Soo Locks*.

133 *it would cost the U.S. economy eleven million jobs*: interview with Michelle Briggs; U.S. Army Corps of Engineers—Detroit District, *Soo Locks*.

136 *swarms of bugs that drove the Zugs crazy*: see Neil Rubin, "Mill Workers at Zug Island Steel Themselves for the End," *Detroit News*, April 19, 2020, www.detroitnews.com/story/business/2020/04/19/mill-workers-zug-island-steel-themselves-end/2957131001.

139 *one in New York to unload the garbage barges*: see Railroad Street, "Cleveland's Forgotten Hulett Unloaders," Railroad Street YouTube channel, 21:06, February 10, 2022, accessed February 3, 2025, www.youtube.com/watch?v=S2B-V2n4b34.

IX: THE SAILOR'S LIFE

147 *more than one hundred million tons of cargo annually*: Correspondence with James H. I. Weakley, president of the Lake Carriers Association, and Glen Nekvasil, vice president of the LCA.

157 *"But we didn't think we had a hit"*: interview with Elliot Lurie.

160 *changed his mind—and his life*: interview with Craig Ellquist.

161 *then move on to the next hatch cover*: Stonehouse, *Wreck*, 16.

162 *very helpful on the sticky clamps*: Stonehouse, *Wreck*, 16.

X: THE VETERANS

172 *"Toivo died. Truck for sale"*: Bacon, *Blue Ice*, 76.

173 *that most valued of Southern qualities, chivalry*: Larson, *Demon of Unrest*, 6–7.

173 *twenty-nine men filling thirteen different roles*: Numerous interviews with former *Edmund Fitzgerald* crewmen and Great Lakes sailors.

177 *"I'd go down with the boat"*: see National Park Service, "An Immigrant Story—Ransom E. Cundy," Keweenaw National Historical Park, accessed February 3, 2025, www.nps.gov/kewe/learn/historyculture/an-immigrant-story-ransom-e-cundy.htm.

177 *"He turned into a sad and beaten man"*: see "Ransom E. Cundy," SS *Edmund Fitzgerald* Online, accessed February 3, 2025, https://ssedmundfitzgerald.org/ransom-e-cundy.

181 *"nothing is ever sure"*: Kevin T. McGee, "Mystery of *Fitz* Lost in the Deep," *Detroit Free Press*, November 10, 1986, 1A, 12A.

188 *"You do not call me Buck"*: interview with Debbie Champeau Gomez.

192 *"I don't think Dad met too many people he didn't like"*: interview with Heidi Brabon.

192 *"working-man's hands—rough, like sandpaper"*: interview with Frank Kobasic.

215 *"Drop a big engine"*: Daniel Charles Ross, research file produced for the author.

XI: THE ROOKIES

218 *"get things done for the next generation"*: interview with Patrick Devine.

225 *"I really couldn't believe it—but it happened"*: interviews with Cindy Reynolds Berlincourt.

XII: LUNCH WITH THE CAPTAIN

231 *suffered her share*: Michael Schumacher, *The Mighty* Fitz*: The Sinking of the* Edmund Fitzgerald (University of Minnesota Press, 2005), 18.

231 *cracks in the hatch covers, which are very common*: Stonehouse, *Wreck*, 28–30.

232 *"nothing is ever sure"*: Kevin T. McGee, "Mystery of *Fitz* Lost in the Deep," *Detroit Free Press*, November 10, 1986, 1A, 12A.

XIII: ONE LAST RUN

239 *"Home is the sailor"*: Robert Louis Stevenson, "Requiem."

240 *entrusted the ring to a friend in Duluth*: Susan R. Pollack, "*Edmund Fitzgerald* Tragedy Still Draws Reverence," *Detroit News*, November 4, 2014, www.detroitnews.com/story/life/2014/11/04/edmund-fitzgerald-legend-lives/18488647.

242 *"just under" Lake Superior by Monday night*: Department of Transportation, U.S. Coast Guard, *Marine Casualty Report, SS* Edmund Fitzgerald*; Sinking in Lake Superior on November 10, 1975, with Loss of Life*, Report No. USCG 16732/64216, July 26, 1977, 18, www.dco.uscg.mil/Portals/9/DCO%20Documents/5p/CG-5PC/INV/docs/boards/edmundfitz.pdf (hereafter USCG Report 16732/64216); Hugh E. Bishop, *The Night the* Fitz *Went Down* (Lake Superior Port Cities Inc., 2009), 9–10.

243 *cheat a few more inches on the Plimsoll line*: Lynn and Winters, *The Legend Lives On*, 24.

243 *more than fifty thousand gallons of No. 6 fuel oil*: Lynn and Winters, *The Legend Lives On*, 11.

244 *watch the* Fitzgerald *make its way out to the open seas*: Lynn and Winters, *The Legend Lives On*, 11.

249 *full speed of 16.3 miles per hour*: Lynn and Winters, *The Legend Lives On*, 11.

252 *Dudley J. Paquette, captain of the* Wilfred Sykes, *sensed trouble*: Bishop, *The Night the* Fitz *Went Down*, 14.

256 *"I can't stay with you"*: Bishop, *The Night the* Fitz *Went Down*, 14.

257 *"something wasn't right when I heard that"*: Bishop, *The Night the* Fitz *Went Down*, 14.

259 *from the Keweenaw Peninsula toward Whitefish Bay*: interview and correspondence with David Schwab.

259 *would rush down to Lake Superior's edge to witness the spectacle*: interviews and correspondence with Pat Schutte.

261 *"a temperature of 41 degrees (F), and waves of ten feet"*: USCG Report 16732/64216, 20.

262 *The only question was when*: USCG Report 16732/64216, 20–21.

266 *to keep the* Fitzgerald *in sight*: USCG Report 16732/64216, 23.

269 *"we're just getting our asses kicked"*: interviews with Rick Barthuli.

275 *"Canadian authorities have been consulted"*: USCG Report 16732/64216, 85–86.

275 *"even as a hazard," let alone the lethal one that it is*: National Transportation Safety Board (NTSB), *Marine Accident Report, SS* Edmund Fitzgerald *Sinking in Lake Superior, November 10, 1975*: Report No. NTSB-MAR-78-3, May 4, 1978: 21, 23.

276 *"Caribou Island disappears on that chart"*: interviews with Tom Wiater.

279 *"no one was permitted on deck"*: Great Lakes Shipwreck Historical Society, "Through the Eyes of Capt. Cooper: The Night the *Edmund Fitzgerald* Went Down" (video interview with Bernie Cooper), 3:52, n.d., GLShipwreckSociety YouTube channel, November 10, 2011, accessed February 10, 2025, www.youtube.com/watch?v=3VXY6tuZ5eU.

279 *"I'm checking down"*: Accessed May 2025 at https://www.mlive.com/news/2021/11/wreck-of-the-edmund-fitzgerald-see-photos-of-the-great-lakes-most-famous-ship.html.

280 *"felt that it indicated any real concern"*: USCG Report 16732/64216, 26.

284 *increase its weight up to 7 percent*: NTSB, *Marine Accident Report*, 10.

286 *when the* Anderson *neared Caribou Island*: USCG Report 16732/64216, 28.

288 *For the remainder of the journey*: Thom Holden and Julius F. Wolf, *Julius F. Wolff Jr.'s Lake Superior Shipwrecks*, 2nd expanded ed. (Lake Superior Port Cities, 1990), 219.

289 *a safety broadcast*: Lynn and Winters, *The Legend Lives On*, 13.

289 *thirty-five miles from Whitefish Point*: USCG Report 16732/64216, 28.

290 *Cedric Woodard, the captain of a Swedish ship called the* Avafors, *responded*: NTSB, *Marine Accident Report*, 6.

291 *They found the* Fitzgerald*'s forward winch:* Wendolyn R. Goerl, *Five Theories on the* Fitz*: And What They Reveal About the Politics of Disaster*, CreateSpace Independent Publishing Platform, 2018.

294 *they won't hesitate: November 10, 1975*: John U. Bacon, "Mighty Mac," *Detroit News*, September 6, 1998.

294 *she got hit broadside with a series of waves twenty-five feet or higher*: USCG Report 16732/64216, 28.

299 *"the worst possible place, at the worst possible time"*: Thomas R. Hultquist, Michael R. Dutter, and David J. Schwab, "Reexamination of the 9–10 November 1975 '*Edmund Fitzgerald*' Storm Using Today's Technology," *Bulletin of the American Meteorological Society* 87, no. 5 (2006): slide 43, www.glerl.noaa.gov/pubs/fulltext/2006/20060016.pdf.

300 *the last known words from the* Edmund Fitzgerald: USCG Report 16732/64216, 28–29.

XIV: THE SAILOR'S CODE

303 *his crew had little doubt that the* Fitzgerald *would pull through*: Lynn and Winters, *The Legend Lives On*, 15; Hultquist, Dutter, and Schwab, "Reexamination," slide 42.

303 *the* Anderson*'s signal was loud and clear*: Lynn and Winters, *The Legend Lives On*, 15.

304 *no response on Channel 12*: Stonehouse, *Wreck*, 41.

304 *Cooper's most ominous radio transmission thus far*: USCG Report 16732/64216, 34.

305 *"I just hope he didn't take a nosedive"*: USCG Report 16732/64216, 30.

305 *the* Fitzgerald *did not respond*: USCG Report 16732/64216, 34.

305 *the Coast Guard rescue coordination center in Cleveland, Ohio*: Lynn and Winters, *The Legend Lives On*, 15–16; USCG Report 16732/64216, 34.

305 *to inform them of the* Fitzgerald*'s situation*: USCG Report 16732/64216, 34.

306 *forced her back into the dock until 9 a.m. the next day*: Lynn and Winters, *The Legend Lives On*, 16.

308 *the question he'd hoped not to hear*: Lynn and Winters, *The Legend Lives On*, 16–19.

309 *"I finally decided I'd go out"*: Great Lakes Shipwreck Historical Society, "Through the Eyes of Capt. Cooper."

311 *back to Whitefish Bay within thirty minutes*: USCG Report 16732/64216, 37.

311 *"because of the severe weather conditions"*: USCG Report 16732/64216, 36–37.

312 *three Canadian ships:* USCG Report 16732/64216, 38.

316 *thinking about his friends on the ship that night*: interviews with Craig Ellquist.

317 *everyone from Elvis Presley to Sarah McLachlan*: Lynn and Winters, *The Legend Lives On*, 33.

317 *"from an old Irish folk song"*: Gordon Lightfoot, "Gordon Lightfoot here. Singer/songwriter for over 50 years whose work has been performed by everyone from Elvis to Barbra. AMA!" Reddit, August 21, 2014, accessed February 10, 2025, www.reddit.com/r/IAmA/comments/2e8cjz/gordon_lightfoot_here_singersongwriter_for_over.

317 *"It must've been awful"*: Nicholas Jennings, *Lightfoot* (Penguin, 2016), 147.

318 *"hitting the clubhouse, where we were"*: interviews with Doug Frericks.

319 *Then their phone rang*: interview with Bonnie Church Kellerman and Marilynn Church Peterson.

320 *"A Great Lake ship is feared lost on Lake Superior"*: see clip of *ABC Evening News* (with Harry Reasoner), November 11, 1975, in "The Wreck of the Edmund Fitzgerald" (tribute video), Joe Fulton YouTube channel, 6:38, April 21, 2009, accessed February 10, 2025, www.youtube.com/watch?v=hgI8bta-7aw.

321 *"My dad wasn't on it, but I knew my uncle Grant was"*: interviews with and columns by Tom Walton.

322 *"he wasn't coming home"*: interviews with Heidi Brabon Wilhelm.
323 *"I think David was on that ship"*: interviews with Cindy LoCicero Sauer.
324 *"Not at all"*: interviews with Pam Woodman Wittig.
324 *"They say it might have gone down"*: interviews with Cindy Reynolds Berlincourt.

XV: SEARCHING

329 *"eavesdropping on the captains talking to one another"*: interviews with Harry Atkins.
333 *"'let's band together and get it done'"*: interview with Jim Gaines.
336 *"But he did it"*: interview with James D. MacDonald.
337 *would affect Candace's blood pressure and endanger the baby*: interview with Heidi Wilhelm Brabon.
338 *seventeen miles from the entrance*: NTSB, *Marine Accident Report*, 6.
338 *back to Duluth in somber silence*: interviews with Michael Zronek.
339 *which used to comprise the middle of the ship*: USCG Report 16732/64216, 50–51.
340 *"like a diving board after somebody has jumped off"*: Wolff and Holden, *Lake Superior Shipwrecks*, 227.
340 *did not ask Burgner to testify*: Wolff and Holden, *Lake Superior Shipwrecks*, 227.
342 *Dick Race, to explore Six Fathom Shoal*: interviews with John Tanner, Ed Wiltse, and Earl Zuelke.
344 *"Dick has since been involved"*: Mark Fellows, "Anchor Aweigh! . . . and Away," *Harbor Light/Summer Life* (August 31–September 6, 1983).
344 *confidential report for Oglebay Norton*: Fellows, "Anchor Aweigh!"
345 *footage from Dick Race's exploratory dives on Six Fathom Shoal*: interview with Peter Groh.
346 *"That's pretty basic"*: interview with Matthew Collette.

XVI: ALL THAT REMAINS

352 *wore Eddie's anniversary ring the rest of her life*: see Pollack, "*Edmund Fitzgerald* Still Draws Reverence."
352 *"probably the worst day of his life"*: Lynn and Winters, *The Legend Lives On*, 21.
352 *"He didn't like to talk about it"*: Lynn and Winters, *The Legend Lives On*, 21.
353 *"I know David wanted to transfer ships. Why didn't he?"*: interviews with John Tanner.
354 *"this is final. He's gone"*: interviews with Debbie Champeau Gomez.
356 *deserved more than a half page in a national news magazine*: Jennings, *Lightfoot*, 148.
356 *"got everything in chronological order"*: Lightfoot, "Gordon Lightfoot here."
357 *"I never played a single beat on it"*: interviews with Barry Keane.
361 *"the shipwreck song on FM"*: interviews with Barry Keane.
362 *"That's some old-school troubadour stuff, a ballad in the classic sense"*: interview with Christian Hoard.
363 *"As simple and pure as it gets"*: interview with Rick Haynes.
364 *"I was really irritated"*: interviews with Patrick Devine.
366 *"It's stood the test of time"*: Roger LeLievre, "Lightfoot Still Follows His Own Path," *Ann Arbor News*, April 25, 2002.
366 *"So close to safety. It gets you"*: interview with Rick Haynes, longtime bassist, Gordon Lightfoot Band.
367 *"I don't know how I did it"*: interviews with Cindy Reynolds Berlincourt.

371 *"They are more cautious now"*: interviews with Guy Meadows.

374 *the centerpiece of the Great Lakes Shipwreck Museum*: Lynn and Winters, *The Legend Lives On*, 28–29.

374 *a permanent grave marker*: Lynn and Winters, *The Legend Lives On*, 29–30.

374 *the surface of Lake Superior at 1:25 p.m.*: Lynn and Winters, *The Legend Lives On*, 30.

375 *thirty thousand sailors who have lost their lives on the Great Lakes*: Lynn and Winters, *The Legend Lives On*, 30.

375 *"That's my closure. I'm done"*: interviews with the *Fitzgerald* families, Whitefish Point.

EPILOGUE

382 *"I just crawled down into a bottle and hid"*: interviews with Patrick Devine.

384 *"It took me a long time to come to terms with it"*: interviews with Cindy LoCicero Sauer.

385 *"So his brother Tom and I picked it up"*: interviews with Debbie Champeau.

386 *"'He'd be fifty now. I can picture him'"*: interviews with Pam Woodman Wittig.

387 *a piece of the father she never met*: interviews with Cindy Reynolds Berlincourt.

389 *"A* family—*truly"*: interviews with Heidi Wilhelm Brabon.

BIBLIOGRAPHY

ABC Evening News [with Harry Reasoner]. November 11, 1975. Clip of news footage in "The Wreck of the Edmund Fitzgerald" (tribute video). Joe Fulton YouTube channel, 6:38. April 21, 2009. Accessed February 10, 2025. www.youtube.com/watch?v=hgI8bta-7aw.

Allison, Ira S. "The Giants Range Batholith of Minnesota." *Journal of Geology* 33, no. 5 (July–August 1925), 488–508.

Andra-Warner, Elle. Edmund Fitzgerald*: The Legendary Great Lakes Shipwreck.* North Shore Press, 2006.

Austin, Dan. "Hudson's Department Store." Historic Detroit. Accessed February 10, 2025. https://historicdetroit.org/buildings/hudsons-department-store.

Bacon, John U. "How Immigration Shaped Detroit." *Detroit News*, December 3, 1996.

———. "Mighty Mac." *Detroit News*, September 6, 1998.

———. *Blue Ice: The Story of Michigan Hockey*. University of Michigan Press, 2001.

———. "The Floor Beneath Their Feet." *Michigan History* (May–June 2001), 9–11.

———. "The True Story of 'The Gipper.'" In *The Best of Bacon: Select Cuts*, 151–63. University of Michigan Press, 2018.

Baehr, Carl. "City Streets: The Dreadful Legacy of Charles Nash." Urban Milwaukee. February 16, 2017. Accessed February 10, 2025. https://urbanmilwaukee.com/2017/02/16/city-streets-the-dreadful-legacy-of-charles-nash.

Baime, A. J. *The Arsenal of Democracy: FDR, Detroit, and an Epic Quest to Arm an America at War.* Mariner, 2015.

Bernstein, Peter L. *The Erie Canal and the Making of a Great Nation*. W. W. Norton & Company, 2005.

Bishop, Hugh E. *The Night the* Fitz *Went Down.* Lake Superior Port Cities Inc., 2009.

Bloch, Jim. "Marking the 55th Anniversary of Sinking of Freighter Daniel J. Morrell: Sailor from St. Clair Among 28 Victims." *The Voice*, November 29, 2021.

Braatz, George. "Luxury Cruise on the Great Lakes." *Toledo Blade*, September 1970.

Brown, David G. *White Hurricane: A Great Lakes November Gale and America's Deadliest Maritime Disaster.* International Marine/McGraw-Hill, 2004.

Catton, Bruce. "The Ultimate Storm." *American Heritage* 35, no. 6 (October/November 1984). www.americanheritage.com/ultimate-storm.

Classen, Mikel B. "The Wreck and Rescue of the L.C. Waldo—Keweenaw Peninsula—Lake Superior." Mikel B. Classen on the Road, n.d. Accessed February 10, 2025. https://mikelbclassen.com/the-wreck-and-rescue-of-the-l-c-waldo-keweenaw-peninsula-lake-superior.

Cutler, Elizabeth Fitzgerald, and Walter M. Hirthe. *Six Fitzgerald Brothers: Lake Captains All.* Wisconsin Marine Historical Society, 1983.

Davis, Edward W. *Pioneering with Taconite.* Minnesota Historical Society Press, 1964.

Dennis, Jerry. *The Living Great Lakes: Searching for the Heart of the Inland Seas.* Thomas Dunne Books, 2003.

Department of Transportation, U.S. Coast Guard. *Marine Board Casualty Report, SS* Edmund Fitzgerald*; Sinking in Lake Superior on 10 November 1975 with Loss of Life.* Report No. USCG 16732/64216. July 26, 1977. www.dco.uscg.mil/Portals/9/DCO%20 Documents/5p/CG-5PC/INV/docs/boards/edmundfitz.pdf.

Dick Race Materials, 1979–1986. Box 4, folder 9. Dr. Charles E. and Jeri Baron Feltner Great Lakes Maritime History Collection. Clarke Historical Library, Central Michigan University.

Egan, Dan. *The Death and Life of the Great Lakes.* W. W. Norton & Company, 2017.

Faber, Don. *The Toledo War: The First Michigan–Ohio Rivalry.* University of Michigan Press, 2008.

Fellows, Mark. "Anchor Aweigh! . . . and Away." *Harbor Light/Summer Life,* August 31–September 6, 1983.

Fisher, Ben, and Sean Kery. "A Forensic Investigation of the Breakup and Sinking of the Great Lakes Iron Ore Carrier *Edmund Fitzgerald*, November 10th 1975, Using Modern Naval Architecture Tools and Techniques." Paper presented at the Society of Naval Architects and Marine Engineers Conference, April 27, 2012.

Frump, Robert. *Until the Sea Shall Free Them: Life, Death, and Survival in the Merchant Marine.* Naval Institute Press, 2001.

Galluzzo, John J., ed. *Rescue: True Stories of the U.S. Life-Saving Service.* Avery Color Studios, Inc. and the United States Life-Saving Service Heritage Association, 2011.

Gard. "The Sailor's Champion: Samuel Plimsoll." June 1, 2023. Accessed February 10, 2025. www.gard.no/insights/sailor-s-champion-samuel-plimsoll.

Global Great Lakes. "Lake Superior Overview." Accessed February 10, 2025. https://globalgreatlakes.org/lgl/superior/index.html.

Goerl, Wendolyn R. *Five Theories on the* Fitz*: And What They Reveal About the Politics of Disaster.* CreateSpace Independent Publishing Platform, 2018.

Grann, David. *The* Wager*: A Tale of Shipwreck, Mutiny and Murder.* Doubleday, 2023.

Great Lakes Shipwreck Historical Society. "Through the Eyes of Capt. Cooper: The Night the *Edmund Fitzgerald* Went Down." Video interview with Bernie Cooper, 3:52. n.d. GLShipwreckSociety YouTube channel. November 10, 2011. Accessed February 10, 2025. www.youtube.com/watch?v=3VXY6tuZ5eU.

Hale, Dennis, Tim Jule, Jim Stayer, and Pat Stayer. *Sole Survivor: A Tale of Shipwreck on the Great Lakes and One Man's Survival Against Overwhelming Odds: Dennis Hale's Own Story.* Lakeshore Charters & Marine Explorations, Inc., 1996.

Hancock, Paul. *Shipwrecks of the Great Lakes.* Thunder Bay Press, 2008.

Hawke, David Freeman. *John D.: The Founding Father of the Rockefellers.* Harper & Row, 1980.

Hemming, Robert J. *Gales of November: The Sinking of the* Edmund Fitzgerald. Thunder Bay Press, 1981.

———. *Ships Gone Missing: The Great Lakes Storm of 1913.* Contemporary Books, 1992.

"History of the Soo Locks." Northern Michigan History. n.d. Accessed February 10, 2025. https://northernmichiganhistory.com/history-of-the-soo-locks.

Holden, Thom, and Julius F. Wolff. *Julius F. Wolff Jr.'s Lake Superior Shipwrecks.* 2nd expanded ed. Lake Superior Port Cities, 1990.

Hultquist, Thomas R., Michael R. Dutter, and David J. Schwab. "Reexamination of the 9–10 November 1975 '*Edmund Fitzgerald*' Storm Using Today's Technology." *Bulletin of the American Meteorological Society* 87, no. 5 (2006), 607–22. www.glerl.noaa.gov/pubs/fulltext/2006/20060016.pdf.

Jennings, Nicholas. *Lightfoot*. Penguin, 2016.

Joachim, George J. *Iron Fleet: The Great Lakes in World War II.* Wayne State University Press, 1994.

Junger, Sebastian. *The Perfect Storm: A True Story of Men Against the Sea.* W. W. Norton & Company, 1997.

Kaminsky, Arthur C., and John Powers. *One Goal: A Chronicle of the 1980 U.S. Olympic Hockey Team.* Harper & Row, 1984.

Kantar, Andrew. *Deadly Voyage: The SS* Daniel J. Morrell *Tragedy*. Michigan State University Press, 2009.

Larson, Erik. *The Demon of Unrest: A Saga of Hubris, Heartbreak, and Heroism at the Dawn of the Civil War.* Crown, 2024.

Lear, John. "New Design for Ships Foundered in Red Tape." *Detroit Free Press*, November 10, 1985.

LeLievre, Roger. "Lightfoot Still Follows His Own Path." *Ann Arbor News*, April 25, 2002.

Lightfoot, Gordon. "Gordon Lightfoot here. Singer/songwriter for over 50 years whose work has been performed by everyone from Elvis to Barbra. AMA!" Reddit. August 21, 2014. Accessed February 10, 2025. www.reddit.com/r/IAmA/comments/2e8cjz/gordon_lightfoot_here_singersongwriter_for_over.

Lynn, Bruce, and Christopher Winters. *The Legend Lives On: SS* Edmund Fitzgerald. Running Light Press in partnership with the Great Lakes Shipwreck Historical Society, 2015.

MacInnis, Joseph. Fitzgerald*'s Storm: The Wreck of the* Edmund Fitzgerald. Macmillan Canada, 1997.

Manuel, Jeffrey T. *Taconite Dreams: The Struggle to Sustain Mining on Minnesota's Iron Range, 1915–2000.* University of Minnesota Press, 2015.

Mays, Frank, with Pat Stayer, Jim Stayer, and Tim Juhl. *If We Make It 'til Daylight: The Story of Frank Mays.* Out of the Blue Productions, 2003.

McCullough, David. *The Johnstown Flood.* Simon & Schuster, 1968.

McGee, Kevin T. "Mystery of Fitz Lost in the Deep: Cause of Sinking Still Unknown." *Detroit Free Press*, November 10, 1985.

Michigan History Center Staff. "The Soo Locks." Michiganology, n.d. Accessed February 10, 2025. https://michiganology.org/stories/the-soo-locks.

Michigan State University Michigan Sea Grant Program. "Conclusions of Panel—Important Considerations." *Edmund Fitzgerald* Phase of the Great Lakes Shipwreck Documentation Project. August 1989.

"The Mitten," *Michigan History*, October 2004.

Mixter, Ric. *Tattletale Sounds: The* Edmund Fitzgerald *Investigations.* Airworthy Productions, 2022.

National Park Service. "An Immigrant Story—Ransom E. Cundy." Keweenaw National Historical Park. Accessed February 10, 2025. www.nps.gov/kewe/learn/historyculture/an-immigrant-story-ransom-e-cundy.htm.

National Transportation Safety Board (NTSB). *Marine Accident Report, SS* Edmund

Fitzgerald *Sinking in Lake Superior, November 10, 1975.* Report Number: NTSB-MAR-78-3. May 4, 1978.

Okrent, Daniel. *Last Call: The Rise and Fall of Prohibition.* Scribner, 2010.

Oleszewski, Wes. *The Witch of November: Wicked Winds and Wrecks.* Avery Color Studios Inc., 2021.

Orgel, Richard. *The* Edmund Fitzgerald *Hull Failure:* Edmund Fitzgerald *Crew Vindicated.* Cleo Publishing, 2008.

Philbrick, Nathaniel. *In the Heart of the Sea: The Tragedy of the Whaleship* Essex. Penguin Books, 2000.

Pollack, Susan R. "*Edmund Fitzgerald* Tragedy Still Draws Reverence." *Detroit News*, November 4, 2014. www.detroitnews.com/story/life/2014/11/04/edmund-fitzgerald-legend-lives/18488647.

Railroad Street. "Cleveland's Forgotten Hulett Unloaders." Railroad Street YouTube channel, 21:06. February 10, 2022. Accessed February 3, 2025. www.youtube.com/watch?v=S2B-V2n4b34.

Ramsay, Raymond. *Requiem for the Toledo Express: A Search for Truth.* Keweenaw Media Press, 2009.

"Ransom E. Cundy." SS *Edmund Fitzgerald* Online. Accessed February 10, 2025. https://ssedmundfitzgerald.org/ransom-e-cundy.

Ratigan, William. *Great Lakes Shipwrecks & Survivals.* WM. B. Eerdmans Publishing Company, 1960.

Risen, Clay. "How America Learned to Love Whiskey." *Atlantic*, December 6, 2013. www.theatlantic.com/national/archive/2013/12/how-america-learned-to-love-whiskey/282110.

Rubin, Neil. "Mill Workers at Zug Island Steel Themselves for the End." *Detroit News*, April 19, 2020. www.detroitnews.com/story/business/2020/04/19/mill-workers-zug-island-steel-themselves-end/2957131001.

"Samuel Morse Demonstrates the Telegraph with the Message, 'What hath God wrought?'" History. July 20, 2010. www.history.com/this-day-in-history/what-hath-god-wrought.

Schumacher, Michael. *Mighty* Fitz*: The Sinking of the* Edmund Fitzgerald. University of Minnesota Press, 2005.

———. *November's Fury: The Deadly Great Lakes Hurricane of 1913.* University of Minnesota Press, 2013.

———, ed. *The Trial of the* Edmund Fitzgerald. University of Minnesota Press, 2019.

———. *The Wreck of the* Carl D.*: A True Story of Loss, Survival, and Rescue at Sea.* Indiana University Press, 2008.

Sherman, Casey, and Michael J. Tougias. *The Finest Hours: The True Story of the U.S. Coast Guard's Most Daring Sea Rescue.* Scribner, 2009.

Shipwreck, Edmund Fitzgerald, sts, undated. Folder 32, box 37. Dr. Charles E. and Jeri Baron Feltner Great Lakes Maritime History Collection. Clarke Historical Library, Central Michigan University.

"Special Deputy Marshal Christopher Keenan." Officer Down Memorial Page. Accessed February 10, 2025. www.odmp.org/officer/reflections/22863-special-deputy-marshal-christopher-keenan.

Stonehouse, Frederick. *Blood on the Water: The Great Lakes During the Civil War.* Avery Color Studios, Inc., 2011.

———. *Lake Superior's Shipwreck Coast: Maritime Accidents from Whitefish Bay to Grand Marais, Michigan*. Avery Color Studios, Inc., 1985.

———. *Steel on the Bottom: Great Lakes Shipwrecks*. Avery Color Studios, Inc., 2006.

———. *The Wreck of the* Edmund Fitzgerald. Avery Color Studios, Inc., 1977.

Thompson, Mark L. *Graveyard of the Lakes*. Wayne State University Press, 2000.

———. *Queen of the Lakes*. Wayne State University Press, 2017.

Tobin, James. *Great Projects: The Epic Story of the Building of America, from the Taming of the Mississippi to the Invention of the Internet*. The Free Press, 2001.

Tocqueville, Alexis de. "To Ernest de Chabrol, 9 June 1831." In *Selected Letters on Politics and Society*. Edited by Roger Boesche. University of California Press, 1985.

U.S. Army Corps of Engineers—Detroit District. *Soo Locks: Sault Ste. Marie, Michigan* (informational pamphlet). February 2023.

Walton, Thomas. "33 Years On, the *Fitzgerald* Story Still Haunts." *Toledo Blade*, November 10, 2008. www.toledoblade.com/Tom-Walton/2008/11/10/33-years-on-the-Fitzgerald-s-story-still-haunts/stories/200811100035.

"War Production." *The War*. PBS. www.pbs.org/kenburns/the-war/war-production.

Wolff, Daniel. *Grown-Up Anger: The Connected Mysteries of Bob Dylan, Woody Guthrie, and the Calumet Massacre of 1913*. Harper, 2017.

INDEX

Page numbers in *italics* refer to illustrations and maps.

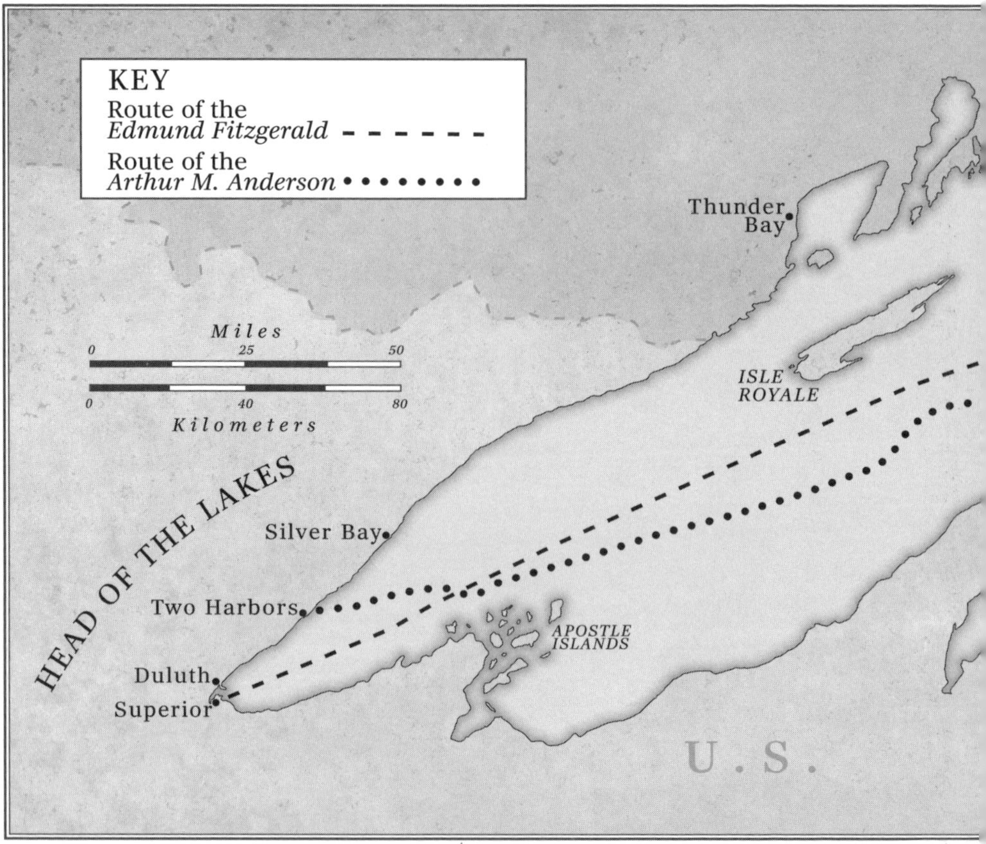

KEY
Route of the *Edmund Fitzgerald* - - - - - -
Route of the *Arthur M. Anderson* • • • • • • • •

Miles
0 25 50
0 40 80
Kilometers

HEAD OF THE LAKES
Thunder Bay
ISLE ROYALE
Silver Bay
Two Harbors
APOSTLE ISLANDS
Duluth
Superior
U.S.

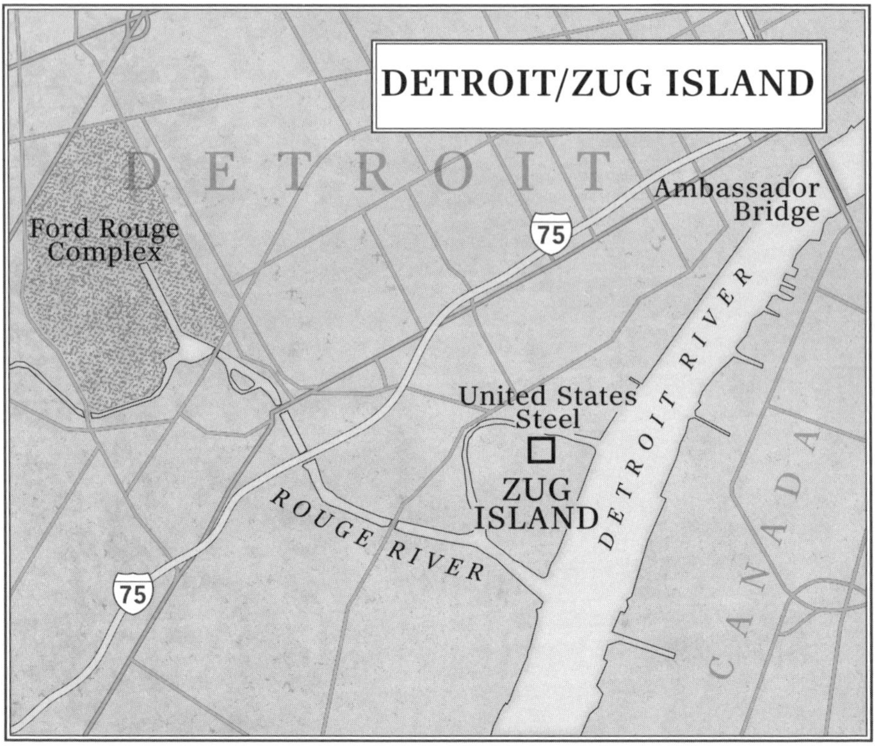

DETROIT/ZUG ISLAND

DETROIT
Ford Rouge Complex
75
Ambassador Bridge
DETROIT RIVER
United States Steel
ZUG ISLAND
ROUGE RIVER
75
CANADA

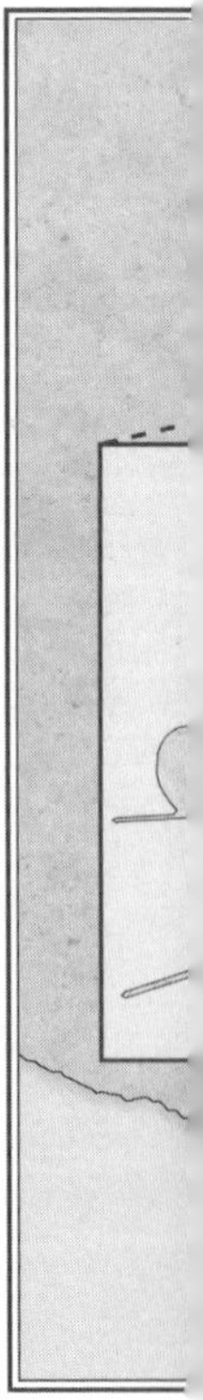